GENDER ROLES IN
DEVELOPMENT PROJECTS

Gender Roles in Development Projects

A Case Book

Editors: **Catherine Overholt**
Mary B. Anderson
Kathleen Cloud
James E. Austin

Printed in the United States of America

Cover design by Marilyn Penrod

First Printing 1984
Second Printing 1986
Third Printing 1988
Fourth Printing 1989
Fifth Printing 1991

Library of Congress Cataloging in Publication Data
Main entry under title:
Gender roles in development projects.

Bibliography: p.
1. Sex role—Developing countries—Case studies.
2. Women—Developing countries—Economic conditions—Case studies.   3.Women in business—Developing countries—Case studies.   4.Women—Employment—Developing countries—Case studies.
I. Overholt, Catherine.

HQ1075.5.D44G46   1985   305.3   84-23325
ISBN 0-931816-15-7

CONTENTS

Acknowledgements.. ix
Foreword x
Preface..., xii
TECHNICAL PAPERS
Women in Development: A Framework for Project Analysis...   3
Catherine Overholt, Mary B. Anderson, Kathleen Cloud, James Austin

Women's Productivity in Agricultural Systems: Considerations
for Project Design..   17
Kathleen Cloud

Technology Transfer: Implications for Women   57
Mary B. Anderson

Small Scale Enterprise and Women............................   79
Maryanne Dulansey
James E. Austin

CASE STUDIES
INDONESIA: East Java Family Planning, Nutrition, and
Income Generation Project 135
David Pyle

TANZANIA: The Arusha Planning and Village Development
Project 163
Liz Wiley

KENYA: Egerton College...................................... 185
Mary B. Anderson

DOMINICAN REPUBLIC: Program for Development of Micro-
Enterprises 215
Susan Sawyer
Catherine Overholt

PERU: Banco Industrial del Peru 243
Credit for the Development of Rural Enterprise
Maria Eugenia Arias
John Ickis
Members of the Research Faculty of the Instituto Centroamericano de Administración (INCAE), Managua, Nicaragua

INDIA: Gujarat Medium Irrigation Project 283
  Dr. C. Gopinath
  Dr. A. H. Kolaro
  Faculty members of the Indian Institute of Management, Ahmedabad, India

KENYA: Kitui District Arid and Semi-Arid Lands Project 309
  Mary B. Anderson

ACKNOWLEDGEMENTS

On behalf of my colleagues, Mary Anderson, Kathleen Cloud, and Jim Austin, I would like to express our deep appreciation to all those who cooperated in this undertaking.

We are particularly grateful to the USAID personnel in field missions and to host country nationals for their generous cooperation in working with case writers to assemble and interpret project information for the development of these case studies. Their cooperation is a clear indication of their willingness to address these issues seriously. We also extend our sincere appreciation to the HIID staff for their administrative assistance and to the staff of USAID WID Office for their encouragement and assistance. We extend a special thanks to Paula Goddard and Sara Tinsley for their vision in undertaking this project and their continued guidance and support in seeing it through to completion.

Our hope is that this effort will assist others in the task of incorporating women into the development process.

Catherine Overholt
Project Director

Cambridge, Massachusetts

FOREWORD

People working in the field of development have long been concerned with how the benefits of development are distributed. Only recently, however, concern with distributional issues has incorporated differences in income and economic power between men and women. Concern with issues of gender, of course, involves more than how gender affects distribution. Understanding the role played by gender in development can also make a substantial difference as to whether growth-oriented projects succeed or fail. Thus, questions of how men and women define their roles, or have them defined for them, influences all aspects of the development process.

HIID's response to the need to address these issues in a systematic manner has three major but linked aims. The first is to learn more about the role of gender through research and through direct involvement in policy and project work overseas. The second is to develop training materials and courses that will convey the knowledge acquired and thus will improve the ability of development planners and practitioners to address the differing ways in which women and men may be involved in and affected by development. The third is to incorporate an informed approach to the role of gender directly into HIID's developing-country projects.

Progress toward the second of these objectives is represented clearly by this volume which presents the materials developed in the first phase of a training project undertaken by members of HIID in collaboration with other members of the Harvard Community. Support for this project came from the Women in Development Office of the United States Agency for International Development. Efforts to make gains in meeting the first and third objectives have been furthered by a grant from the Ford Foundation making it possible for HIID to hire an Institute Associate with primary responsibility for research, teaching, and project work in the Women in Development field.

The need to redress the failure to consider systematically and coherently the different roles of women and men as they engage in and are affected by development activities requires more than *ad hoc* attention. Rather than a band-aid or add-on approach we need to institutionalize successful initiatives in providing the necessary analytical and methodological skills for assessing the significance of gender differences in the development process. One key means is to integrate these skills into the training of development planners and practitioners. This volume is a significant step in that critical process.

Dwight H. Perkins

Director
Harvard Institute for
International Development

In 1973, the Congress of the United States, recognizing that "women in developing countries play a significant role in economic production, family support and the overall development process," required that United States bilateral assistance "be administered so as to give that particular attention to those programs, projects and activities which tend to integrate women into the national economies of foreign countries, thus improving their status and assisting the total development effort."

In direct response to the Amendment, USAID established the Women in Development Office.

In 1982, at the request of the Administrator, M. Peter McPherson, the Agency issued a Policy Paper on women in development which affirmed the Agency's effort to undertake an effective development strategy promoting balanced economic development. One of the premises of A.I.D.'s women in development policy is that gender roles constitute a key variable in the socio-economic condition of any country —one that can be decisive in the success or failure of development plans. Additionally, the policy paper stated that it is critical now for AID to move beyond its initial activities, taking an active role and providing leadership to ensure that women have access to the opportunities and benefits of economic development. The paper also clearly stated that the responsibilty for implementing A.I.D.'s women in development policy rests with all of A.I.D.'s offices and programs at all levels of decision-making. Implementation of this policy was understood to be an important qualitative aspect of A.I.D.'s overall program, one which is crucial to the achievement of the Agency's goals. Thus, it became paramount to increase the knowledge of gender issues among USAID personnel.

The Office of Women in Development has been working with the Harvard Institute for International Development (HIID) for the past several years in the preparation and testing of case studies of AID-funded projects. To date, two workshops, which employ the cases as a data base, have been held in order to introduce new analytical and conceptual skills to senior-level AID staff. An additional four workshops are being planned for 1984-1985—two for USAID's Washington staff and two for overseas personnel.

We expect that the case studies will continue to provide valuable information, not only to AID personnel, but also to persons from other donor agencies, to representatives from private voluntary agencies and universities and to others interested in international development.

Sara Tinsley

Director
Office of Women in Development
USAID

PREFACE

Within the international development community, there is a growing recognition of the importance of women's role in the development process. Major development organizations, such as USAID, have made institutional commitments to increasing their capability to deal effectively with the issues surrounding women in development. The primary vehicles through which most development agencies can have an effect in this area are projects. Thus, the tasks of project design and implementation are critical for determining effects.

There now exists sufficient empirical evidence to conclude that weaknesses in project design and implementation have caused adverse effects on women, reduced benefits accruing to them, or failed to capture fully their contributions to projects and to the development process. Project weaknesses are a reflection of inadequacies in awareness and skills of the staff involved in the preparation and implementation of a project. These inadequacies are not surprising, for the distinctive nature of women's roles in development gives rise to a unique set of project design considerations. Staff require a new set of conceptual and analytical perspectives and skills in order to deal explicitly, effectively, and efficiently with women-related issues in the spectrum of projects in which they become involved. The objectives of the case studies and technical papers assembled in this book flow from these training needs.

The training materials developed by the Case Study and Training Project at the Harvard Institute for International Development are based on the case method of training. The case study method has been highly developed and effectively employed by Harvard and other institutions for training professionals, including those in development agencies. The materials presented here include seven case studies based on actual country projects which received USAID funds, and four technical papers related to substantive issues on the women and development aspects of project analysis.

The book is organized into two sections. The first section is a collection of papers which provide background reading in technical areas and introduce an overall framework for case analysis. The individual cases follow the technical papers and are intended for use as vehicles for group discussion.

The case method has a long history as a particularly effective pedagogical aproach to develop problem solving and decision making skills. It is based on the philosophy that participants must take an active part in, and assume responsibility for the learning process. The basic premise is that active intellectual engagement is essential if the learning experience is to be meaningful.

Case studies are the pedagogical vehicles through which intellectual involvement is generated. Cases are factual descriptions of actual situations facing decision makers in organizations. The case studies do not set forth theories or hypotheses but rather present a slice of the real world of projects that allow the discussion participants to think purposefully about issues which are highly relevant to their own professional work. Thus, the approach is practitioner-oriented and reality-based.

The cases do not include an analysis or evaluation of a situation but rather provide the raw material from which participants can engage in their own analysis and draw their own conclusions. As in the real world, the case situations do not have one "right answer." There may be many reasonable alternatives and defensible recommendations. From the learning perspective, the answer is less important than the problem-solving skills that are developed in the process of deriving systematically a logical and sensible set of conclusions and recommendations.

The HIID Case Study and Training Project has developed teaching notes for each of the case studies which are intended to serve as a guide for case method instructors. These teaching notes may be obtained from:

> Director
> Office of Women and Development
> PPC/WID USAID
> New State
> Washington, D.C. 20523

The priority and urgency of integrating women more fully into the development process dictate that development practitioners and academics strengthen their analytical approaches to this task. This book is a step in that direction and we hope that it, in turn, will stimulate further efforts by our colleagues in the development community.

Catherine Overholt

TECHNICAL PAPERS

CHAPTER ONE

Women in Development: A Framework For Project Analysis

Prepared by Catherine Overholt, Kathleen Cloud, Mary B. Anderson and James E. Austin.

Development planning has failed to recognize fully or systematically women's contribution to the development process or, in turn, the effect of this process on them. This failure has limited development efforts and effects. Economic growth, project efficiency, and social justice call for a new approach to development which systematically includes women.

In her seminal work of 1970, Ester Boserup plainly articulated the state of neglect: "In the vast and ever-growing literature on economic development, reflections on the particular problems of women are few and far between."[1] Over the last decade, the issues regarding the integral involvement of women in national development processes have slowly crept onto the agendas of national and international development agencies. By 1980, many countries and international agencies had explicitly incorporated women's issues into their development plans and had set up special bureaus, offices, or even ministries as the organizational focal point of these new concerns. Furthermore, the barren literature fields observed by Boserup had begun to produce intellectual harvests. By 1981, articles and books in the women in development area were appearing at a rapid rate.

Although there has been much activity, development planning efforts still fail to recognize fully women's actual and potential contribution to the development process or the effect of the development process on them. The imperatives for rectifying these inadequacies are based on both economic and equity concerns. Women are key actors in the economic system, yet their neglect in development plans has left untapped a potentially large economic contribution. Women represent the majority of the population, but they are concentrated at the bottom of the ladder in terms of employment, education, income and status. Both economic growth and social justice call for increased attention to the integration of women into the development process. This paper proceeds from the basis that equity and economic growth are compatible objectives and must be pursued simultaneously.

Projects are among the primary vehicles used by governments and international agencies to channel resources in the development process.[2] One of the barriers[3] to translating research activity about women into effective and beneficial development programming has been the absence of an adequate analytical framework for integrating women into project analysis. Such integration of women is essential for transforming policy concerns into practical realities.[4] The purpose of this paper is to present an analytical framework which will facilitate this process.

ANALYTICAL FRAMEWORK

What women do will have an impact on most projects whether or not women are considered explicitly in their design and implementation. Similarly, most projects will have an effect on women's lives. The framework we propose can improve the definition of general project objectives, assess how these relate to women's involvement with a project, and anticipate the effect of the project on women. The analysis which we introduce here is not intended to be limited in its application to projects which are directed only to women. This analysis is equally applicable, and probably more important, precisely for projects where women's roles and responsibilities have not been explicitly noted but are implicitly assumed in project design and implementation.

Development projects are vehicles for generating change. Project design and implementation, therefore, require an adequate data base. "Visibility" is the starting point for integrating women into development projects and visibility also comes through data. Thus, the cornerstone of the proposed framework is an adequate data base which considers what women do and why. The key challenge, however, is how to organize and present this information so as to facilitate its translation into project terms. The framework we propose uses four interrelated components: Activity Profile; Access and Control Profile; Analysis of Factors Influencing Activities, Access, and Control; and Project Cycle Analysis.

The first component, the Activity Profile, is based on the concept of a gender-based division of labor. The Activity Profile will delineate the economic activities of the population in the project area first by age and gender and then by ethnicity, social class, or other important distinguishing characteristics. In addition, it will indicate the amount of time spent by individuals to accomplish these activities. The second component, the Access and Control Profile, will identify what resources individuals can command to carry out their activities and the benefits which they derive from them.

Analysis of Factors Influencing Activities, Access, and Control focuses on the underlying factors which determine the gender division of labor and gender-related control over resources and benefits. These analyses identify the factors which create differential opportunities or constraints for men's and women's participation in and benefits from projects. Because the work that men and women carry out shifts over time in response to the processes of change, an understanding of the underlying trends within the broader economic and cultural environment must be incorporated into this analysis.

The final component of the analytic framework, Project Cycle Analysis, consists of examining a project in light of the foregoing basic data and the trends that are likely to affect it and/or be generated by it. Together, these four components provide a sufficient basis for designing and implementing projects which can best benefit women and benefit by women's participation.

ACTIVITY PROFILE

To assess the interaction between women and projects, it is important to know what women do. How one categorizes activities conceptually is important. We suggest the following categories:

1) Production of Goods and Services

Too often planners have failed to recognize women's roles as producers. Specific productive activities carried out for all goods and services by men or women should be identified. It is not sufficient to identify only female activities. Male activities must also be specified, because the interrelationships can affect or be affected by the project.

Since general typologies can be very misleading, specific delineation of activities is needed for each country and project setting. Huntington's critique of the early Boserup work emphasized the difficulties of generalizing: ". . . even if the classification and causal relationships of Boserup's conceptualization are pertinent to African societies, they do not hold elsewhere."[5] The work of Deere and Leon in Andean areas reinforces the problem with generalization . . . "Boserup's propositions . . . hold only for the middle and rich states of the peasantry. . . ."[6]

The degree of specificity of the activity listing should depend on the nature of the project. Those areas most directly associated with a project should carry the greatest detail. For example, if the project concerns a new agricultural production technology, then the gender division of labor for each agricultural productive activity should be delineated, e.g. land clearance, preparation, seeding, weeding, processing, etc.

2) Reproduction and Maintenance of the Human Resources

Activities that are carried out to produce and care for the family members need to be specified according to who does them. They might include but are not limited to fuel and water collection, food preparation, birthing, child care, education, health care, and laundry. These activities are often viewed as noneconomic, generally carry no pecuniary remuneration, and usually are excluded from the national income accounts. In fact, these household maintenance tasks are essential economic functions which ensure the development and preservation of the human capital for the family and the nation. Galbraith observed . . . "what is not counted is usually not noticed."[7] In project analyses, not noticing a major activity can lead to defective project design.

Giving explicit attention to these functions is critical. Women's project involvement can depend on whether or how a project affects reproduction and maintenance activities, the production of goods and services, and/or the interrelationship between these activities. The scarcest resource for most low-income women is time. The design of projects which increase time requirements for particular activities must consider these requirements in relation to the time required for other necessary activities.

The activities listed in the above categories need to be further classified to increase their utility for the subsequent project analysis. Three parameters are suggested for describing the activities:

(a) Gender and Age Denomination - identifies whether women, men, their children, or the elderly carry out an activity; reveals gender patterns in the work activities; and is the key to identifying subsequent gender effects.

(b) Time Allocation - specifies what percentage of time is allocated to each activity and whether it is seasonal or daily.

(c) Activity Locus - specifies where the activity is being performed -in the home, in the family field or shop or in the outside community; reveals female mobility; and carries implications for project delivery systems.

Table 1 provides an example of how information on activites can be summarized.

Most projects are not targeted to homogeneous population groups. The gender-based division of labor as well as the access to and control over resources and benefits are likely to differ, often quite substantially, according to socio-economic class or ethnic affiliation. Therefore, it is essential to develop the activity profiles separately for each of the distinct population groups to whom the project is targeted.

ACCESS AND CONTROL PROFILE

Identifying the gender-specific activities in production, reproduction, and maintenance is a necessary, but not sufficient, step in the data preparation for project design and implementation. The flow of resources and benefits is a fundamental concept in the analysis of how projects will affect and be affected by women. Of particular concern is the access that individuals have to resources for carrying out their activities and the command they have over the benefits that derive from these activities. Table 2 illustrates how this information can be usefully summarized.

Two points are important here. First, it is essential to differentiate between access and control. Access to resources does not necessary imply the power to control them. To control a situation is to impose one's own definition upon the other actors in that situation.[8] In other words, access can be determined by others, but control implies that one is the determining force.

Second, it is also important to differentiate between access to and control over the use of resources, on the one hand, and access to and control over the benefits derived from the mobilization of resources. Even where women have unrestrained use of resources, they are not always able to realize the gains from their use. Huntington's observation on female-dominated African agriculture illustrates this situation. Men have power and control over the fruits of women's labor because "tradition gives men a position of authority over women. . . . Men get their wealth, their livelihood and their leisure from women's labor."[9] By focusing on both resources and benefits, one obtains an accurate assessment of the relative power of members of a society or economy and can utilize this knowledge to analyze the probable interaction of women with a project and its likely effect on them.

ANALYSIS OF FACTORS INFLUENCING ACTIVITIES, ACCESS, AND CONTROL

The factors which determine who does what in any population subgroup and what access and control individuals will have to resources and benefits are broad and interrelated. They could be categorized in numerous ways. We suggest the following:

(a) general economic conditions, such as poverty levels, inflation rates, income distribution, international terms of trade, infrastructure;

(b) institutional structures, including the nature of government bureaucracies and arrangement for the generation and dissemination of knowledge, technology, and skills;

(c) demographic factors;

(d) socio-cultural factors;

(e) community norms, such as familial norms and religious beliefs;

(f) legal parameters;

(g) training and education;

(h) political events, both internal and external.

The reason for specifying these determining factors is to identify which can facilitate or constrain a project. Some factors, if not most, will not be amenable to change by a project. Therefore, the task for project design and implementation is to assess the above factors in terms of whether and how they will have an effect on or be affected by a project.

In addition, it is important to identify the exogenous trends or dynamic forces which are already affecting change on what men and women actually do. Projects are not implemented and carried out within the static environment implied by the Activity and Access and Control Profiles. Dynamic forces—political, social, environmental, or physical—can either enhance the accomplishment of a project's objectives or seriously impede it.

The consideration of exogeneous trends and dynamic forces, while always important, is even more so in relation to women. There are a number of forces affecting women on a world-wide basis. Life-expectancy is rising, particularly for women. Availability of birth control information and techniques combined with declining infant mortality rates have the potential to change a fundamental determinant of women's activities; women may have fewer births and/or raise the same number or fewer children. Women are taking up productive activities previously undertaken by men as men migrate to cities or as women assume responsibilities as heads of their households. Women are increasingly entering wage labor occupations in order to survive or to maintain a standard of living. Women are gaining increasing access to permanent wage labor in some areas.

In many areas, the number of women-headed households is increasing, although there tends to be a cultural lag in acknowledging this fact. Bangladesh provides an important case in point. The number of women who were left destitute, widowed, or abandoned after the war has had a significant effect on the Bangladesh cultural norm that all women should be under the care and protection of a man. Decreasing land availability is also challenging the norm that children are an asset. Children now cannot be absorbed onto family land, but must be educated in order to earn a living. Costs of education raise the costs of childrearing significantly. Decreasing land/human ratios also mean that it is more difficult for a man to support all the dependent female family members. The trend is towards an abdication of this traditional responsibility. While these forces have direct and important effects on women's lives and the activities they perform, they are part of a much larger dynamic process. The status of women and their involvement in work external to the household is changing in Bangladesh without anyone's having designed this process. Project design and implementation for Bangladesh must take these forces into account in order to understand the context in which a project will be working and the forces which will affect it.

While Bangladesh provides an example of broader national trends that influence projects, there are also a number of international trends which affect local circumstances. World-wide inflation, international transfers of labor, the impact of technologies, international tensions including the Cold War, all change over time and can affect project outcomes. Events within a project may be better understood when these larger forces are explicitly noted and considered in project planning, implementation and evaulation.

PROJECT CYCLE ANALYSIS

The remainder of the analytical framework consists of examining a project in light of the foregoing basic data. The process is to ask which activities the project will affect and how the issues of access and control relate to these activities. The factors which determine who undertakes particular activities and with what access and control are critical because they act as mediators for the project's effects on women. The analysis will help pinpoint areas of a project which have to be adjusted in order to achieve the desired outcome.

At the project identification stage, questions which relate to women as project clientele need to be addressed. This includes defining project objectives in terms of women, identifying the opportunities and/or constraints for women's project involvement, and, finally, identifying possible negative effects on women. In the design stage of the project, questions related to the impact on women's activities, access and control of resources and benefits need to be raised. For project implementation, questions regarding the relationship of women in the project area to project personnel, organizational structures, operations, logistics, etc. need to be considered. Finally, data requirements for evaluating the project's effects on women must be addressed. Specific questions related to project cycle analysis are detailed in Annex 1.

The activity analysis and the access and control analysis applied to the project cycle analysis provide the basis for good project development. They guide project identification by revealing where women are and what they are doing. They assist project design by highlighting the problem areas and their causes. The challenge is to find ways to deal with the problem areas either by removing them, by-passing them, or adjusting project expectations within them. Project implementation has to be considered in the design process and can benefit from the analytical data, too. It is important to recognize that no standard project design is possible. Each country's situation is unique and will require specific responses.

CROSS-CULTURAL USES OF THE ANALYTICAL FRAMEWORK

The analytical framework which we have provided here is a useful device for understanding the roles of men and women in a society and the external forces which may affect project planning The analysis is generalizable in every context in that it is relevant to determine the gender-based division of labor and to understand the forces which act as constraints on this division or which act to change it.

In applying any generalized analysis across projects and across cultures, it is important to bear in mind its precise use and its clear limits. When activity analysis shows that women are involved in certain productive tasks in one area and that these tasks have certain implications for the division of resources and of power in that context, it is unlikely that even this same division of labor will have exactly the same implications for the division of power in any other culture or project location. Traditions, customs, and political processes interact with economic and social activities differently in different settings. Transference of conclusions and interpretations across projects and cultures is unlikely to be accurate. Nonetheless, there may be similarities in the mode of analysis which may be applied to understand these interactions. While the analytical framework suggested here raises questions that are applicable in all settings insofar as it is designed to gather critically relevant information for project design, one must apply it to specific project settings. Good project design requires actual data on what work women do and in what context, together with clear specification of the issues of prestige, power, access and control.

A decade has passed since the Percy Amendment required that U.S. bilateral assistance programs

> "be administered so as to give particular attention to those programs, projects and activities which tend to integrate women into the national economies of foreign countries, thus improving their status and assisting the total development effort."[10]

This legislative mandate requires that women be cast as contributors and agents of economic development as well as its beneficiaries. Planners, therefore, must guard against the negative effects of their projects on women and focus on the need to enhance women's productivity, raise their income, and promote their access to economically productive resources as a means to achieving overall national economic growth.

CONCLUSION

The foregoing framework should be viewed as a flexible instrument rather than a rigid format for accomplishing this objective. It does not pretend to be a definitive work, but rather one upon which others can build. Only in that spirit can we continue to learn together, and that collective process is essential to the progress we pursue.

TABLES

Table 1   Activity Profile

	Gender/Age[1]							
Socioeconomic Activity	FA	MA	FC	MC	FE	ME	TIME[2]	LOCUS[3]
1. *Production of Goods and Services*								
a. Product/Services								
1. Functional Activity								
2. Functional Activity								
3. Functional Activity								
b. Product/Services								
1. Functional Activity								
2. Functional Activity								
3. Functional Activity								
2. *Reproduction & Maintenance of Human Resources*								
a. Product/Services								
1. Functional Activity								
2. Functional Activity								
3. Functional Activity								
b. Product/Services								
1. Functional Activity								
2. Functional Activity								
3. Functional Activity								
1. Functional Activity								
1. Functional Activity								

Code:1/ FA = Female Adult; MA = Male Adult; FC = Female Child; MC = Male Child; FE = Female Elder; ME = Male Elder
2/ Percentage of time allocated to each activity; seasonal; daily
3/ Within home; family, field or shop; local community; beyond community

Table 2   Access and Control Profile

Resources	Access (M/F)	Control (M/F)
Land		
Equipment		
Labor		
Production		
Reproduction		
Capital		
Education/Training		

Benefits	Access (M/F)	Control (M/F)
Outside Income		
Assets Ownership		
In-Kind goods		
(Food, clothing, shelter, etc.)		
Education		
Political Power/Prestige		
Other		

ANNEXES
Annex 1

The following sets of questions are the key ones for each of the four main stages in the project cycle: identification, design, implementation, evaluation.

WOMEN'S DIMENSION IN PROJECT IDENTIFICATION
A. **Assessing Women's Needs**
1. What needs and opportunities exist for increasing women's productivity and/or production?
2. What needs and opportunities exist for increasing women's access to and control of resources?
3. What needs and opportunities exist for increasing women's access to and control of benefits?
4. How do these needs and opportunities relate to the country's other general and sectoral development needs and opportunities?
5. Have women been directly consulted in identifying such needs and opportunities?

B. **Defining General Project Objectives**
1. Are project objectives explicity related to women's needs?
2. Do these objectives adequately reflect women's needs?
3. Have women participated in setting those objectives?
4. Have there been any earlier efforts?
5. How has present proposal built on earlier activity?

C. **Identifying Possible Negative Effects**
1. Might the project reduce women's access to or control of resources and benefits?
2. Might it adversely affect women's situation in some other way?
3. What will be the effects on women in the short and longer run?

WOMEN'S DIMENSION IN PROJECT DESIGN
A. **Project Impact on Women's Activities**
1. Which of these activities (production, reproduction & maintenance, socio-political) does the project affect?
2. Is the planned component consistent with the current gender denomination for the activity?
3. If it plans to change the women's performance of that activity, (i.e., locus of activity, remunerative mode, technology, mode of activity) is this feasible, and what positive or negative effects would it have on women?
4. If it does not change it, is this a missed opportunity for women's roles in the development process?
5. How can the project design be adjusted to increase the above-mentioned positive effects, and reduce or eliminate the negative ones?

B. **Project Impact on Women's Access and Control**
1. How will each of the project components affect women's access to and control of the resources and benefits engaged in and stemming from the production of goods and services?
2. How will each of the project components affect women's access to and control of the resources and benefits engaged in and stemming from the reproduction and maintenance of the human resources?

3. How will each of the project components affect women's access to and control of the resources and benefits engaged in and stemming from the sociopolitical functions?
4. What forces have been set into motion to induce further exploration of constraints and possible improvements?
5. How can the project design be adjusted to increase women's access to and control of resources and benefits?

WOMEN'S DIMENSION IN PROJECT IMPLEMENTATION
A. Personnel
1. Are project personnel sufficiently aware of and sympathetic toward women's needs?
2. Are women used to deliver the goods or services to women beneficiaries?
3. Do personnel have the necessary skills to provide any special inputs required by women?
4. What training techniques will be used to develop delivery systems?
5. Are there appropriate opportunities for women to participate in project management positions?

B. Organizational Structures
1. Does the organizational form enhance women's access to resources?
2. Does the organization have adequate power to obtain resources needed by women from other organizations?
3. Does the organization have the institutional capability to support and protect women during the change process?

C. Operations and Logistics
1. Are the organization's delivery channels accessible to women in terms of personnel, location and timing?
2. Do control procedures exist to ensure dependable delivery of the goods and services?
3. Are there mechanisms to ensure that the project resources or benefits are not usurped by males?

D. Finances
1. Do funding mechanisms exist to ensure program continuity?
2. Are funding levels adequate for proposed tasks?
3. Is preferential access to resouces by males avoided?
4. Is it possible to trace funds for women from allocation to delivery with a fair degree of accuracy?

E. Flexibility
1. Does the project have a management information system which will allow it to detect the effects of the operation on women?
2. Does the organization have enough flexibility to adapt its structures and operations to meet the changing or new-found situations of women?

WOMEN'S DIMENSION IN PROJECT EVALUATION
A. Data Requirements
1. Does the project's monitoring and evaluation system explicity measure the project's effects on women?
2. Does it also collect data to update the Activity Analysis and the Women's Access and Control Analysis?
3. Are women involved in designating the data requirements?

B. **Data Collection and Analysis**
  1. Are the data collected with sufficient frequency so that necessary project adjustments could be made during the project?
  2. Are the data fed back to project personnel and beneficiaries in an understandable form and on a timely basis to allow project adjustments?
  3. Are women involved in the collection and interpretation of data?
  4. Are data analyzed so as to provide guidance to the design of other projects?
  5. Are key areas for WID research identified?

NOTES

1. Ester Boserup, *Women's Role in Economic Development* (London: George Allen and Unwin Ltd., 1970).

2. This focus on "projects" rather than processes, institutions, and policies can inhibit rather than promote development if not managed appropriately. See David C. Korten, "Community Organization and Rural Development: A Learning Process Approach," *Public Administration Review* 40, (1980), pp. 480-503. Our attention to projects does not carry a normative judgment on this approach but rather reflects a concern to improve the existing modalities.

3. The perceptions or biases of "planners" concerning women constitute another barrier. See Barbara Rogers, *The Domestication of Women: Discrimination in Developing Societies* (London: Tavistock Publications, 1980).

4. See Gloria Scott, *The Invisible Woman* (Washington, D.C.: World Bank, 1980).

5. Sue Ellen Huntington, "Issues in Women's Role in Economic Development: Critique and Alternatives," *Journal of Marriage and the Family* (November 1975), p. 104.

6. C. Deere, and M. Leon de Leal, *Women in Andean Agriculture: Peasant Production and Rural Wage Employment in Columbia and Peru* (Geneva: ILO, 1982).

7. Kenneth Galbraith, "The Economics of the American Housewife," *Atlantic Monthly* (August 1973,) p. 79.

8. Alan Dawe, "The Two Sociologies," *The British Journal of Sociology* 21 (1970) p. 207; also cited in Rogers, *op. cit.*

9. Huntington, *op. cit.*

10. U.S. Congress Foreign Assistance Act of 1973, Sections 103-107.

CHAPTER TWO

Women's Productivity In Agricultural Systems: Considerations For Project Design

Prepared by Kathleen Cloud

The analytic formulation of this paper is based on work undertaken collaboratively with Catherine Overholt in 1981-1982 under funding from the Ford Foundation and the Agricultural Development Council. Our original paper was presented at the 1982 International Agricultural Economics Meetings in Jakarta. For invigorating discussions and helpful comments on that paper, and its subsequent transformation, I am grateful to Jim Austin, Mary Anderson, Elsa Chaney, Richard Goldman, Christine Jones, Jane Knowles, Martha Lewis, Peter Moock, Richard Meyer, Kathleen Staudt, Peter Timmer, Woods Thomas, Francille Firebaugh, and Abe Weisblatt.

INTRODUCTION

This paper is intended to help development professionals think systematically about the work that women do in agricultural systems. Because increasing the productivity of agricultural systems is a key concern of developing countries and international development agencies, many development projects are directed to this end. Effective project design requires identification of the key economic actors and an understanding of their incentives and constraints. Failure to do so increases the risk of ineffective project interventions.

Evidence has mounted over the past decade that women are important actors in most agricultural production systems, that many responsibilities are gender-specific, and that failure to address women's roles within a specific system undercuts the degree of project success. In some cases, such omission may contribute directly to project failure. Because women are so deeply involved in agricultural production, it is important to think systematically about factors that affect their functioning not only for equity reasons, but also for the sake of efficiency. The AID Women and Development policy paper notes that though there is now sufficient evidence of women's contribution to agriculture:

> "there is equal proof that women are often farming without benefit of the improved inputs and services required for a more productive and remunerative agriculture. The paradox is most obvious in the African setting, where it is estimated females do 60-80 percent of all agricultural work. Yet these same females are rarely systematically targeted for training, extension, research, technology, or improved inputs. It is predictable, then, that efforts to improve access to resources and thereby to increase productivity in the agricultural sector will need to be better directed to the female population, if goals for growth are to be achieved."[1]

Gender-specific economic analysis of food production and distribution systems can contribute significantly to improving system performance. Such economic analysis also has strategic value. While many development professionals are sensitive to cultural differences and unwilling to be accused of cultural imperialism for proposing change in the social relationships between the sexes, it is commonly accepted that development projects can appropriately attempt to intensify economic change and move it in desired directions. Shifting discussion of farm women's roles from social to economic terms has the advantage of permitting rational discussion using commonly accepted analytic tools and arguments. It *pays* to deliver resources to women in agricultural systems. This argument is easily understood, and, one hopes, persuasive. Under the pressure of increasing populations, agricultural systems throughout the world are changing, for better or worse. As systems change, it is often possible to use efficiency arguments honestly for promoting productivity-enhancing changes in inequitable situations.

II. AN ANALYTIC FRAMEWORK FOR AGRICULTURAL PROJECTS

This paper will provide tools for improving the correspondence between current knowledge of women's roles in agricultural production and the programming designed to increase agricultural production. The framework for agricultural projects runs parallel to that outlined in "Women in Develpment: A Framework for Project Analysis." The basic elements are
- analysis of women's productive activities within the agricultural system,
- identification of factors influencing women's productivity,
- application of this knowledge to each stage in the project process.

Each of these elements is addressed in turn by the paper. A discussion of the major patterns of activities undertaken by rural women is followed by a discussion of the factors influencing women's productivity in agricultural systems. Such factors include women's relative size and strength, their reproductive roles, their access to productive resources and the incentive structures they face. In the final section, the paper provides an agriculturally focused adaptation of the project cycle analysis.

III. IDENTIFYING WOMEN'S ACTIVITIES IN AGRICULTURAL PRODUCTION SYSTEMS

A. Macro Data on Women's Agricultural Activities

Although there is increasing recognition that women are involved in the world's agriculture, until recently it has been difficult to gain a clear picture of where, when, and under what circumstances women participate in farm work. Although the number of microstudies documenting the importance of women's roles has risen steadily, national statistics have tended to undercount women's agricultural labor due to their definition of economic activity, their sampling patterns and their interviewing procedures.

As the number of detailed empirical studies of women's roles in local production systems has grown, there has been increasing pressure for more accurate estimates of women's contributions to national production systems. A number of such efforts has been undertaken. The latest, largest and most reliable is that of Dixon[2], who estimated female percentages of the agricultural labor force for 82 developing countries. She used regression analysis on three types of national data (the 1977 ILO labor force estimates and projections 1950-2000, FAO's 1970 agricultural censuses and national population census data) to arrive at the most reliable figures for each country. For the 82 countries combined, she found the proportion of women in the agricultural labor force to be 42%; for Sub Saharan Africa the regional average was 46%; for North Africa and the Middle East 31%; and for Asia 45%. Latin American data were not adequate for analysis. There were important differences between countries within each region, and indeed, within each country. Her comments on the differences between data sets are useful in considering data collection strategies for project purposes as well as for understanding patterns of women's participation.

Of the three major sources of agricultural labor force data reviewed . . . the population censuses . . . generally yield the lowest proportions of females in the agricultural labor force, whereas the censuses of agriculture conducted under the sponsorship of FAO yield the highest proportions. As unpaid family helpers and seasonal workers become progressively incorporated into definitions of the labor force, the sex composition changes. More specifically, contrasts between sources confirm that the total farm labor force is generally larger, and that women (and children) form a higher proportion of the total, when the definition of economic activity includes:

- farm production for subsistence only, as well as production intended in whole or in part for sale or exchange;

- unpaid work by family helpers;

- homestead-based crop processing, preparation of crops for storage, transport to markets, raising small animals and poultry, and cultivating kitchen gardens, in addition to field-based production and processing. activities.

The proportion of females is also generally higher when:

- a low minimum of days or hours of work is specified as a criterion for inclusion in the labor force,

- a longer reference period is defined during which economic activity is to be assessed, for example, during the preceding cropping season or year rather than the preceding day or week,

- the survey is conducted during the peak season of agricultural activity, especially if the reference period is brief,

- respondents are asked for a secondary activity or occupation as well as a main activity, and a usual activity as well as a current one

- the interviewer probes the specific activities, based on knowledge of the crops and animals raised, rather than accepting without question the woman's definition of herself as housewife, or her possible assumption that farm work refers only to wage-earning employment

- the interviewer questions women in the household directly rather than asking male household members to report women's activities

- the work of children between the ages of 10 and 15 is routinely included.[3]

The picture that emerges from this comparison of macro data sets is not a complete description of women's agricultural work, but some inferences can be made. In addition to the substantial number of women documented in national agricultural labor force data, many additional women and girls work as unpaid family laborers. Many are primarily involved in production of the family food supply; many work intensively in the fields only during the peak labor season; many girls between 10 and 15 do substantial amounts of agricultural labor, particularly in North Africa and the Middle East. Finally, many women consider their work in agricultural production to be subsidary to other roles.

B. Women's Roles in Agricultural Households

Rural women *do* play multiple roles in the world's agricultural systems. They may be mothers, housekeepers, wage laborers, agricultural processors, market women, and entrepreneurs as well as agricultural producers. Most rural women make constant tradeoffs in allocating labor time and productive resources among their roles and obligations. Most farming systems display mixed patterns of women's agricultural responsibilities, combining production cycles where one sex is primarily responsible with crops where responsibility is shared.

Women are often responsible for the livestock, vegetables and tree crops cared for near their dwellings. They are more likely to be involved in cereal production in hoe cultures and irrigated rice systems than in extensive plow cultures. Class also influences women's participation in agricultural production. Studies in Bangladesh, Indonesia, and Peru all found that women in more affluent farm families devoted less time to field work and more time to cooking for hired laborers. Although in low technology systems poor women are likely to do more field work than more prosperous women, in highly mechanized systems, many women in prosperous farm households do substantial amounts of field work.[4]

1. Agricultural Household Production Models

Few people live alone in rural societies. Agricultural production is intrinsically a collaborative endeavor, with the agricultural household as the most common unit of production and consumption. Because of this, we suggest that project analysis of women's productive work be undertaken within the household context, taking account of the activities and demands of household members of all ages. The *agricultural household*, as the term is used here, is a kinship-based group engaged in both production and consumption with corporate ownership of some resources and a degree of joint decision making among members. Its boundaries are assumed to be permeable and to change over time, as well as under different macroeconomic conditions. Such a definition can include monagamous, polygamous, and women-headed households, as well as compounds or extended families.

Recent economic models of the agricultural household have made women's productive work much more visible, both because they have enlarged the definition of farm production and because they have viewed women's labor time as a rationally allocated productive resource. As it becomes increasingly clear that the home and the fields compete for allocations of capital resources and family labor, the definition of the "products" of the farm enterprise has expanded. Without a definition of output that includes all the productive uses of household time, it is impossible to understand correctly the opportunity costs of member's time, and the underlying rationality of the tradeoffs they make in allocating their time and other productive resources among activities. Fortunately, this research is increasingly convergent in its definition of the output of the family farm firm. Studies in Nepal, Java and the Phillipines, Malaysia, Bangladesh, Kenya, Romania, and the United States have used somewhat different categories for classifying the goods and services produced by the agricultural household.[5] When the various categories are integrated and rationalized, they include the following:[6]

- *agricultural production:* the output of crops and livestock for home consumption or market sale (cereals, vegetables, tree crops, live stock, dairy products, poultry)

- *household production:* goods and services produced within the household for home consumption or market sale (food processing and preparation, provision of household water and cooking fuels, laundry, cleaning, health care, house buildig and maintenance)

- *human capital production:* childbearing, child care and the transmission of skills and knowledge

- *self-employment in the informal market sector:* off-farm activities such as marketing and personal services

- *wage-labor:* paid employment, whether in agriculture or other sectors

Much of the recent farming system research also addresses interactions of production and consumption behaviors, as well as the tradeoffs between on-farm and off-farm labor. However, this research has been much slower to explicitly incorporate household and human capital production in their analysis.[7]

2. Household Resource Allocation Strategies

Several kinds of models have been developed to understand the resource allocation choices made by farm households. Small farmers are no longer viewed as ignorant, tradition bound and resistant to change. They are now seen to be allocating scarce resources of capital and labor rationally to achieve the greater benefit (utility) for the household. In this view they are "efficient by necessity," responsive to prices, and willing to adopt improved technology when it pays to do so. The most recent household models also acknowledged that because farm families consume part of what they produce, production and consumption behaviors are closely entwined and that distinctions between the two are not always clear. Much farm household consumption could also be seen as productivity-increasing investments in the health, education and nutrition of the household's human capital. Allocative choices are constantly being made about the levels of time and resource that will be devoted to each area of household activity. Produce is processed and consumed by the household, or sold, and the profits used to purchase inputs or to pay school fees. Such choices are affected by the level of resources the household possesses, the size and age structure of the household, the availability and cost of technology, and the prices in local markets as well as the cropping systems possible in the environment.

Most household models assume that farm households and the people within them, will do first the things that are necesarry for survival. To provide their basic needs for food, water, shelter, and clothing, a kind of "safety first" strategy is used by most small farms in allocating their resources. Risk reduction strategies are used to assure the household a supply of the things necessary for survival. Many cropping strategies are chosen for their reliability rather than for maximum productivity. If it is necessary to walk long distances to obtain drinking water, or cooking fuel, hours of labor time may be taken from agricultural and household production and locked into these essential activities.

A second assumption is that work is organized and resources are deployed to give the maximum returns compatible with safety. Ben White, in his study of poor Javanese households, describes it this way:

"If we were to rank the various productive opportunities in order of their returns to labor . . . we would expect to find that households would, whenever possible, choose the available combination of activities with the highest total returns to labor. Thus for example, women will often stop or reduce their trading or mat-weaving activity during harvest time to take advantage of the better returns in harvesting. Men may remain at home, cooking and babysitting to free their wives for the harvest; young children may herd livestock or cut fodder when there are wage-labor opportunities for their fathers, or they may cook and babysit while their father cuts fodder and their mother is planting rice. . . . Each household survives on a basis of extreme 'occupational multiplicity' and a highly flexible division of labor among household members. Since the returns to labor in most occupations can barely support an adult, let alone a whole household, the burden of subsistence is shared by men, women and children together. Each household's income is derived from a great variety of sources which constantly change in response to available opportunities according to the season, the state of the market and even the time of day."[8]

Gender Roles in Development Projects

Figure 1

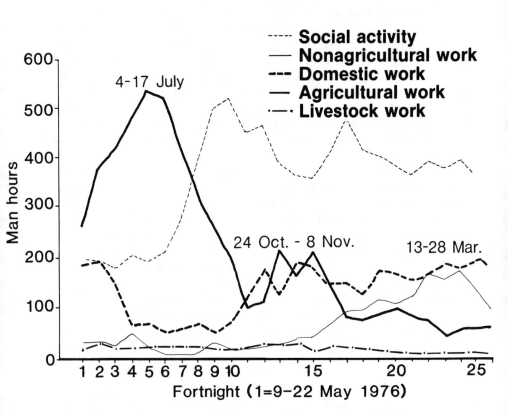

Figure 1. Mean Total Household Labor Hours Each Fortnight By Category of Work, Upper Volta.

Source: Norman, D.W., Newman, M.D. and Ouedrago, I., 1981.
Farm and Village Production Systems in the Semi-Arid Tropics of West Africa: An Interpretive Review of Research, Research Bulletin No. 4, Vol. 1. Pantancheru, A.P., India (ICRISAT)

Although this description emphasizes the rationality of the household's labor allocation decisions, it is clear that such choices are also affected by the power relationships within the household and the community. Such a description ignores the question of *how* decisions are made within the households. Women and men may have different production priorities. One may wish to invest more resources in subsistence production while the other favors cash crops, or wishes to invest more in the nutrition or education of the children. Purchases of household production technology such as improved stoves may compete for capital with purchases of agricultural technology. The relative bargaining power of the two sexes within the household will influence the allocation of productive resources as much as purely economic considerations.

In many systems there are gender-specific responsibilities for producing certain crops or supplying certain kinds of household income, as well as responsibilities for making certain kinds of household expenditures. Many rural households utilize both pooled and non-pooled income streams. Those familiar with American farms will remember the discretionary power of women's butter and egg money, which often contributed substantially to the family's well being. In many developing countries, greater proportions of household income flows may be separate. According to AID's Women and Development policy paper:

> "Research findings for Sub-Saharan Africa, the Carribean, South and South East Asia indicate . . . a pattern of separate and distinct income streams and expenditures, where males and females meet financial responsibilities to the family individually with little or no access to each other's cash or other resources."[9]

In intervening in such systems it is important that projects address the reality of the income flows in project households and not undercut women's income sources, or lessen the base of their bargaining power in other ways.

The economic convention of assuming a household utility function in which a household acts in its own best interest given its resources, its economic environment and its technology, obscures the fact that what is in the best interests of the household may not be in the best interests of the particular members. The unpaid family labor of women or its younger members may increase the income, status and living standard of the household, yet they may not receive an equitable share of the benefits. In placing women within the household context, therefore, we must emphasize that although individuals in households have *shared* interests, they also have *separate* interests, and they may sometimes have *opposing* interests. The separate and opposing interests of women and men may be either acknowledged and institutionalized within the community or they may be vigorously denied. In systems where public norms define women's role as that of economic dependent and restrict them to unpaid labor, women's defense of their own interests is likely to be subtle and difficult to perceive. Nevertheless, it can generate profound impacts on the agricultural economy. Consider the consequence of dependent women's need for sons who will support them in their old age.

We would caution project analysts that while it is often a useful assumption that households act in a relatively rational and equitable manner to maximize benefits to their members, it is also important to be alert for situations of separate or conflicting interests within the household that may affect project functioning.

C. Patterns of Women's Participation in Agricultural Production

Possible arrangements of agricultural responsibilities and tasks are almost limitless. Fortunately for project analysis, there do seem to be patterns. During the past decade, one of the liveliest fields of research on women has centered on factors that influence these patterns of rural women's work. Economic rationality, culture, demography, colonialism, capitalism, capitalist exploitation, patriarchy, the physical safety of women and children, and the type of cropping system have all been cited as influences.

One of the most influential explanations was offered by Boserup in 1970. She noted that in sparsely populated areas such as Africa where shifting hoe cultivation is the rule, men take part in cultivation, primarily in land clearing, but women do most of it. Such areas were contrasted with more densely populated areas of Asia where the agricultural system is that of extensive plow cultivation. Here, men perform the farm tasks associated with the plow, and the hand operations, or some of them, are left for women to perform. In regions of intensive cultivation of irrigated lands, both men and women must work in the fields to support a family on small holdings. In linking population density and the consequent differences in modes of production to women's roles within the production system Boserup makes an implicitly evolutionary argument which identifies population pressure as the engine that propels agricultural intensification and technical change. The unfolding of this scenario removes women from control of land and other productive resources, thus marginalizing them, and constraining their productivity.

"As agriculture becomes less dependent on human muscular power, differences in productivity between the sexes might be expected to fall. In actual fact, this is far from the case. Men monopolize the use of new equipment and modern methods. . . . In all developing countries, and most industrialized countries women perform simple manual tasks in agriculture while more efficient types of equipment, operated by animal or mechanical power, are used primarily by men. Often men apply modern scientific methods of cultivation to cash crops while wives continue to cultivate food crops by traditional methods. Thus, in the course of agricultural development, men's labor productivity tends to increase while women's remain more or less static. . . . The tendency toward a widening gap is exacerbated by the fact that it is cash crops men are taught to cultivate . . . because men can use part of the earnings to invest in improvement of production, while women producing food crops for the family have no cash income for improving their farming techniques.[10]

This thesis has stimulated considerable debate. As more and better information becomes available, the picture seems more complex, with a larger number of factors at play. Traditional systems present more variation, and the dynamics of change are more variable than Boserup's arguments reflect. Nevertheless, there do seem to be systematic underlying regularities, although they are not yet well understood.

Because current generalizations are tentative and have numerous exceptions, it is important to understand the reality of the specific systems the project is intended to affect. Five common patterns of women's agricultural responsibilities are described briefly below.

1. **Separate Crops.** In this pattern, women and men are responsible for production and disposal of different crops within the household production system. Alternatively, women may specialize in certain crops as well as participating with men in the production of others. There may be a division between

- women's subsistence crops and men's cash crops
- women's horticultural crops and men's cereal crops
- between two cereal crops such as millet and rice
- women's swamp rice and men's irrigated rice
- between women's goats and men's cattle.

Alternatively, women may specialize in

- poultry
- vegetable or tree crops
- small ruminants
- gathering of wild crops
- beans, cowpeas and other legumes.

2. **Separate Fields.** In this pattern, women produce the same crops as those controlled by men but in different fields. Such crops are usually

for household consumption, but some may also be marketed. This pattern is found in West African systems, where women's fields are usually part of a larger system in which labor of both sexes is also contributed to the communal fields of the extended household. In these cases, there may be three interlocking production systems: the fields of each wife, the husband's field and the joint field of the extended family.

3. **Separate Tasks.** In this pattern, some or all of the tasks within a single cycle are assigned by gender. Common tasks assignments include the following:

- Men prepare the ground; women plant or transplant the crop. This pattern is particularly prevalent in rice production and in African hoe culture.
- Seed selection and storage is done by women in many systems.
- Plowing is done by men in most systems.
- Certain types of plant protection may be assigned to women.
- Certain kinds of harvesting tasks may be assigned by gender. Climbing trees to harvest crops is usually done by males.
- Post harvest processing and storage of cereals, vegetables, tree crops and dairy products are often women's tasks.
- Care of animals when they are young or sick is often women's work.
- Men and boys often supervise grazing of herds far from home.
- Milking is often assigned to one sex or the other. Sometimes this differs by animal. Among the Malian Tuareg, men milk camels, women milk goats, both may milk cattle.

4. **Shared Tasks.** In this pattern, which overlaps with the other patterns to varying degrees, men and women undertake the same tasks on the same crops. Some systems are marked by jointness in most tasks; in other systems, only labor intensive tasks such as weeding and harvesting are shared.

5. **Women-Managed Farms.** These are two types, *de facto* and *de jure*. In *de facto* systems, men work away from the farms for days, weeks or even years, leaving the women to manage in their absence. In some situations as in the Indonesian example, men work off-farm but return each evening. Kenyan and Japanese women manage farms during the week while their husbands work in the city. In Nepal, absences extend for several months. In Jamaica, Lesotho, Botswana, Yemen, Zimbabwe and the Senegal river basin, male migration abroad may last for years. While in some highly patriarchal systems, farm management and the investment of remittances may remain in the hands of older men, in

many systems, women become the effective farm managers. Many of these farms command significant resources but women managers may lack legal authority to sign credit agreements and commit resources.

De jure women headed households are increasing on a world wide basis. Such women may be widowed, divorced, abandoned or simply never married. Such women-headed households may represent as much as one third of the households in some rural communities. They tend to be among the poorest farming households, underresourced and suffering serious labor constraints. Yet there are many who depend on them for survival.

In patterns of separate crops and separate fields, women are likely to be responsible for management, labor, and disposal of production. Often the produce is primarily for household consumption, but there may be significant surplus for sale. Labor exchange is common in these systems, paid labor less so. In patterns of separate tasks and shared tasks, women's labor may be either unpaid family labor or paid wage labor. On family farms, management of this labor is likely to be a shared household responsibility. Control of the proceeds is variable and usually complex. In cases of plantation agriculture or communal farms, management rests further afield and control of wages may rest either with the individual worker or the household head. For women-managed production systems, women are more likely to control proceeds and usually provide most of the labor, though they may also hire labor or supervise the labor of younger household males. Most agricultural households display mixed patterns of responsibility and control, combining production cycles for which one sex is primarily responsible with those where responsibility is shared or interlaced.

Systems vary both not only in the tasks they assign by gender, but also in the flexibility with which the tasks can be shifted. Children may take over tasks of the parents as they mature, sons replacing mothers in field work or milking. Seasonal shifts in the labor devoted to different kinds of production are often linked to the agricultural cycle. during seasonal labor bottlenecks such as harvesting, every able bodied person may be drawn into agricultural work while other work is put aside. Sometimes this means that everyone goes into the fields. In other systems women work to process the harvest and prepare meals for field workers. Women's field labor may also be divided by class. Poorer women may work in the fields for pay while women in more prosperous households process and cook the food.

Figure 1 provides a particularly striking example of household time tradeoffs in Upper Volta. During the July peak agricultural labor period, the average mean hours of domestic labor per fortnight drops from 200 to 50 and then to 25 as the agricultural labor climbs from

250 to 550 hours. Later, as the agricultural labor hours drop back to 100, the average domestic labor returns to 200, with two sharp dips in October and November mirroring brief upswings in agricultural labor demand. Non-agricultural work-time is very low during the agricultural season and increases during the dry season, while livestock work continues steadily at a low level straight through the year.

Such a pattern clearly reflects women's transfer of labor time from household production to agricultural production during periods of peak labor demand, together with a burst of "catch up" household production time immediately after each agricultural peak subsides. Because the data is not disaggregated by sex, the other gender-related shifts in labor allocation patterns within the household are less visible, although certainly present.

D. Women's Roles in Management of Agricultural Production

Because increased productivity is related to management decisions, it is important to understand not only who is doing the work, but who is making the decisions about cropping patterns, seed selection, use of purchased inputs, use of family and hired labor and crop disposal. It is also important to understand who is implementing the decisions, with what resources and at what level of skill. Unfortunately, the burgeoning literature on farm management and farming systems has given scant attention to issues of gender influence on intra-household decision making and resource allocation.

By contrast, anthropological studies have consistently documented the patterns of women's responsibilities for management of their own animals and crops as reflected in previous pages. Systematic studies of male and female influence on management decisions in integrated systems are increasing in a number of social science literatures. Acharya and Bennet, in an elegant study of women's time use and decision making in eight Nepalese villages, concluded that:

> "Nepalese women are not just silent workers who take directions from men; on the contrary, their managerial role in the agricultural production appears to be commensurate with the level of their labor input into the family farm enterprise (which is 57% for all villages averaged) . . . In decisions. . . , about the disposal of what is produced, and the management of household assets, we find that in these later types of decisions women's labor input into subsistence production no longer seems to have a consistently positive effect across communities. Instead what appears to be more important is the degree to which women in a given community participate in the market economy . . . and the home production of crafts for sale . . . Moreover it appears that cultural factors affect both the

structure of female economic participation and female input into the decision making process . . . there are, however, a number of other factors acting at the household and individual levels such as the economic status of the household, the individual woman's age, the availability of child care, which also affect the structure of female economic participation and decision making in the household."[11]

White and Hatusi, in studying decision making in Javanese households, make the following observations:

Women are often involved in production decisions, and, in significant number of cases they are the dominant influence in these decisions. Since we are dealing with households whose primary source of income is from agriculture, we find no confirmation of the notion that production decisions are firmly in the hands of "male farmers." Any researcher who carries out farm management surveys in rural Java quickly learns that men do not monopolize the details of production management. Normally, the interviewer sits in the front room and addresses questions to the (male) "farmer" in implicit endorsement of the general norm that farming is "men's business." However, detailed questions on fertilizer or labor use, yields and so on, seem very often to require prior consultation with the "housewife" (who may be crouching modestly out of sight in the back room) before they can be answered: "Mak (mother), how much fertilizer did we use? Where did we get the seed? How many laborers helped in the planting and how much did you pay them?" and so on. pgs.[12]

They also note that for some households the involvement of women on production decisions is a necessity because their husbands are physically absent. Either the men are working in the fields of others or in another type of wage labor.

E. Importance of Identifying the Gender Related Responsibilities

Identifying the gender division of responsibility for labor, management, and disposal of all types of households production is crucial to project analysis because the segmentation of control and responsibility has practical effects. Technical assistance given to one family member does not assure its use in all the household's landholdings. Increasing household income will not necessarily make productivity increasing inputs available for all activities if household income is not completely pooled. Targeting improved technologies efficiently demands an understanding of who is likely to use the technology. When labor is segmented by gender, care must be taken in project analysis that labor supply estimates reflect this to avoid creating gender-specific labor bottlenecks.

F. Developing Activity Profiles of Agricultural Households

Table 1 provides an outline for developing a gender-specific profile of agricultural household activities. It should be recognized that although some farming systems projects are beginning to collect detailed micro-level data, existing data would seldom be sufficient to complete such a profile. Nonetheless, it is important to know what information is missing so that a decision can be reached whether to invest additional resources in gathering data or to proceed with project design based on certain tentative assumptions regarding the missing data pieces. Perhaps the major value of an attempt to develop such a *projile* at the micro level is to make programers aware of what they *are* assuming and somewhat more cautious in proceeding.

Such household level analysis is only useful to the degree that it is integrated into project level planning and implementation. *The particular aspects of the household production system likely to be affected by the project should receive the most attention in data collection, and the findings should be explicitly related to project level analysis throughout the project cycle.* For example, if household level analysis shows seed selection and preservation to be women's responsibility, then institutional interventions to develop or disseminate new seeds should take this into account. If household level analysis shows women to be responsible for production and marketing of poultry, dairy products or vegetables, interventions in areas should address this reality.

Such attention does not demand that traditional roles are to be preserved at any costs. It does demand that the analysis of the costs and benefits of differing project strategies explicitly attend to gender roles, as well as to the gender differences in control over resources and benefits that will be addressed in the following section.

IV. FACTORS INFLUENCING WOMEN'S PRODUCTIVITY IN AGRICULTURAL SYSTEMS

There are a number of factors that influence rural women's productivity. They can be seen as three overlaping constellations: the physical factors associated with size, strength and reproduction; the socio-cultural factors influencing role ascriptions and family incentive structures and the institutional structures which affect access to factors of production; and to public incentive structures. Although institutional factors are most amenable to project intervention, and will occupy the major share of this discussion, it is useful to begin by discussing the influence of physical and social factors connected to women's size, strength, and nurturing responsibilities, since so many discussions not only begin, but end, there.

A. Women's Relative Size and Strength

Women's relatively smaller size and strength are often cited as reasons for assuming their productivity is lower than men's in farm labor and off-farm employment. There is a tradition in farming systems work of weighting women's productivity at .75 or .8 of a man's. Recent empirical analysis of input-ouput data does not support these weights. In Kenya, women's overall productivity was found to be as high as men's in agricultural labor, while in Sri Lanka women's rice transplanting, in Upper Volta women's weeding and in West Africa women's cotton picking were all found to be as productive as men's labor in the same activity.

In Bangladesh, by constrast, women's productivity was lower than men's when carrying earth and rocks for road building. It seems likely that women's and men's productivity differences based on size and strength vary by task and are greatest for tasks that demand the most body mass and strength in the upper torso. This view is reflected in a survey of Peruvian peasant farmers where over 70 percent of the respondents considered the time of men and women equally productive in planting, weeding and harvesting by hand, while only 33 percent felt women to be as productive in hoeing, digging with a pick or harvesting with a sickle, tasks that do require both tools and greater strength.[13] The problem is of more than passing interest in farming systems research. Norman recommends more rigorous data collection and analysis to establish realistic weight ranges for tasks.

"There is difficulty in measuring work by different family members and reducing it to a common denominator in terms of productivity. Different approaches to this problem have led to the *actif* concept in Francaphone countries, and the male equivalent concept in Anglaphone Africa. The male equivalent approach is often used in situations where labor flow data is being collected . . . the system need only reflect differences in productivity per unit of time of labor. Arbitrary weights by task is rarely done, an unfortunate fact which could result in spurious conclusions. *The weighting systems employed are critical in determining the validity of the results. Unfortunately, it's not always clear what weighting system was employed, and why specific weights were chosen* . . . Weights have been used that reflect differences in levels of consumption rather than in terms of work productivity. It is important to distinguish . . . between consumption units and work units since such weighting systems are useful for different purposes . . . Relevant weights are further complicated by the facts that productivity of individuals of different sex and age will vary according to the task and its urgency. . . . This is a major problem and makes comparison of studies difficult."[14]

B. Women and the Production of Human Capital

Women have a clear comparative advantage in the production of human capital due to their unique capacity to produce new human beings through pregnancy. Without this capacity societies could not continue to exist. In many cultures women achieve both power and status by exercising this capacity, while at the same time carrying out a great deal of other productive work. After childbirth, women continue to carry out this productive work while simultaneously attending to the needs of their children.

Although increasing amounts of child care can be delegated to others as children grow older, a stream of joint productive work is characteristic for many women in farm households, particularly during periods when they are pregnant and nursing. On the one hand, woman's agricultural or market time may be shortened by the need to nurse a baby or the need to attend to children while working may increase the time needed to complete a task. Yet, at the same time, women are also producing human capital. In the past, such joint productivity seemed difficult for economists to handle. Now, despite the methodological problems, economists studying American farm households are beginning to develop models that reflect joint production, arguing:

> "For farm households, the possibilities for joint production are much greater than for wage earning households. . . . The wife's household time may simultaneously be spent preparing dinner and listening to farm market and weather information. Farm records can be prepared while supervising children, and farm and household inputs can be purchased on the same trip to town.[15]

Much of women's work in agricultural households involves this kind of double or triple layer of simultaneous productive activities. It is characteristic of mother-child interactions that they are pulsed, occurring in brief bursts, separated by attention to other tasks on the part of both mother and child. Such an activity pattern demands both skill and judgement in coordinating a great variety of different activities. Mead Cain in his discussion of Asian households notes:

> "The particular work activities of females are of shorter duration and are more integrally linked than those of males. Thus managerial skills must be applied more frequently and efficiency is best judged overall rather than for specific activities."[16]

C. The Issue of Time

Discussions of time and its relationship to women's productivity are threaded through this paper. We have alluded to short run, daily allocations of time, medium run seasonal cycles of time use, and long run effects of major changes in the economic, political or physical environments.

THE SHORT RUN

Because labor time is the primary productive resource for many of the rural poor, we have assumed that both sexes allocate it rationally, given the constraints they face. Women in most agricultural systems have different patterns of time use than men, both day by day and across the seasons. As noted above, women are more often engaged in joint production, managing two or three activities simultaneously, changing activities more often in the course of the day. Across the world, rural as well as urban women work three to four hours a day more than men in the same society.[17]

At least three reasons have been advanced to account for this difference. Many households and human capital production tasks must be done repeatedly and consistently in order to sustain life at an acceptable level. Food processing and cooking, supplying fuel and water, caring for children and the sick are all activities that must be done daily no matter what other work is undertaken. These tasks, assigned overwhelmingly to women in rural societies, consume large amounts of time, and add to the length of the work day. A second explanation is that labor-reducing technology is less available to women in all areas of their production; therefore, women's labor hours are longer, though their total production may be no greater than that of men in their households. These two arguments are not mutually exclusive, and are often assumed to be interactive.

A third argument made by an interesting assortment of Chicago school economists and feminist scholars, argues that women's joint production is so valuable to the household that it is economically rational for women to work longer hours. Feminist scholars cite distortions in labor markets and incentive structures and women's constrained options as ways of reconciling the high value of joint production with women's relative lack of benefits from this value. The Chicago school argument begs the question of the intra-household distribution of benefits from women's work, submerging the issue in the household utility function. Whatever the explanation, the fact remains that women in rural households work very long hours, trading off the value of time used in one activity against the value in another. Women's time is a scarce resource, and its opportunity costs must be considered in project interventions.

There are a number of ways that the time constraint can be addressed in project design. Using the kind of Activity Analysis suggested in *Table 1*, it is possible to estimate how time is spent and to project how proposed changes may effect household time use. If changes in any part of the system are likely to increase the demand for women's time, several questions can be asked:

- What benefits will women gain from increasing their labor time: Direct? Indirect? Uncertain?

- What other activities are likely to be displaced by this increased time use? What effects will this have on the household in general? What effect on children?

- What kinds of technologies might be introduced to relieve the pressure on women's time? Will they lessen her paid labor time or her unpaid labor time?

- How might such technologies be funded? Credit to households or to women directly? Higher incomes? For whom? Government provision of public services such as wells and electricity?

Among the successful strategies to increase the productivity of women's time have been provision of closer water points, addressing the fuelwood problem with improved stoves or fuel sources, and introduction of household or community grain mills. Basic health and sanitation programs can also release time spent caring for the sick, and rural electrification can transform rural time use.

Aside from technological innovations, it is often possible to free up time for training or for regular health care by paying for it, directly or indirectly. Many poor people can release themselves for a morning, a day, or even a week, if they can pay someone else to assume their responsibilities. Many American poverty programs have used this strategy successfully. In developing countries, maternal/child health clinics often distribute a family flour allotment on the days the mothers come for appointments. In Upper Volta a female literacy program succeeded by purchasing a deisel grinding mill. Three days a week, lessons were held before the mill was turned on. In other places, mills have been combined with radio lessons to provide both flour and literacy in time previously devoted to hand pounding.

One final project intervention is support of child care arrangements which release the time of both women and girls, as well as assuring the safety of children. Often, traditional systems rely heavily on girls for child care. When education becomes available, the opportunity cost of their time rises sharply. In Tanzania, day care centers were organized in many villages, to release girls for school. In other places, older women, or nursing mothers have been informally assigned responsibility while mothers are in the fields. Otherwise, mothers may take the children along and tend them as they work. Support of appropriate child care arrangements can contribute significantly to long term gains in the productivity of both women and girls.

THE MEDIUM AND LONG RUN

In the long run, women's activities and productivity will be influenced by the larger forces at work in the environment. Male migration, changes in technology and increase of production for market affect both the control and the allocation of household resources. Demand for women's agricultural labor may increase, decrease, or change in nature. Shifts in allocation may take place smoothly and swiftly, or slowly and with great difficulty. Control over resources of land, labor, capital, tools, and information may shift between the sexes, as new resources become available. Aside from Boserup's path-breaking work, until recently there had been little attention paid by mainstream economists in the relationships between shifts in the macrocontext and shifts in the gender-related resource allocation patterns of agricultural households. Recently, however, forward and backward linkages between the national economy and decisions made within farm families are receiving more attention. For example, Marc Nerlove cities the effect of a shift in allocation of resources to human capital development:

"... demographic changes which accompany agricultural transformation ... . are a crucial element in agricultural supply response ... Many demographic changes have their roots in individual decision of farm people to make greater investment in human capital in the form of more education and better nutrition . . . and to have fewer children . . . As labor markets improve and there is increased awareness of opportunities outside of the agricultural sector, such demographic changes alter the nature of agri-cultural production, leading to the increased use of non-traditional inputs and to a greater reliance on markets, and thus alter the nature of supply response to prices and other factors."[18]

D. Gender Differences in Access to Productive Resources

One way that agricultural development proceeds is by making resources available for increasing farm productivity. The most common productivity-increasing resources are improved seeds, fertilizers, technology, credit and information. In some cases, land may also be redistributed or new land brought into production. Infrastructure such as irrigation systems, roads and rural health programs are often introduced, and rural industries may be encouraged. Such inputs are intended to increase the productivity of the entire system by increasing the productivity of farm households and the individuals within them. In land-short systems efforts are generally directed toward increasing productivity per acre through the use of "soft" technologies such as improved seed, fertilizers and irrigation. In labor-short systems, the efforts generally focus on increasing productivity per labor hour through the use of machinery and tools.

Systems differ in the degree of access to productive resources they permit to various groups. Often, those who control the greatest share of the current resources gain the largest share of the new. The heirarchial distribution of social power, income and productive resources by *class* has been extensively explored in development literature. There is a second system of stratification present in many societies, that of patriarchial social relations between sexes. Mead Cain defines *patriarchy* as:

> "a set of social relations with a material base which enables men to dominate women. In Bangladesh, patriarchy describes a distribution of power and resources within families where power and control of resources rests with men, and women are powerless and dependent on men. The material base of patriarchial control are interlocking and include elements of the kinship system, political system and religion."[19]

Systems vary greatly in the equity of their relationships. In many agricultural systems, household resource allocation decisions are relatively equitable. In other systems the strong exploit the weak for their own advantage. To the extent that class or patriarchial stratification characterizes an agricultural system, women's access to productivity-increasing resources will be constrained either by their household's status, their gender, or both. Since women consistently contribute well over half the labor hours in rural households, constraints on women's access to resources systematically depress the productivity of half of the available rural labor. This seems shortsighted, yet there is substantial evidence that in many rural systems women have less access to land, capital, credit, technology, wage markets and training than men in the same system. Effective project design must identify which of these barriers to women's access are operative with the project and find ways to deal with them, either by removing them, passing them by, or adjusting project expectations to them.

1. *Women's Access to Land*

Women's access to land is generally greater in systems of low population density, such as Africa where use rights to land are still in force. Even in such areas, women may lose access to good land as a growing population increases pressure on the land. Cleave's African studies show women walking farther than men to their fields in areas where increased cash cropping makes land more valuable. Palmer in Indonesia, Smale in Mauritania and Hanger and Morris in Kenya all document women's loss of secure access to land when the introduction of irrigation increased the productivity of the land. Effective loss is often accompanied by changes in the legal code that register all land in the name of the head of a household. Such legal changes have been documented recently in Kenya and Sri Lanka.

The 145 countries attending the 1979 FAO-sponsored World Conference of Agrarian Reform and Rural Development (WCARRD) recommended a different course of action. The program of action recommended that countries:

> "Repeal those laws which discriminate against women in respect to rights of inheritance, ownership and control of property, and promote understanding of need for such measures . . . promote ownership and co-ownership of land to effectively give women with absentee husbands the legal right to make decisions on the land they manage (Section IV, A i, ii)."

The government of India has incorporated this recommendation into their sixth Five Year Plan, and AID is exploring with the Indian government possible arrangements for implementing co-registration of land title in the resettlement accompanying the Marharashtra Irrigation Project. Similiar discussions are underway between AID and the participating governments to assure women's access to land (and water) in the Senegal River Basin Development.[20]

2. *Women's Access to Capital, Credit and Agricultural Technologies*

Women's lack of access to cash assets, which results from their role as unpaid family laborers and subsistence producers, when combined with constraints on their access to paid labor markets, limits their ability to invest in productivity-enhancing agricultural inputs. Compounding this problem is the reality that where women are responsible for separate crops, separate fields, or management of the total farm enterprise, it is often difficult for them to belong to the government sponsored cooperatives and water users associations which control distribution of new seeds, production packages, water and credit. Not only is women's access to credit constrained by their lack of access to membership in farmers' associations and cooperatives, but their lack of secure title to property often cuts them off from other sources of credit. Henn cites this lack of access to capital as a major constraint on African women's use of agricultural inputs. Since African women are major agricultural producers, such a pattern is a serious constraint to increasing African food production.

Despite all these difficulties, women farmers often do surprisingly well with the resources they have. In one of the few empirical investigations of the relative productivity of men and women farmers, Moock did intensive input-output analysis of maize farms in a Kenyan district where 40% of the farm managers were women. He found women equally productive per hectare despite the fact that the women had less capital and used fewer purchased inputs. They substituted additional labor for other inputs and maintained productivity per hectare, though not per hour. However, in a nearby area with a higher level of government services (all directed to men), women's relative productivity was falling behind men's. Additional time could no longer compensate for improved technologies.[21]

A complicating factor is that packages for improving productivity of "women's crops" often simply do not exist because such crops have low priority in government research and extension. It is noteworthy that when AID asked a panel of international experts to specify agricultural research priorities in areas that would be of great benefit to the world's poor, the top priority crops were small ruminants (sheep and goats), millet/sorghum and beans and cowpeas. All of these neglected crops are women's crops in much of the developing world. Collaborative research involving American and developing country institutions is now going forward on all these crops, with specific attention to women's roles in their production.

Among projects targeted specifically to "women's crops", there have been a number of successful vegetable production projects. The Gambian Ministry of Agriculture set up a project to train 30 women in production of onion crops for export. Fertilizer and seed were provided and the government purchased the crop at an agreed price. Within two years the project grew to involve 900 women in 32 different projects, providing women with income and opportunities to join cooperatives.[22] In Jamaica, USAID financed a women's vegetable production component as part of a larger integrated rural development project. Here, the intention was to improve the nutritional balance in the family food supply of poor hill farmers. The gardens were designed to produce year round with low labor inputs. Thirty young women high school graduates were trained as extension agents, and of these 20 were employed by the larger project. The gardens are rapidly spreading and visitors from a number of Carribean countries have been trained there to develop similiar projects.[23]

Common problems with agricultural projects for women are inadequate attention to crop preservation, and lack of markets for sale of excess production. Both of these problems have been successfully addressed in the Indian Project Flood, where women have been successfully integrated into the cooperatives that produce milk for sale in the city. Because women traditionally cared for the cows, they were involved in the decisions of villages to join the cooperatives. They have received training about animal care and nutrition, and generally they receive payment for the milk because they are the ones responsible for the care and feeding of the animals.[24]

3. Women's Access to Household Technology

If women's lack of capital and credit is a serious constraint to use of improved agricultural technology, it is an even more serious constraint to use of improved household technology. In developing countries, low levels of household technology for the provision of water, domestic fuel and the milling of grain are particular problems. Projects for provision of domestic water sources and social forestry are often justified because they release women's time for more productive activities. In labor-short African agricultural systems, when labor-saving household technology such as cooperative grinding mills have been introduced, women use them most intensely during peak agricultural periods, investing the saved time into cooking an evening meal after their field work or additional time in the fields. By contrast, in labor-surplus situations such as Indonesia, when mechanical milling replaced hand pounding by paid labor, the effect was to deprive poor women of a crucial source of income. Once again, it is important to understand the specific system before intervening.

4. Women's Access to Rural Labor Markets

In land-short situations, women's participation in rural labor markets may be necessary for family survival. In other cases, women may need wage labor to meet certain obligations or to purchase productivity increasing inputs. Studies of such markets show distinct male and female segments. Many tasks are assigned by gender, women's wages are generally lower, and their unemployment rates are higher. Binswanger, in citing ICRASAT's village studies in India, says:

"Males would hardly desire to participate in female submarkets; male wages . . . are roughly 80% higher than female wages, and male possibilities of employment are much higher . . . The segmentation clearly works in favor of the males and at the expense of the females . . . Low wages are attributed - by males and females - to the lack of physical strength and stamina of women. One need only see the loads carried by them, and the discipline of their paddy transplanting lines to realize that the large observed wage differentials can hardly be explained this way."[25]

Projects can and should be designed to provide employment at fair wages for women as well as men in areas such as forestry, seed multiplication facilities, professional and paraprofessional service delivery, agroindustries and other rural enterprises.

In some circumstances, women have also worked to improve their own employment opportunities. Many Kenyan women have organized themselves into self-help groups that exchange labor with one another, and also hire out as a group one or two days a week. They often use their wages as capital for group enterprises. In 1950, a small group of Sri Lankan women organized themselves into the Women's Transplanting Society. Every year since then, women in the group travel to paddy growing areas to transplant rice for 2-3 months, moving from farm to farm. Because they assure steady reliable work, they have been able to bargain for an agreed wage, nutritious free meals, free transport and separate lodging for the group. "By organizing themselves . . . the women are able to work with security in areas distant from their homes, to command reasonable working conditions, and to earn important income."[26]

5. Women's Access to Education and Training

A major factor influencing women's productivity is the extent to which they have access to education and training. There is general agreement that education increases productivity and a substantial literature exists documenting the positive effects of women's education on human capital development[27], paid labor force participation[28] and agricultural production.[29] A recent comprehensive Indian study found that formal education of farm wives enhances the productivity of *all* farm inputs, including a husband's time in farm production.[30]

Yet, according to UNESCO (1977), women compose less than one-third of the primary school students in the low income nations of every region except Latin America. According to Safilious-Rothschild:

"Rural women have consistently lower literacy than rural men, but also lower literacy than urban women . . . Educational wastage is higher in rural areas and for girl students . . . Although girl students show greater rates of educational wastage than boys, their wastage is more often due to repetition of grades . . . girls attrition from primary school seems, therefore, to be less due to a failure to be promoted than to withdrawing from school for non-scholastic reasons. The obstacles to rural women's access to elementary education can be grouped in the following categories: 1) competing household and childcare tasks and responsibilities; 2) competing involvement in productive economic activities; 3) parents', and especially fathers' parents' limited financial and educational resources; 5) shortage of schools; 6) shortage of women elementary school teachers combined with male teachers' negative attitudes; 7) dropping out of school because of pregnancy or marriage."[31]

Remedies that have been suggested include rearranging the school schedule to accomodate cropping cycles, policies and programs to decrease the excessive time spent by rural women in household and agricultural work, development of day care and rotating childcare arrangements to free girls' time for school, the increased training of women as teachers and assistant teachers, and increasing the number of paid professional and paraprofessional women in rural programs to establish the economic and social status pay-off of girls education.

Such efforts to increase the number of rural women with a primary education must be supplemented by systematic efforts to increase the number of women receiving higher education. According to AID's policy paper:

"Women who combine the skills provided by modern education with an understanding of traditional values and local realities affecting women contribute a great deal to successful development programming. Thus, AID must take measures to provide access for women to training programs and higher education, especially in management and administration of the sectors . . . in most countries it is the functional ministries that bear primary responsibility for integrating women into their programs and for insuring the relevance of their program to the particular needs of women and girls."[32]

This concern with the integration of professionally trained women into all aspects of agricultural institutions is particularly relevant to institution-building projects that include participant training. Care must be taken that women are actively recruited and supported in a training for a range of professional roles in agriculture in order to assure that the needs of women in agricultural households will be adequately addressed by agricultural institutions.

E. Access to and Control Over the Benefits of Production: The Problem of Incentive Structures

Much of women's productive work is unpaid. Women subsidize the world's economies through unpaid household and human capital production. Farm women also undertake significant amounts of agricultural labor without pay. What benefits do they receive from this work? How can their labor be accounted for in terms of women's economic rationality? Two explanations are possible. One is that women are altruists. They derive their utility from the satisfaction of others, from seeing their families healthy, well cared for and well fed. The other explanation is that women have little choice. Societies are arranged in such a way that women's independent access to productive resources, to labor markets, to information, to political and legal rights are seriously constrained. Society permits them only limited control of their own reproductive capabilities. The obligations of childbearing and child raising are thrust upon them and they must labor within households to assure their children's survival as well as their own.

It is reasonable to assume that both explanations contain some truth, though their weight certainly varies between societies. In modern American society, where reproductive control is widespread, women devote significant amounts of unpaid time to the care of families, apparently because they derive altruistic satisfaction from doing so. Their access to labor markets and productive resources is great enough so that most North American women also have independent cash incomes. Nevertheless, there are significant gender differences in access to the highest paying work and resources for the most productive investments, which makes women's relatively greater contribution to household production economically rational, at least while their children are young. In most rural societies in the developing world, women's alternatives are more sharply constrained and the benefits they receive more limited.

Whatever the range of available incentives, it is safe to say that people will exert more effort, will become more productive in an activity, if they can see benefits flowing from their increased effort. These benefits may be in cash, in kind, in power, respect, or in the satisfaction of seeing others well cared for. Benefits may also include relief from difficult or unpleasant tasks or from feelings of guilt.

Recent research documents that in societies where women participate in the market economy in some way, where women have direct access to cash, their power is greater in intra-household decision making, and the status of women is higher in the communities.[33] The incidence of wife beating also seems to be lower in such societies.[34] These are all benefits, over and above the value of the cash, yet linked to cash income. Therefore, in analyzing agricultural systems for possible project intervention, it is useful to think about intra-household income flows.

- which productive work is paid? unpaid?
- who receives the pay? all the family workers individually or the head of household for the whole family?

- who controls disposal of the different household products?
- who receives cash from the sales? the producer? someone else?

Intra-household disbursement patterns are also important. Women's income may all flow to purchase the household's basic needs, to food and clothing, although her husband may have disposable income to use for productive inputs as well as for consumer goods such as transistor radios and beer. Where this is the case, the targeting of additional income specifically to women may be necessary. Simply "raising family incomes" will not serve.

Project Flood presents one successful way to channel income directly to women. Women's producers are paid directly by the co-op. Although this income is channeled back into the family budget, the report notes that the contribution women make enhances their importance. The same effect was described by Cerna in Rumania:

> "The organizational and economic structure of the producer co-op has had a particular impact . . . by institutionalizing women's participation and paying them directly for farm work . . . The previous pattern of the individual family farm prevented a wife's distinct contribution to its welfare from being measured: this favored and strengthened the position of the family head who was the owner of the fruit of the family's toil. Now, on the contrary, each cooperative farm member's output of work and corresponding forms of payment are computed on an individual basis, whatever a person's family status may be . . . This is a tremendous change which enhances the partnership status of the wife, favors more independent behavior of women and creates conditions which will promote, in the long run, their equal status within the house."[35]

Such payment structures have also been used with success in an AID PVO resettlement project in Senegal where membership in the productive cooperative is by individual rather than by household.

In contrary cases where women are not paid directly for their work, productivity often suffers, especially in systems with little pooled income. Women with high levels of responsibility for the provision of the family's basic needs and little access to cash are forced to substitute their labor, and that of the children they create, for the productivity-increasing inputs they cannot afford.

F. Developing Profiles of Gender Access to, and Control over, Resources and Benefits

Table 2 provides an outline for developing a gender-specific profile of access to and control over resources and benefits. Such a profile by its very nature has both efficiency and equity implications. The kind and degree of women's access to productive resources conditions the productivity of their labor, as do the incentive structures they face. The degree of control they exercise over resources and benefits affect their ability to increase production and their ability to increase production and their ability to bargain to protect their own interests. Because each of these factors has implications for project design and implementation, developing such a profile is a useful exercise in clarifying assumptions. It also permits a clearer picture of possible areas of project intervention.

V. ADDRESSING WOMEN'S PRODUCTIVE ACTIVITIES IN AGRICULTURAL PROJECTS

Factors that influence women's productivity have been identified in the previous section to include women's differential access to land, capital, credit, agricultural and household technologies, education and training as well as to rural labor markets. Programmers should try to indentify the nature and seriousness of the barriers to women's access to such productive resources and relieve them wherever possible. We have also noted the importance of identifying distortions in the incentive structures facing women not only for reasons of equity, but also because they influence the kinds of activities women undertake and the levels of productivity they can attain. Such analyses provide focal points for project interventions.

Straightforward economic analysis, when disaggregated by sex, often provides convincing efficiency arguments for removing institutional barriers to women's productivity; but, in order to make efficiency arguments, it is necessary to have data. The first step is specification of the productive activities women engage in within agricultural households. It is also necessary to understand the level of resources women command and the incentives structures that influence their behavior. This understanding can then be applied to each step in the project process. An outline of questions for addressing women's roles throughout the project cycle is included as Table 3.

Such a project cycle analysis requires a dynamic view of changes over time. Because projecting changes accurately with the present limited knowledge base is a risky business, the analysis emphasizes the need for regular monitoring of project effects and flexibility in project implementation. It also emphasizes the need to evaluate projects in such a way that the lessons learned can be accumulated and that, over time, e can increase our ability to design equitable and efficient agricultural projects.

TABLES
Table 1   Activity Profile of an Agricultural Household

% of Total House- hold Time	Type of of Production	Who Acquires Inputs	Who Manages Production	With What Labor	With What Resources[2]	Who Controls Disposal
AGRICULTURAL						
*Separate Crops**						
Crop 1						
Crop 2						
Separate Fields						
Crop 1						
Crop 2						
Separate Tasks						
*Crop						
Task 1						
Task 2						
*Crop						
Task 1						
Task 2						
Shared Tasks						
Crop						
Task 1						
Task 2						
Women Managed Farm						
*Crop 1						
*Crop 2						
HOUSEHOLD						
Product 1						
Product 2						
Product 3						
HUMAN CAPITAL						
Task 1						
Task 2						
INFORMAL MARKET SECTOR						
Task 1						
Task 2						
WAGE LABOR						
Task 1						
Task 2						

*Crops include agricultural, horticultural and animal products

Table 2   Gender Profile of Access to, and Control Over, Resources and Benefits in Agricultural Systems

	Sources of Access		Degree of Control	
	M	F	M	F
I. RESOURCES				
Land				
Technology				
Labor				
Production				
Reproduction				
Capital				
Education/Training				
Rural Labor Markets				
Entrepreneurial/Markeing Resources				
II. BENEFITS				
Outside Income				
Assets Ownership				
In-kind Goods				
Food, Clothing, Shelter				
Information/Knowledge				
Offspring — Reproduction of the Group				
Social Insurance				
Care in Disaster and Old Age				
Political Power/Prestige				
Other				

Table 3   Project Cycle Analysis: Agriculture

I. WOMEN'S DIMENSION IN PROJECT IDENTIFICATION

A. Defining General Project Objectives

1. Are the project objectives explicity related to women's economic and social roles?
2. Do these objectives adequately reflect women's needs?
3. Have women participated in setting these objectives?

B. Assessing Women's Needs and Opportunities

1. What needs and opportunities exist for increasing women's productivity and/or production?
   a. In agriculture?
   b. In household production?
   c. In human capital production?
   d. In the informal sector?
2. What needs and opportunities exist for increasing women's access to and control over resources?
3. What needs and opportunities exist for increasing women's access to and control over benefits?

Table 3 (Continued)

4. How do these needs and opportunities relate to the country's other general and sectoral development needs and opportunities?
5. Have women been directly consulted in identifying such needs and opportunities?

C. **Identifying Possible Negative Effects**
   1. Might the project reduce women's access to or control of resources and benefits?
   2. Might it adversely affect women's situation in some other way?
   3. What are the potential effects on women in the short run? The longer run?

II. **WOMEN'S DIMENSION IN PROJECT DESIGN**

A. **Project Impact on Women's Activities**
   1. Which activities will the project affect in:
      a. agricultural production?
      b. household production?
      c. human capital production?
      d. informal sector production?
      e. wage labor production?
   2. Is the planned component consistent with the current gender denomination for these activities?
   3. If it plans to change the women's performance of activities, is this feasible, and what positive or negative effects would it have on women?
   4. Where there are no planned changes in activities, is there a missed opportunity for improving women's roles in development process?

B. **Project Impact on Women's Access and Control**
   1. How will each of the project components affect women's access to and control over *productive resources* such as:
      a. land
      b. water (domestic and agricultural)
      c. capital
      d. credit
      e. agricultural technology
      f. household technology
      g. firewood and other fuels
      h. information
      i. rural wage markets
      j. resources in the informal sector
      k. their own labor
      l. the labor of others
   2. How will each project component affect women's access to and control over *benefits* such as:
      a. wages
      b. revenue from sale of goods
      c. revenue from sale of services
      d. subsistence goods
      e. social insurance (care in sickness, old age, etc.)
   3. How can project design be adjusted to increase positive effects and eliminate or reduce negative ones?

III. WOMEN'S DIMENSION IN PROJECT IMPLEMENTATION
A. **Organizational Structures**
1. Does the organizational form enhance women's access to resources?
2. Does the organization have adequate power to obtain resources needed by women from other organizations?
3. Does the organization have the institutional capability to support and protect women during the change process?

B. **Operations and Logistics**
1. Are the organization's delivery channels accessible to women in terms of personnel, location and timing?
2. Do control procedures exist to ensure dependable delivery of the goods and services?
3. Are there mechanisms to ensure that the project resources or benefits are not usurped by males?

C. **Finances**
1. Are funding levels adequate for proposed tasks?
2. Is preferential access to resouces by males avoided?
3. Is it possible to trace funds for women from allocation to delivery with a fair degree of accuracy?
4. Do funding mechanisms exist to ensure program continuity?

D. **Personnel**
1. Are project personnel sufficiently aware of women's productive activities and sympathetic toward women's needs for resources and benefits? If not, is it possible to increase staff responsiveness through incentives and training?
2. Do personnel have the skills necessary to provide the specific inputs required by women in the project area? If not, are training and/or additional staff possible?
3. Are there appropriate opportunities for female participation in project management positions?

E. **Flexibility**
1. Does the project have a management information system which will allow it to detect the effects of the operation on women?
2. Does the organization have enough flexibility to adapt its structures and operations as changes occur and new information is processed?

IV. WOMEN'S DIMENSIONS IN FORMATIVE AND SUMMATIVE EVALUATION
A. **Data Requirements**
1. Does the project's monitoring and evaluation system explicity measure the project's on-going and end-of-project effects on women?
2. Are women involved in designating the data requirements?

B. **Data Collection and Analysis**
1. Are the data collected with sufficient frequency so that necessary adjustments could be made during the project?
2. Are the data fed back to project personnel and beneficiaries in an understandable form and on a timely basis to allow project adjustments?
3. Are women involved in the collection and interpretation of data?
4. Are data analyzed so as to provide guidance to the design of other projects?
5. Are key areas for further research on women's roles in agricultural systems identified?

NOTES

1. U.S. Agency for International Development, *AID Policy Paper: Women in Development.* (Washington, D.C., Bureau for Program and Policy Coordination, 1982), p. 3.
2. Ruth B. Dixon, "Women in Agriculture: Counting the Labor Force in Developing Countries," *Population and Development Review* (8, no. 3, 1982).
3. Ibid., pp. 561-562. Excerpted with the permission of the Population Council.
4. For Japan, see Japanese Ministry of Agriculture, Forestry and Fisheries, *Publication for Mid-Decade Conference* (Copenhagen, 1980); for Eastern Europe, see Elizabeth Croll, "Women in Rural Production and Reproduction in the Soviet Union, China, Cuba, and Tanzania: Socialist Development Experiences," *Signs* (7, no. 2, 1981); for France, see Ministere du Travail, Comite du Travail Feminin, *La Formation des Femmes*, Government of France; for the United States, see Calvin Jones and Rosenfield, *American Farm Women: Findings from a Survey*, Report no. 130 (Chicago: National Opinion Research Center, 1981).
5. For Nepal, see Meena Acharya and Lynn Bennett, *Women and the Subsistence Sector, Economic Participation and Household Decision making in Nepal* (Washington, DC: The World Bank, 1982); for Java, see Gillian Hart, "Patterns of Household Labor Allocation in a Javanese Village" in *Rural Household in Asia*, Binswanger, ed. (Singapore: Singapore University Press, 1980); for the Philippines, see R. Evenson, "Time Allocation in Rural Philippine Households" *American Journal of Agricultural Economics*, (60, no. 2, 1978); for Malaysia, see J. DaVanso and D.L.P. Lee, *Compatibility of Child Care with Labor Force Participation and Non-Market Activities: Preliminary Evidence from Malaysia Time Budget Data*, (Rand Paper Series, 1978), and H. Barnum and L. Squire, *A Model of an Agriculture Household: Theory and Evidence*, (Baltimore: World Bank Occasional Papers no. 27, 1979); for Bangladesh, see Mead Cain et al, *Class, Patriarchy and the Structure of Women's Work in Rural Bangladesh*, Population Council Working Paper no. 43 (New York: The Population Council, 1979); for Kenya, see Jane Hanger and Jon Morris, "Women and the Household Economy" in *An Irrigated Rice Settlement in Kenya* R. Chambers and J. Moris eds. (Munich: Weltform Verlag, 1973); for Rumania, see Michael Cernea, *Macroeconomic Change, Feminization of Agriculture and Peasant Women's Threefold Economic Role* (Washington, D.C., The World Bank, 1979); for the United States, see W. Huffman and M. Lange, *Farm Household Production: Demand for Wives Labor, Capital Services and the Capital Labor Ratio*, Yale University Discussion Paper No. 408 (New Haven: Economic Growth Center, 1982).
6. Kathleen Cloud and Catherine Overholt, "Women's Productivity in Agricultural Systems: A Overview," Proceedings of the International Agricultural Economics Meetings, (Jakarta, Indonesia, 1982), p. 167.
7. David Norman, Mark Newman and Ismael Ouedraogo, *Farm and Village Production Systems in the Semi-Arid Tropics of West Africa: An Interpretive Review of Research*, Research Bulletin No. 4 (Hyderabad, India: International Crops Research Institute for the Semi-Arid Tropics, 1981), p. 6.
8. Benjamin White, "Population, Involution and Employment in Rural Java," *Development and Change*, (7, 1976), p. 280.
9. USAID, Policy Paper, p. 3.
10. Ester Boserup, *Women's Role in Economic Development* (New York: St. Martin's Press, 1970).
11. Meena Acharya, and Lynn Bennett.
12. Benjamin White and E.L. Hastuli, *Different and Unequal: Male and Female Influence in Household and Community Affairs in Two West Javanese Villages* (Indonesia: Bogar Agricultural University, Indonesia, 1980), pp. 32-33.

13. Carmen Diana Deere, "The Division of Labor by Sex in Agriculture: A Peruvian Case Study," *Economic Development and Cultural Change* (30, 1982), p. 810.
14. Norman, Newman, and Quedraogo, p. 244.
15. Huffman and Lange, p. 243.
16. Mead Cain, "The Economic Activities of Children in a Village in Bangladesh" in *Rural Households in Asia*, H. Binswanger, ed. (Singapore: Singapore University Press, 1980), p. 243.
17. Alexander Szalsi, *The Situation of Women in the Light of Contemporary Time Budget Research*, Report submitted to the United Nations World Conference of the International Women's Year (Mexico City, 1975), p. 11.
18. Marc Nerlove, "The Dynamics of Supply: Retrospect and Prospect," *American Journal of Agricultural Economics* (1979), p. 885.
19. Cain et al, p. 2.
20. For India, see "USAID Project Paper, Maharashtra Irrigation" (Vol. 1), p. 43; for Senegal, see "USAID Project Paper, OMVS Agricultural Research II" (Vol 2), p. 21.
21. Peter Moock, *Managerial Ability in Small-Farm Production: An Analysis of Maize Fields in the Vehiga Division of Kenya* unpublished dissertation (New York: Columbia University, 1973); and Kathleen Staudt, "Agricultural Productivity Gaps: A Case Study of Male Preference in Government Policy Implementation," *Development and Change* 9, 1978.
22. International Women's Tribune Center, *Women and Food Newsletter*, No. 10, p. 10.
23. E. Chaney and M. Lewis, *Creating a Women's Component: A Case Study in Rural Jamaica* (Washington, D.C.: USAID, 1980).
24. World Food Program, *A Flood of Changes: World Food Program in India* (Rome, 1979).
25. H. Binswanger, et al, *Common Features and Contrasts in Labor Relations in the Semi-Arid Tropics of India* Progress Report 13 (Hyderabad, India: ICRISAT, 1982), pp. 18-19.
26. International women's Tribune Center, p. 12.
27. See J. DaVanzo and D.L.P. Lee, 1978.
28. Cynthia Lloyd and Beth Neimi, *The Economics of Sex Differentials (New York: Columbia University Press, 1979).*
29. See Peter Moock, 1973.
30. See M. Rosenzweig, "Neoclassical Theory and the Optimizing Peasant: An Econometric Analysis of a Market Family Labor Supply in a Developing Country," *The Quarterly Journal of Economics, 1980.*
31. C. Safilios-Rothschild, *Access of Rural-Girls to Primary Education in the Third World: State of the Art, Obstacles and Policy Recommendations* (Washington, DC: AID/WID, 1979), pp. 2, 3, 8.
32. USAID Policy paper, p. 8.
33. See Meena Archarya and Lynn Bennett, 1982; and P. Sanday, "Female Status in the Public Domain" in *Women, Culture and Society* M. Rosaldo and L. Lamphere editors (Stanford: Stanford University Press, 1974).
34. R.L. Blumberg, "A Paradigm for Predicting the Position of Women" in *Sex Roles and Social Policy*, Bernard Lipman-Blumen ed. (London: Sage, 1979).
35. Michael Cernea, p. 119-120.

BIBLIOGRAPHY

Abbott, Susan. "Full-Time Farmers and Weekend Wives: An Analysis of Altering Conjugal Roles." *Journal of Marriage and the Family* 38, no. 1 (1976).
Aboul-Seoud, Khairy, and Farag, Flora. *The Role of Women and Youth in Rural Development With Special Emphasis on Production and Utilization of Foods.* Cairo: 1979. Mimeograph.
Acharya, Meena. *Time Use Data and the Living Standards Measurement Study.* LSMS Working Paper no. 18. Washington: The World Bank, 1982.

Acharya, Meena, and Bennett, Lynn. *Women and the Subsistence Sector, Economic Participation and Household Decisionmaking in Nepal.* Washington, D.C.: Staff Working Paper no. 526. The World Bank, 1982.

Barnum, H., and Squire, L. *A Model of an Agricultural Household: Theory and Evidence.* World Bank Occasional Paper no. 27. Baltimore: The World Bank, 1979.

Binswanger, H.; Evenson, R.; Florencio, C.; and White, B. *Rural Households in Asia.* Singapore; Singapore University Press, 1980.

Binswanger, Doherty; Balarmeah, Bhende; et al. *Common Features and Contrasts in Labor Relations in the Semi-arid Tropics of India.* ICRISAT Progress Report 13. Hyderabad, India: ICRISAT, 1982.

Blumberg, R. L. "A Paradigm for Predicting the Position of Women." In *Sex Roles and Social Policy,* edited by Bernard Lipman-Blumen. London: Sage, 1979.

Boserup, Ester. *Women's Role in Economic Development.* New York: St. Martin's Press, 1970. Reprinted by permission of publisher.

Burfisher, Mary, and Horenstein, Nadine. *Sex Roles in the Nigerian Tiv Farm Household and the Differential Impacts of Development Projects.* Case Studies of The Impact of Large-Scale Development Project on Women, Study no. 2. New York: The Population Council, 1983.

Cain, Mead. "The Economic Activities of Children in a Village in Bangladesh." In *Rural Households in Asia,* by H. Binswanger, et al. Singapore: Singapore University Press, 1980.

Cain, Mead, et al. *Class, Patriarchy and the Structure of Women's Work in Rural Bangladesh.* The Population Council Working Paper no. 43. New York: The Population Council, 1979.

Cernea, Michael. *Macrosocial Change, Feminization of Agriculture and Peasant Women's Threefold Economic Role.* Paper submitted to the World Bank. Washington, D.C.: The World Bank, 1979.

Chaney, E., and Lewis, M. *Creating a Woman's Component: A Case Study in Rural Jamaica.* Paper submitted to USAID/WID. Washington, D.C.: USAID/WID 1980.

—. *Women, Migration and the Decline of Small Holder Agriculture.* Paper presented to the Board for International Food and Agricultural Development, Washington, D.C., 1980.

Chayanov, A. V. *The Theory of Peasant Economy,* edited by Thorner, Kerblay and Smith. Homewood, Ill. Richard D. Irwin, Inc., 1966.

Chen, Marty. *A Structural Analysis of Women's Work in Rural Bangladesh.* Paper presented at the 1st Women, Work, and Public Policy Workshop. Cambridge, Mass.: Harvard Institute for International Development, 1981.

Cleave, John. *African Farmers: Labor Use in the Development of Smallholder Agriculture.* New York: Praeger, 1974.

Cloud, Kathleen. "Sex roles in Food Production and Distribution Systems in the Sahel." In *Proceedings of The International Conference on Women and Food.* Washington, D.C.: USAID/WID, 1978.

Cloud, Kathleen, and Overholt, Catherine. *Women's Productivity in Agricultural Systems: An Overview.* Proceedings of the International Agricultural Economics Meetings, Jakarta, Indonesia, 1982.

Collinson, M. P. *Farm Management in Peasant Agriculture: A Handbook for Rural Development Planning in Africa.* New York: Praeger Publishers, 1972.

Croll, Elizabeth. "Women in Rural Production and Reproduction in the Soviet Union, China, Cuba and Tanzania: Socialist Development Experiences." *Signs* 7, no. 2 (1981).

Danish Agricultural Council. *Rural Women in Denmark.* Copenhagen: Danish Agricultural Council, 1980.

DaVanzo, J., and Lee, D. L. P. *Compatibility of Child Care with Labor Force Participation and Non-Market Activities: Preliminary Evidence from Malaysian Time Budget Data.* Rand Paper Series, Santa Monica, Calif.: The Rand Corp. 1978.

Deere, Carmen Diana. "The Division of Labor by Sex in Agriculture: A Peruvian Case Study." *Economic Development and Cultural Change* 30 (1982).

Deere, Carmen Diana, and Leon de Leal, Magdalena. *Women in Andean Agriculture.* Geneva, Switzerland: International Labour organization, 1982.

Dey, Jennie. "Gambian Women: Unequal Partners in Rice Development Projects." *The Journal of Development Studies,* 17, no. 3 (1981).

Dixon, Ruth B. "Women in Agriculture: Counting the Labor Force in Developing Countries." *Population and Development Review* 8, no. 3 (1982).

Evenson, Robert. "Food Policy and the New Home Economics." *Food Policy,* vol. 6 no. 3 (1981).

—. *Measurement of Time Allocation and Household Income.* Rockefeller Foundation Workshop. New York: The Rockefeller Foundation, 1982. Mimeograph.

—. "Time Allocation in Rural Philippine Households." *American Journal of Agriculture Economics* 60, no. 2 (1978).

Folbre, N. *Household Production in the Philippines: A Non-neoclassical Approach.* Women in International Development Working Paper no. 26. East Lansing, Mich.: Michigan State University, 1983.

Food and Agriculture Organization of the United Nations. *Report of the World Conference on Agrarian Reform and Rural Development,* Rome, 1979.

Fortman, Louise. *Women and Tanzanian Agricultural Development.* Economic Bureau 77.4. Tanzania: University of Dar Es Salaam, 1978.

Gasson, Ruth. *The Role of Women in British Agriculture.* Report commissioned by the Women's Farm and Garden Association, Colchester, Essex, England, 1980.

Hanger, Jane, and Moris, Jon. "Women and the Household Economy." In *An Irrigated Rice Settlement in Kenya,* by Robert Chambers and Jon Moris. Munich: Weltforum Verlag, 1973.

Hart, Gillian. "Patterns of Household Labor Allocation in a Javanese Village." In *Rural Households in Asia* by Binswanger, Evenson, Florencino, and White. Singapore: Singapore University Press, 1980.

Henn, Jeanne. *Women Farmers in Africa: Why Are They Using The Short Handled Hoe?* Paper presented at the 2nd Women, Work and Public Policy Workshop. Cambridge: Harvard Institute for International Development, 1982.

Huffman, W., and Lange, M. *Farm Household Production: Demand for Wives' Labor, Capital Services and the Capital Labor Ratio.* Yale University Discussion Paper no. 408. New Haven: Economic Growth Center, 1982.

International Center for Research on Women (ICRW). *The Productivity of Women in Developing Countries: Measurement Issues and Recommendations.* Washington, D.C.: USAID/ WID, 1980.

International Women's Tribune Center (IWRC). *Women and Food, Newsletter* no. 10. New York: IWRC, 1979.

Japanese Ministry of Agriculture, Forestry and Fisheries. *Publication for Mid-Decade Conference,* Copenhagen, 1980.

Jones, Calvin, and Rosenfield, Rachel. *American Farm Women: Findings from a Survey.* Report no. 130. Chicago: National Opinion Research Center, 1981.

Johnston, Bruce F., and Kilby, Peter. *Agriculture and Structural Transformation.* New York: Oxford University Press, 1975.

Jones, Christine. *Women's Labor Allocation and Irrigated Rice Production in North Cameroon.* Paper prepared for the International Association of Agricultural Economists, Jakarta, Indonesia, 1982.

Jones, Christine. *The Effects of the Intrahousehold Organization of Production and the Distribution of Revenue on the Participation of Rice Cultivators in the Semry I Rice Project.* Cambridge, Mass.: Mimeograph, 1982.

Kusnic, Michael, and DaVanzo, Julie. *Income Inequality and the Definition of Income: the Case of Malaysia.* Paper submitted to USAID, no. R-2416. Santa Monica, Calif.: The Rand Corp., 1980.

Lele, Uma. *The Design of Rural Development: Lessons from Africa.* Baltimore: The John Hopkins University Press, 1975.

Lloyd, Cynthia, and Niemi, Beth. *The Economics of Sex Differentials.* New York: Columbia University Press, 1979.

Lloyd, Cynthia, ed. *Sex, Discrimination and the Division of Labor.* New York: Columbia University Press, 1975.

Loose, Edna. *Women in Rural Senegal.* Muncie, Ind.: Purdue University, 1979. Mimeograph.

McSweeney, Brenda Gale. "Collection and Analysis of Data on Rural Women's Time Use." *Studies in Family Planning* 10 nos. 11/12 (1979): 379-382.

Mellor, John W. *The Economics of Agricultural Development.* Ithaca: Cornell University Press, 1966.

Ministere du Travail, Comité du Travail Feminin. *La Formation des Femmes en Millien Rural.* Paris, Government of France, 1974.

Moock, Peter. "The Efficiency of Women as Farm Managers: Kenya." *American Journal of Agricultural Economics* vol. 56, no. 5, (1976).

—. *Managerial Ability in Small-Farm Production: An Analysis of Maize Yields in the Vihiga Division of Kenya.* Unpublished dissertation. New York: Columbia University, 1973.

Nerlove, Marc. "The Dynamics of Supply: Retrospect and Prospect," *American Journal of Agricultural Economics* vol. 61, no. 5, (1979).

Newman, M.; Ouedraogo, I.; and Norman, D. "Farm Level Studies in the Semi-Arid Tropics of West Africa." In *Socioeconomic Constraints to Development of Semi-Arid Tropical Agriculture,* by J. Ryan, Hyderabad, India: International Crops Research Institute for the Semi-Arid Tropics, 1981.

Norman, David; Newman, Mark; and Ouedraogo, Ismael. *Farm and Village Production Systems in the Semi-Arid Tropics of West Africa: An Interpretive Review of Research.* Research Bulletin 1, no. 4. Hyderabad, India: International Crops Research Institute for the Semi-Arid Tropics, 1981.

Palmer, Ingrid. *The Nemow Case: Case Studies of the Impact of Large Development Projects on Women.* Working Paper 7. New York: The Population Council, 1979.

Rosenzweig, M. "Neoclassical Theory and The Optimizing Peasant: An Econometric Analysis of a Market Family Labor Supply in a Developing Country." *The Quarterly Journal of Economics,* vol. 94, no. 1, (1980).

Safilios-Rothschild, C. *Access of Rural Girls to Primary Education in the Third World: State of the Art, Obstacles and Policy Recommendations.* Paper submitted to USAID/WID, Washington, D.C., 1979.

Sanday, P. "Female Status in the Public Domain." In *Women, Culture and Society,"* by M. Rosaldo and L. Lamphere. Stanford: Stanford University Press, 1974.

Schultz, Theodore. "The Value of the Ability to Deal with Disequilibria." *Journal of Economic Literature* vol. 13, no. 3, (1979).

Secretary-General of the World Conference of the UN Decade for Women in Collaboration with the Department of International Economic and Social Affairs. *Report on Women in Rural Areas.* Item 8b of the agenda, World Conference of the UN Decade for Women, Copenhagen, July, 1980 A/Conf. 94128.

Smale, Melinda. *Women in Mauritania: the Effect of Drought and Migration on Their Economic Status and Its Implications for Development Programs.* Report for USAID/WID and USAID Mauritania PASA AG/MAU 300-1-80, Washington, D.C. 1980.

Spencer, Dustan, and Byerlee, Derek. "Technical Change, Labor Use and Small Farmer Development: Evidence from Sierra Leone." *American Journal of Agricultural Economics,* vol. 58, no. 5, (1976).

Spring, Anita, and Hansen, Pat. *Women's Agricultural Work in Rural Zambia: From Valuation to Subordination.* Report submitted to African Studies Association Annual Meeting, Los Angeles, Calif. 1979.

Staudt, Kathleen. "Agricultural Productivity Gaps: A Case Study of Male Preference in Government Policy Implementation." *Development and Change* 9 (1978).

Szalsi, Alexander. *The Situation of Women in the Light of Contemporary Time-Budget Research.* Report submitted to the United Nations World Conference of the International Women's Year, Mexico City, 1975.

Tinker, Irene. *Women and Energy: Program Implications.* Paper submitted to USAID/WID under contract no. AID/otr-C 1808, Washington, D.C., 1980.

Timmer, C. Peter. "Choice of Techniques in Rice Milling on Java." *Indonesia Economic Studies* 9, no. 2 (1973).

UNESCO. *Development of School Enrollment: World and Regional Statistical Trends and Projections 1960-2000.* Paper submitted to the International Conference on Education, Geneva, 1977.

U.S. Agency for International Development. *India Maharashtra Irrigation Technology and Management,* vol. 1. Project Paper. New Delhi: U.S. Agency for International Development, 1982.

—. *OMVS Agricultural Research II,* vol. 2. Project Paper. Dakar, Senegal: U.S. Agency for International Development 1982.

—.Bureau for Program and Policy Coordination. *AID Policy Paper: Women in Development.* Washington, D.C.: U.S. Agency for International Development, 1982.

Weil, Peter. "The Staff of Life: Food and Female Fertility in a West African Society." *Africa* 46, no. 2. (1976).

White, Benjamin. "The Economic Importance of Children in a Javanese Village." In *Population and Social Organization,* edited by Moni Nag. The Hague: Mouten, 1975.

—. "Population, Involution and Employment in Rural Java." *Development and Change* 7, (1976).

White, Benjamin, and Hastuti, E. L. *Different and Unequal: Male and Female Influence in Household and Community Affairs in Two West Javanese Villages.* Working paper of the Project on Rural Household Economies and the Role of Women. Indonesia: Bogor Agricultural University, 1980.

Wharton, Clifton R., Jr., ed. *Subsistence Agriculture and Economic Development.* Chicago: Aldine Publishing Company, 1968.

Woodhall, M. "Investment in Women: A Reappraisal of the Concept of Human Capital." *International Review of Education* 19 (1973).

World Food Program. *A Flood of Changes: World Food Program in India.* No. 1/9326/ E/9.78/2/5000. Rome: World Food Program, 1979.

CHAPTER THREE

Technology Transfer: Implications For Women

Prepared by Mary B. Anderson

INTRODUCTION

Much of the literature on technology transfer now acknowledges that technologies are not value free or value neutral. Two important volumes by Stewart and Goulet[1] which came out in 1977 represent a turning point in this recognition. Technologies are seen to be embedded in, and to carry, social values, institutional forms, and culture—even as they also reflect resource endowments and the organization of production.

It is also true, though less often acknowledged, that technologies are not gender neutral. Because in every society there is a gender-based division of labor (or, as it is called in the industrialized countries, occupational segregation), technologies have different and differential impacts on men and women. Technologies as techniques affect the ways in which people do things; technologies as systems of knowledge affect the ways in which people think about what they do. If men and women do different things, then any particular technology will affect the roles of men and women differently. When technologies are transferred across boundaries where the roles of men and women differ from those in the originating country, the impact on men and women will be different in the receiving country from that in the sending country. As technologies affect the ways in which people think about what they do, the transfer of a technique from an area with one set of norms affecting work roles to another with different expectations, beliefs, and norms will often bring about surprising (and sometimes unfortunate) outcomes.

A. K. N. Reddy, in his effort to devise an appropriate science and technology policy for India, cautions any recipient country regarding the impact of an imported technology. He writes, "Technology can be considered to resemble genetic material which carries the code of the society which conceived and nurtured it and which, given a favorable milieu, tries to replicate that society."[2] In technology transfer it is not enough either to determine the terms of trade by which one country may purchase another's technology or to ensure that a given imported technology utilizes the recipient country's resource base appropriately. The cultural, social and political "codes" carried by technologies must be considered if unexpected, and often negative, impacts in the receiving countries are to be avoided.

How can we understand the socio-political biases and gender implications of technologies? What are the most useful ways of thinking about transfers of technology from one area to another to ensure the best possible outcomes? How can we ensure desired economic results while maximizing beneficial social/political impacts and minimizing negative effects on people and the environment? This paper will examine the issues of technology transfer and will provide a framework for understanding the relationships between technology transfer and women's involvement in development. We shall address specifically those issues which are most important in designing projects that are effective both in engaging women in the development process and in assuring women's participation in project benefits to the greatest possible degree.

Transfers of technologies involve both a sender and a receiver. Two underlying assumptions about technology and economic development have emerged historically. It is useful to make these assumptions explicit before proceeding.

The experience of Europe and North America during the Industrial Revolution, as well as the unprecedented material abundance produced by coupling scientific discovery, technological innovation, and industrial production, have shaped the very definitions of modernity which influence today's attempts at development. Progress has been equated with the emergence of technological capacity for transforming resources into material abundance and, even more important, with a mind set that holds that nature can and should be controlled through science and technique to serve human ends.

The success of this period in producing wealth brought with it an optimism that all problems were amenable to scientific/technological solution. In 1934, Richie Calder proposed that the British House of Lords be replaced by a Senate of Scientists because, he claimed, such a body would have the knowledge and technique to solve all the problems then confronting England. Science could solve not only scientific and material problems, he and others claimed, but also any social, political or human problem as well. There was no better examplar of this belief than Buckminster Fuller who expressed it this way: "...for every human problem there is a technical solution...You may...ask me how we are going to resolve the ever-accelerating dangerous impasse of world-opposed politicians and ideological dogmas. I answer, it will be resolved by the computer...all politicians can and will yield enthusiastically to the computer's safe flight-controlling capabilities in bringing all of humanity in for a happy landing."[3]

Even as the experience of the Third World has not substantiated this optimism, the basic assumption persists that technical solutions can be found for any problem. Efforts to develop Science Policy Institutes in many developing countries, to negotiate systems for the equitable transfer of technical knowledge, to develop international journals for the publication and dissemination of discoveries—even the appropriate technology movement—all rest on the assumption that a technological "fix" may be found. If we can only get the technology "right," then the assumption is that progress and development in the Third World will be inevitable. Many advocates of women's involvement in development are now searching for the "right" technologies for women to assure their participation in and benefit from development.

What is behind this? Again, from the history of the development of science and technology in Europe and North America emerges another strongly held and influencing belief about science. This belief is that science and technology, because based in nature, are separate from all normative and political influence and free from cultural or class bias. In fact, there is evidence to the contrary. Among scientists there is an increasing acknowledgement of the interactions of their discoveries and knowledge with their social experience. In attempts to transfer technological know-how from the cultures of the North to those of the South, experience has shown that the history of colonialism, existing power and wealth disparities, and ideoligical differences affect and influence the transfer process.

These two assumptions—that all things are possible through science and technology, and that the affairs of these fields are free from political bias—should be recognized. Once both the senders and receivers of technologies understand the force of these assumptions and distinguish the realistic elements within them from the unrealistic, they will be able to analyze the interactions of technology transfers in context. They may also assess the linkages between the access to and control of knowledge and the effective application of technologies in development.

A FRAMEWORK FOR UNDERSTANDING TECHNOLOGY
TRANSFER AND WOMEN

This technology framework will bring together three strands. First, we shall look at the ways in which technologies affect and alter productive activities. Second we shall examine the characteristics of technologies which reflect the context of their origin as these influence and work through technological impacts. Third, we shall discuss the systems or mechanisms for technology transfer and the way in which these shape the impact of technology transfers.

The three parts of this framework for understanding technology transfer and women relate directly to the analysis of productive activities and of access to and control over resources presented in the initial paper of this volume, "Women in Development: A Framework for Project Analysis." The relation arises from the fact that technologies affect the ways in which people work and the ways in which they think about their work. The Analytical Framework shows that every society has a recognized set of productive roles for men and women. The rigidity or flexibility of these roles for controlling and using resources is historically, pragmatically, culturally and/or religiously based. The effect of technical innovation on gender-based roles itechnologies may have an effect on production. In each of these, the potential n project design and implementation.

A. The Effects of Technologies on Production

There are five basic categories of impacts through which for different and differential impacts on women and men is important.

1. The Doer of a Productive Activity.

The first and most obvious impact of any technology is to change the doer of an activity, the producer. The introduction of any device, technique or organizational arrangement which alters the role assignments of men and women in production may have a number of ramifications in status, in access to and control over resources and income, and in the opportunity for leisure.

In technology transfers from industrialized to Third World countries, the changes in the gender of a producer induced by the introduction of a technology arise in one of two interrelated ways. The first is through an implicit expectation that the operator or manager of a technology in the originating country will be replicated in the receiving country. Second, as new technologies are introduced into an area, the ability to handle them is usually associated with relatively high status. Thus, when a technology is introduced, those who either already enjoy higher status or who are in a position to corner it may move into tasks that were previously low status when done without the benefit of the new technology.

An ILO study conducted for the United Nations Commission on the Status of Women in 1967 provides illustrations of these shifts. The study analyzed the impact of scientific and technological progress on employment and work conditions in the metal trades; textiles, clothing, leather and footwear trades; food and drink industry; and printing and allied trades. In every case where machinery was introduced in activities traditionally done by women, men either completely replaced women or the activity became sub-divided and men took over the tasks that used the technology and required greater skill while women were relegated to the less skilled, menial tasks. These shifts were accompanied by loss of income earning opportunities or marginalization and lower income for women.

In Java, when rice mills were introduced, women who had traditionally earned their only monetary income from hand milling were displaced as men assumed the positions in the factories.[4] In Korea, when the government installed rice mills, men in the mills did jobs previously done by women.[5]

In the Ivory Coast, women were traditionally responsible for growing and spinning cotton which men then wove into cloth. Women, however, controlled the cloth production and gained wealth, status and power from it. With the change of cotton into a cash crop resulting from the colonizer's need for increased supplies, technological innovations were introduced to increase cotton output. Extension agents and technologists worked with men, and male heads of households were required to pay a cash head tax for family members. Thus, cotton growing became the domain of men. However, because women were displaced from their primary role in cotton production, they were subsequently hired into newly built textile mills as weavers using machinery. In this example, technological innovations induced a series of changes in gender assignments in the tasks associated with cloth production.[6]

In addition, a technology may alter the components of a productive task, breaking it into separate functions in a way that alters the gender roles in the separate, changed parts of an activity. A technology may focus on a single component of a job rather than the entire task and, by doing so, alter productive relations between men and women. In Upper Volta, an AID/NASA project installed a solar pump to save women the work of lifting water. As it turned out, lifting the water was the least time consuming and least difficult part of the water collection task of women; they spent most time and energy in carrying buckets of water from the well to their homes. The pump, in fact, aided male cattle herders far more than women in that the women only used a few buckets of water a day in home consumption while herders used many buckets for watering their cattle. For a technology to ease the work of women, it should have been concentrated on piping water rather than on pumping it.[7]

Technologies affect doers of activities by saving labor or generating employment. In certain circumstances, a decision to employ a labor-intensive technology may draw women into the labor force to tasks not previously and traditionally theirs. Sometimes, status is increased in this process. The period of the Chinese Revolution from the 1950s through the mid-60s provides a good example. Decisions to employ low-capital techniques to construct water irrigation and storage tech-nologies resulted in increased demand for women, as well as men, to be mobilized in large numbers for construction. Because the status of the worker was high in that revolution, women gained as they adopted the worker role alongside men. In Java, the massive involvement of labor in building irrigation systems and the mobilization of large amounts of female labor produced a similiar result.[8]

As technologies of production influence who does what, technologies of marketing and trade can also have this effect. In colonial India, the importation of cotton from England displaced many Indian workers, primarily women, from the jobs of spinning and weaving on which they previously depended. The English production and transportation technologies were sufficiently inexpensive and effective to make this a viable economic alternative to Indian production.

In cultures where women and men both engage in trade but there are distinctions as to quantities and types of products traded by each, the introduction of carts, roads, or trucks can alter these distinctions. Transportation technologies may either favor the trader of larger goods or they may open opportunities for traders who were previously limited in their ability to carry produce.

Finally, technologies may introduce processes which, because of social or cultural restraints, make them inaccessible for use by a certain group. For example, when bicycle pumps have been introduced in some societies, women have been prevented from using them because of taboos that prohibit women sitting astride the bicycle.

Thus, technologies may change the doer of a productive activity by changing the production process itself. The effects may be employment-generating or labor-saving. The impact on women relative to men can only be analyzed in context when the division of labor and its social/cultural basis is known.

2. The Location of the Productive Activity.

Technologies may affect production by relocating activities. In many societies, women have different patterns of mobility from those of men. In some they are confined to certain private, "female" places, such as the household compound, by social or religious traditions. They may be required to travel in pairs or groups, or always with a spouse or a father, or only in certain kinds of conveyances. Women may also be restricted in their movements by their other productive and household obligations such as child care, food preparation, or livestock care.

When technologies change the location of any task, they may result either in the exclusion of women from the work or in changes in traditional work patterns. Some women limited by purdah may not accept employment in a situation where both men and women work; nor may they work outside their compounds. A rice mill, located in a central area for ease of access, may not provide employment opportunities for Bangladeshi women who formerly were responsible for all rice processing because they are not free to accept work in such a location. When a technology centralizes productive activities and women may not go to this location, men move into productive activities where women previously held sway. Such a process tends to reinforce the belief that men work with technologies and women do not, or that men do "modern" work while women only work in subsistence sectors. The real issue, however, is only where the technology is located.

Changes in the location of production in situations where women are not restricted by religion or tradition but only by their home-based productive obligations may cause women to move out of traditional patterns and undertake new activities. When the owners of the wool mills of western New England wanted to attract cheap female labor in the 19th century, they built dormitories (and installed chaperones!) to house the young girls who took employment. In China, as women moved into factory labor, nurseries and child care centers were built in the factories to allow women to meet their nursing obligations and to provide substitute child care. Electronics factories in southeast Asia and others in Mexico have recruited mainly young, unmarried women in order to avoid having to provide these services. In West Africa, urban women who have undertaken economic activities outside their homes have worked out a variety of alternative systems for providing food to their families, including rotating the responsibility for food preparation among members of a neighborhood group. Street food vendors clearly help meet this need as well.

3. The Timing of Production.

A technology may eliminate or lessen the time it takes to accomplish a job, may change the time of day or year when a job must or may be done, or may lessen the time spent on some aspect of a job while increasing the requirements for other aspects.

A recent publication on women and technology shows a photograph of two sweating and miserable women in southern Africa using a solar stove designed by an expatriate technician. The purpose of the technology was to eliminate the need for women to walk for as much as six hours a day to gather decreasingly available firewood. The technician, however, did not know that these women traditionally cook in the early morning or late afternoon precisely in order to avoid the heat of midday. Utilizing solar energy involved a significant rescheduling of the daily activities by the users. Although the technician understood resource endowments, he did not consider the time requirements of his innovation relative to other uses of time in the recipient society.[9]

A technology designed to increase output/acre through applications of fertilizers or insecticides may force increased labor applications over that acre, changing the time allocations of workers. If those laborers who are responsible for the fertilizer or insecticide applications are already overburdened, as is the case with many African women agriculturalists, the technology will have a differential impact on different workers. In much of the world, women are carriers of water, and water is necessary in backpack insecticide sprayers. Women often weed, the requirements for which increase with fertilizers. If tractors plow more land, the cultivators, weeders, harvesters and food processors—often women—have more work.

The impact of a technology on one part of a productive process will be felt not only on that component, but also on related processes. When various parts of a productive chain are assigned by gender, it is important to know this in order to understand labor constraints, opportunities, and characteristics. When a technology saves labor on one aspect of production but increases it on another, planners have assumed that the labor freed from the former will be available to the latter. When gender determines functions, this is not the case.

Even within the jobs that are women's, a technology may save labor in one aspect while increasing it in another. A new cooking stove may, for example, reduce the quantity of wood a woman must collect and thus save time. It may also require wood of a shorter length or smaller diameter, thereby increasing the time spent on chopping wood. Enclosing the flame of a fire inside a fuel-efficient stove may force women to cook and/or serve meals during daylight hours because of the loss of firelight. A stove and its chimney or flue requires maintenance for efficient performance and this takes time.

Linkages, attendant activities, and gender roles complicate the introduction of technologies. To assess accurately a gain in time savings, one must consider shifts in time of day when a task must be done, shifts in amounts of time spent on an activity and all its attendant activities, and shifts among workers (and genders) of time allocations in the processes affected by the technology.

4. Skills Needed for Productive Activity

A technology may alter the skills needed for doing a particular job. Skills are required both in production with a technology and in its maintenance and repair. Access to and control over the knowledge required to acquire a technology and to use it may determine who does a particular job and who gains from that production. Gender biases are built into the systems of training, education, and skills acquisition which often comprise a part of technology transfers. Educational systems shape access to and knowledge of technologies in several ways. First, in most societies more male children go to school than female, and fewer males drop out of school than females. The ability to read, exposure to a broader world and the options it contains, and training in science and mathematics all support a subsequent ability to understand, respond to, use, and control technologies which have originated elsewhere. Advanced training follows basic training, so the chain is reinforcing; those who lose out early are virtually prohibited from later involvement.

In most rural areas of the world, schooling provides the only way for children to learn to speak a more widely used language beyond that of their village, tribe, or cultural group. The ability to communicate with outsiders is an essential part of gaining access to knowledge and technique which come from outside.

Schooling also transmits and reinforces expectations about who does what in "modern" society. Gender roles, as they have emerged in the technology-creating societies, are taught even as information about these societies and their modernization process is taught.

5. Related Attributes of Activities of a Productive Task.

Many productive activities are associated with some ceremonial, social or familial activity which, if the production is changed, is also changed. This effect may occur in home-based production more than elsewhere and, therefore, may be a more important consideration to women than to others. The Loreno stove, by enclosing the fire, utilizes wood efficiently, but at the same time deprives the household of firelight around which, in many parts of the world, the family traditionally gathers in the evening for conversation and decision-making. At an even more practical level, the same stoves that have reduced smoke and incidence of respiratory disease have also been associated with increases in malaria and other insect borne disease because the smoke had been effective in killing insects. Smoke also is thought by some women to be helpful in making thatch roofs more resistant to rain.

Women have traditionally used the time of long walks to fetch water and firewood for social organization, conversation and interchange. Technologies which alter these functions eliminate these opportunities, so that other social forms have to be found. Technologies which gather women in certain areas, such as grain mills, can have the opposite effect. They can facilitate social activity and opportunities for education. For example, women in Asia have received literacy training while they wait for their rice to be ground at mills and women in Africa have received nutrition training while waiting in line at clinics.

The cotton weaving in the Ivory Coast, discussed above, traditionally involved an important element of aesthetics. Prestige was derived from the beauty and patterns of the weaving more than from the income produced. The changes in production that resulted from cash cropping undermined this prestige value, and other means for satisfying it have had to be found.

By their nature, technologies are disruptive of old patterns precisely because these old patterns have not been sufficiently productive. People look for and adopt technologies in order to increase economic output and security. However, for a technology to be effectively adopted, the gains to recipients must outweigh losses. Some of these gains and losses are non-economic. Marilyn Hoskins, summarizing a range of case studies on the transferrence of household technologies to women in many countries, notes that ". . . costs appear to be a relatively less important consideration than many implementers had expected and that of aesthetics relatively more important."[10]

Projects which are designed on the assumption that the suitability of technology transfers can be assessed by economic criteria alone are, therefore, likely to result in unexpected failure. Experience has shown that economic rationality is not the only, or even the primary, motivator of all decisions in many parts of the world. This is particularly true in the spheres of activity which are not entirely within the market. Because many of women's productive activities fall outside the market sphere, such a caution might be especially relevant to understanding potential technological impacts on women or to developing any predictive capability regarding these impacts.

B. The Effects of Technologies on Consumption

Related to the division of labor in production, but requiring additional empirical research and analysis, is the division of labor in consumption. Some aspects of consumption seem to have gender implications. Partly, this division is related to production in that who produces what determines who consumes what. Partly, it is the result of traditional role divisions.

Some consumption technologies would seem to be entirely gender-neutral. In practice, they may have gender implications. For example, a radio provides access to information on a broad and unlimited scale. A radio may be listened to, a television may be watched, a telephone may be used equally by male and female ears, eyes and voices. However, if a radio is placed in a traditional gathering place for men, such as a beer hall or the village council, and if women are restricted socially from access to this place, then men will gain access to additional information not available on an equal basis to women. The technology itself becomes a reinforcer of patterns of access and control which already exist in the society.

A technology may alter consumption patterns in relation to the goods and services it is designed to produce. The solar water pump, referred to above, was designed to facilitate women's access to water but, in fact, benefitted cattle herders more. Whereas the herders had traditionally moved away from the watering place when the rainy season came, the pump made water access so much easier for them that they remained close at hand all year round. This forced the women to wait in line for water each time they came. Also, the cattle in the area began to feed on small, new plant growth which women had previously used for food, handicrafts and medicines. Utilization of the water supply increased markedly, straining it beyond its capacity. Women had to wait in line longer, walk farther for the plant growth, and risk periodic loss of this resource as a result of the technological innovation. This technology had a productive intent, but in practice changed women's consumption patterns for the worse.

In some areas of Africa, women note that because they now grind their meal at a mill only a few times a week, rather than grinding the family ration at home daily, their children use the meal for snacks. This may improve nutrition. It may also put stress on food supplies if the productive process of daily pounding at home had operated as a rationing system for consumption.

In Ghana, a project that had apparently been successful in getting women to use a fuel efficient stove was later found to have failed to sustain this use. The women explained that the new stoves did not accomodate the large cooking pots necessary for the Ghanian type of cooking. In this case, a refusal to change consumption patterns caused the productive technology to be abandoned.[11]

Table I shows a scheme for tabulating the effects of technologies on production and on consumption which we have discussed and for noting the implications of each of these impacts on women in particular. With this part of our three part framework in place, we shall turn now to examine the characteristics of technologies and of transfer processes which form the other cornerstones of this analysis.

C. Technology Characteristics

Technologies may be small or large, simple or complex, cheap or expensive, labor-saving or employment-generating, locally-based or imported, etc. That is, any technology has a series of definable characteristics which influence its transfer from one context to another and, specifically, through the analysis of effects above, the impact of its transfer on women in the development process. These characteristics are both material and non-material.

The "appropriate technology" movement, which stressed the importance of fitting a technology's resource requirements to local resource endowments, grew out of a recognition of the misfit of physical characteristics of imported technologies to recipient environments. E. F. Schumacher's *Small is Beautiful* subsequently led many people to believe that an appropriate technology is always small, simple, cheap and labor-intensive. Much effort has been put into the invention and development of such "appropriate" technologies to be disseminated around the world. In fact, the characteristics of technologies are more complicated than this. Appropriateness implies a link to some external factor and a judgment about correctness in relation to something else such as resources, goals or values. Furthermore, scale, complexity and expense are not always positively correlated. It is possible for a large machine to be both simple and cheap and for a small one to be highly complex and expensive. The characteristics of technologies can be combined in a number of different ways and these combinations incorporate both physical and non-physical elements.

Thomas P. Hughes writes about these combinations as technological "style." He notes that mechanical technologies were primarily developed in the United States where energy was abundant and labor short while Europe, with the opposite resource endowments, relied more heavily on chemical technologies.[12] Biological technologies emerged in 19th century Europe but were elaborated in America through the application of genetic science to large-scale agriculture. Because climatic conditions, disease vectors and crop types vary widely among geographic areas, it is obvious that biologically-based technologies require more adaptation for effective transference than do mechanically and chemically-based technologies. With all three types, however, adaptations have not been adequate because even when they have occurred, they have usually taken account only of the physical resource base characteristics of technologies and not of the non-physical characteristics.

Technological style requires more exploration. Hughes illustrates the concept by comparing the development of the Volkswagen with the oversized American car. While one is energy efficient and the other is not, these styles also embody and reflect generalized cultural style, including a set of explicit values (grandeur vs. utilitarianism), class attitudes (conspicuous consumption vs. a "people's" car), and intended use (to spend a lot of time, to travel long distances, to go to drive-in movies vs. to get around town and through narrow streets conveniently). Hughes writes about the transfer of technology from Britain to colonial America which was striving for its independent technology, "British engineers transferring technology would have used iron and steam because they knew it; Americans used wood and water because they had it."[13] But the development of the Mississippi river boat in one country and the shipbuilding industry in another reflects not only these resources, but also the fact that the British required a means for moving beyond their small island to explore distant lands while the Americans wanted to navigate the large rivers of their continent and had little desire to cross any oceans. Technological styles are composites of many factors.

What difference might technological style make to gender? What should we understand about it in order to design projects that engage women as effectively as possible in development? Table II provides a system for tabulating the importance of those characteristics of technology which make up this "style" in projects involving women.

We look first at the physical requirements of technologies in the originating environment. These include the factors of production— land, labor, and capital. When the uses of these resources in the original technology are identified, then two questions, related to its transfer, should be asked. First, are these resources available in sufficient quantity and quality in the recipient country? Second, who in the recipient country owns, or controls, these resources? Men and women, by virtue of tradition and tasks, frequently have different access to and control over resources, and the patterns of this gender-based division vary from country to country and from context to context within countries. Often patterns of resource control are changing. In Kenya, for example, new land ownership laws are transferring title to land almost exclusively to men. Under traditional systems, women enjoyed assurance of access to land, and this access was central to their roles as primary subsistence producers. As land laws change, women's abilities to farm are changing. Technologies which affect farming patterns will have differential impacts on men and women with their different access to and control over land.

In all societies, it is important in technology transfer to determine who has access to adequate capital to buy and maintain a technology. Also, men and women have differential access to and control over labor. Women may command the labor only of their children or they may form interchangeable labor units among kinship groups. Men may hire men, but in some societies women may not. In some societies women may work for wages, but in others they are restricted from wage activity by tradition. Resource inputs to effective technology usage are among the most important factors for anaylsis in understanding the impacts of technology transfer.

The physical characteristics of technologies and their gender implications in Table II include mechanical, chemical, and biological purposes. It is important that the purposes behind the development of the technology where it originated be made explicit. What questions or problems was the technology originally designed to answer? Who decided? How were the priorities set regarding which problems to solve? In all three areas a number of technological developments have been made in response to productivity needs in the market sphere. Returns to research and development have been calculated to determine the profit rate of investment.

In the Third World there are a number of areas where profits can be realized through technological innovation. New questions based in Third World experience are being posed to the mechanical, chemical and biological technologies, but these tend still to be concentrated in certain types of activities like those found in industrialized countries. Women are not often included in the decision-making to determine priority areas for research. There are two reasons for their absence. First, men have more access to and control over traditional decision-making and capital resources. Second, women's work is disproportionately concentrated in the nonmonetized or small scale enterprise sectors of the economy. These areas are not seen as those which are most likely to produce profits on a scale to justify technological innovation. While this calculation may be correct, it is also true that women's productive sectors are increasingly recognized as central to many countries' overall productivity. Subsistence agriculture feeds the majority of people and produces the majority of food in many lands. Understanding the basis on which technologies have been developed in the originating countries is an essential first step to determining what other considerations should be included in the decisions about where to focus them in developing countries.

Non-physical characteristics of technologies are also important in their potential differential impacts on women and their roles. These include such things as organization, level of skills required, type of discipline required, degree of cooperation and scale of operation.[14] A technology originated in an area where production is organized hierarchically will not necessarily be suitable where production is carried out cooperatively. In situations where women's productive work is organized differently from that of men, as is the case where women's mobility is restricted, a technology which meets the oganizational setting of the one will not necessarily suit the other. The connection of the analysis of the non-physical characteristics of technologies with the related attributes or activities of any productive activity is obvious. When a technology provides water to women individually at their homes, they may, as we saw, lose an opportunity for interaction which was important in the ways they had previously organized their water gathering work. The purpose of this analysis is to make explicit the variety of characteristics of different technologies which will affect their successful transfer and to relate this to the definable separate roles of men and women so that the differing impacts may be seen at early stages in project design.

D. Mechanisms for Technology Transfer

There are three basic mechanisms by which technologies are transferred in assistance programs.[15] These are 1) through direct projects or programs 2) through personnel and 3) through education and training programs. Usually the three are combined in a project. A project will introduce a new technology making it available physically to project participants. Personnel will bring it, assemble it, demonstrate its use and maintenance. Training systems for its use will complete the transfer as project beneficiaries learn to use and maintain the technology. Personnel also, of course, do the training.

Much of the previous discussion was concerned with elements which define the technology (the equipment or technique) itself. To complete the analysis, more discussion is in order here regarding the personnel in charge of transfer.

The person who transmits a technique, or knowledge of it, can affect or determine who finds out about it and who can have access to using it. There is growing documentation of the problems which have emerged as a result of the fact that, in many societies, male extension agents or teachers and instructors do not have access to women who may be potential or actual users of technologies.

The effect of the agent in technology transfers is more important and more subtle than direct gender access implies. The characteristics of the possessor of knowledge about a technology or of the person who controls a technology communicate a message about who may have technological knowledge or control. This occurs in two ways that usually reinforce each other. The possessor/controller may believe that only people like himself can manage technologies. Thus, he looks for people like himself to be the recipients of his efforts to disseminate, sell, give or demonstrate a technology. Others who observe that men handle technologies will make the assumption that this is inevitable. In agriculture, there is an additional, insidious, related belief which follows. Because women have, in many parts of the world, been responsible for subsistence agriculture, there is a sense that the modernization of agriculture through the application of technologies requires, at the same time, the masculinization of agriculture.[16] This same process is found in industry and the belief that it is inevitable follows. As rice milling became industrialized in Indonesia, men ran the mills. The modernization of milling brought also its masculinization.

Technologies that originated in Europe and North America often carry this message. In the history of the development of technologies in these societies, for a variety of reasons not necessarily replicated in other cultures and places, technologies have been for the most part invented, developed, controlled and used by men. Ironically, many technologies obviate gender differentiations based on size, weight, strength or speed. Anyone, for example, can push a button or drive a power steering tractor. It becomes impossible to claim that women are too weak or fragile to do certain tasks when a technology overcomes physiological differences. The gender-based division of labor has not disappeared, however. As physical differences between men and women have been obviated by technologies, we have substituted limits believed to be imposed by mental capacity, talents, acumen, and inclination. We developed the belief that women "don't do" math and that women "don't like" to work with machines. Women tinker with a machine with a hairpin; men repair a machine with tools. As western assistance agencies approach development projects and programs in which they transmit a technology, the staffs of these agencies often carry these attitudes and preconceptions and assume that the more complex the technology, the more inevitable it is that they will need to locate men to whom to transfer it.

Even those concerned with broader access to technique are often trapped into these gender-based expectations. One U.S. agency, which is designed to transfer appropriate technologies to all askers from any area of the world, quite recently still carried photographs in its major publicity pieces which showed only men working with technologies. A line drawing showing women washing clothing on rocks was the only pictorial representation of women. Its technical assistance experts are predominantly male, as is true for most such agencies. Thus, in a subtle way even this organization devoted to increasing technological access conveys the mesage that technologies are more for males than females.

For project design purposes, consideration of the messages represented by the agents of technology transfer, as well as by the systems of transfer, is important to increasing women's involvement in and benefit from technologies.

CONCLUSION

In the discussion above, we have presented categories for analyzing the impacts of technologies on production and consumption and for thinking about the characteristics which may affect these impacts. We have also noted the central importance of the transmitting agent. The discussion should have made it clear that there is no simple, technological solution to the problems of development or to the problems of technology transfer.

Simply having smaller technologies will not bring development. Simply recruiting women to work as instructors of technology use will no more solve problems of development for women than the corresponding process has done for men.

What is needed is the development of systems for transferrence of technologies in their broadest sense, including know-how and technique, in a manner which promotes the recipient's own ability to become, him or herself, a technologist.[17] How does one develop the capacity to invent? Familiarity with existing technologies is certainly one part of the answer. This is why issues of access to both knowledge and use of technologies is so crucial for longer term development. Those who do not have access to technological knowledge or experience are never as likely to become developers of their own technological solutions as those who do.

Technological familiarity does several things. It instills the idea that some things can be done better, with less effort, with more favorble results, or with less cost. It also teaches that a person can make this occur by control over a technique. It teaches various mechanical, chemical and biological processes which form the bases for new discoveries, inventions and adaptations. It gives people the ability and power to solve their own problems of production. Thus, the marginalization of any group in relation to technology development and use not only leaves them out of current benefits to be derived from technology, but also consigns them to an inferior position in relation to future developments. It limits, if not prohibits, their ability to participate in self-sustaining development based on the invention and application of techniques and technological systems.

TABLES

Table I   Technology Transfer and Women: A Framework for Analysis

I. **Effects of Technology on Productive Activities**
  A. *On doer*
      1. Traditional doer
      2. Doer with technology
      3. Implications for women
  B. *On location*
      1. Location of traditional production
      2. Location of production w/technology
      3. Implications for women
  C. *On timing*
      1. How long activity traditionally took
      2. How long activity takes with technology
      3. Implications for women
      4. Time of day/week/month/year activity traditionally done
      5. Time of day/week/month/year activity done with technology
      6. Implications for women
      7. Segmentation of time as activity traditionally done
      8. Segmentation of time as activity done with technology
      9. Implications for women
  D. *On skills needed for activity*
      1. Skills used to do activity traditionally
         i. Where acquired
         ii. How acquired
      2. Skills used to do activity with technology
         i. Where acquired
         ii. How acquired
      3. Implications for women
  E. *Attendant benefits or activities*
      1. Linked benefits/activities when done traditionally
      2. Linked benefits/activities when done with technology
      3. Implications for women

II. **Effects of Technology on Consumption Activities**
  A. Through technology itself
  B. Through products of technology

Table II   Characteristics of Technologies

Physical Characteristics

Requirements Originating Country	Availability in Recipient Country	Control in Recipient Country
Land		
Labor		
Capital		
Implications for Women		

	Purpose in Originating Country	Suitability in Recipient Country
Mechanical		
Chemical		
Biological		
Implication for Women		

Non-Physical Characteristics

	Originating Country	Recipient Country
Skills		
Organization		
Discipline		
Cooperation		
Scale		
Implications for Women		

NOTES

1. Frances Stewart, *Technology and Underdevelopment* (London: The Macmillan Press, Ltd, 1977); Denis Goulet, *The Uncertain Promise* (New York: IDOC/North America, Inc., 1977).
2. A. K. N. Reddy, *Mazingira: The World Forum for Environment and Development*, no. 8, 1979.
3. Thomas P. Hughes, *Changing Attitudes Toward American Technology* (New York: Harper & Row, Publishers, 1975), p. 41.
4. C. Peter Timmer, "Choice of Technique in Rice Milling in Java," *Bulletin of Indonesian Economic Studies* 9, (July, 1973).
5. Marilyn W. Hoskins with Fred R. Weber, "Household Level Appropriate Technology for Women: Part II." (Washington, DC: Office of Women in Development, U.S. Agency for International Development, 1981), p. 51.
6. Mona Etienne, "Women and Men, Cloth and Colonization: The Transformation of Production - Distribution Relations Among the Boule" *Cahiers d'Etudes Africaines* 65 (1978).
7. Hoskins with Weber, p. 43.
8. Gilian Hart, *Power, Labor and Livelihood: Processes of Change in Rural Java* (forthcoming).
9. ISIS, *Women in Development* (Geneva: ISIS International Women's Information and Communication Service, 1983).

10. Hoskin with Weber, p. 72.
11. Ibid., 47.
12. Thomas P. Hughes, "Another Point of View: Comment on Paper Read by Amulya Kumar N. Reddy at the University of Pennsylvania," May 30, 1981 (unpublished).
13. Ibid., p. 6.
14. Mary B. Anderson, "Rural Development Through Self-Reliance: Implications for Appropriate Technology," In *New Dimensions of Appropriate Technology: Selected Proceedings of 1979 Sympisium Sponsored by the* IAAATDC (Ann Arbor: University of Michigan, 1980), p. 108.
15. There is extensive literature on the processes of technology transfer through trade and commerce which includes implications of technology packages, components, servicing contracts, licensing, patenting, etc. A particularly good analysis of the implications of various technology aid and trade packages may be found in Hans Singer, *Technologies for Basic Needs* (ILO, 1982), pp. 29-50. Because we are concerned with project design and implementation by agencies involved in providing aid to developing countries, we are focusing here only on the aid transfer mechanisms.
16. Roslyn Dauber and Melinda L. Cain, eds., *Women and Technological Change in Developing Countries* (Boulder: Westview Press, 1980), pp. 33-50.
17. Mary B. Anderson and Peter Buck, "Scientific Development: The Development of Science, Science and Development, and the Science of Development," *Social Studies of Science* 10, (1980), p. 229.

BIBLIOGRAPHY

Anderson, Mary B. "Rural Development through Self-Reliance: Implications for Appropriate Technology." In *New Dimensions of Appropriate Technology: Selected Proceedings of 1979 Symposium Sponsored by the IAAATDC* Ann Arbor, Mich.: University of Michigan, 1980.

Anderson, Mary B., and Buck, Peter. "Scientific Development: The Development of Science, Science and Development, and the Science of Development." *Social Studies of Science* 10, (1980).

Canada's role in Science and Technology for Development. Proceedings of the Symposium, Ontario Science Centre, Toronto, Canada, 10-13 May 1979.

Carr, Marilyn. "Women and Technology in Rurally Oriented Projects" (Washington, D.C.: The World Bank, 1981).

Dauber, Roslyn and Cain, Melinda L., eds. *Women and Technological Change in Developing Countries.* Boulder, Colo.: Westview Press, 1980.

de Cubas, Jose. *Technology Transfer and the Developing Nations.* New York: Council of the Americas and Fund for Multinational Management Education, 1974.

Driscoll, Robert E., and Wallender, Harvey M., III, eds. *Technology Transfer and Development: an Historical and Geographical Perspective.* New York: Fund for Multinational Management Education and Council of the Americas, 1974.

Dulansey, Maryanne. "Can Technology Help Women Feed Their Families?" Paper prepared for AAAS Workshop on Women and Development, Brookings Institution, Washington, D.C., March 26-27, 1979.

Elzinga, Aant, and Jamison, Andrew. *Cultural Components in the Scientific Attitude to Nature: Eastern and Western Modes.* Lund, Sweden: Research Policy Institute, 1981.

Foster, George M. *Traditional Societies and Technological Change.* New York: Harper & Row, Publishers, 1973.

Goulet, Denis. *The Uncertain Promise.* New York: IDOC/North America, Inc., 1977.

Hart, Gilian. *Power, Labor and Livelihood: Processes of Change in Rural Java* (forthcoming).

Hoskins, Marilyn W., with Weber, Fred R. "Part I: Issues and Project Considerations;" "Part II: Appropriate Technology Efforts in the Field: Issues Reconsidered;" "Part III: Field Training Manual: Selection, Introduction and Evaluation of Appropriate Technologies for Women." In "Household Level Appropriate Technology for Women." Washington, D.C.: Office of Women in Development, U.S. Agency for International Development, 1981.

Hughes, Thomas P. "Another Point of View: Comment on Paper Read by Amulya Kumar N. Reddy at the University of Pennsylvania," May 30, 1981 (unpublished).

—. *Changing Attitudes Toward American Technology*. New York: Harper & Row, Publishers, 1975.

—. "Technology." In *The Holocaust: Ideology, Bureaucracy, and Genocide*, edited by Henry Friedlander and Sybil Milton. Milwood, NY: Kraus International Publications, 1980.

ISIS. *Women in Development*. Geneva: ISIS International Women's Information and Communication Service, 1983.

Rabinowitch, Eugene, and Rabinowitch, Victor eds. *Views of Science, Technology and Development*. Oxford: Pergamon Press, 1975.

Restic, Slobodan. *The Collective Self-Reliance of Developing Countries in the Fields of Science and Technology*. Japan: The United Nations University, 1980.

Ribes, Bruno, et al. *Domination or Sharing*. Paris: The UNESCO Press, 1981.

Rothschild, Joan. "Technology, Women's Work and the Social Control of Women." In *Women, Power, and Political Systems*, edited by Marguerita Rendel. London: Croom Helm, 1981.

Sagafi-Nejad, Tagi and Belfield, Robert. *Transnational Corporations, Technology Transfer and Development*. New York: Pergamon Press, 1980.

Singer, Hans. *Technology for Basic Needs*. Geneva: International Labor Organization, 1982.

Solo, Robert A., Rogers, Everett, M. *Inducing Technological Change for Economic Growth and Development*. East Lansing, Mich.: Michigan State University Press, 1972.

Stewart, Frances. *Technology and Underdevelopment*. London: The Macmillan Press, Ltd., 1977.

Timmer, C. Peter. "Choice of Technique in Rice Milling on Java." *Bulletin of Indonesian Economic Studies* 9 (July 1973).

Volti, Rudi. *Technology, Politics and Society in China*. Boulder, Colo.: Westview Press, 1982.

JOURNALS

Bhaneja, Balwant, and Walker, J. A. S. "Comment." *Impact of Science on Society* 28 (1978): 95-104.

Bourguiba, Habib, Jr. "Development and Transfer of Technology." *Culture* 3, nos. 3-4 (1976): 126-130.

Brown, Richard Harvey. "Appropriate Technology and the Grassroots: Toward a Development Strategy from the Bottom Up." *The Developing Economies* (Sept. 1977): 253-279.

Brozen, Yale. "Invention, Innovation, and Imitation." *American Economic Review* 41 (1951): 239-257.

—. "Technological Change, Ideology, and Productivity." *Political Science Quarterly* 70 (1955): 522-542.

Carroll, James D. "Participatory Technology." *Science*: 647-653.

Dean, Genevieve C. "Science Technology and Development: China as a 'Case Study'." *China Quarterly* (July 1972): 520-534.

—. "A Note on the Sources of Technological Innovation in the People's Republic of China." *Journal of Development Studies* 9, (1972-73): 187-199.

Eckhaus, Richard S. "Notes on Invention and Innovation in Less Developed Countries." *American Economic Review* 56, nos. 1-2, (1966): 98-109.

Etienne, Mona. "Women and Men, Cloth and Colonization: The Transformation of Production-Distribution Relations Among the Baule." *Cahiers d'Etudes Africaines* 65 (1978): 41-65.

Goulet, Denis. "The Suppliers and Purchasers of Technology: A Conflict of Interest." *International Development Review* 18, no. 3 (1976): 14-20.

Jackson, M. N. "Science and Depoliticization." *Impact of Science on Society* 28 (1978): 359-367.

Sagasti, Francisco. "Underdevelopment, Science and Technology: The Point of View of the Underdeveloped Countries." *Science Studies* 3 (1973): 47-59.

CHAPTER FOUR

Small-Scale Enterprise and Women

Prepared by Maryanne Dulansey and James Austin

I. INTRODUCTION

Small-scale enterprises (SSEs) represent an important means of earning income for women in developing countries. SSEs typically constitute a significant sector of the economy in such countries, and women play a major role within SSEs.

The purpose of this paper is to provide guidance for the analysis of SSE projects, with the hope that they can be designed so as to encourage the participation of women and to improve women's welfare.

II. WOMEN AND SSE

A. Significance of the SSE Sector for Development

The SSE sector is important to the economy of developing countries. It provides employment and income for many people while supplying needed products and services.[1] The sector has become more important as experience has proven large-scale enterprise incapable of providing large shares of employment in developing countries, as employment in agriculture declines, and as migration from the countryside swells urban populations.[2]

Agriculture is of paramount importance to economic development and to women. Nonfarm income also plays a critical role, however, both for those who share in the returns from agricultural development and for those who do not. With economic growth, agriculture inevitably comes to represent a smaller part of total output, income, and employment.[3] Enterprises unrelated to agricultural production account for an increasingly large share, until ouput, income, and employment from nonfarm enterprises surpass those derived from farming.

As subsistence farming gives way to marketed production, there is more need for specialized marketing, transport, processing, and packaging. In the industrialized economies, these activities produce more value added and employment than does agriculture itself. In countries or regions where the majority of the population is still in rural areas, and where transport of raw materials and/or products is costly and difficult, small-scale enterprise is often more efficient than large-scale operations, and thrives particularly under conditions of agricultural prosperity.[4]

Small-scale enterprise is an even more important provider of income, products, and services under less favorable economic conditions. The very poor, the landless, and women who live in rural areas but fail to share in the returns from agricultural development are dependent on nonfarm enterprises, as are those who live in urban areas. "Nonfarm income is particularly important for the very poor," the World Bank has reported. "In countries as different as India, Republic of Korea, and Sierra Leone, landless or nearly landless households earn about half their income from nonfarm sources."[5]

The importance of SSEs increases as the size of the locality decreases. In Haiti, the percentage of the population "directly employed" by SSEs rises from 2.2 percent in the capital, Port-au-Prince, to 8.4 percent in the localities with population between 1,000 to 2,000. The SSE contribution to total Haitian employment would loom much larger if the extremely small localities could be considered.[6]

If poverty is chronic in rural areas (over 90 percent of the world's poor, estimated at 1 billion, are rural people), it is becoming acute in urban areas where the need for income is growing rapidly.[7] It is estimated that the Third World will need 782 million new jobs between 1980 and the end of the century. Since city populations are growing, often by more than 5 percent per year, an increasing proportion of these new jobs must be created in urban areas. Currently 20-50 percent of those working in cities are employed in the urban informal sector in businesses ranging from street vending to tailoring to furniture making. A growing share are working in the informal sector because larger-scale businesses have not expanded rapidly enough to provide the jobs.[8]

B. Significance of the SSE Sector for Women

Small-scale enterprise is particularly important for women who need to earn income. It is more flexible and less restrictive than employment in larger enterprises, which may require education, training, and/or experience that women lack; such jobs may also require that work be done at times and in places that are culturally unacceptable or difficult for women with family responsibilities. SSEs can be built upon knowledge and skills women acquire in the family, can be engaged in part-time and within the household if desired, and can facilitate the transition from agricultural employment as it begins to decline.

Although women's economic activities in both agricultural[9] and nonagricultural production are undoubtedly underreported, data compiled from the Yearbook of Labor statistics for 1970, 1974, and 1977 show that for Latin America and Asia, the percentage of the economically active population that is female is higher in nonagricultural production than in agriculture; in the Middle East it is equal, and in Africa it is lower.[10]

Migration of women to urban areas has risen recently. In Tanzania, female participation in agriculture is strong, migration is traditionally male-dominated, and the percentage of population living in urban areas is smaller than in other regions. Nontheless, women in growing numbers are migrating to the cities, many in search of income. A World Bank study found "a sharp increase in the proportion of female urban migrants" during the 1960s in Africa. "In Tanzania the proportion of migrants who are women rose from 33 percent of all those migrating before 1950 to 54 per cent by 1971. The analysis indicates that while the proportion of female migrants who came as economic dependents remained high, the pull of the city as a source of employment and education contributed to the increase in the number of female migrants. . . . [with] great implications for labor utilization."[11]

Small-scale enterprise is difficult for people newly arrived in the city. With all its demands and challenges to someone who does not know the ropes, however, it still provides greater access for women than other sectors, which often require educational qualifications beyond those held by women. In the Tanzania case, women represented 53 percent of the SSE sector in urban areas, with steet trading and small plot cultivation the most common occupations.[12] The PISCES studies, covering urban micro-enterprise projects in several countries of Africa, Asia, and Latin America, came to a general conclusion that such "projects mostly assist women entrepreneurs. In general, the smaller the size of the business reached, the larger the proportion of women business owners."[13]

III. PROJECT IDENTIFICATION: THE CRITICAL STARTING POINT

The starting point of the project process is the identification of an opportunity for development, or of a problem or block to be solved or removed. The two cardinal rules of project design, as applied to women, are:

1) Do no harm: do not worsen the situation of women by virtue of the project intervention.

2) Assist the chosen development process in appropriate ways; help women with the totality of tasks and concerns, and do so in their way.

To follow these rules requires information about women and their roles. This paper proposes a twofold methodology for collecting and considering this information at the project identification stage, when it can be most valuable in shaping the project. The Small-Scale Enterprise Participation Profile, as described below, specifies the relevant data and provides a useful means of arraying them. In addition, we suggest that preliminary project analysis give explicit attention to the barriers to women's participation in SSEs.

The use of the SSE participation profile and barriers analysis will help in small-scale enterprise project design. The participation profile should be used not only to identify numbers and types of SSEs, but also to assess the level of experience and skill in the various management categories (organization, personnel, production, marketing, finance). It then serves as an early indicator of project feasibility, which can help prevent waste of resources. In particular, the profile can help overcome the common tendency to neglect marketing considerations at the first stage of the project process. Deficiencies and problems in other management categories may be addressed by selected project interventions, but it is very difficult to improve demand, particularly in the populations targeted for development assistance. There is widespread consensus that "marketing proves to be one of the most difficult obstacles to creating viable economic enterprises based on the small-scale production of most rural women's projects."[14]

Used in conjunction with general indicators (for example, criteria on participation, access, control, status and indicators of physical, economic, and social well-being), the participation profile and barriers analysis can make it easier to identify and design projects that are not specifically SSE interventions, but may affect women's economic interests. Small-scale enterprise is a major mode of income generation for women, especially women with limited financial and human capital.

For virtually any project with economic ramifications, the SSE participation profile and barriers analysis can be useful in determining the
conditions under which women are least likely to be disadvantaged,
either absolutely or relative to men.[15]

Because project identification usually follows a broader country or
sectoral development strategy, the intended beneficiaries are often not
defined in terms of gender. Women within the beneficiary group (e.g.,
small-scale entrepreneurs) may be invisible and, as women, may actually
be hurt by the project intervention.

A few common project goals that vitally affect women's economic
interests are:

1) Increasing GNP; increasing foreign exchange; accelerating economic growth; decreasing poverty.

2) Increasing employment.

3) Increasing family income.

4) Decreasing rural-urban migration.

The interventions chosen for the first goal set often harm women's
economic interests by affecting them as producers of basic necessities
(food, clothing, household utensils, and furnishings). Interventions
that favor large industries, products for export, and modernization
requiring capital, land, and human resources tend to exclude women
from participation. Since women are producers, often very efficient
producers, of basic necessities, projects that do not include them and
their productive functions, or even create competition that may drive
women out of the market, will not achieve their maximum potential
macroeconomic impact. The projects may increase income, but if the
returns are not channeled to the producers of society's basic needs, the
long-run effect will be to widen the economic gap within the population.

Small-scale enterprise interventions are gaining favor among planners as a means of increasing employment. Women's employment, in
terms of time spent in producing goods and services, can hardly be
increased. Poor women cannot afford to be unemployed. Their time is
already fully occupied; the issue is not occupation but compensation,
the returns to them from their investment of time and effort.

Planners have learned that interventions aimed at increasing family
income tend to fall short of the goal if they fail to take into account
women's major responsibility to support their children. Projects that
channel resources only to men and/or perpetuate constraints on
women's access to inputs and earnings have often failed to improve
the income and the quality of life for women and children. Because
women entrepreneurs are well represented among the poor, assistance

to them will ameliorate poverty—both for the women as individuals, and for their children.

Efforts to improve rural life in hopes of decreasing migration to urban areas must include women, in their role of primary producers of basic goods and services. The increase in the numbers of women migrants indicates their difficulties in meeting increasing economic responsibilities in a rural setting.

Other commonly cited project goals may signal women's participation, yet their economic interests may be overlooked as a factor, for example in goals to:

1) improve nutritional status and health of at-risk groups;

2) decrease population growth rates; increase family planning practice; or

3) increase literacy and/or education levels.

The importance of women's earnings to the attainment of these goals is increasingly being recognized. They need additional income to purchase nutritional foods, to boil or filter water, and to acquire medicine and health care. Population/family planning project experience indicates that income-generating activities are "the most effective type of intervention when trying to reach the poor."[16] Literacy and education for females are important for development; but women who are already fully occupied with the daily struggle to subsist frequently do not see literacy or education projects as immediately productive investments of time and energy. Thus, for example, the beneficiaries of the Upper Volta Equal Access to Education for Women and Young Girls program modified the project to give priority to their basic tasks.[17]

It is precisely at the project identification stage that determined steps must be taken to counteract women's invisibility. If their roles and interests are not explicitly considered as an intrinsic part of the project process at the early stages, an adverse impact on women is more likely. The project identification stage must also include attention to social norms that may act as formidable barriers to women in their economic roles. Philip Coomb's observation about rural development projects is equally applicable to projects affecting women's economic activities:

> One of the clearest lessons to emerge from ICED's case studies is that the impact and continuity of any rural development project are strongly influenced by deep-rooted social, cultural, and political factors in the project's environment, and these differ considerably from one locality to another. Failure to give adequate attention to such factors *before* designing the project has often led to disappointing results."[18]

As we have seen, women are already in small-scale enterprises, and for each woman visible there may well be others who have not been picked up in the employment statistics, SSE censuses, and project data. For each woman engaged in an SSE, there are others who need income and would like to be involved. To estimate numbers and types of existing women's SSEs, and to assess need and feasibility for new ventures, one can base projections on whatever data are available, then spot-check them by interviews with women from the targeted beneficiary population. Reliability of community group interviews can be high, as AITEC discovered in Costa Rica.[19]

The crucial first step was the perception of the conditions, problems, and solutions to problems as defined by the people who lived in the regions. Comprehensive interviews with key groups (selectmen in town government, farmers, local club members and agency personnel, teachers, businessmen, unemployed laborers) were conducted, in which topics ranging from migration to employment to production and community services were discussed.[20] (As was commonplace some ten years ago, the participatory methods of this project identification did not quite extend to women.)

If such a comprehensive program is not feasible at the project identification stage, attempts should be made to interview the most knowledgeable persons accessible—for example, female home economists, agricultural or health extension agents, members of women's organizations, or personnel from the host country government, development assistance agencies, or local research and educational institutions. However, there is no substitute for asking the women themselves.

Within any relatively poor group that would be the clientele of development assistance efforts, it is safe to assume that women are involved in productive activities and have economic interests and responsibilities. The challenge is to find them (for women in their economic roles are sometimes invisible even to themselves) and to discover how their interests and roles contribute to and are affected by the chosen project goals and interventions—to see and support women within the family, the community, and the economy.

A. Participation Profile

Women in small-scale enterprise suffer from a double invisibility. Although the importance of SSEs to development has recently received greater recognition, most such businesses are very small indeed, and it is very difficult to "see" the smallest "microenterprises," especially in rural areas. It is even more difficult to see women in SSEs: (1) often neither they nor men think of women as businesspeople; (2) the habit of working without remuneration renders women's participation in small-scale enterprise less visible; and (3) women's enterprises are often on the borderline with their subsistence occupations.

The first step toward assessing women's participation in SSEs is thus to specify the activities they engage in and where, when, and how they perform them. These activities should not be identified in isolation, but rather examined relative to male counterparts within the sector.

Thus it is necessary to define the SSE sector and its role within the larger economy. Much of the literature defining SSEs has used an "informal-formal sector" dichotomy. Although this has been usfeul in drawing attention to the neglected SSE portion of the economy, initial research for this paper led Mary Beth Wertime to suggest that a more useful conceptual approach for project analysis is to analyze the SSEs in terms of several descriptive parameters describing their positions along a continuum or within segments. Enterprises are heterogeneous, and project design must take this diversity into account. Within this sectoral profile the women's position can then be explicitly identified.

A useful way to capture the diversity of SSEs is to relate a set of common descriptive characteristics to two parameters that will significantly shape project design: enterprise size (in terms of human resources) and type of good or service produced. The descriptive characteristics can be categorized into the main functional areas of management: organization, personnel, production, marketing, and finance.

The format for an SSE participation profile combining these descriptive characteristics with the enterprise size parameter is shown in Table 1; Table 2 shows the analogous profile with the goods and services parameter. Seldom, if ever, would existing data be sufficient to fill out such matrices completely. Nonetheless, it is very important for an analyst to know what information is missing so that a decision can be made either to gather the data or to proceed with project design on the basis of certain assumptions regarding the missing data.

Three principal sources of data are useful in assessing the role of women in providing labor to small-scale enterprises and/or deriving income from them:

1) labor statistics compiled by the International Labor Organization (ILO) from national data;
2) census or research data on employment or small scale enterprises; and
3) project data.

None of these sources provides much information disaggregated by sex. Since it is difficult to "see" small-scale enterprises and particularly the women within them, available data have to be used creatively. Approximations may be derived from whatever disaggregated data may be available on nonagricultural economic activity. Breakdowns for status categories are then compared with data from census and project sources.

Women in nonagricultural labor are represented in all status categories of the ILO International Classification as employers, own-account workers, employees, unpaid family workers, and members of producers' cooperatives.[21]

The available data suggest that the various roles women play in the SSE sector are influenced by the skills and experiences they have garnered, primarily in the family. Other factors shaping their roles are the practices and traditions of the society, which may result in women's domination of a particular industry. The roles may differ from place to place and may change over time. Garment-making is an example. In Jamaica, all the dressmaking is done by women.[22] Conversely, in Sierra Leone men dominate tailoring, the industry that accounts for the greatest share of employment and value added.[23] Men also predominate in carpentry, blacksmithing, baking, goldsmithing, and watch repair. However, over 80 percent of the owners of tie-dye (*gara*) SSEs in Sierra Leone are women.[24]

Women's participation in particular types of SSE's may change over time, influenced by the level of development and the conditions of the economy. In the Philippines, women are moving from household-based to establishment-based textile/wearing apparel manufacture and are shifting out of manufacturing into commerce and services.[25]

The following pages illustrate the variety of roles played by women in SSEs. The information is organized in the Participation Profile framework.

1) ORGANIZATION

a) Number of Units

This statistic reveals the degree of fragmentation and the number of contact points that would be needed to ensure adequate outreach and coverage for the project. Gender-specific analysis would then show how many units were owned by women.

In countries where a census of SSEs has been made or SSE data have been derived from analysis of employment data,[26] there has been a tendency to concentrate on manufacturing (or industry). Anderson identifies three overlapping phases in the development of a country's manufactures:

1) a phase in which household manufacturing is predominant, accounting for one-half to three-quarters or more of total manufacturing employment;

2) a phase in which small workshops and factories emerge at a comparatively rapid rate, displacing household manufacturing in several sectors; and

3) a phase in which large-scale production becomes predominant, displacing the remaining household manufacturing activities and much of the production of workshops and small factories.[27]

The number of SSE units cannot be determined through analysis of labor force data unless the average number of workers in SSEs and the SSE share of the labor force are known. A census may tend to undercount household manufacturing and SSEs located in rural areas. It seems likely, however, that if other factors are equal, the number of SSE units is likely to be highest in the household and small workshop phases of development. In the Philippines and perhaps in many countries, manufacturing outside the household employs mostly men;[28] as a result women have a comparatively larger share of employment in household manufacturing. (See "Production Location" below.)

The existence of many relatively small SSE industrial units, in both the household and the small workshop phases, may be economically and socially rational, even though problems arise in:

- meeting volume requirements in export and some local markets;
- getting the price advantages from bulk purchases of raw materials;
- covering the costs of specialized technical, managerial, design, or R&D staff; and
- affording necessary equipment.[29]

Small units are a more efficient alternative when labor, raw materials, and markets are dispersed in rural areas; transport and infrastructure are poor; work is irregular or the job cannot be standardized; and products have low scale economies and serve small markets.[30] The convenience and flexibility of household units are highly valued by some women. In a Chilean cooperative, for example, women who knitted in production groups in their homes were asked whether they would be interested in doing the same work "at four times the pay, but in a nine to five factory setting. Not one of them considered the alternative feasible, giving as a reason the primary importance of their family responsibilities."[31]

b) Number of Female Employees

This information is needed to determine which types of SSE are the main sources of income for women. Certain types of SSE may be significant employers of women even if not owned by them.

Four categories of workers are found in SSEs—entrepreneur, family, apprentice, and hired.[32] Usually only the hired worker is paid wages, either in cash or in kind. The apprentice may provide labor in exchange for learning or may be required to pay. In Sierra Leone, the *gara* industry requires an average of 1.7 years of apprenticeship, and an average fee of 15.5 Leones, with higher fees in rural areas.[33] The ratio of employed to owners of SSEs is very low in Kenya[34] and other countries for which data are available; many SSEs are one-person businesses.

Hired workers seem to be more important than family workers in Jamaican and Haitian SSEs. A survey of Jamaican nonfarm SSEs found hired workers to be the second largest category (after entrepreneurs). Hired workers' share ranged from a high of 77.3 percent of the work force in food enterprises to a low of 5.4 percent in craft, which is dominated by women and also has the highest proportion of family workers, 35.9 percent. In Haiti, apprentices represented 35 percent of small manufacturing and repair SSE employment, hired workers 31 percent. Jamaican hired workers and trainees, in contrast, together make up only 42.6 percent of the manufacturing SSE work force.[35]

The amount of employment for women afforded by small-scale enterprises in a particular service or product seems to depend on the extent of female ownership. For example, in Haitian small manufacturing entrprises, women dominate the pastry and candy-making businesses and are well represented in tailoring, straw products, and baking. Female workers make up two-thirds of the employees of Haitian women entrepreneurs, but only 6 percent of those employed by men entrepreneurs.[36] In Jamaica, women are predominantly found in craft and dressmaking enterprises; employment opportunities for unskilled females are very poor except in those categories.[37]

The incidence of paid employment for women is SSEs is difficult to determine without conducting micro studies. Sometimes it can be approximated if labor force breakdowns are available for male/female and family/hired. From the Ilocos (Philippines) cottage industries data cited in a World Bank study,[38] for example, one can draw the conclusion that garmentcraft, loom-weaving, and needlecraft provide employment for women. However, these SSEs are very small, almost one-person enterprises, and thus provide little if any paid employment to non-owners.

Comparing data from various sources may raise more questions than it answers. The ILO figures for Haiti on paid employment in manufacturing show more women than men. Yet the census shows women with only a 16 percent share in manufacturing and repair SSEs. Is there significant large-sale manufacturing that employs mostly women? The census covered SSEs employing fewer than 50 persons; data on larger firms are either nonexistent or not comparable. Or is women's share of employment in SSEs underreported? The census was not able to gather data in localities below 1,000 in population, which account for 80 percent of the population in Haiti.[39]

The national-level, detailed data disaggregated by sex from the Jamaica and Haiti SSE surveys indicate women do not have much of a share in the relatively small amount of wage employment in SSEs. While women owners of SSEs were 49.3 percent of the total in Jamaica, women were only one-third of workers in all categories.[40] In Haiti, women were 18 percent of owners and 16 percent of workers.[41] As the PISCES studies[42] and other project data indicate, women in SSEs are primarily owner-operators, predominantly in commerce, services, and "traditional" manufacturing activities. In both countries, the SSEs clustered at the 1-5 worker size category.

c) Legal Status

Different legal statuses (e.g., sole proprietorship, partnership, corporation, cooperative, other, or none) may call for different administrative responses.

Census data indicates that sole proprietorships are the dominant ownership form, constituting 94.3 percent of the SSEs surveyed in Jamaica.[43] Information on legal status or form of ownership is not included in the very useful sample questionnarie Allal and Chuta append to their work on cottage industries.[44] It is probably not needed in the case of very small enterprises; it is usually neither necessary nor advantageous to define their status formally, nor are the resources available to do so.

When forms of organizations, such as cooperatives and corporations, or business functions, such as credit and marketing, are subject to legal regulation, women often find it difficult to deal with the legalities.

Little information on the sex of SSE owners is readily available, even in studies of SSEs. Two censuses, for Jamaica and Haiti, provide some of this information, however. The Jamaica census of small-scale manufacturing enterprises finds that "an equal number of men and women are owner/operators (proprietors) of small scale enterprise."[45] In Haiti, women are owners or managers of 18 percent of the small manufacturing and repair enterprises surveyed.[46] In both cases, the proportions of women undoubtedly would have been higher had nonmanufacturing SSEs been included. This category includes commerce and service occupations, in which women are strong and which usually dominate manufacturing. In Jamaica, for example, manufacturing SSEs account for 63 percent of all workers and roughly the same percentage of establishments.[47]

Some indications can be garnered from labor data. The categories with the highest numbers of women, according to the most recent ILO statistics, are own-account workers and employees.[48] Own-account or self-employed workers may be considered the same as owner-operators of small-scale enterprises. Approximately one-third as many women as men are found in this category in the countries providing data in the 1982 ILO Yearbook of Labour Statistics.

Differences among data collectors in the definition of self-employment make it difficult to identify many female owner-operators in small-scale enterprises. Census definitions used in three African countries illustrate the problem. In Zambia (1969), the self-employed are defined as having their own place of business and determining their own hours of work and work program; in Ghana (1970), a person working for two or more individuals is self-employed; and in Swaziland, a person is self-employed if he or she is paid for the job done or goods sold, as opposed to receiving a stable salary.[49] A further difficulty in compiling an accurate picture is that many women fail to identify their activities as work.

Dixon has documented regional differences in the percentage of women among self-employed workers in the 1970s.

"Sub-Saharan Africa shows the highest median at 43 percent; South/ Southeast Asia and Central/South America [are] considerably lower at 22 and 16 percent; and North Africa/Middle East the lowest at 4 percent. The extremely low figures are not all in North Africa or the Middle East, however, for 10 percent or fewer of the self-employed are female in Sri Lanka, Pakistan, Panama, Costa Rica, and Cuba. The highest figures for women entrepreneurs (40 to 63 percent) are in Botswana, Tanzania, Ghana, and Malaysia."[50]

2) PERSONNEL

a) Literacy, Training, and Formal Education

These are factors that affect productivity and income, and that differ by sex. Fewer women than men have achieved functional literacy and numerical ability, which are very useful, if not essential, skills in SSEs.

Participation in job-related training may differ between men and women, in terms of both types of skills (e.g., machine repair vs. food processing) and access to training, especially on-the-job training (e.g., apprenticeships). Vocational and basic education are also significant factors.

Whereas many employers require workers to meet certain formal education requirements, 77 percent of the proprietors of small-scale industry in Sierra Leone had no formal education at all; the figure is 87 percent within the predominantly female *gara* industry.[51] Thirty-nine percent of the market women in a Honduras project had never been to school and were presumed to be illiterate.[52] In Tanzania, 65.7 percent of all women in the informal sector have no formal education.[53] The owner of the largest tie-dye business in The Gambia reported that she could not "do sums."[54] Success in the SSE sector seems to depend on factors other than education, such as entrepreneurial ability and experience.

Women in the SSE sector earn relatively little, both in absolute terms and in comparison with men in SSEs. Some evidence indicates that this effect is linked to women's relative lack of education and experience, which in turn is conditioned by their sex; other data, however, indicates that women may do better than men in realizing an economic return on their education. In a study of women in the urban labor market in Tanzania, regression analyses indicated that women with relatively high education and experience made more money than men at the same level. Furthermore, there was no sex discrimination in the job market when the number of years of schooling was controlled for, and experience (especially for illiterate women) was positively related to earnings.[55] Skills needed in small-scale enterprise are usually acquired through on-the-job experience, within the family or as an apprentice.

b) Marital Status

People's needs depend in part on their marital situation. Distinct patterns for men and women are likely. Single, married, and head of household are relevant categories.

Most female small-scale entrepreneurs are married or in a nonlegalized union. In a project for Honduran market women, 19 percent were legally married, 50 percent were in nonlegalized unions, 29 percent were single mothers, and 2 percent were widows.[56] In a sample of twenty-five borrowers in the Self-Employed Women's Association— SEWA—of Ahmedabad (India), 76 percent were married, 20 percent widowed, and 4 percent single.[57]

c) Household Size

An SSE's viability may be affected by how many household members depend on income from it and contribute labor, support services, or other income to it.

A small-scale enterprise usually provides only a portion of the entrepreneur's total income. SSE earnings may be reinvested in that or another business, or may go toward personal or family consumption. Because women tend to devote income to family consumption, the number of dependents they must support is a factor in gauging both economic necessity and the viability of an SSE, which may depend on reinvestment of earnings.

Household size may be relatively large, and women often contribute half to nearly all of the resources required. Assumptions about women's economic dependency on men have been substantially modified by research showing a significant and growing number of women-headed households.[58] It has been estimated that women represent 20 percent of heads of households in Ecuador; a study of 159 women SSE candidates for credit in Quito found 30.2 percent.[59] Almost half of the families of Philippine vendors had seven or more members, but 70 percent had only one or two income earners.[60] A study of SEWA borrowers estimates that at least one-fourth of them were household heads, 12 percent were widows, and 26 percent contributed more than the husband to household income.[61]

d) Age

There are likely to be significant differences in the average ages of women and men in SSEs. This reveals constraints to participation at earlier ages and may also suggest special needs related to age.

Women in SSEs are older than men, probably because they become active when the needs of their growing children call for additional resources and because they are less culturally constrained from operating in public as they grow older. Women in SSEs in Colombo, Sri Lanka, were concentrated in the 40-49 age group, men in the 20-29 age group.[62]

Households in San Salvador, El Salvador are heavily involved in small-scale enterprise, with 85 percent engaged in businesses, mostly run by women, that provide half or more of the family income. The women in a SSE credit project in San Salvador were fairly evenly distributed in age categories: 29 percent in their twenties, 35 percent in their thirties, and 24 percent forty or older.[63]

e) Time Commitment

Whether the workers are full-time, or part-time, or seasonal workers is quite important for project design. This issue is particularly relevant for women, given their significant household responsibilities. It is also important to ascertain whether limitations on time arise from the SSE (e.g., seasonal demand or marginal and uncertain return) or from the worker (time required for agricultural pursuits and/or family duties).

Women, like men, engage part-time in SSEs as one of a mix of income-generating activities; because of their household and family responsibilities, women can devote less of their total time to business than men. When the men are absent from the household, women must also assume their responsibilities. Male migration from rural to urban areas leaves women to head the household and take responsibility for operating and maintaining the smallholding.[64] In Kenya, estimates based on the 1969 census indicate that about 25,000 rural households did not have a male head, with another 400,000 effectively headed by women whose husbands were away in the town.[65]

3) PRODUCTION

a) Geographical Location

Knowing whether the SSE is located in a rural, semi-urban, or urban area or concentrated in certain regions of a country is an essential input to project design. Infrastructure and delivery system requirements can vary considerably. Collecting this information on a gender-specific basis may reveal concentrations of female-owner SSEs.

Small-scale enterprises are found in both rural and urban settings. The only census of SSEs that adequately covers both urban and rural areas and provides data disaggregated for sex is that of Jamaican small-scale manufacturing. That census found that women are more often engaged in SSEs in rural than in urban areas, which may be because small SSEs, in which women are most likely to participate, are more common in rural areas. It may also indicate that SSEs at the owner-operator, self-employment level provide "last resort" income for women in rural areas, while those in urban areas have access to other income-generating opportunities. In Jamaica, women represented a much higher percentage of female proprietors—64.7 percent—in the Enumeration Districts with fewer than 2,000 people than in any of the other three size categories. In the capital city, women accounted for 14.3 percent, in major towns (20,000-100,000) for 7 percent, and in rural towns (2,000-20,000) for 6.7 percent.[66]

The Haitian study was unable to cover localites with population below 1,000, which account for 80 percent of total population; thus, the finding of fairly uniform employment of women across locality sizes holds true only for "urban" areas.[67]

The urban-focused PISCES studies of SSE assistance projects in several countries of Africa, Asia, and Latin America found that "projects most commonly assisted women entrepreneurs. . . . in general, the smaller the size of the business reached by a project, the larger the proportion of women business owners."[68]

b) Operating Location

It is important to note by gender where the goods or services are produced. The main categories would be purchased or rented locale, donated locale, household, street (fixed or shifting), and mobile.

Women in SSEs are more likely to be found engaged in commerce as street or market vendors, or in household-based manufacturing or service occupations, rather than in a factory or workshop setting. Although household-based enterprises eventually give way to the next phases of industrial development, they persist over long periods of time, even growing in relative and absolute terms when industrialization is rapid.[69]

Household-based SSEs have both advantages and disadvantages for women. They may be more convenient and economical, but it may be difficult for women in household SSEs to receive compensation for their productive efforts. Home enterprise tends to be seen as "women's work," and devalued accordingly. Men generally do not consider the activities of women "real work," as a Togolese farmer put it. And even women think that their household, family, and agricultural activities, and their petty commerce as well, are not "work."[70] Although women do much of the work in home enterprise, the returns may be controlled by male family members. Thus, removing production from the home can ensure that women are paid for their economic activities directly, rather than working as a part of a labor unit in which the husband or father is the employer handling negotiations with the outside world, marketing the product, and controlling the household income.[71]

c) Technology

Information on the level of technology of the SSE, again recorded by gender, will reveal both constraints and opportunities relevant to project design (See "Technology Transfer: Implications for Women").

The productivity of small-scale enterprises can often be increased through improvements in technology, either machinery ("hardware") or methods of working ("software"). The availability of new power sources in rural areas carries a potential for significant technological change and an increse in productivity. Household manufacturing is particularly important in rural areas. About three-quarters of household manufacturing is located in rural areas in East Africa, West Africa, and India; the rural share is one-half in Colombia and the Philippines, and two-fifths in Korea. Thus, the availability of electric- or petroleum-powered equipment suitable for small-scale manufacture of food, clothing, implements, and utensils can have a substantial impact on employment and earnings.[72] However, improvements in technology have sometimes harmed rather than helped women in small-scale food processing enterprises. The introduction of petroleum- or electric-powered mills and presses for processing major food grains, tubers, and oils in various parts of the world has not always increased women's productivity. In fact, it has sometimes displaced them from the industry and even increased their household expenses.

In Upper Volta, for example, women have traditionally been responsible for processing millet flour. "It takes 4 to 6 hours to prepare for a hot meal and most of this is the pounding of millet," an AID study found. "When technical help is devised, the process usually becomes the domain of men. This means that something that used to be laborious and time-consuming but which cost nothing and sometimes was a source of income for women, is taken over by machines run by men. Women now have to pay for the service . . . If women wish to buy modern products, this new demand for money comes at the very time their sources of money from traditional products is declining."[73] On the other hand, the time saved might be used for more productive activities.

The choice of appropriate production technologies, both hardware and software, is crucial to productivity, profitability, and the best use of relatively scarce capital and relatively abundant labor in small-scale industries. Allal and Chuta indicate that "technologies that are neither the most labor-intensive nor the most capital-intensive have proven to be optimal at the given opportunity cost of resources," citing a case of the bread industry in Sierra Leone. An "obsolete technology," the rotary peel oven, was the most profitable, combining "the advantages of high-quality bread and considerable turnover of the modern bakery with much less capital-intensity." The traditional peel brick or mud oven was the next most profitable overall and was considered appropriate for smaller markets, while the most advanced technology was the least profitable.[74]

In terms of ratios of output to capital, output to labor, and labor to capital, traditional technologies may sometimes be the most rational.

In the female-dominated *gara* industry in Sierra Leone, enterprises using traditional technology (natural indigo versus imported synthetic dye) had the highest average capital productivity, an output-to-capital ratio of 82.7, as well as the highest labor-to-capital ratio, 98. The lowest output-to-capital rated industry using traditional technology was tailoring, with 7.5. The high and low for modern processes were 72 for *gara* and 0.5 for blacksmithing.[75]

d) Productive Activity

The small-scale entrepreneur's activities in the production/marketing cycle potentially include acquisition of raw materials, financing, processing/production, stocking/storing, transportation, and sale to an intermediate market channel or the final customer. Some SSEs cover a broad range of activities; others are more focused. Where the SSE is located within the production cycle will influence the nature of the project.

Women in SSEs are active in the production of both services and goods. In urban areas they seem to be found more often in services, particularly vending, than in production of goods, although in some countries urban women are concentrated in food production.

A sample of 26 entrepreneurs in the Manila Community Services Inc. (MCSI) program, 90 percent of whom were women, were engaged in the following productive activities in an urban setting:

> 18 in selling (buying and selling bottles, fruit, vegetables, cooked food, comic books, magazines, ready-made dresses, peanuts, used clothes, cooked corn, sweepstakes tickets, costume jewelry, bread, toys, candy and the running of *sari-sari* stores which usually involved selling of kerosene, soft drinks, cigarettes and rice, plus other necessities); 7 in manufacturifng (toy making, box making, welding cement molds, candy making, fancy crafts, tailoring); and 1 in service (shoe repair).[76]

Small-scale sellers represented 48 percent of a sample of SEWA (India) borrowers, while 40 percent were home-based producers.[77] Urban informal workers in Tanzania were classified as service (transport, porter, street trading, shopkeeper hotel/bar, and house rental) and goods-producing (craft manufacture, contractor, *shamba* [gardening] (and fishing). Women were concentrated in *shamba* and street trading, where they were 50.3 and 34.3 percent of the total workers. Other categories in which women had high percentages of participation were hotel/bar (47.5 percent), house rental (38.3 percent), transport (37.2 percent), and craft manufacture (37.2 percent).[78]

Rural women seem to concentrate on production, primarily of food and clothing, and to engage to a lesser extent in services such as vending, although it is not uncommon for rural women also to sell their produce at market. Work by home economists has found that rural women from Latin American and Caribbean countries seem to concentrate on small-scale food production

> Eleven of sixteen reports were of agriculturally oriented projects where women were involved in the production of food . . . Only in Panama were women involved in a large production enterprise: they had acquired 20 hectares of land for rice production and were able to supply the local independent mills and the Agricultural Marketing Institute . . . In three of the sixteen reports, women worked in handcrafts, clothing, embroidery, and fish selling . . .[79]

In Cameroon, food production is also important for rural women

> Agriculture and the related areas of livestock raising, fishing and exploita-tion of forest resources were the occupations of 94 percent of the eco-nomically active rural women—90 percent were in food crop production, 2 percent in industrial and export crops . . . less than one percent . . . are involved in trading activities. . . . Other important areas for rural women were manufacturing—primarily dress making and tailoring . . .[80]

4) MARKETING

a) Market Destination

An SSE's production can be primarily for the producer's own house-hold or for rural, urban, or export markets. It may or may not be directed to a market segment in which competition from large industry is a factor. These patterns may differ by gender.

Small-scale entrepreneurs often identify marketing as their most serious problem. They have trouble selling their goods or services, perhaps because of lack of demand, competition, or factors they cannot identify. When owners of small-scale manufacturing enterprises in Jamaica were asked to indicate the relative importance of demand, finance, raw materials, import license, spare parts/machinery, utilities, fuel, and transportation as business problems, 38 percent selected inadequate demand as the most important problem facing them; two-thirds named demand as one of the top three problems. In the rural Enumeration Districts, demand problems were cited as most important by 46 percent and as among the top three by 77.6 percent of pro-prietors. In these rural areas, women represent 64.7 percent of pro-prietors, compared with 49.3 percent nationally.[81]

Small-scale entrepreneurs' primary markets are nearby and small, defined not only by local demand but also by the entrepreneurs' ability to reach the market: to know the needs and preferences of the market segment to which they target their product, to know about market channels and competition, and to be physically able to deliver the goods or services. Nearby markets have the advantage of being more easily researched and serviced by small-scale entrepreneurs, but they often have disadvantages as well: low effective demand due to relative poverty, and saturation due to commonality of raw materials and skills, and therefore products, in the area. Among beneficiaries of the MCSI program in urban Manila, almost all of whom were women, 80 percent did both purchasing and marketing in their own neighborhoods. Of those interviewed from another Manila-based program, 85 percent "sell their products either to individuals, usually neighbors, or to small local stores." That program, run by the Ministry of Industry, has learned that "institutional markets, in spite of the 'clout' of government agencies, are difficult to penetrate. Products produced by the client groups do not meet high quality requirements."[82]

In Niger, markets are divided according to sex. The men are in *official* markets where export crops (peanuts, cotton) are sold; the women are in *traditional* markets, which are held every week in important villages and serve as intervillage exchanges. It is in these markets that women sell their production (both agricultural and livestock). Even more often women sell some processed products, to which their labor has added value, as in the oil they make from peanuts harvested from their personal fields. They also offer a whole range of cooked dishes, and some sell crafted objects such as decorated calabashes and water jugs. Undoubtedly these transactions do not bring them large sums of money. But the traditional markets function all year long, whereas the official markets are open only two or three months a year. The fact that women can receive cash income more regularly is an important point in the financing of all development operations. No matter how modest, it is evident that women may have a steadier cash flow than men.[83]

Although small-scale entrepreneurs, especially women, are often limited to nearby markets with low effective demand, people usually try to improve their markets. An example is the predominantly female beneficiaries of the PRIDECO program, most of whom reside in the slums of San Salvador:

> Fifty-three percent of the businesses are located outside the owner's community, indicating that they are providing goods and services to the generally wealthier surrounding communities. Almost 41 percent of these businesses belong to street vendors.[84]

b) Sales Value

Larger enterprises are likely to have higher sales, but there may be significant variation by product type. Again, the gender delineation might point to patterns.

Figures on sales are difficult to obtain; the majority of SSEs do not keep books, and entrepreneurs are generally not willing to divulge sales figures when they are available. Income data from loan projects can be used as an indicator in the absence of sales figures.

For the smallest enterprises, and those in which women operate, the sales or income from services may be quite small, yet still constitute an important part of the family budget. Among 286 borrowers from the SEWA bank, women's monthly earnings averaged 234 Rs. (about $30 at an exchange rate of 8:1) and represented 46 percent of the combined family earnings. Women in SEWA had income about 50 percent higher than the 157 Rs. average monthly income of self-employed women in Ahmedabad.[85]

5) FINANCE

a) Capital

Lack of capital is a major problem for very small entrepreneurs. More than 80 percent of the participants in the Manila Community Services Inc. program said it was their critical constraint.[86] It is generally regarded as a sector-wide problem.[87] Studies of closures of small firms in the Philippines, however, suggest that "access to finance for fixed or working capital seems not to be a 'barrier to entry,' though it may well place more of a restriction on expansion or the maintenance of output when the firms are larger."[88]

The amount of capital used to start up a SSE may be very small, especially for what PISCES defines as micro-enterprises, "the smallest-scale economic enterprises of the poor. They are normally run by a single owner-manager, and employees, if any, average less than two. Capital required for start-up is minimal, anywhere from a few dollars to one or two hundred dollars."[89] Women are generally concentrated in SSEs that require little capital, such as selling.

Low capital investment, however, usually means low profits. Interviews of SSE project beneficiaries carried out by PISCES in the Philippines indicate that investments in service are higher than in selling. Absolute profits were also higher for services but percentage returns on investment were greater for selling.[90]

b) Financing Sources

The lending sources could be institutions (e.g., banks, credit unions), professional money lenders, traditional "savings" groups, friends, or relatives. The equity sources could be retained earnings, family, private investors, or government. Distinct patterns by gender might emerge.

The small-scale enterprise sector is generally self-financed. Whether because of exclusion from commercial and governmental financing or because of personal preferences, small-scale entrepreneurs use their own and their families' and friends' resources to start their businesses. This is true in middle-income, industrialized countries such as Korea and Taiwan as well as in low-income countries such as Haiti and Sierra Leone. Personal savings accounted for 72 percent of initial capital in Haitian SSEs and 60 percent in Sierra Leone; money lenders, credit unions, and banks accounted for less than 6 percent in Haiti and 2 percent in Sierra Leone. Recurring expenditures follow the same pattern.[91]

In some places, particularly Africa, women have developed strong traditional savings organizations from which they may finance SSEs. In Cameroon, for example:

Groups usually meet regularly, e.g., weekly, bi-weekly or monthly. If it is a mutual aid group, a small fixed sum is paid which is held by the organization until it is needed by some member to meet the costs of an illness or a funeral. There is no reciprocity in these hand-outs and the criterion for receiving the fund is simply that of need. A second payment may be made which goes to cover the expense involved in holding the meeting. Finally, a third payment may be made which is for savings purposes (in some groups this is the only payment made). Many different descriptions were found of how this function might be organized. Members might simply put whatever amount they wished in at each meeting and the amounts contributed by members would be kept in a box or in a joint bank account. Periodically, usually once a year just before Christmas, the fund would be shared out and each member would receive back the amount she had put in, plus interest if a bank had been used.[92]

Some form of rotating share-out is the more usual form found in rural areas (and in many urban groups as well). In this case no use is made of banks or other formal financial institution. Instead, one member in turn receives the amounts contributed by all other members of the association. The order in which members receive the share-out is determined in a variety of ways—it may be fixed in advance, lots may be drawn, it may be auctioned off, or it may be given to a member who has an emergency need. (However, each member can receive the share-out only once in each round.) Obviously, the members who receive the share-out early in a round are the debtors of other members of the group, who have their turn later. Accordingly, elaborate arrangements are sometimes made to even out the benefits received, for example, by paying more money to those who receive their shares late in the round.[93]

Guy Belloncle observes that in Niger "there seems to exist among the women a capacity for self-organization and self-financing superior to that of the men. One cannot but be struck by the importance of the sums which the 'Local Women's Unions'—which themselves seem to be supported by the most traditional organizations—are capable of collecting."[94]

c) Financial Management

To gain access to formal credit systems, SSEs must keep written financial accounts. Women may be disadvantaged in this area.

Keeping books is important not only for the immediate success of the business but also for its potential improvement and expansion through institutional credit. Small firms in the Philippines that went bankrupt showed a "noticeably lower . . . tendency to keep books and records, to separate business and family accounts, and to use the services of professional accountants."[95] In fact, small-scale entrepreneurs seldom keep books, particularly in very small SSEs and in rural areas. In rural Bangladesh, only 6 percent kept books, and in Sierra Leone, the national rate was 17 percent.[96] About 10 percent of Jamaican small-scale manufacturing enterprises overall kept books, with the rate ranging from 4 percent in the smallest Enumeration Districts to 29 percent in the capital city. The size of the enterprise was apparently the most important factor determining whether records were kept.[97]

The female-dominated *gara* industry in Sierra Leone, by contrast, showed the highest industry rate of record-keeping, 50 percent. It should be noted that the sample was the smallest of all the industries, comprising only eight cases, and that none was located in the smallest size locality.[98] In Jamaica, the industries dominated by women, dressmaking and crafts, have only a 1.9 and 1 percent rate of record-keeping respectively.[99]

How can women compensate for a lack of bookkeeping skills? Togolese borrowers from the African Enterprises Program, part of the Entente Fund in West Africa assisted by the Agency for International Development, agreed to use the part-time services of an accountant. Thirty-nine percent of these borrowers were women, mostly the famous cloth sellers who, though illiterate, "can figure into millions of francs and keep their records entirely in their heads. The legend of their ability to calculate mentally is probably quite accurate: she who counts wrong gets out of business quickly. Bankers being less charmed by mental bookkeeping than are tourists, the lack of accounting is one factor which has kept the market women ineligible for credit."[100]

d) Earnings

Inadequate financial management often makes it difficult to ascertain an SSE's earnings or profit. Some entrepreneurs have only marginal earnings, while others make more than the prevalent wage. Many SSEs that are not profitable in themselves have other kinds of utility, both economic and social. For example, the SSE may provide cash during an off-period in another occupation, often agriculture. it may provide occupation for a family member, have value in the portfolio of enterprises, or offer the entrepreneur an improved social status or a preferred work style. A woman selling crafts in The Gambia found it difficult, time-consuming, and costly to make other arrangements to handle her family and household tasks; still, she explained, "I like to be in the market much better than to work at home."[101] The independence afforded by self-employment is valued by many, including 46 percent of interviewees in Philippine SEEs, of whom over three-fourths were women.[102]

Women who could make more money elsewhere may nevertheless opt for their preferred work style and location. Women of a small Honduran village, for example, sought assistance in increasing their income from the production and sale of *rosquillas,* biscuits made of corn and cheese. With a loan from Save the Children, they purchased a motor-driven mill, which saved time and energy grinding the corn and permitted them to increase sales. The loan was repaid and, encouraged by their success, the women decided to form a baking cooperative to produce *rosquillas* more efficiently. It soon became apparent, however, that the women really preferred to work in their own homes for whatever reasons of individual differences or family demands, the women of this community were not inclined toward a cooperative project. The mill continues to serve the community and the women appreciate their additional income and time.[103]

In many cases, people engage in a marginally profitable SSE simply because there are no better alternatives. The PISCES studies found that "many of the poorer artisans and traders in squatter settlements engage in entrepreneurial activity as a matter of survival rather than choice and, in many instances, would prefer secure wage employment if it were available."[104]

This is probably the case for many women. They earn less than men and are concentrated in types of SSEs with lower earnings. In urban

Tanzania, 47 percent of the self-employed women (compared with 4 percent of the men) had labor incomes of not more than 100 shillings.[105] The predominant activity of women entering SSEs in the Philippines is selling, but two-thirds of those in this type of SSE earned below $1.40 per day (slightly more than the minimum wage).[106]

6) SIZE OF SSE

Women are found predominantly in very small "micro-enterprises" (one to five workers), especially in owner-operated enterprises that employ one other worker on average. Some data indicate that more women are found in the smallest SSEs, and as size increases, women's participation decreases. The PISCES study found that, in the projects examined in Africa, Latin America, the Philippines, and India, the entrepreneurs most commonly assisted were women, and they were at the bottom of the scale. "In general, the smaller the size of the business reached by a project the larger the proportion of women business owners."[107]

7) TYPE OF PRODUCT OR SERVICE

Women are concentrated in certain occupations, both as owners and as employees. In a particular country women may predominate in either services or products, depending on the level of development and the range of occupations open to them. They usually concentrate in businesses in which they have skills and access to raw materials.

Sexual division of labor in a particular culture may also influence the choice of SSEs. For example, in Haitian small manufacturing enterprises, women dominate the pastry and candy-making businesses and are well represented in tailoring, straw products, and baking. Women account for only 1-3 percent of the employees in metal working and the repair of shoes, cars, and machines, and are not represented in leather working, watch repair, tire repair, or mattress making, either as proprietors or employees. In Jamaica, all the dressmaking and most of the straw work are done by women.[109] In rural small-scale enterprises in Guatemala, women contribute 65 percent of the work force in commercial services, 50 percent in textiles, 47 percent in food processing and baking, and 17 percent in leather working.[110]

B. Barriers Analysis

Our description of women in small-scale enterprise has not considered those who might wish to be active but for one reason or another cannot. As Anderson aptly points out in his overview issue paper on small industry in developing countries, researchers have skewed the sample by neglecting those who have not been able to enter or to remain in SSEs.[111]

People in small business often rank finances, markets, and raw materials as critical problems. Women participants at the International Women's Year Seminar on Third World Craftswomen and Development unanimously chose money (for raw materials), markets, and management as the priority needs of developing country craftswomen.[112] Women in SSEs have problems similar to those of men and face similar constraints. Yet the women's situation is exacerbated by their gender. In addition to the normal difficulties of small business—marketing, undercapitalization, lack of credit—women's businesses face some obstacles that are specific to their being run by women.[113] Difficulties and constraints become barriers, sometimes to entry into business, sometimes to the types of SSEs that provide more income, and sometimes to increases in size, efficiency, and profitability.

Women in SSEs may encounter difficulties in any of the functional management areas: in getting organized, for example, or in acquiring adequately trained personnel, producing appropriate quality, finding markets for their goods, or obtaining sufficient credit. One should first try to identify the nature and seriousness of the problems in the functional areas. They will vary from situation to situation, but similarities across areas will emerge. This analysis provides focal points for project design.

A second step is to specify the causes of these problems. Project design can then attempt to address causes rather than than symptoms. Problems may stem from women's inadequate access to the control of key external resources (including inputs such as capital and training, as well as markets). But it is important then to identify the access barriers, which fall into five interrelated categories: societal norms, institutional structures, legal aspects, economic factors, and political factors.

Availability of information will be a problem in barriers analysis. Micro studies are needed for problem identification. Furthermore, estabishing causal relationships is a slippery affair. Nonetheless, one should attempt these tasks because they are important inputs to the project design process.

1) SOCIETAL NORMS

Religious, historical, familial, and cultural factors create attitudes that may act as barriers to women's participation in SSEs (though some may facilitate access).

Social attitudes concerning women's value, abilities, and proper roles, often internalized by women themselves, are the single most serious barrier to women's entry and success in small-scale enterprises. The combination of these negative attitudes with women's commitments to raising a family further intensifies and strengthens the barrier.

A task is devalued when it becomes "women's work" in a given society, and even financially successful women are held in low esteem. Planners and policy makers reflect societal attitudes, often regarding women and their productive activities as nonexistent, unproductive, or critically limited by women's childbearing and childrearing roles, all contrary to evidence.

These attitudes have little basis in objective reality. As we have seen, women already play a considerable role in small-scale industries, especially when some correction is made for the "invisibility." Nor are women unproductive. They create goods and services that produce wealth and value; but because of societal constraints on women, the wealth and value does not always accrue to the producers in full measure. An AID study noted that women are "not an 'underutilized' human resourse, as the planners are fond of referring to them, but 'overutilized' in a very basic way. They work hard, all day, with few visible benefits from their labors."[124]. Some evidence indicates that women, though comparatively disadvantaged with regard to both financial capital and human capital, make comparatively more efficient use of investments (for example, in the *gara* industry in Sierra Leone).

Attitudes of society toward women act directly, reflexively, and indirectly to impede women in business. Disapproval may directly keep women out of SSEs; women may reflect society's attitudes and regard business as unattainable for them; and society's views influence the institutions, laws, economy, and policies to discriminate against women.

Notions of impropriety and inability are used to keep women out of business in general and certain businesses in particular. Restrictive concepts of impropriety are particularly strong in Muslim and Hindu societies, although their effect is eroded by the necessity to work brought on by poverty. An AID study found that in Bangladesh, Pakistan, India, and Nepal, "the girls and women defined as being economically active are drawn disproportionately from the non-Hindu and non-Muslim minorities (especially tribals, Christians, Buddhists), from low-caste and scheduled-caste groups in the Hindu community, and from the lowest socioeconomic ranks among the Muslims."[115]

The notion of women's inability in certain areas is particularly strong with regard to machinery. This widespread idea may have arisen from the need to assign a domain to men, particularly as their traditional roles as hunters and protectors declined over time while women's roles remained constant. Perhaps not only outsiders bearing technology but also overburdened women saw men as the group to be concerned with machines. At the International Women's Decade midpoint meeting in Copenhagen, leaders of women's organizations in Francophone Africa argued that the point of rural development was to decrease women's work and free up some of their time. Women could not do everything. So in the case of a grain mill in Senegal partly donated by UNICEF, "the mill was operated by a man who had been employed (and had to be paid a salary that the milling fees could not support) . . . . Why was it a man who was running the mill? To give the men a feeling that they participate, to keep their cooperation. We should not be overly concerned to feminize everything." In another case, women "refused to sew because men are already doing it and women have plenty to do."[116]

Both men and women devalue women's economic production. "In many traditional rural settings," one report noted, "female respondents are not conscious of themselves as economic beings, despite the fact that they are de facto involved in productive-market production. The self-perception of women, who though economically active, continue to 'declare themselves' as 'only housewives' is a crucial factor in the underestimation of the female work force."[117]

The family is a powerful focus of male disapproval of women's economic activities. Disapproval may be turned to acquiescence, especially if the human relations are handled well and the economic contribution women make to the family is needed. The Inter-American Foundation observed that "many women's projects have foundered because of (husbands', fathers', and brothers') opposition—which often can only be alleviated by time and the women's persistence. In many instances, however, these problems can be minimized by efforts of a supporting organization to explain to the men the purposes of the project, to discuss with them the benefits to be derived, and to enlist their support."[118]

A representative of the National Union of Malian Women noted that "The liberation of women cannot take place against men because the structure demands that men agree. Women who participate in meetings have to report back to the husband and if he is not agreeing, he can forbid her to participate—he can threaten divorce and send her back home."[119] Nevertheless, male family members may be persuaded by economic necessity to change their views. Women participating in a YWCA handicraft training program in Dacca, for example, "contribute so heavily to the family income, husbands find their initial objections appeased by the extra money."[120]

2) INSTITUTIONAL STRUCTURES

Institutions reflect societal norms and so may create administrative and organizational barriers.

Schools, banks, and businesses may create institutional barriers to women's entry and advancement in small-scale enterprise. These institutional barriers may affect both human and financial capital formation required for SSE success. Furthermore, the effect of institutional structures that discriminate against women may be cumulative. As a World Bank researcher notes, "Cumulative discrimination occurs whenever a worker has low productivity and therefore low wages because of past discrimination. For example, when choices concerning the type of training and levels of education of younger women are affected by job patterns of older women who have been victims of past discrimination in jobs or education."[121]

3) LEGAL ASPECTS

Laws may impede women's access to or control over key resources, intentionally or unintentionally.

Although many nations have subscribed to the United Nations Convention on the Elimination of All Forms of Discrimination against Women, many retain laws that treat women as minors, without legal power. Women often have no legal person of their own and must depend on male relatives for legal status. Legal barriers to organizing a business and obtaining credit are common. In parts of Latin America, for example, "businesses owned by women cannot obtain legal status and must be registered either in their husbands' names or operate within a larger organization. Indian women, many of whom do not speak Spanish, are particularly dependent on men for outside business dealings. Sometimes organizations that helped establish businesses have been unwilling to subsequently relinquish authority to the women owners. . . . Even successful women-owned businesses have been denied commercial credit when husbands or other males were unwilling to co-sign or guarantee loans."[122]

4) ECONOMIC FACTORS

Macroeconomic conditions may exacerbate other barriers (e.g., credit availability) or make it easier to overcome them (e.g., societal restrictions on role behavior may give way to economic necessity).

Changes created by modernization, urbanization, and industrialization have increased the need for monetary tansaction. Women must have money to get things they need for themselves and their families—things that can only be acquired in exchange for money (such as transportation or schooling); things that require too much work and time to produce at home; and things that could be produced at home but which seem to be better, have more appeal, or carry more status value because of the way they are produced and packaged.[123]

Women also need money because social changes have left them increasingly responsible for the economic support of the family. An estimated 15-22 percent of women are heads of households, depending on the region.[124]

Self-employment in personal service occupations or in trade and marketing is feasible for some, but is not very productive economically. Dixon argues that the "single most important factor retarding rural development is the lack of money in poor households and the lack of control over what money exists contributes to the low status of women and increases their motivation for frequent childbearing." She reports that a woman member of the Provincial Assembly in Punjab, India, decided in 1966 that "the key to women's problems was their lack of control over money" and remarks on "how rarely people have come to this particular conclusion regarding the needs of rural women."[125]

The traditional small-scale enterprises engaged in by women, such as food processing and the making of household utensils, are giving way to competition from industrialized products that have status value and are competitively priced. In India, for example, the absolute number of women in nonagricultural jobs dropped between 1911 and 1971. Particularly sharp declines appear in the economic activities traditionally employing large numbers of rural women—cottage industries, including spinning and weaving; paper making; jute handicrafts; bidi (cigarette) making; rice processing and oil processing; and trade and commerce. Women in these occupations have been increasingly forced into competition with factory producers in the expanding industrial sector and with wholesalers and intermediaries in marketing. The control over income that many women had derived from marketing their own food or handicrafts has largely been lost.[126]

Women are invariably found at the bottom of the economical scale, as indicated by the project experience of the Inter-American Foundation. Even within their own communities, women are generally at the bottom of the ladder. If Peruvian Indians are poor, Peruvian Indian women are poorer. If Honduran children have few schooling opportunities, Honduran girls have fewer. If laws discriminate against Ecuadorian blacks, they discriminate more against Ecuadorian black women.[127] Since there is basis in experience for the truism that the rich get richer and the poor poorer, economically disadvantaged women have every expectation of remaining so.

5) POLITICAL FACTORS

Changes in political leadership may bring either greater repression or greater equality to women.

Politics governs life at all levels, and men most frequently control politics. Women are accustomed to dealing with male power and may be able to chart a successful course through the political currents. But when politically powerful men realize that their position may be affected by women, they often act against women's interest.

Many of the organizations seeking to help women in SSEs have had political difficulties. One of the most interesting cases is to be found in SEWA, a trade union of 5,000 poor women workers in Ahmedabad, India. Emerging from the activities of the Women's Wing of the Textile Labor Association, SEWA was established as a union in 1972, achieved a notable success, and, after efforts to extend the protection of existing labor laws to self-employed women, became independent in 1981. It was forced into independence because neither the Textile Labor Association (TLA) nor the National Labor Organization (NLO), of which it was an affiliate, felt the political advantages outweighed the disadvantages of women activists in their ranks. At the session during which SEWA was expelled, the NLO's president commented, "I built SEWA during the emergency days to protect TLA against Indiraji's [Indira Ghandi's] attacks. I built a wall of poor women around TLA. Now I am expelling SEWA because it is dangerous for TLA."[128]

IV. PLANNING, DESIGN, AND IMPLEMENTATION

The considerations we have noted as relevant to project identification are even more important in the actual design of the project. Steps must be taken to correct for "the invisible women" within the project population. Searching out, collecting, and producing disaggregated data; using women designers; collecting data on women's roles (using the SSE Participation Profile for economic roles); using local organizations and individuals; exploring women's needs with them, especially at the village level; translating working documents into the language of the host country and distributing them to collaborating organizations—all have been suggested as means to bring women into the planning process, guard against negative impact, and provide an intervention that will assist them.[129]

All planners agree that investments made during planning will pay off in the implementation state. Yet because relatively little importance is attributed to women's economic activities, planning resources are seldom allocated to assessing women's participation, which often requires more time, effort, and consequently money than "established" types of data.[130]

A recent AID evaluation study on SSEs recommended the development of a diagnostic profile to capture "knowledge of local production technologies and of firm profitability, by type, as well as of employment patterns and skill levels, particularly of women and the poorest generally". The Participation Profile advocated in this paper is an attempt to meet that need. "[T]he more comprehensive the profile and participatory process of developing it," notes the AID study, "the more complete the picture it provides of the commercial sector and its social setting, the more likely the eventual attainment of project goals . . . it is possible to argue that an accurate pre-analysis may give more scope for knowledgeable, shared decisions later—in the implementation phase."[131]

Certain design elements—simplicity, flexibility, appropriateness to the project milieu, and ownership and control by the intended beneficiaries—are likely to prove crucial in implementation. At this stage projects are likely to stray inadvertently from their goal of benefiting women, focusing rather on other goals.[132] Women's participation needs to be monitored on an ongoing basis, and project administrators must have the authority to make needed adjustments. The barriers analysis may be particularly useful, since psychosocial difficulties may well impede implementation. The following brief notes suggest how the participation profile and barriers analysis can be related to stages of the project process.

1) **Avoid Negative Impact** - Channeling resources to other parties often hurts women in SSEs by creating competition at all levels, from raw materials to markets. Women are also often hurt by regulations intended to improve business or industry, such as licensing of SSEs, standardization, or purity regulations (e.g., in the food industry).[133] Improvements in the marketing system may also exclude women by making it too costly for them to participate or removing control over pricing.

2) **Foster Positive Impact** - Women can be assisted in their economic
function by giving them time to engage in small-scale enterprise.
This was the accomplishment of the *mabati* movement in Kenya.
With tin roofs, rainwater can be saved and stored, releasing women
from the daily chore of fetching water, which normally takes two
to ten hours per household. The women used the traditional
rotating societies to accumulate cash to buy the tin roofs. Each
woman contributed money to a communal pool, which was distributed to members in turn, with the order determined by lot. With
the time saved because rainwater was available, and often with
cash earned by selling some of the water, the women increased
their production of vegetables, chickens, and pigs for sale in the
urban markets.[133]

Projects will be more helpful if they take into account the totality of
women's activities and the meeting of priority needs. Day care is an
obvious example, but sometimes the needs are even more basic.
Women of the most arid and remote part of Upper Volta, for example,
were in favor of the AID-sponsored Training Women in the Sahel
Project, with its emphasis on appropriate technology and income
generation, but wanted to know if it would help them get water.

The information gathered about barriers occasioned by social norms
will indicate how production and marketing in the SSE might be best
organized and carried out to suit the particular women participants.
Experience has shown the wisdom of not attempting too great a
departure from social norms. Dixon finds that "women have more
direct access to project benefits when planners explicitly recognize the
prevailing sexual division of labor and design activities that build on
women's work and enable them to control their earnings."[135]

Women need help in overcoming the problem of low social esteem,
which may impede their SSE activities. Hunt finds the psychosocial
obstacle to enterprise creation and success of "surpassing importance
to entrepreneurs in general."[136] Surely it is still more important for
women, and must be explicitly considered in any project attempting to
assist women to enter SSEs.

Interventions of different types, intensities, and durations are
required for SSE projects intended to assist women entrepreneurs at
different levels of experience and need. The PISCES study divided
projects into those that aim to assist existing SSEs and those that
create new ones. Projects were studied on the basis of their objectives
(ranging from the narrow "assistance to existing business" to the
broad "diversifying the economic base of the community by encourag-
ing self-sufficiency and linkages to nearby rural areas"). Interventions
were made at three levels: community, group, and individual. The

study found that community and group interventions seemed to fit better with projects having comprehensive objectives and those aimed at new businesses. "In general, the needier the population, the more long-term, intensive, and comprehensive is the program." Credit is the most sought input among urban clients, many of whom are women in the very smallest enterprises. "In general, the smaller the size of the businesses reached, the larger proportion of women business owners."[137]

* * *

Small-scale enterprises will continue to play for many decades a significant role in Third World economies. The importance of women's roles in SSEs makes gender an important variable in enhancing SSE project performance and the benefits accruing for women. The Participation Profile and Barriers Analysis provide one means of more systematically carrying out gender-based analysis for project identification, design, and implementation.

TABLES

Table I   Enterprise Size

		Number of Workers Per Unit			
	1	2-5	6-10	11-20	21-50

Organization
  1) Number of Units:
    — Male owned
    — Female owned
  2) Number of Workers:
    — Male
    — Female
  3) Legal Status (number):
    — Sole proprietorships
    — Partnerships
    — Corporations
    — Cooperatives
    — Other
    — None

Personnel
  4) Levels of Literacy, Training
    Formal Education:
    — Male
    — Female
  5) Marital Status:
    — Married
        M
        F
    — Single
        M
        F

Table I   Enterprise Size (Continued)

		Number of Workers Per Unit			
	1	2-5	6-10	11-20	21-50

— Head of Household
  M
  F
6) Household Size and Female
   Economic Contribution (%):
7) Age:
  M
  F
8) Time Commitment:
  — Full Time
    M
    F
  — Part Time
    M
    F
  — Seasonal
    M
    F

Production
9) Geographical Location:
  — Rural
    M
    F
  — Semi-Urban
    M
    F
  — Urban
    M
    F
  — Regional Concentration
    M
    F
10) Operating Locations:
  — Household
    M
    F
  — Donated Locale
    M
    F
  — Rented/Purchased Locale
    M
    F
  — Mobile
    M
    F

Table I   Enterprise Size (Continued)

	Number of Workers Per Unit				
	1	2-5	6-10	11-20	21-50

11) Technology:
  — Traditional
    M
    F
  — Semi-Modern
    M
    F
  — Modern
    M
    F

12) Productive Activity:
  — Physical Production
    M
    F
  — Processing
    M
    F
  — Wholesaling
    M
    F
  — Retailing
    M
    F
  — Financial
    M
    F
  — Transporting
    M
    F
  — Storing
    M
    F

Marketing
13) Market Destination:
  — Household
    M
    F
  — Rural
    M
    F
  — Urban
    M
    F
  — Export
    M
    F

Table I   Enterprise Size   (Continued)

	Number of Workers Per Unit				
	1	2-5	6-10	11-20	21-50
14) Sales Value:					
— M SSEs					
— F SSEs					
Finance					
15) Capital:					
— Debt					
M					
F					
— Equity					
M					
F					
16) Financing Sources:					
— Personal, Family, Friends					
M					
F					
— Savings Associations					
M					
F					
— Money Lenders					
M					
F					
— Cooperatives					
M					
F					
— Banks					
M					
F					
17) Financial Management:					
M					
F					
18) Earnings:					
M					
F					

Table 2   Type of Good or Service

	Services			Goods		
	Vending	House-hold	Personal	Food Products	Clothing	Other
Organization						
1) Number of Units:						
— Male owned						
— Female owned						
2) Number of Workers:						
— Male						
— Female						
3) Legal Status (number):						
— Sole proprietorships						

Table 2   Type of Good or Service (Continued)

		Services			Goods	
	Vending	House-hold	Personal	Food Products	Clothing	Other
— Partnerships						
— Corporations						
— Cooperatives						
— Other						
— None						

Personnel
4) Levels of Literacy, Training
Formal Education:
— Male
— Female
5) Marital Status:
— Married
    M
    F
— Single
    M
    F
— Head of Household
    M
    F
6) Household Size and Female
Economic Contribution (%):
7) Age:
    M
    F
8) Time Commitment:
— Full Time
    M
    F
— Part Time
    M
    F
— Seasonal
    M
    F

Production
9) Geographical Location:
— Rural
    M
    F
— Semi-Urban
    M
    F
— Urban
    M
    F
— Regional Concentration
    M
    F
10) Operating Locations:
— Household
    M
    F
— Donated Locale
    M
    F

Table 2   Type of Good or Service (Continued)

	Services			Goods		
	Vending	House-hold	Personal	Food Products	Clothing	Other
— Rented/Purchased Locale						
M						
F						
— Mobile						
M						
F						
11) Technology:						
— Traditional						
M						
F						
— Semi-Modern						
M						
F						
— Modern						
M						
F						
12) Productive Activity:						
— Physical Production						
M						
F						
— Processing						
M						
F						
— Wholesaling						
M						
F						
— Retailing						
M						
F						
— Financing						
M						
F						
— Transporting						
M						
F						
— Storing						
M						
F						
Marketing						
13) Market Destination:						
— Household						
M						
F						
— Rural						
M						
F						
— Urban						
M						
F						
— Export						
M						
F						
14) Sales Value:						
M						
F						

Table 2   Type of Good or Service (Continued)

	Services			Goods		
	Vending	*House-hold*	*Personal*	*Food Products*	*Clothing*	*Other*
Finance						
15) Capital:						
— Debt						
M						
F						
— Equity						
M						
F						
16) Financing Sources:						
— Personal, Family, Friends						
M						
F						
— Savings Associations						
M						
F						
— Money Lenders						
M						
F						
— Cooperatives						
M						
F						
— Banks						
M						
F						
17) Financial Management:						
M						
F						
18) Earnings:						
M						
F						

NOTES

1. Dennis Anderson, *Small Industry In Developing Countries: Some Issues,* World Bank Staff Working Paper no. 518 (Washington, D.C.: Development Economics Department, The World Bank, 1982), p.1.

2. Ibid.; Enyinna Chuta and Carl Liedholm, *Rural Non-Farm Employment: A Review of the State of the Art,* MSU Rural Development Paper no. 4 (East Lansing, Mich.: Department of Agricultural Economics, Michigan State University, 1979), p. 6; Michael Farbman, ed., *The PISCES Studies: Assisting the Smallest Economic Activities of the Urban Poor* (Washington, D.C.: Office of Urban Development, Bureau for Science and Technology, U.S. Agency for International Development, International Development Cooperation Agency, 1981), p. 12.

3. The World Bank, *World Development Report 1982* (New York: Oxford University Press for the World Bank, 1982), p. 43.

4. Anderson, p. 32.

5. The World Bank, p. 79.

6. Steve Haggblade, Jacques Defay, and Bob Pitman, *Small Manufacturing and Repair Enterprises in Haiti: Survey Results,* Working Paper no. 4, MSU Rural Development Series (East Lansing, Mich.: Department of Agricultural Economics, Michigan State University, 1979), pp. 10-12.

7. The World Bank, p. 78.

8. Farbman, p. ix.

9. See Kathleen Cloud, *Women's Productivity in Agricultural Systems: Considerations for Project Design* (Cambridge, Mass.: Harvard Institute for International Development, 1983).

10. In South/Southeast Asia, women account for 26 percent of nonagricultural production and 20 percent of agricultural production; in Central and South America the figures are 15 percent and 4 percent; in North Africa and the Middle East 4 percent and 4 percent; and in Sub-Saharan Africa 6 percent and 26 percent. Ruth B. Dixon, *Jobs for Women in Rural Industry and Services* (Washington D.C.: Office of Women in Development, U.S. Agency for International Development, 1979), pp. 5-6.

11. Nwanganga Shields, *Women in the Urban Labor Markets of Africa: The Case of Tanzania*, World Bank Staff Working Paper no. 380 (Washington, D.C.: The World Bank, 1980), p. 27.

12. Ibid., p. 49.

13. Farbman, p. 45.

14. Ruth Dixon, *Assessing the Impact of Development Projects on Women*, AID Program Evaluation Discussion Paper no. 8 (Washington, D.C.: Office of Women in Development and Office of Evaluation, Bureau for Program and Policy Coordination, U.S. Agency for International Development, 1980), p. 47.

15. Ibid.; Subcommittee on Women in Development of the Committee on Development Assistance, American Council of Voluntary Agencies for Foreign Service, Inc., *Criteria for Evaluation of Development Projects Involving Women* (New York: Technical Assistance Information Clearing House/American Council of Voluntary Agencies for Foreign Service, Inc., 1975).

16. Irene Tinker with Laura T. Raynolds, *Integrating Family Planning and Women's Enhancement Activities: Theory and Practice* (Washington, D.C.: Equity Policy Center for Office of Population, U.S. Agency for International Development, 1982), p. II-6.

17. United Nations Educational, Scientific and Cultural Organization, *Women, Education, Equality: A Decade of Experiment* (Paris: The UNESCO Press, 1975), p. 22. See also NFE Information Center, "Literacy and Development," in issue no. 17 of *The NFE Exchange* (East Lansing, Mich.: Institute for International Studies in Education, Michigan State University.)

18. Philip H. Coombs, *New Strategies for Improving Rural Family Life* (Essex, Conn.: International Council for Educational Development, 1981), p. 65.

19. Maryanne L. Dulansey, ed., *Approaches to Appropriate Evaluation: Report on a Series of Workshops on Evaluation* (New York: American Council of Voluntary Agencies for Foreign Service, Inc./Technical Assistance Clearing House, 1978), p. 90.

20. Jeffrey Ashe, *Rural Development in Costa Rica* (New York: Interbook Inc. for ACCION International, 1978), pp. 14-15.

21. International Labour Office, *Yearbook of Labour Statistics, 1982* (Geneva: International Labour Office, 1982).

22. Yacob Fisseha and Omar Davies, *The Small-Scale Manufacturing Enterprises in Jamaica: Socioeconomic Characteristics and Constraints*, Working Paper no. 16, MSU Rural Development Series (East Lansing, Mich.: Department of Agricultural Economics, Michigan State University; Kingston, Jamaica: The Institute of Social and Economic Research, University of the West Indies, 1981), p. 15.

23 .Carl Liedholm and Enyinna Chuta, *The Economics of Rural and Urban Small-Scale Industries in Sierra Leone*, African Rural Economy Paper no. 14 (East Lansing, Mich.: Department of Agricultural Economics, Michigan State University, Njala, Sierra Leone: Department of Agricultural Economics, Njala University College, University of Sierra Leone, 1976), p. 14.

24. Enyinna Chuta, *The Economics of the Gara (Tie-Dye) Industry in Sierra Leone*, African Rural

Economy Working Paper no. 26 (East Lansing, Mich.: Michigan State University, 1978), p. 2.

25. Dennis Anderson and Farida Khambata, *Small Enterprises and Development Policy in the Philippines; A Case Study*, World Bank Staff Working Paper no. 468 (Washington, D.C.: The World Bank, 1981), p. 93.

26. The MSU studies on Sierra Leone, Haiti, Jamaica; The World Bank Papers on small Industry, The Philippines, Korea, Taiwan; The ILO Kenya study.

27. Anderson, p. 6.

28. Anderson and Khambata, p. 94.

29. Nancy Barry, "Small Industry as Big Business" (Internal paper, The World Bank, 1981), p. 5.

30. Anderson, pp. 20-25.

31. Maryanne Dulansey, "Duenas de Algo: A Case Study of an Enterprise Owned and Managed by Women Artisans in Santiago, Chile" (Washington, D.C.: Consultants in Development, 1980), p. 29.

32. See the MSU studies on Sierra Leone, Jamaica, and Haiti previously cited. They include child labor under family worker, while a recent ILO publication retains it as a separate category. See M. Allal and E. Chuta, *Cottage Industries and Handicrafts; Some Guidelines for Employment Promotion* (Geneva: International Labour Office, 1982), p. 178.

33. Liedholm and Chuta, pp. 46-47.

34. Ian Livingstone, *Rural Development, Employment and Incomes in Kenya* (Addis Ababa: International Labour Office, Jobs and Skills Programme for Africa (JASPA, 1981)), p. 12.

35. Fisseha and Davies, p. 15; Davies, Fisseha, and Kirton, p. 29. *Small-Scale, Non-Farm Enterprises in Jamaica: Initial Survey Results*, MSU Rural Development Series, Working Paper no. 8 (East Lansing, Mich.: Department of Agricultural Economics, Michigan State University; Kingston, Jamaica: Institute of Social and Economic Research, University of the West Indies, 1979.

36. Haggblade, Defay, and Pitman, pp. 24-25.

37. Fisseha and Davies, pp. 15, 23, 25.

38. Andersdon, p. 85.

39. International Labour Office; Haggblade, Defay, and Pitman, pp. 12, 24.

40. Fisseha and Davies, pp. 13, 23.

41. Haggblade, Defay, and Pitman, p. 24.

42. Farbman.

43. Fisseha and Davies, p. 19.

44. Allal and Chuta, Annex VIII.

45. Fisseha and Davies, p. 15.

46. Haggblade, Defay, and Pitman, p. 24.

47. Omar Davies, Yacob Fisseha, and Claremont Kirton, p. 15.

48. International Labour Office.

49. International Center for Research on Women, *The Productivity of Women in Developing Countries: Measurement Issues and Recommendations* (Washington, D.C.: Office of Women in Development, U.S. Agency for International Development, 1980), p. 42.

50. Dixon, 1979, p. 9.

51. Liedholm and Chuta, pp. 50-53.

52. Farbman, p. 231.

53. Shields, p. 49.

54. Interview with Maryanne Dulansey, September 1975.

55. Shields, pp. 102-4.

56. Farbman, p. 231.

57. Jennefer Sebstad, *Struggle and Development Among Self-Employed Women: A Report on the Self-Employed Women's Association, Ahmedabad, India* (Washington, D.C.: Office of Urban

Development, Bureau for Science and Technology, U.S. Agency for International Development, 1982), p. 99.

58. Mayra Buvinic and Nadia H. Youssef, with Barbara Von Elm, *Women-Headed Households: The Ignored Factor in Development Planning (Washington, D.C.: International Center for Research on Women, 1978).*

59. Carlos C. Luzuriaga, *Situacion de la Mujer en El Ecuador* (Quito: Graficas San Pablo, 1982), pp. 47-49.

60. Farbman, p. 264.

61. Sebstad, pp. 94, 99.

62. International Labour Office, *The Informal Sector of Colombo City (Sri Landa)* Colombo: Marga Institute, 1979), p. 85.

63. Farbman, p. 174.

64. Elsa M. Chaney and Martha W. Lewis, "Women, Migration and the Decline of Smallholder Agriculture" (Washington, D.C.: Office of Women in Development, U.S. Agency for International Development, 1980).

65. Livingstone, pp. 2-11.

66. Fisseha and Davies, p. 13.

67. Haggblade, Defay, and Pitman, pp. 10, 24.

68. Farbman, p.ix.

69. Anderson, pp. 16-18.

70. "Revaloriser le travail de la femme," *Agripromo* 27 (October 1979): 14. Translation by Dulansey.

71. Ruth B. Dixon, *Rural Women at Work: Strategies for Development in South Asia* (Baltimore: Johns Hopkins University Press for Resources for the Future, 1978), p. 26.

72. Anderson, pp. 16-17.

73. Societe Africaine d'Etudes et de Developpement, *Social and Economic Development in Upper Volta: A Woman's Perspective* (West Africa: Regional Economic Development Services Office, U.,S. Agency for International Development, 1978), p. 25. For a more thorough discussion of this point see: Irene Tinker, *New Technologies for Food Chain Activities: The Imperative of Equity for Women* (Washington, D.C.: Office of Women in Development, U.S. Agency for International Development, 1979), p. 17.

74. Allal and Chuta, pp. 17, 24-25.

75. Liedholm and Chuta, pp. 79-83.

76. Farbman, p. 285.

77. Shields, p. 51.

78. Sebstad, p. 100.

79. American Home Economics Association/International Federation for Home Economics, *Income Generation for Rural Women: Proceedings of Workshop* (Washington, D.C.: American Home Economics Association, 1981), p. 33.

80. Judy C. Bryson, "Women and Economic Development in Cameroon" (Yaounde: U.S. Agency for International Development, 1979), p. 79.

81. Fisseha and Davies, pp. 28-30 and 13.

82. Guy Belloncle, *Femmes et developpement en Afrique sahelienne: L'experience nigrienne d'animation feminine (1966-1976)* (Dakar: Nouvelles Editions Africaines and Paris: Les Editions Ouvrieres, 1980), p. 41. Translation by Dulansey.

83. Farbman, pp. 285, 273-74.

84. Ibid., pp. 172-73.

85. Sebstad, p. 268.

86. Farbman, p. 285.

87. Anderson, p. 49.

88. Anderson and Khambata, p. 116.

89. Farbman, p.8.

90. Ibid., p. 270.
91. Samuel P. S. Ho, *Small-Scale Enterprises in Korea and Taiwan,* World Bank Staff Working Paper (Washington, D.C.: The World Bank, 1980), p. 103; Liedholm and Chuta, p. 36.
92. Bryson, pp. 91-92.
93. Ibid.
94. Belloncle, p. 212.
95. Anderson and Khambata, p. 109.
96. Chuta and Liedholm, p. 50; Liedholm and Chuta, p. 54.
97. Fisseha and Davies, p. 90.
98. Liedholm and Chuta, p. 54.
99. Davies, Fisseha, and Kirton, p. 49.
100. Philomena Friedman, "Women and the African Enterprise Program" (Abidjan: West Africa Regional Development Services Office, U.S. Agency for International Development, n.d.), pp. 9-10.
101 Interview with Delansey, September 1975.
102. Farbman, p. 270.
103. Marion Fennelly Levy, *Bringing Women into the Community Development Process: A Pragmatic Approach,* Occasional Paper 2 (Westport, Conn.: Save the Children, 1981), pp. 24-25.
104. Farbman, p. 145.
105. Shields, p. 88.
106. Farbman, pp. 270, 264.
107. Ibid., p. ix.
108. Haggblade, Defay, and Pitman, p. 25.
109. Fisseha and Davies, p. 15.
110. Samuel Daines and G. Smith, *1978 Rural Enterprise Survey* (Guatemala: Ministry of Agriculture, 1978) quoted in Allal and Chuta, p. 15.
111. Anderson, p. 35.
112. Jacqui Starkey and Maryanne Dulansey, "Expanding the External Market for Third World Crafts: The Role of Alternative Marketing Organizations" (Washington, D.C.: Consultants in Development, 1976) Appendix A: Recommendations Made by Participants in the Seminar on "Third World Craftswomen and Development" held at the International Women's Year Conference, in Mexico City, June 20, 1975.
113. Ann Hartfiel, "In Support of Women: Ten Years of Funding by the Inter-American Foundation" (Washington, D.C.: The Inter-American Foundation, 1982), p. 16.
114. Dixon, 1978, pp. 112-13.
115. Ibid., . 106.
116. The Exchange, "Notes on Session 1, Developpement Rural Integre, Copenhagen, 1980" (New York: The Exchange, 1980), pp. 8-9.
117. International Center for Research on Women, p. 28.
118. Hartfiel, pp. 28-30.
119. The Exchange, p. 7.
120. Dixon, 1978, p. 108.
121. Shields, p. 110.
122. Hartfiel, pp. 16-17.
123. American Home Economics Association, p.6.
124. Buvinic and Youssef, p. 39.
125. Dixon, 1978, pp. 13-14.
126. Ibid., pp. 21-22.
127. Hartfiel, pp. 1-2.
128. Sebstad, p. 340.
129. Dixon, 1980.
130. See the experiences of WID Development Practitioners distilled in a report of

workshops conducted in 1980-81 by the Office in Development of the New TransCentury Foundation: Pat Hersch, "Women in Development Workshops"; Maryanne Dulansey, "Women in Development Program Concerns in Francophone Sahel; Report of a Workshop, July 5-7, 1979, Bobo-Dioulasso, Upper Volta" (Washington, D.C.: Office of Women in Development, U.S. Agency for International Development, 1979); and Caroline Pezzulo, *Women and Development Guidelines for Programme and Project Planning*, (Santiago de Chile: CEPAL Economic Commission for Latin America, 1982).

131. Robert W. Hunt, *The Evaluation of Small Enterprise Programs and Projects: Issues in Business and Community Development*, AID Evaluation Special Study no. 13 (Washington, D.C.: U.S. Agency for International Development, 1983), pp. 26-27.

132. See Farbman, pp. 39-46 for characteristics of effective urban SSE projects.

133. See Daniel Santo Pietro, ed., *Evaluation Sourcebook for Private and Voluntary Organizations* (New York: American Council of Voluntary Agencies for Foreign Service, 1983), especially pages 52-53.

134. Tinker, p. 17.

135. Dixon, 1980, p. 30.

136. Hunt, p. 30.

137. Farbman, pp. 19-23, 41-45.

BIBLIOGRAPHY

Part I: Small-Scale Enterprise

Allal, M., and Chuta, E. *Cottage Industries and Handicrafts: Some Guidelines for Employment Promotion*. Geneva: International Labour Office, 1982.

Anderson, Dennis. *Small Industry in Developing Countries: Some Issues*. World Bank Staff Working Paper No. 518. Washington, D.C.: Development Economics Department, The World Bank, 1982.

Anderson, Dennis, and Khambata, Farida. *Small Enterprises and Development Policy in the Philippines: A Case Study*. Washington, D.C.: The World Bank, 1981.

Anderson, D., and Leiserson, M. W. "Rural Non-Farm Employment in Developing Countries." *Economic Development and Cultural Change* 28, no. 2 (1980).

Baranson, Jack. *Informal Small Scale Enterprise Sector of the Urban Economy: Problems and Suggested Approaches*. Washington, D.C.: Office of Urban Development, U.S. Agency for International Development, 1976.

Barry, Nancy. "Small Industry as Big Business." World Bank Internal paper. Washington, D.C.: The World Bank, 1981.

Bear, Marshall; Jackelen, Henry; and Tiller, Michael. *Microenterprise Development in the Urban Informal Sector: Case Studies from Brazil and the Philippines*. Washington, D.C.: A. T. International, 1982.

Bouman, F. J. A. "Indigenous Savings and Credit Societies in the Third World." *Development Digest* 16 (July 1978): 36-47.

Bromley, R., and Gerry, C., eds. *Casual Work and Poverty in Third World Cities*. New York: John Wiley and Sons, 1979.

Centro de Estudios para el Desarrollo Cooperativo, CEDEC. *Approximaciones al Concepto y Funcionamiento del Sector Informal en Chile*. Serie no. 15. Chile: Centro de Estudios para el Desarrollo Cooperativo CEDEC, 1982.

Chuta, Enyinna, and Liedholm, Carl. *Rural Non-Farm Employment: A Review of the State of the Art.* MSU Rural Development Paper no. 4. East Lansing, Mich.: Department of Agricultural Economics, Michigan State University, 1979.

Coombs, Philip H. *New Strategies for Improving Rural Family Life.* Essex, Conn.: International Council for Educational Development, 1981.

Cortes, M., and Berry, A. *Small and Mediuim Scale Industries in Colombia.* World Bank Draft Monograph. Washington, D.C.: The World Bank, 1982.

Cortes, M., and Ishaq, A. *Determinants of Economic Performance and Technical Efficiency in Colombian Small and Medium Enterprises.* Washington, D.C.: World Bank, 1981.

Culbertson, Robert; Jones, Earl; and Corpeno, Roberto. *Private Sector Evaluation: The Dominican Republic.* AID Evaluation Special Study no. 16. Washington, D.C.: U.S. Agency for International Development, 1983.

Davies, Omar; Fisseha, Yacob; and Kirten, Claremount. *Small Scale Non-Farm Enterprises in Jamaica: Initial Survey Results.* Working Paper no. 8, East Lansing, Mich.: Michigan State University; Kingston: University of the West Indies, 1979.

de Vries, Barend A. *Industrialization and Employment: The Role of Small and Medium Sized Manufacturing Firms.* Reprint 116. Washington, D.C.: The World Bank, 1980.

Dick, H.W. and Rimmer, P.J. "Beyond the Formal and Informal Sector Dichotomy: Towards an Integrated Alternatve." *Pacific Viewpoint* 21 (1980): 26-41.

Farbman, Michael, ed. *The PISCES Studies: Assisting the Smallest Economic Activities of the Urban Poor.* Washington, D.C.: Office of Urban Development, Bureau for Science and Technology, U.S. Agency for International Development 1981.

Fass, Simo. *The Economics of Survival: A Study of Poverty and Planning in Haiti.* Washington, D.C.: Office of Urban Development, U.S. Agency for International Development, 1980.

Fisseha, Yacob, and Davies, Omar. *The Small-Scale Manufacturing Enterprises in Jamaica: Socioeconomic Characteristics and Constraints.* Working Paper no. 16 MSU Rural Development Series. East Lansing, Mich.: Michigan State University; Kingston: University of the West Indies, 1981.

Fonstad, Carmenza, et al., comps. *The Smallest Businesses of the Poor: An Annotated Bibliography.* Cambridge, Mass.: Accion International/AITEC, 1982.

Geertz, Clifford. "The Rotating Credit Association: A 'Middle Rung' in Development". *Economic Development and Cultural Change* 10, no. 3 (April 1962): 241-263.

Goldmark, Sue, and Rosengard, Jay. *Evaluating Small-Scale Enterprise Promotion: State-of-the Art Methodologies and Future Alternatives.* Washington, D.C.: Development Alternatives, Inc. 1981.

Gross Martinez, Alberto, et. al. *Approximaciones a una Metodologia de A.T. para el Sector Informal Urbano en Chile.* Serie no. 16 Santiago. Chile: Centro de Estudios para el Desarrollo Cooperativo (CEDEC), 1982.

Hageboeck, Molly, and Allen, Mary Beth. *Private Sector: Ideas and Opportunities.* Paper no. 14. Washington, D.C.: Office of Evaluation, U.S. Agency for International Development, 1982.

Haggblade, Steve; Defay, Jacques; and Pitman, Bob. *Small Manufacturing and Repair Enterprises in Haiti: Survey Results.* Working Paper no. 4 MSU Rural Development Series. East Lansing, Mich.: Department of Agricultural Economics, Michigan State University, 1979.

Ho, Samuel P. S. *Small-Scale Enterprises in Korea and Taiwan.* World Bank Staff Working Paper no. 384. Washington, D.C.: The World Bank, 1980.

Hunt, Robert W. *The Evaluation of Small Enterprise Programs and Projects: Issues in Business and Community Development.* Washington, D.C.: U.S. Agency for International Development, 1983.

Kilby, Peter, ed. *Entrepreneurship and Economic Development.* New York: The Free Press, 1971.

Liedholm, Carl, and Chuta, Enyinna. *The Economics of Rural and Urban Small-Scale Industries in Sierra Leone.* Paper no. 14. East Lansing, Mich.: Michigan State University and Njala: University of Siera Leone, 1976.

Livingstone, Ian. *Rural Development, Employment and Incomes in Kenya.* Addis Ababa: International Labor Office, Jobs and Skills Program for Africa (JASPA), 1981.

Malley, Raymond C., et al. *Assisting Small Business in Francophone Africa: The Entente Fund African Enterprises Program.* Washington, D.C.: U.S. Agency for International Development, 1982.

Marris, Peter. "The Social Barriers to African Entrepreneurship." *The Journal of Development Studies 11 (March 1973): 29-38.*

Marsden, Keith. "Creating the Right Environment for Small Firms." *Economic Development and the Private Sector.* Washington, D.C.: The World Bank, 1981.

Mazumdar, D. *A Description Analysis of the Role of Small Enterprises in the Indian Economy.* Draft Working Paper. Washington, D.C.: The World Bank, 1979.

—."The Urban Informal Sector." *World Development 4 (1976): 665-79.*

McFerson, Hazel M. *The Private Sector: Ethnicity, Individual Initiative, and Economic Growth in an African Plural Society: The Bamileke of Cameroon.* AID Evaluation Special Study no. 15. Washington, D.C.: U.S. Agency for International Development, 1983.

Page, John M., Jr. *Small Enterprises in African Development: A Survey.* World Bank Staff Working Paper no. 36. Washington, D.C.: The World Bank, 1979.

Pratt, Robert, et al. *Costa Rica Private Sector Study.* no. 9. Washington, D.C.: U.S. Agency for International Development, 1983.

Reyes, S., and Claudio, Juan. *Hacia Una Conceptualizacion del Sector Informal.* Serie Estudios e Investigaciones no. 17 Santiago, Chile: Centro de Estudios para el Desarrollo Cooperativo (CEDEC), 1983.

Schiavo-Campo, Salvatore, et al. *The Tortoise Walk: Public Policy and Private Activity in the Economic Development of Cameroon.* Washington, D.C.: U.S. Agency for International Development, 1983.

Sethuraman, S. V. ed. *The Urban Informal Sector in Developing Countries.* Geneva: International Labour Organisation, 1981.

Simmons, Emmy B. *The Small Scale Rural Food Processing Industry in Northern Nigeria.* Food Research Institute Studies 14, no. 2. Stanford, Calif.: Stanford University, 1975.

Staley, E., and Morse, R. *Modern Small-Scale Industry for Developing Countries.* New York: McGraw-Hill, 1965.

Standing, Guy. *Labour Force Participation and Development.* Geneva: International Labour Office, 1978.

Steel, William F. *Small-Scale Employment and Production in Developing Countries: Evidence from Ghana.* New York: Praeger, 1977.

—.*The Intermediate Sector, Unemployment, and the Employment-Output Conflict.* Working Paper no. 301. Washington, D.C.: The World Bank, 1978.

Tendler, Judith. *Ventures in the Informal Sector, and How They Worked Out in Brazil.* Washington, D.C.: Office of Private and Voluntary Cooperation, U.S. Agency for International Development, 1983.

Tokman, Victor E. "An Exploration into the Nature of Informal-Formal Sector Relationships." *World Development* (September-October 1978).

"Why Small Businesses Fail." *Small Business Report* 3 (March 1982): 24-27. Monterey, Calif.: Small Business Monitoring & Research Co., Inc., 1982.

Wolgin, Jerome, et al. *The Private Sector and the Economic Development of Malawi.* AID Evaluation Special Study no. 11. Washington, D.C.: U.S. Agency for International Development, 1983.

World Bank, The. *Employment and Development of Small Enterprises: Sector Policy Paper.* Washington, D.C.: The World Bank, 1978.

Part II: Women

"Alternative Education for Maquiladora Workers." *Grassroots Development, Journal of the Inter-American Foundation* (Winter 1982/Spring 1983): 41-45. Washington, D.C.: Inter-American Foundation, 1982.

American Council of Voluntary Agencies for Foreign Service, Inc., Subcommittee on Women in Development. *Criteria for Evaluation of Development Projects Involving Women.* New York: Technical Assistance Information Clearing House/ACVAFS, 1975.

American Home Economics Association, International Federation of Home Economics. *Income Generation for Rural Women: Proceedings of Workshop.* Washington, D.C.: American Home Economics Association, 1981.

Belloncle, Guy. *Femmes et developpement en Afrique sahelienne: L'experience nigerienne d'animation femnine (1966-1976).* Dakar: Nouvelles Editions Africaines and Paris: Les Editions Ouvrieres, 1980.

Bisilliat, Jeanne. "La place de la femme dans le developpement (son role dans une economie de services non remuneres)." Paris Centre de Developpement, (O.E.C.D.), n.d.

Boulding, Elise, *Women in the Twentieth Century World,* New York: John Wiley & Sons, 1977.,

Bryson, Judy C. *Women and Economic Development in Cameroon.* Yaounde: U.S. Agency for International Development, 1979.

Buvinic, Mayra; Sebstad, Jennifer; and Zeidenstein, Sondra. *Credit for Rural Women: Some Facts and Lessons.* Washington, D.C.: International Center for Research on Women, 1982.

Buvinic, Mayra, and Youssef, Nadia H., with Von Elm, Barbara. *Women-Headed Households: The Ignored Factor in Development Planning.* Washington, D.C.: International Center for Research on Women, 1978.

Chaney, Elsa M. *A Women in Development Project in Swaziland, Skills Training for Income Earning.* New York: United Nations Department of Technical Co-operation for Development, 1982.

—."The Women Who Go . . . and the Women Who Stay Behind." *Migration Today* 10 (1982): 8-13.

Chaney, Elsa M. *Women, Migration and the Decline of Smallholder Agriculture.* Washington, D.C.: Office of Women in Development, U.S. Agency for International Development, 1980.

Chen, Marty. "The Working Women's Forum: Organizing for Credit and Change." *Seeds.* 6 (1983).

Chuta, Enyinna. *The Economics of the Gara (Tie-Dye) Industry in Sierra Leone.* African Rural Economy Working Paper no. 26. East Lansing, Mich.: Michigan State University, 1978.

Cloud, Kathleen. *Women's Productivity in Agricultural Systems: Considerations for Project Design.* Cambridge, Mass.: Harvard Institute for International Development, 1983.

Conteh, Al-Hassan; Mends-Cole, Joyce; and David, Magdalene. *A Profile of Liberian Women in Development.* U.S. Agency for International Development, 1982.

Daines, Samuel, and Smith, G. *Rural Enterprise Survey.* Guatemala: Ministry of Agriculture, 1978.

Dixon, Ruth B. *Assessing the Impact of Development Projects on Women.* AID Program Evaluation Discussion Document no. 8. Washington, D.C.: Office of Women in Development and Office of Evaluation, PPC, U.S. Agency for International Development, 1980.

—.*Jobs for Women in Rural Industry and Services.* Washington, D.C.: Office of Women in Development, U.S. Agency for International Development, 1979.

—.*Rural Women at Work: Strategies for Development in South Asia.* Baltimore: Johns Hopkins University Press for Resources for the Future, 1978.

Dulansey, Maryanne L. *Duenas de Algo: A Case Study of an Enterprise Owned and Managed by Women Artisans in Santiago, Chile.* Washington, D.C.: Consultants in Development, 1980.

—.*Factors Which Improve the Viability of Small Business Projects in Developing Countries: COMARCHI.* Washington, D.C.: Consultants in Development, 1981.

—.*Women in Development Program Concerns in Francophone Sahel. Report of a Workshop July 5-7, 1979 in Bobo-Dioulasso Upper Volta.* Washington, D.C.: Office of Women in Development, U.S. Agency for International Development, 1979.

Edmunds, Marilyn, and Helzner, Judith F. *Peru-Mujer: Women Organizing for Development.* Pathpapers no. 9. Chestnut Hill, Mass.: The Pathfinder Fund, 1982.

Friedman, Philomena. Women and the African Enterprise Program. Abidjan: West Africa Regional Development Services Office, U.S. Agency for International Development, n.d.

"Generating Income Through Group Action." *The NFE Exchange* 16 (1979). East Lansing, Mich.: Institute for International Studies in Education, Michigan State University, 1979.

Germain, Adrienne, "Poor Rural Women: A Policy Perspective." Reprint from *Journal of International Affairs,* 30 (1966-67). New York: The Ford Foundation, n.d.

Gladhart, Peter Michael, and Winter, Emily. *Northern Ecuador's Sweater Industry: Rural Women's Contribution to Economic Development.* Working Paper 81/01. East Lansing, Mich.: Michigan State University, 1981.

Sweater Production, Income Generation and Its Uses Among Women of Northern Ecuador. East Lansing, Mich.: Michigan State University, 1982.

Grant, James P. *The State of the World's Children* and *The Gardens: A Report from the Slums and Shanties of Colombo, Sri Lanka.* New York and Geneva: United Nations Children's Fund, 1982.

Hartfiel, Ann. *In Support of Women: Ten Years of Funding by the Inter-American Foundation.* Washington, D.C.: The Inter-American Foundation, 1982.

Hersch, Pat. *Women in Development Workshops.* Washington, D.C.: Office of Women in Development, U.S. Agency for International Development. and New TransCentury Foundation, 1981.

Hoskins, Marilyn, W. *Women in Forestry for Local Community Development.* Washington, D.C.: Office of Women in Development, U.S. Agency for International Development, 1979.

International Center for Research on Women. *Bringing Women In: Towards a New Direction in Occupational Skills Training for Women.* Washington, D.C.: International Center for Research on Women, 1980.

—.*Keeping Women Out: A Structural Analysis of Women's Employment in Developing Countries.* Washington D.C.: International Center for Research on Women, 1980.

—.*Policy and Program Recommendations for Enhancing Women's Employment in Developing Countries,* Washington, D.C.: International Center for Research on Women, 1980.

—.*The Productivity of Women in Developing Countries: Measurement Issues and Recommendations.* Washington, D.C.: International Center for Research on Women, 1980.

International Labour Office. *Equal Opportunities and Equal Treatment for Men and Women Workers: Workers with Family Responsibilities.* Geneva: International Labour Office, 1981.

—.*Labour Market Information Through Key Informants.* Geneva: International Labour Office, 1982.

International Women's Tribune Center, Inc. *Women's Money & Credit.* Newsletter 15. New York: International Women's Tribune Center, Inc. 1981.

Laird, Judith Fincher. *Rural Women in Paraguay: The Socioeconomic Dimension.* Republica del Paraguay: Ministerio de Hacienda, Direccion General de Estadistica y Censos; U.S. Agency for International Development 1979.

"L'Artisinat rural." *Agripromo* 31 (October 1980). Abidjan: INADES-FORMATION, 1980.

Lele, Uma. *The Design of Rural Development, Lessons from Africa.* Baltimore: The Johns Hopkins University Press for the World Bank, 1975.

Levy, Marion Fennelly. *Bringing Women into the Community Development Process: A Pragmatic Approach.* Occasional Papers 2. Westport, Conn.: Save the Children, 1981.

Lewis, Barbara C., ed. *Invisible Farmers: Women and the Crisis in Agriculture.* Washington, D.C.: Office of Women in Development, U.S. Agency for International Development, 1981.

Lewis, Martha. "Developing Income Generating Opportunity for Rural Women." *Horizons* 2 (January 1983): 28-31. Washington, D.C.: Office of Public Affairs, U.S. Agency for International Development, 1983.

Luzuriaga, Carlos C. *Situacion de la Mujer en El Ecuador.* Quito: Graficas San Pablo, 1982.

Massiah, Joycelin. *Women in Barbados: Some Demographic Aspects of Their Employment.* Washington, D.C.: Office of Women in Development, U.S. Agency for International Development, 1977.

"Notes on Session 1, Developpement Rural Integre, Copenhagen, 1980." New York: The Exchange, 1980.

Palmer, Ingrid. *The Nemow Case: Case Studies of the Impact of Large Scale Development Projects on Women: A Series for Planners.* Working Paper no. 7. New York: The Population Council, 1979.

Pezzullo, Caroline. *Women and Development Guidelines for Programme and Project Planning.* Santiago de Chile: CEPAL (Economic Commission for Latin America), 1982.

Piepmeir, Katherine Blakeslee. *Women's Organizations: Resources for Development.* Washington, D.C.: Office of Women in Development, U.S. Agency for International Development, 1980.

Reno, Barbara Morrison, ed. *Credit & Women's Economic Development.* Washington, D.C.: World Council of Credit Unions, Inc. with the Overseas Education Fund, 1981.

Reno, Barbara Morrison, et al. *Report of the Bilingual Regional Seminar, Dakar, Senegal, March 2-6, 1981: Increasing Women's Access to Credit Through Credit Unions in West Africa.* Nairobi: Africa Co-operative Savings and Credit Association, 1981.

"Report." Conference on the Role of Women's Organizations in Development. Washington, D.C.: Office of Women in Development, Agency for International Development, 1979.

"Report." Researchers and Development Practitioners Conference, Women in Development. U.S. Agency for International Development, 1978.

"Revaloriser le travail de la femme." *Agripromo* 27 (October 1979): 14 Abidjan: INADES-FORMATION, 1979.

Schumacher, Ilsa; Sebstad, Jennefer; and Buvinic, Mayra. *Limits to Productivity: Improving Women's Access to Technology and Credit.* Washington, D.C.: International Center for Research on Women, 1980.

Sebstad, Jennefer. *Struggle and Development Among Self-Employed Women.* Washington, D.C.: Office of Urban Development, Bureau for Science and Technology, U.S. Agency for International Development, 1982.

Shields, Nwanganga. *Women in the Urban Labor Markets of Africa: The Case of Tanzania.* World Bank Staff Working Paper No. 380. Washington D.C.: The World Bank, 1980.

Smucker, Jacqueline Nowak. *The Role of Rural Haitian Women in Development.* Port-au-Prince: U.S. Agency for International Development Mission, 1981.

Societe Africaine d'Etudes et de Developpement. *Social and Economic Development in Upper Volta: A Woman's Perspective.* West Africa: Regional Economic Development Services Office, U.S. Agency for International Development, 1978.

—.*Etude sur les besoins des femmes dans les villages de l'A.V.V. et proposition d'un programme d'intervention.* Quagadougou: Ministere du Developpement Rural, Republique de-Haute-Volta, 1977.

Society for International Development, Workgroup, *Proceedings of the Program on Women and Urbanization: Some Innovative Programs.* Washington, D.C.: Society for International Development, Women in Development Workgroup, 1983.

Starkey, Jacqui, and Dulansey, Maryanne. *Expanding the External Market for Third World Crafts: The Role of Alternative Marketing Organizations.* Washington, D.C.: Consultants in Development, 1976.

Stegall, Lael Swinney. *Women's Organizations and Development: Capacities for Technical Assistance in Sri Lanka and Thailand.* Washington, D.C.: Office of Women in Development, U.S. Agency for International Development, 1979.

Tinker, Irene. *New Technologies for Food Chain Activities: The Imperative of Equity for Women.* Washington, D.C.: Office of Women in Development, U.S. Agency for International Development, 1979.

Tinker, Irene, with Reynolds, Laura T. *Integrating Family Planning and Women's Enhancement Activities: Theory and Practice.* Washington, D.C.: Equity Policy Center for Office of Population, U.S. Agency for International Development, 1982.

United Nations. *Convention on the Elimination of All Forms of Discrimination Against Women.* New York: United Nations, n.d.

United Nations Educational, Scientific and Cultural Organization. *Comparative Report on the Role of Working Mothers in Early Childhood Education in Five Countries.* Document Paris: UNESCO ED-78/WS/71 1978.

United Nations General Assembly. *Resolutions and Decisions Referring Specifically to Women, UN General Assembly 36th Session 1981.* New York: International Women's Tribune Centre, Inc., 1981.

U.S. Agency for International Development. Bureau for Program and Policy Coordination. *AID Policy Paper: Women in Development.* Washington, D.C.: U.S. Agency for International Development, 1982.

Voluntary Fund for the United Nations Decade for Women. *A Guide to Community Revolving Loan Funds.* New York: The Voluntary Fund for the United Nationsl Decade for Women, 1982.

Wijayaratne, C. M.; Gunawardana, A .M.; and Asmar, Samir. *Study of Income-Generating Activities for Farm Women.* Research Study Series no. 25. Washington, D.C.: Office of Women in Development, U.S. Agency for International Development, 1978.

"Women and Production." *The NFE Exchange* 22 (1981) East Lansing, Mich.: College of Education, Michigan State University, 1981.

"Women in the Third World." *The Exchange Report.* New York: The Exchange, 1981.

Working Group on World Conference on Agrarian Reform and Rural Development (WCARRD), U.S. Agency for International Development. *Background Papers for the United States Delegation.* Washington, D.C.: U.S. Agency for International Development, 1979.

World Bank, The. *Recognizing the "Invisible" Woman in Development: The World Bank's experience.* Washington, D.C.: The International Bank for Reconstruction and Development in association with The World Bank, 1979.

Youssef, Nadia Haggag. *Women and Work in Developing Societies.* Berkeley, Calif.: University of California, 1974.

Part III: General

Abu-Luhhod, Janet, and Hay, Richard Jr. *Third World Urbanization.* New York: Methuen, 1977.

Bates, Robert H. *The Regulation of Rural Markets in Africa. Washington, D.C.: U.S. Agency for International Development, 1983.*

Belassa, Bela. *A "Stages Approach" to Comparative Advantage.* Washington, D.C.: World Bank Reprint Series no. 136, 1977.

Cernea, Michael. *Modernization and Development Potential of Traditional Grass Roots Peasant Organizations.* Reprint Series no. 215 Washington, D.C.: The World Bank, 1981.

Chernichovsky, Dov. *The Economic Theory of the Household and Impact Measurement of Nutrition and Related Health Programs.* World Bank Reprint Series no. 121 Washington, D.C.: The World Bank, 1979.

International Labour Office. *Yearbook of Labour Statistics, 1982.* Geneva: International Labour Office, 1982.

Kahler, David W. *Literacy at Work: Linking Literacy to Business Management Skills.* Washington, D.C.: Creative Associates, Inc. for the U.S. Agency for International Development, 1982.

Kahler, David W., et al. *Literacy at Work: Linking Literacy to Business Management Skills: An Annotated Bibliography.* Washington, D.C.: Creative Associates, Inc. for the U.S. Agency for International Development, 1982.

Lal, Deepak. *Market Access for Semi-manufacturers from Developing Countries.* World Bank Reprint Series no. 130. The WOrld Bank, 1979.

—.*Shadow Pricing and Wage and Employment Issues in National Economic Planning.* World Bank Reprint Series no. 130. Washington, D.C.: The World Bank, 1979.

"Literacy and Development." The NFE Exchange. East Lansing, Mich.: Institute for International Studies in Education, Michigan State University, 1980.

Non-Formal Education Information Center. *NFE Core Bibliographies.* East Lansing, Mich.: College of Education, Michigan State University, 1981.

Schulz, Theodore W. *Investing in People, The Economics of Population Quality.* Berkeley, Calif.: University of California Press, 1981.

United Nations Childrens Fund. *Moving Towards Universal Primary Education and Literacy.* Document E/ICEF/Misc. 401, 11 April 1983. New York: UNICEF, 1983.

—.*Office of Development Information and Utilization. Selected Statistical Data by Sex: Latin America: El Salvador.* Washington, D.C.: U.S. Agency for International Development, 1981.

—.*Selected Statistical Data by Sex. Africa: Swaziland.* Washington, D.C.: U.S. Agency for International Development, 1981.

U.S. Agency for International Development. Printout of Database on locator words, small business/small industry projects. Washington, D.C.: U.S. Agency for International Development, June 1983.

U.S. Department of Commerce, Bureau of the Census. *Illustrative Statistics on Women in Selected Developing Countries.* Washington, D.C.: U.S. Government Printing Office. 1980.

Visaria, Pravin, *Demographic Factors and the Distribution of Income: Some Issues.* World Bank Reprint Series no. 129. Washington, D.C.: The World Bank, 1979.

World Bank, The. *World Development Report 1982.* New York: Oxford University Press for The World Bank, 1982.

CASE STUDIES

CASE STUDIES

The case studies in this volume have been prepared by individual authors under the supervision of the staff of the Harvard Institute for International Development Case Study and Training Project. The cases are intended to serve as a basis for group discussion rather than to illustrate either effective or ineffective handling of projects.

CHAPTER FIVE

Indonesia:
East Java Family Planning, Nutrition, and Income Generation Project

Prepared by David F. Pyle

CONTENTS

I. Country and Project Context

II. Culture and Women in Indonesia and East Java

III. Integrated Family Planning-Nutrition-Credit Project

    A. Program Design

    B. Implementation and Operation

    C. Project Progress

TABLES

ANNEXES

After having been briefed at the BKKBN (National Family Planning Coordinating Board) headquarters in Jakarta, Ann Carter arrived in Surabaya, the capital of East Java, to meet with the provincial-level officials. Dr. Pangestu, BKKBN chief for East Java, gave her a warm welcome and reviewed the remarkably successful family planning program he had supervised for the past four years. He related how the program had moved into a new stage which integrated nutrition and income-generating activities with the agency's already well-established population efforts. Having attained a high level of contraceptive prevalence, the BKKBN was concerned with achieving high continuation rates and making the promised "small, happy, prosperous family" norm a reality. Ann was scheduled to tour the province to observe the pilot phase of an income-generating credit project for women funded by USAID, referred to by its Indonesian acronym, P2K. Based on her findings, a decision would be made as to whether the approach should be expanded.

I. COUNTRY AND PROJECT CONTEXT

Ann had several years of experience working in Indonesia and was familiar with the country and its problems. The basic facts and figures were well-known to her (Table 1). Indonesia is the world's fifth most populous country. The country is made up of some 13,600 islands, 1,000 of which are inhabited. The archipelago is the western segment of the "Ring of Fire" and has over 400 volcanoes, approximately 75 of them active. Java contains only 7 percent of the land area, yet is called home by 63 percent of the country's population, making it one of the most densely populated areas in the world. The province of East Java has almost 30 million people and a density of over 600 per square kilometer.

Although Ann had spent most of her time on Java, she had travelled extensively and had gained an appreciation for the ethnic and cultural diversity of the country. Over the centuries, peoples from China, Arabia, Polynesia, mainland Southeast Asia, the Subcontinent, and Europe have migrated to Indonesia. Indonesian history is made up of wave after wave of migrations of peoples who either absorbed earlier arrivals, killed them off or pushed them into less favorable regions (jungle, high mountains, remote islands). The Malays were followed by the Hindu believers, and the country was influenced by Hinduism, Islam, as well as the Portugese, English and Dutch. When it achieved independence in 1945, Indonesia was an ethnological goldmine where 366 different groups could be identified. Some 250 distinct languages are spoken although, *Bahasa Indonesian* is the official national language.

The country is really a collection of local nations reflected in the Indonesian expression "lain desa, lain adat" (other villages, other customs). Ann herself had seen some of the cultural variety —including the matrilineal Minangkaban culture of western Sumatra and the syncretic, hierarchal Javanese; animist villagers and orthodox Muslim landlords; religious minorities, including Christians, Buddhists and Hindus. While this cultural variety may be greatest on the outer islands, one can find considerable cultural mix on Java as well.

Farming is the primary source of livelihood in rural Indonesia. However, over three-quarters of all farmers own less than half a hectare of land. Rice is the major crop, and a typical wet rice farmer holds .15 hectare of land. The introduction of technological change (i.e. mechanized tillers and hullers) in the 1970s improved rice farm productivity, and rice production increased impressively from less than 18 million tons in 1979 to an estimated 23.5 million tons in 1983. East Java, with its population density, produces 120 percent of its needs and exports rice to other provinces. The government recently reported that the country had achieved self-sufficiency in rice. Despite this achievement, the country is expected to import one million tons of rice in 1983.

Despite impressive improvements in per capita income over the last decade, poverty remains a major Indonesian problem. According to 1976 estimates, 57 percent of the population of Java were poor, 34 percent were very poor, and 17 percent were destitute. Some estimate that the landless comprise approximately a third of the population of Java. Landlessness increased when productivity of rice farms increased and surpluses were captured disproportionately by larger farmers. Although the annual per capita income in East Java was estimated (1982) at approximately $400, some 30 percent of East Java population was considered to be below the poverty line ($90 per capita per year). Many of them were fishermen along the north coast.

There is a strong tradition of sharing and "communitiness" in Javanese villages. The best known is *gotong royong*, or mutual assistance in farming. In addition, there is the tradition of *tanggung renteng*, the principle of mutual responsibility in which villagers, male and female, look out for the well-being of their neighbors and expect the same in return. Another form of community action is the *lumbung desa*. A percentage of the crop harvested from land belonging to the village council is placed in a "paddy bank." In several East Java villages Ann visited, between one third and one half of the yield from the council's land was put into the *lumbung desa*. This grain reserve is distributed to needy families if and when emergencies arise, or is borrowed by those who run short of rice before harvest and is repaid with no interest after the new crop is in.

Although the traditional social system makes allowances for the poor, this tradition is being slowly eroded. Farmers find it too expensive to share the harvest (one-sixth to one-eighth of what they harvest for neighbors to one-tenth to one-twelfth for those from outside) with a large number of *gotong royong* members. Smaller teams of men complete the job more quickly for less money. In a labor surplus economy like Java, wage labor is cheap. Moreover, as the price of rice has risen, the traditional *gotong royong* harvesting shares have become too costly.

Family planning has been a high priority of the government of Indonesia since 1970, when the BKKBN was created as an independent agency reporting directly to the president. According to USAID (1982), family planning services were offered primarily at health clinics in the six provinces of Java and Bali until 1974 (Phase I). (See Tables 2 and 3 for information on national health statistics and health coverage.) Village-level outreach was emphasized in 1974 as part of Phase II. At the same time, family planning services through health clinics began in ten large provinces (Outer Islands I); by 1977 they were converted to the village family planning system. In 1979, the remaining eleven provinces started clinic-based family planning activities (Outer Islands II).

East Java, the third most densely populated of the 27 provinces, has consistently out-performed the country as a whole in family planning acceptance rates (Table 4) and by January, 1983 had a current user rate of 67.6 percent. In 1982, special emphasis had been placed on increasing the percentage of accepters using IUDs in order to decrease dropout rates and the need for continuous intensive program-client interaction. In early 1983, 49.4 percent of the contraceptive accepters in East Java were utilizing IUDs. The program had been run through the governmental structure with the appointed village headman (*lurah*) responsible for promoting family planning in the community. The deferential tradition of Java, particularly East Java, gives the *lurah* considerable power, since villages follow his word with little questioning. As Dr. Haryono (National Chairman of the BKKBN) told Ann, this accounts for the family planning program in Java reversing what Westerners have traditionally accepted to be the normal sequence: people have adopted and practiced contraception before their knowledge and attitude changed.

Malnutrition is another major concern of the government. Approximately 30% of the children under five years of age in Indonesia are estimated to be malnourished; 3 percent suffer from severe protein-calorie malnutrition. In addition, 7 percent of the pregnant women and 3 percent of the lactating mothers are classified as malnourished. Iron deficiency anemia and iodine deficiency are two other nutritional problems. At least 63,000 cases of xerophthalmia (severe vitamin A deficiency) are reported in under fives each year in the rural areas.

In the past several years, the government, with international donor assistance, launched the Family Nutrition Improvement Program (UPGK) to address the malnutrition problem. The program devotes maximum effort to weighing all the children under five in the village in order to identify those who are not maintaining proper growth rates or are severely malnourished. Each child's progress is charted on a growth chart. The program is monitored by four figures which are placed on a bar chart each month: number of children in the village;

number of children with weight charts; number of children weighed during the month; number of children gaining weight during the past month. Participation rates and nutritional status are calculated on a monthly basis. Nutrition education, home gardening, as well as health activities (e.g., immunization, oral rehydration therapy, and massive dose vitamin A capsule distribution) are integral parts of the UPGK Program. The Ministry of Health is responsible for administering the program and relies upon a corps of mostly female volunteers (*kader*) to oversee the weighing sessions.

According to USAID (1983b), the per capita daily consumption of calories in Indonesia in 1978 was approximately 2000; in East Java it was 1639. Protein intake was 51 grams for Indonesia, compared to 42 in East Java. On the average, 74 percent of a family's total expenditure is for food; the lowest income groups (40 percent of the population) spend more than 80 percent and nearly half of this for staple foods. Calories and protein intake by income group are given in Table 5. The primary source of calories (77 percent) and protein (71 percent) are cereals and starch foods (rice, cassava, corn, sweet potatoes). The consumption of rice increases sharply as income increases (from 45 percent of staple food calories in the lowest income group to over 90 percent in the higher incomes); conversely, the consumption of cassava and corn decreases as incomes increase (from 25 to 30 percent for each to virtually nothing).

II. CULTURE AND WOMEN IN INDONESIA AND EAST JAVA

Because of the cultural diversity of Indonesia, it is difficult to generalize and describe a single Indonesian culture. One can find ways of life which are 5000 years apart, ranging from the Neolithic to the Nuclear Ages. Over three-fourths of the population still resides in the rural areas and, as has been the case for centuries, most of their lives revolve around rice cultivation. Village life has changed very little over the years. Many of people's actions are guided by the *adat* (common or customary law), which has evolved from ancient times when villages were largely self-governing.

Ann was pleased that this assignment involved Java because she was not as knowledgeable on the cultures and women's position in the Outer Island societies. She felt comfortable in Rural Java where she was familiar with the customary law (*adat*). On Java, women's rights are generally the same as those of men with respect to marriage, divorce, inheritance and property rights. They have a considerable degree of economic independence and initiative. Women exercise significant social power and are not subordinate, as in China and the subcontinent. Although the province of East Java is overwhelmingly Muslim, it has not been a negative influence on women's traditionally high status. Instead, religious beliefs and practices have adapted themselves to the traditional women's role and position in Java. Female children are not considered a negative economic factor, since a daughter provides labor and brings a bride price from the husband. In addition, a married daughter may live for a short time with her family before she and her husband procure a house of their own. This may explain why there is no strong desire to have sons among Indonesian women; if there is a preference, it is to have children of both sexes.

The Javanese wife dominates or enjoys equal status in the household decision-making process regarding both production as well as consumption issues. The woman can be described as being the silent head of household (has the "informal" power). The husband is the family representative (has the "formal" power). All income is turned over to the wife and she decides how it will be spent, consulting her husband only on major purchases. Many families, therefore, are dependent on the wives' financial capabilities.

Although women enjoy high status, they do not always share equally in opportunities in the development process. Ann reviewed recent census figures on women-related issues. In education, government efforts during the 1970s virtually eradicated the gap between male and female attendance rates in the primary school years. Women, however, are involved in household and family work from an early age. At seven years old, they begin to tend animals and fetch water; by age ten, girls are helping to plant and harvest rice. Use of their labor contributes to higher female absenteeism and dropout rates in school. In addition, parents feel that girls will become "just housewives," thus see no need for as much schooling as boys. An additional educational disincentive is provided by the fact that many villages have no schools beyond the primary level. Children, therefore, are forced to leave the village and enter a boarding facility if they are to continue their education. Significantly lower school attendance rates among girls of higher age groups as well as lower educational attainment figures (Tables 6, 7) are attributable to this situation. Employment opportunities vary directly with educational levels achieved.

A higher percentage of women are economically active in the rural areas than in the cities, with from one-third to almost a half of all village women between the ages of 15 and 65 working (Table 8). The main employment for rural women is agriculture, either on the family's land or as hired labor. Men do the heavy work of field preparation and terrace construction; women plant, transplant, hoe, weed and harvest.

However, within the past decade, the employment opportunities for women in agriculture have decreased dramatically. As the price of rice has increased, the traditional mutual assistance (*gotong royong*) system (where neighbors help plant and harvest each other's crops for a share of the grain reaped) decreased. Often, a family will harvest together or will hire laborers at low wages and sell the crop. Accordingly, instead of harvesting rice with light, hand-held knives, more productive, heavier steel sickles are used, but only by men. This has drastically changed labor patterns—reducing 200 women days of harvest work to 70 men days. Moreover, new rotary weeders used only by men are replacing women who used to weed by hand, reducing 20 women days of work to 8 men days.

Simultaneously, rice is now machine-milled instead of hulled by women hand-pounding. The proportion of hand-pounded rice fell from 80 percent in the early 1970s to 50 percent in 1973, and soon to less than 10 percent. The small Japanese rice-hulling machines, with government-assisted financing through decreased import duties and favorable credit, were faster, cheaper, and made the rice somewhat more decay-resistant during storage. An estimated 125 million women days of work were lost per year, involving an income of $55 million. This equals 8.3 months of half-time, relatively well-paying work for 1,000,000 women. The only alternative economic activity for women has been to become petty traders. An estimated 40 percent of women can be classified as small traders. Some say that currently there are more women traders than customers in some rural markets.

The other major source of income for rural women is in elementary processing. Food and drink preparation, preservation, sales are all common forms of income generation as are tapping palm trees and making brown sugar (*gula*) from it, extracting oil from coconuts, and collecting herbs and producing traditional remedies.

Alternative employment opportunities and sources of income for rural women are severely limited. While modernization in production is accepted, labor is remunerated in a traditional manner. Skilled labor of both sexes, who are better educated and more aware of their worth, are able to command higher wages. Handicrafts and cottage industries have limited economic appeal since village women are largely unorganized and cannot compete with manufactured products in terms of either cost or quality. An exception is woven bamboo products like mats and hats which are utilized in the village itself (Table 9).

Javanese women tend to work longer hours and earn less for their labor than men. Ann remembered an early 1970 study carried out in Java which compared women's working hours with men's. Poor women put in longer hours than their wealthier counterparts since they cannot afford to hire anyone to assist them with the heavy burden of domestic work (e.g., food preparation and water fetching). In agriculture, women do the lighter work and get paid 20 to 30 percent of men's wages for heavy work. Female wages remain at a low level as the labor-intensity of agriculture decreases. This has particularly serious consequences in the poorer families since women contribute a greater percentage to the household income. For families owning less than .2 hectares, females contribute one-third or more to the total family income; over .2 hectares the percentage falls to 15 percent; the figure is 4.4 percent in the highest income groups.

The problem is particularly acute for female-headed households. Family instability is a serious concern in Indonesia and especially in Java. Indonesia is noted for its high divorce rate. In 1974, 24 percent of all marriages ended in divorces, with East Java having 28 percent. Economic problems are the cause for a significant portion of the break-ups and desertions. It is estimated that 16 percent of all households are headed by women with slightly higher rates in rural areas. The marital status of female-headed households in rural Indonesia is: 1 percent never married; 15 percent married but husband absent (deserted, migrated for work); 13 percent divorced; 71 percent widowed. Over 62 percent of all widows and 74 percent of all divorcees in a rural sample were found to be economically active. Thirty-two percent of the economically active were able to support a single person's need; 49 percent were unable to earn enough to support themselves.

Currently, about two thirds of rural women from low income households must contribute to achieve a minimum level of household income through income-generating activities. Poor women already have the longest working hours, spending most of their time searching for work and earning just enough for the next days meals while carrying out household responsibilities.

While both males and females technically have the same access to credit, in reality men receive credit from formal lending agencies and women depend on informal sources for theirs. Title to property is held in the man's name. This is the greatest constraint for a woman's gaining access to credit since land (i.e., rice field) is required as collateral. Additionally, social convention considers a man's actions more binding than a woman's. Consequently, women have relied upon such traditional sources as the *arisan*, a rotating savings association. Women meet on the basis of friendship, occupation or neighborliness, generally once a month. Each member contributes an agreed upon amount. Lots are drawn so that one member wins; no one can win twice. Once all had their turn, the group is disbanded. It has a social as well as economic function. It can be considered more a form of forced savings (without interest) rather than credit. Women are able to set aside money and receive a large amount at one time which enables them to invest to start or increase an income-generating activity. One woman Ann met had purchased equipment to establish a small bakery with the proceeds.

Another informal savings and loan group at the village level is the *simpan pinjam* in which members contribute what they want which entitles them to borrow at low interest rates when in need. Any profits derived from the operation are divided among the members. Most often, savings are put into such tangibles as jewelry, fine batik, chickens or even roof tiles, which can be sold in the event of need. Usually women operate on a very small scale due to limited capital; ones day's or market's earnings finances the next. One program (*Chandak Kulak*) makes small-scale loans (Rp.20,000 to 30,000) to women traders. Of course, there are always the traditional money lenders who charge exorbitant rates but are preferred to formal lending institutions because they are accessible, require no forms be filled out, are more flexible about repayment, and do not insist on complete repayment before new loans are made.

The poor live on the social, economic, political, and geographical periphery of the village. Poor women generally do not have either the status or the time to involve themselves in formal women's activities such as the PKK (Family Welfare Education). The PKK is the National Women's Movement with a branch in each village. The local chapter must, by law, oversee all women's activities in the village. The wives of the administrative officials at each level head the PKK organizations. In each village, the PKK is under the direction of the *lurah's* wife. The organization has devoted most of its energies to teaching domestic arts (e.g., sewing). The *lurah's* wife is assisted by several of the most educated and economically advantaged women of the village, and she controls women's activities in the community. Thus, the social hierarchy for women parallels that for men through the wives of the administrative officials at the province, regency (*kabupatan*), country (*kecamatan*) and village levels, and social power relates to social class.

III. INTEGRATED FAMILY PLANNING —
NUTRITION —CREDIT PROJECT

A. Program Design

The program was designed to facilitate and promote integration of family planning, nutrition and income-generating activities. Funders included the Government of Indonesia, UNFPA, World Bank, USAID. and ASEAN (Table 10). Total USAID funding for the life of the project was $10,000,000. The amount of credit allocated to each village varies considerably from program to program as well as from village to village.

The National Family Nutrition Improvement Program (UPGK) was begun with UNICEF and USAID support in the late 1970s and was carried out in conjunction with the Ministry of Health infrastructure. By early 1983, that program had been started in some 21,000 villages of the approximately 60,000 villages in Indonesia. In East Java, almost 5,300 villages out of 8,340 had the UPGK Program. Beginning in 1980, the nutrition program activities were coordinated more closely with the BKKBN structure which had been so successful in reaching the village and achieving a high level of contraceptive practice. Village-level *kaders* were supported and supervised by the BKKBN field worker. The fieldworkers were equally divided among male and female, and each was assigned to two or three villages and a population of approximately 12,000 or more. They, in turn, are supervised by group leaders (one per county). The BKKBN staff were assisted in the program by the local health center personnel. In addition, the fieldworkers from the Agriculture Department helped with such activities as upgrading the nutritional quality of home gardens. The income-generating aspect started at the same time the UPGK and family planning activities were combined.

In concept, the East Java, USAID-supported, integrated income generation program was similar in many respects to the other small loan projects elsewhere in Indonesia. However, a few variations are noted. First, in Central Java, the funds were allocated to sub-village administrative units called *kelompoks*. (Villages in Java usually have from three to six kelompoks although Sidomulyo has 13.) The reason for this was to encourage small group formation and operation. The geographical dispersion of Javanese villages provided an incentive for program administrators to bring credit activities closer to the borrowers. A second major difference was that the other loan programs were open to both men and women, and men received the disproportionate percentage of the loans. The USAID scheme was the only one designed explicitly and exclusively for female participants.

Contraceptive acceptance was one of the two principal criteria to become a borrower. The second was being a mother of a child under five years of age. Orientation and regular follow-up meetings for the loan project were to be coordinated with the monthly weighing sessions and thereby serve as an incentive for participation in the nutrition activities. Each sub-village administrative unit or *kelompok* was to have a women's group to discuss every loan application and vote on its acceptance (i.e., worthiness and ability of the borrower to repay the loan). Mutual responsibility for members' debts and peer pressure for repayment would eliminte the need for collateral. Moreover, accountability was to be established through open management, which would help maintain the scheme's integrity once the BKKBN and USAID were no longer involved in supervision.

Maximum loans were fixed at Rp. 50,000. This is not an insignificant amount, since most women in the village earn between Rp. 10,000 and 20,000 per month. During the first phase of the loan program, credit was directed at women with existing productive skills. New technical capabilities requiring outside training and/or equipment were to be introduced during Phase Two when cooperative formation also would be featured.

Loans were to be repaid according to an established schedule of three or seven months, depending on the amount. Loans below Rp. 10,000 were to be paid back in six installments over a three-month period with a total interest of 20 percent. Loans over Rp. 10,000 were to be repaid over a seven-month period with a total interest of 40 percent. As the repayment schedule in Annex A demonstrates, half of the interest payment was designated as administrative costs (i.e., nutrition programming, program administration expenses and *kader* incentives). The exact amount allocated to each category was left to the discretion of the individual villages. The second half of the interest payment was termed compulsory savings, which was credited to the woman's name, but could not be withdrawn until the individual withdrew from the loan program. The money was to accelerate capital formation.

Each month, each village was to pay Rp. 14,000 to the bank toward the repayment of the start-up capital. The money, when fully repaid, would be utilized to initiate the credit program in new villages. Repayment would be increased to Rp. 30,000 per month once the second installment was made to the villages.

B. Implementation and Operation

The USAID pilot integrated KB-Gizi credit program began in 1982 and became known as P2K. Twenty-four villages in five *kabupatans* and 15 *kecamatans* were selected, based upon their high current contraceptive user rates and good performance in the UPGK Program. Eighteen of the villages received their first installment of Rp. 700,000 ($700) during September 1982. The final six villages received their first "drop" in early June 1983. Three officers (leader, secretary, treasurer) of the village, organized to administer the small loan program, were brought to Surabaya for four days of training in mid-June 1982. The training consisted mostly of technical details relating to income-generating activities and loan procedures/record keeping. The village women were informed that good performances (i.e., rapid capital accummulation, good repayment record, good program administration) would result in the second and final installment of Rp. 800,000 being given to each village.

The program was administered by the same infrastructure that was responsible for running the Family Planning-Nutrition Program and the BKKN programs, the volunteer *kader* in the village, and the BKKBN workers in the *kecamatans*. The leaders of the P2K credit activities and organization on the village level were usually the same as the top PKK or women's movement officials.

C. Project Progress

After being in operation for slightly more than seven months, the credit program had accomplished a lot. Almost 4000 villages throughout the country had received funds for small loans. The most active province was Central Java which had over 3,300 villages with income-generating activities. East Java will have almost 200 villages with credit programs by March 1984. A total of nearly Rp. 200,000,000 has been budgeted for the East Java small loan program over its four years of operation.

Ann Carter started her six-village visit by meeting with a group of *kabupatan* level officials from the various departments which played a role in the integrated program headed by the *bupati*, the top official in the regency. She then proceeded to the *kecamatan* in which the first two villages were located. The *camat*, the official responsible for overall administration and operations at the *kecamatan* or sub-agency level, and the BKKBN group leader briefed Ann on the program. To compare could afford the time and/or lived close to the weighing post. With the villages being so spread out, as much as six to seven kilometers from the village center, distance was often a concern, especially in the mountainous areas along the southern coast of East Java. There was little evidence that special attention was being paid to the children who were found either to be below 60 percent of standard (third degree malnutrition) or not gaining weight for three consecutive months.

The women who joined the P2K program were generally from the middle or upper socio-economic groups in the village. Several P2K officials explained that this was necessary at the early stages of the program to provide an example for others and reduce fear in the loan procedure. The number of households in the six villages ranged from approximately 1000 to almost 1700; the number of women receiving loans ranged from 84 to 148. A high percentage of loans in all six villages were concentrated in or around the central *kelompok:*

Sumboroto	- 68.5% of loans in the central kelompok;
Rejosari	- 55.4% of loans in the central kelompok;
	90.4% in two of four kelompok;
Bandung rejo	- 83.7% of loans in the central kelompok;
Sidomulyo	- 57.5% of loans in the central kelompok and
	94.3% in two of four kelompok.

The further one got from the center, the fewer loans could be found. Some of the borrowers were over forty years of age, but were considered good credit risks. In Rejosari, 27.7 percent of the borrowers were over 40 years old, the oldest being 55. In Nglaran, 36.4 percent of the borrowers were family planning acceptors, 12.8 percent had *balita*, 37.5 percent were both acceptors and had young children; 13.3 percent were neither. Few female heads of household received loans—four in Nglaran and three in Bandungrejo and none in the other four villages.

The women used the loans for a variety of activities—small business (production and marketing of such things as palm sugar, coconut oil, tempi), trading, handicrafts (e.g., bamboo mats and hat making), agriculture (purchase of fertilizer), livestock raising (rabbits, chickens, goats). Examples of how individual women utilized their loans and benefits derived are provided in Annex B. In the vast majority of cases, the loan generated products which were sold in the village markets. No examples were found of women who hired other community members to work with them to increase production, hence profits. If extra labor was required, it was recruited from within the family unit (parents, in-laws, children). Moreover, no one provided instructions in skills to those in the village without a trade or skill. The early loans

performance since the beginning of the credit project, she asked
and was provided with data on family planning program performa
in the *kabupatan*, the *kecamatan* and on any of the villages having
integrated credit program (Tables 11-12). In addition, in each vill
she visited she collected performance figures for the nutrition progr
over the past year (Table 13) to establish progress since September

At the first village Ann Carter visited, the performance of the lc
program was very impressive. The same was found in the other fi
villages as well. Capital had accumulated rapidly (more than doubled
one village). Loan repayments were virtually perfect. Only one case
inability to repay was reported, but the woman involved had request(
and had been allowed to pay over an extended period and was doir
so. Loan records were being maintained in a generally neat and order)
fashion.

When inquiring about who received loans, Ann was told that a larg
percentage of the PKK/P2K officials and *kaders* were among the firs
borrowers, often for the maximum amount. Loan applications wer(
submitted to the women in charge of program operations at the
kelompok level who, in turn, would pass them on to the head of the P2K.
The decision to grant a loan was made by the three P2K officials and
the *lurah*. In the six villages visited, no case of a loan being turned
down was reported.

The amounts of money being set aside for nutrition activities,
administration and incentives differed greatly from village to village
(Table 14). In several villages, no funds had been taken by the P2K
leaders so that the capital would accumulate more rapidly. The money
for the nutrition fund that had been spent was used for demonstratior
feeding at the weighing centers to educate the mothers in what to fee(
their *balita* and the proper way to prepare it, so as to preserv(
nutritional value. This was in accordance with the guidelines from th
provincial BKKBN office which stated that nutrition funds could b
utilized for demonstration feeding, first aid, referral of seriously ma
nourished children or supplementation of the diets of the severe)
malnourished. In fact, the exercise appeared to Ann to be a distributic
program to encourage women to come to the weighing center ea(
month.

From recent census figures, it was evident that the nutritional stat
of all children was not being monitored. In Sempu, for example, 4
children between 0 and 4 years were enumerated in March 1983,
they used only 292 figures for the monthly nutrition report. Sumber
had a similar case. The average participation rate in the project villa
ranged from 50 to 70 percent of the total number of under fives.
women who attended the weighing sessions appeared to be those (

were now repaid and second, even a few third, loans were being made to women who had borrowed money before.

Observing a weighing session, Ann spotted a malnourished child and interviewed the mother. It was not difficult to tell that she was poor. She had not taken out a loan since she had no productive skill or anything to invest in. She expressed an interest in studying a skill if it were made available in the village.

Three of the six villages contained health posts, and there was some evidence that immunization and vitamin A distribution were being carried out with varying regularity. In Sidomulyo, a very active and innovative nurse-midwife had mapped the village according to nutritional status (i.e., number of first, second, and third degree malnutrition cases by *kelompok*). Immunization and vitamin A distribution were also much more regular in Sidomulyo than in the other five villages. Ann did not encounter any agricultural extension officers during her village visits. The most active and involved person in the integrated credit program was inevitably, and often exclusively, the PLKB who maintained surveillance over the family planning, nutrition activities as well as ensured that the loan program was being administered properly and records were being kept accurately.

At the conclusion of her field visits, Ann returned to Jakarta to debrief the BKKBN and USAID officials and to draft her report on whether the credit program was achieving its objectives, whether the second installment should be made to the first eighteen villages, and finally, whether the program should be expanded on a larger scale in East Java and elsewhere in Indonesia.

TABLES

Table 1   Data on the Republic of Indonesia

	1971	1981	
Population (1981)			153,000,000
Area (sq. km.)			144,000
% of Population in Rural Areas			77.6
% of Eligible Couples as Active Contraceptive Users (1982)			39
Birth Rate (per 1000 population)	46	32	
Death Rate (per 1000 population)	19	12.5	
Infant Mortality Rate (per 1000 live births)			100+
Population Growth Rate (1981)			1.8%
Population Doubling Rate			39 years
% of Population below 15 years old (1980)			40.9
Average Income/Capita (1981)			$520
Annual Inflation Rate			8%
% of Children Enrolled in Primary School (7-12 years old)			85
Agriculture's Share of GDP (1980)			26%
Agriculture's Share of Labor Force (1980)			58%
Literacy Rate (> 10 years old) (1980)	Female		63.8
	Male		80.5
Life Expectancy	Female		57.2
	Male		54.5

Table 2   Communicable Diseases as Causes of Death

Respiratory Diseases	19.9%
Diarrheal Diseases	18.8%
Tuberculosis	8.4%
Tetanus	6.5%
Typhoid	3.3%
Other Communicable Diseases	3.0%
Other	40.1%
Total	100.0%

Source: Health Sector Paper, Jakarta: USAID (January, 1983).

Table 3 Health Coverage of Vulnerables by Public Health Services (1980)

	% of Infants Attended	Children 1-4	Pregnant Women
All Indonesia	42%	10.8%	35%
Province with Highest Coverage	76% (East Java)	23% (East Java)	47% (Jakarta)
Province with Lowest Coverage	18% (South Kalimantan)	2% (Jakarta)	14.5% (South Kalimantan)

Source: Health Sector Paper, Jakarta: USAID (January, 1983).

Table 4 Indonesia and East Java Contraceptive Prevalence Rates (1971-82)

	1971	*1972*	*1973*	*1974*	*1975*	*1976*	*1977*	*1978*	*1979*	*1980*	*1981*	*1982*
Indonesia	1	2	6	9	13	17	19	23	27	31	36	39
East Java	—	4	12	20	28	31	34	40	50	57	60	69

Source: Health Sector Paper, Jakarta: USAID (January, 1983).

Table 5 Calorie And Protein Intake by Income Group (1976)

Expenditure Group (Rp per capital per month)	% of total population	Per capital daily consumption	
		Calories (Kcals)	Protein (Grams)
Less than 2000	15.3	1381	22.2
2000-2999	23.8	1870	32.3
3000-3999	19.5	2034	40.2
4000-4999	13.6	2084	47.0
5000-5999	8.8	2280	52.7
Over 6000	19.0	2760	69.2
Average intake/capita	100.0	2064	43.2
Minimum intake reqiurement		1900	39.2
Average availability		2231	

Source: Hutabarat: *Proyeksi Distribusi Konsumsi Kalorie Menurut Kelompok-kelompok Pendapatan di Indonesia Tahum, 1990;* Sekolah Pasca—Sarjana IPB, 1979.

Table 6   Percentage of Persons who are Attending School by Age and Sex: 1971 and 1980

Umur	*Laki-Laki/Male*		*Perempuan/Female*	
Age	*1971*	*1980*	*1971*	*1980*
(1)	*(2)*	*(3)*	*(4)*	*(5)*
5	0.0	10.5	0.0	13.1
6	15.2	32.1	15.8	35.9
7	39.9	70.6	39.9	73.2
8	57.7	84.2	56.0	84.0
9	68.3	88.4	64.8	87.8
10	70.1	89.2	65.9	88.3
11	74.8	89.4	68.9	89.3
12	66.0	83.8	57.8	80.8
13	61.5	77.1	57.1	69.8
14	51.0	66.7	39.0	57.9
15	37.2	54.3	26.2	42.8
16	34.6	49.6	22.1	35.3
17	28.3	38.8	15.8	25.0
18	21.9	28.9	10.1	16.2
5- 6	7.6	21.0	7.9	24.3
7-12	61.7	83.9	57.9	83.5
13-15	49.4	65.6	38.7	56.3
16-18	27.9	38.8	15.4	24.7
19-24	12.1	12.6	4.1	5.5
25+	0.8	0.8	0.2	0.4
Tak terjawab Not stated	21.8	8.9	13.4	1.5
Jumlah Total	21.2	28.4	16.4	24.1

Sumber: Ulasan singkat hasil Sensus Penduduk, 1980.
Source: A brief note on 1980 Population Census results. Jakarta, Indonesia (unpublished).

Table 7   Percent Distributions of the Surveyed Population Aged 15 and Over by Age, Sex, Educational Attainment: East Java, 1980

Age Group	*Percent Distribution by Educational Attainment*					
	No Education	Primary Grades 1-3	Primary Grades 4-6	Primary Complete	Junior High +	Totals
	Both Sexes					
15-19	13.0	15.2	23.4	22.2	26.2	100.0
20-24	16.6	15.2	22.1	25.7	20.4	100.0
25-29	22.9	16.2	21.0	23.6	16.3	100.0
30-34	30.5	16.3	18.7	20.1	14.4	100.0
35-39	42.5	16.7	14.0	16.5	10.4	100.0
40-44	54.2	16.7	10.5	11.4	7.1	100.0
45-49	60.7	16.6	8.9	9.4	4.4	100.0
50-54	64.5	14.7	7.5	9.5	3.7	100.0
55-59	67.5	13.6	5.7	10.1	3.1	100.0
60-64	78.0	10.3	4.3	5.7	1.7	100.0
65+	84.6	7.4	3.2	3.9	0.9	100.0
Totals	39.9	15.1	15.3	16.9	12.9	100.0
	Males					
15-19	9.7	14.8	23.7	21.6	30.3	100.0
20-24	11.2	12.6	21.0	28.3	26.9	100.0
25-29	15.4	13.6	21.8	28.7	20.5	100.0
30-34	19.3	16.0	21.1	25.2	18.5	100.0

Indonesia

Table 7 (Continued)   Percent Distributions of the Surveyed Population Aged 15 and Over by Age, Sex, Educational Attainment: East
Java, 1980

Age Group	No Education	Primary Grades 1-3	Primary Grades 4-6	Primary Complete	Junior High +	Totals
	Percent Distribution by Educational Attainment					
35-39	27.7	17.8	17.3	22.0	15.2	100.0
40-44	36.9	20.4	14.9	16.3	11.4	100.0
45-49	44.0	21.7	13.7	13.6	6.9	100.0
50-54	46.2	21.8	11.7	15.0	5.4	100.0
55-59	49.0	20.9	9.5	15.6	5.1	100.0
60-64	60.1	17.5	8.1	11.2	3.1	100.0
65+	69.4	14.2	6.3	8.2	1.9	100.0
Totals	28.2	16.8	17.5	20.7	16.8	100.0
	Females					
15-19	16.3	15.6	23.2	22.9	22.1	100.0
20-24	21.0	17.4	23.0	23.6	15.1	100.0
25-29	30.0	18.7	20.3	18.7	12.3	100.0
30-34	41.0	16.6	16.5	15.3	10.6	100.0
35-39	56.1	15.6	10.9	11.3	6.0	100.0
40-44	69.6	13.4	6.6	7.1	3.3	100.0
45-49	76.3	11.7	4.3	5.5	2.1	100.0
50-54	83.5	7.5	3.1	3.9	2.0	100.0
55-59	86.7	6.1	1.8	4.4	1.0	100.0
60-64	92.1	4.7	1.3	1.3	0.6	100.0
65+	95.9	2.4	0.9	0.7	0.2	100.0
Totals	50.5	13.6	13.3	13.3	9.3	100.0

Source: 1980 Baseline Round of the East Java Population Survey: A Final Report (Chapel Hill: International Program of Laboratories for Population Statistics (POPLAB), June, 1982, p. 39.

Table 8   Economically Active Women Classified by Age for Rural and Urban Areas, 1971

Age	Rural	Urban	Total
	Economically Active Women (%)		
10-14	15.3	6.9	13.7
15-19	33.8	19.2	30.8
20-24	35.8	24.2	33.4
25-29	37.2	26.1	35.3
30-34	40.8	29.6	39.0
35-39	43.2	31.9	41.4
40-44	46.6	34.6	44.7
45-49	47.0	34.2	44.9
50-54	44.7	33.1	43.0
55-59	42.3	27.9	40.0
60-64	36.3	24.9	34.7
65-69	31.6	20.4	29.9
70-74	25.3	16.2	24.0
75-+	16.8	9.3	15.4
Total	35.3	23.2	33.1

Source: Pudjiwati Sajogyo, "The Integration of Rural Women in National Development in Indonesia." Home Economics and Social Programmes Service, FAO, 1977, p. 16; and UNDP, "Rural Women's Participation in Development" Evaluation Study #3 (New York: June, 1980), p. 137.

Table 9   Percent of Working-Time Devoted to Various Activities by Adult Men and Women (Aged 15 and Over) in a Sample of 20 Households, November 1972-October 1973

Activity	Percent of total working hours Men (N=31)	Women (N=33)
1. Childcare	4.2	9.3
2. Housework	0.9	9.4
3. Food Preparation	1.2	24.5
4. Firewood Collection	2.4	0.8
5. Shopping	0.5	2.5
6. Handicrafts	5.1	20.9
7. Food Preparation for sale	3.9	3.7
8. Animal Care and Feeding	15.2	1.3
9. Trading	8.3	12.9
10. Garden Cultivation (own)	8.4	0.9
11. Sawah Cultivation (own)	21.7	3.7
12. *Gotong Royong*	8.8	1.4
13. Wage or Exchange Labour (agricultural)	3.4	6.9
14. Wage or Exchange Labour (non-agricultural)	12.8	1.5
15. Other	3.2	0.3
Average hours of all work per day:	8.7	11.1
Average hours of directly productive work per day (no's 6-15 only):	7.9	5.9

Source: UNDP, Rural Women's Participation in Development Evaluation Study #3 (New York: June, 1980), p. 132.

Table 10   Funding For East Java Small Loan Program

Year	Source	Number of Villages	Amount of Capital/Village (Rp)		Total (Rp)
1980-81	GOI	16		700,000	11,200,000
1981-82	GOI	21	6 x	300,000	
			4 x	450,000	
			11 x	900,000	13,500,000
1981-82	UNFPA	4	3 x	400,000	
			1 x	669,000	1,869,000
1982-83	GOI	18	6 x	500,000	
			12 x	1,000,000	15,000,000
1982-83	GOI	20	4 x	675,000	
			16 x	1,350,000	24,300,000
1982-83	World Bank	9	1 x	637,291	
			4 x	700,000	
			1 x	757,000	
			1 x	824,000	
			2 x	2,000,000	9,018,291
1982-83	USAID	24	18 x	700,000	12,600,000
1983-84	ASEAN	8	8 x	3,856,625	30,853,000
1983-84	GOI	75	75 x	1,000,000	75,000,000
	Totals	195			193,340,291

Table 11 Credit Program Performance (as of end April, 1983)

	Rejosari	Sumberoto	Bandungrejo	Sidomulyo	Nglaran	Sempu
			Villages			
Total number of loans	177	130	104	113	209	120
Number of individ. borrowers	137	115	89	86	148	84
Average amt. of loan (Rp)	14,070	13,908	17,202	21,858	12,774	18,900
Outstanding loans (Rp)	1,216,545	1,035,700	1,061,000	1,314,000	1,255,900	1,113,450
Current value (Rp)	1,316,940	1,145,125	1,161,975	1,417,500	1,353,900	1,255,550
Cumulative amt. loaned (Rp)	2,490,400	1,808,000	1,789,000	2,470,000	2,669,800	2,268,000
Inc. in Capital Fund (Rp)	569,440	445,125	461,875	717,500	653,900	555,550
(%)*	76.2	63.6	66.0	102.5	93.4	79.4

*All villages received initial capital of Rp. 700,000 except for Rejosari which received an additional Rp. 47,500 from Kabupatan BKKBN funds.

Table 12 Kabupatan, Kecamatan, Village Family Planning Program Performance March, 1982-March 1983

		Kabupatan Malang	Kecamatan Bantur	Village Sumberoto	Kabupatan Pacitan	Kecamatan Village	Village Nglaran
March 1982	CU*	57.1	72.3	87.4	77.6	69.2	n/a
	IUD**	37.2	20.7	83.4	96.2	98.6	n/a
April 1982	CU	50.9	75.5	87.3	n/a	n/a	n/a
	IUD	36.1	20.0	83.7	n/a	n/a	n/a
May 1982	CU	54.4	78.7	86.8	n/a	n/a	n/a
	IUD	39.1	19.5	83.7	n/a	n/a	n/a
June 1982	CU	56.6	56.8	87.1	n/a	n/a	n/a
	IUD	37.9	27.2	83.8	n/a	n/a	n/a
July 1982	CU	56.9	72.0	86.5	76.3	68.3	n/a
	IUD	37.7	21.6	83.9	96.3	98.8	n/a
August 1982	CU	50.8	65.8	87.0	76.2	68.2	n/a
	IUD	38.9	23.5	84.0	96.3	98.8	n/a
September 1982	CU	52.9	80.7	88.2	76.7	68.4	73.2
	IUD	37.3	19.4	84.3	96.5	98.8	99.4
October 1982	CU	n/a	n/a	91.3	n/a	n/a	73.4
	IUD	n/a	n/a	85.0	n/a	n/a	99.4
November 1982	CU	59.5	82.9	93.0	76.8	68.5	73.9
	IUD	41.8	24.7	86.1	96.3	98.8	99.4
December 1982	CU	62.6	88.7	93.8	77.8	69.3	77.3
	IUD	41.5	27.1	86.7	96.5	98.8	99.4
January 1983	CU	61.9	86.4	93.3	79.1	72.0	77.0
	IUD	42.3	27.9	86.8	96.4	98.9	99.4
February 1983	CU	63.5	88.1	93.2	79.2	72.3	77.1
	IUD	41.6	27.4	86.8	95.6	98.9	99.2
March 1983	CU	61.9	86.8	93.4	80.4	75.4	89.1
	IUD	43.1	27.8	87.0	96.4	98.7	99.3

*CU = % of Eligible Currently Using Contraception
**IUD = % of Current Users using IUD as Method of Contraception

Table 13   Nutrition Program Performance P2K Villages

		Kab. Malang		Villages	Kab. Pacitan	
	Rejosari	Sumberoto	Bandungrejo	Sidomulyo	Nglaran	Sempu
1982						
Baseline						
W/N*	85.8	23.9	62.6	98.4	51.0	53.1
G/W**	50.3	50.0	42.6	96.8	26.7	37.2
September						
W/N	n.a.	n.a.	n.a.	60.3	33.1	56.3
G/W	n.a.	n.a.	n.a.	58.0	76.0	39.4
October						
W/N	59.2	21.3	45.2	60.0	36.5	52.6
G/W	59.9	35.2	70.8	63.9	66.7	42.8
November						
W/N	57.4	23.0	44.9	59.3	33.1	45.3
G/W	63.0	39.7	70.3	64.6	76.0	49.3
December						
W/N	64.4	21.1	37.1	66.6	39.4	44.1
G/W	56.9	33.0	89.6	51.0	70.5	75.2
1983						
January						
W/N	25.0	18.6	37.2	43.2	69.9	56.9
G/W	25.0	44.6	50.2	64.5	72.5	51.8
February						
W/N	27.1	19.9	39.7	42.7	68.5	55.9
G/W	27.1	34.3	50.8	62.4	74.5	53.3
March						
W/N	17.1	25.9	45.9	55.9	70.8	56.9
G/W	17.2	34.7	52.0	54.9	74.1	58.9

*W/N = participation rate (number of children weighed over total number of under fives reported in village).
**G/W = nutritional status (number of children gaining weight over total number of children weighed).
Note: Figures for Kabupatan Malang (Mar. 1983) are: W/N = 39.0; G/W = 41.1.
     Figures for Kabupatan Pacitan (Apr. 1983) are: W/N = 46.0; G/W = 60.0.
     Denominators for Rejosari, Sidomulyo revised upward in 1983; reverse occurred
     in Nglaran.

Table 14 Use of Service Charge (Rps)

			Villages			
	Rejosari	Sumberoto	Bandungrejo*	Sidomulyo	Nglaran	Sempu**
Nutrition Fund						
%	50	50	15	60	60	—
utilized	20,000	17,550	36,650	10,000	—	12,900
in acct.	149,080	120,100	7,995	249,800	227,310	—
Administration Fund						
%	35	35	35	25	25	—
utilized	10,350	65,200	69,375	37,750	11,600	35,700
in acct.	108,006	31,155	34,330	70,500	83,113	—
P2K Official Incentive Fund						
%	15	15	45	15	15	15
utilized	—	54,000	—	55,575	54,500	30,000
in acct.	50,724	(12,705)	133,335	9,375	2,327	26,445
Dues						
per meeting (Rupiah)	25	25	25	50	—	—
total	16,225	11,925	3,700	37,650	—	—
Compulsory Savings						
total	299,210	233,100	215,350	366,000	356,850	281,100
withdrawn	48,500	—	—	—	—	2,000

*Set aside 5% for charity; nothing utilized and Rp. 14,815 in account.
**Set no percentage for Nutrition and Administration Fund—together Rp. 319,555 are in account.

ANNEXES

Annex A P2K Loan Repayment Tables

1. Loans Under Rp. 10,000 3 months

Amount of Loan	Admin. Cost 1st week	Compulsory Savings 2nd week	Principal Repayment 3rd week (FIRST MONTH)	Prin. Repay. 4th week	Prin. Repay. 1st week	Prin. Repay. 2nd week (SECOND MONTH)	Prin. Repay. 3rd week	Prin. Repay. 4th week
1,000	100	100	100	100	100	100	100	100
2,000	200	200	200	200	200	200	200	200
3,000	300	300	300	300	300	300	300	300
4,000	400	400	400	400	400	400	400	400
5,000	500	500	500	500	500	500	500	500
6,000	600	600	600	600	600	600	600	600
7,000	700	700	700	700	700	700	700	700
8,000	800	800	800	800	800	800	800	800
9,000	900	900	900	900	900	900	900	900
10,000	1,000	1,000	1,000	1,000	1,000	1,000	1,000	1,000

Amount of Loan	Prin. Repay. 1st week	Prin. Repay. 2nd week (THIRD MONTH)	Prin. Repay. 3rd week	Prin. Repay. 4th week	TOTAL
1,000	100	100	100	100	1,200
2,000	200	200	200	200	2,400
3,000	300	300	300	300	3,600
4,000	400	400	400	400	4,800
5,000	500	500	500	500	6,000
6,000	600	600	600	600	7,200
7,000	700	700	700	700	8,400
8,000	800	800	800	800	9,600
9,000	900	900	900	900	10,800
10,000	1,000	1,000	1,000	1,000	12,000

2. Loans Over Rp. 10,000   7 months

Amount of Loan	Admin.Cost FIRST MONTH		Compulsory Savings SECOND MONTH		Principal Repay. THIRD MONTH		Principal Repay FOURTH MONTH		TOTAL
	1st	2nd	1st	2nd	1st	2nd	1st	2nd	
15,000	1,500	1,500	1,500	1,500	1,500	1,500	1,500	1,500	21,000
20,000	2,000	2,000	2,000	2,000	2,000	2,000	2,000	2,000	28,000
25,000	2,500	2,500	2,500	2,500	2,500	2,500	2,500	2,500	35,000
30,000	3,000	3,000	3,000	3,000	3,000	3,000	3,000	3,000	42,000
35,000	3,500	3,500	3,500	3,500	3,500	3,500	3,500	3,500	49,000
40,000	4,000	4,000	4,000	4,000	4,000	4,000	4,000	4,000	56,000
45,000	4,500	4,500	4,500	4,500	4,500	4,500	4,500	4,500	63,000
50,000	5,000	5,000	5,000	5,000	5,000	5,000	5,000	5,000	70,000

Amount of Loan	Principal Repayment FIFTH MONTH		Principal Repayment SIXTH MONTH		Principal Repayment SEVENTH MONTH	
	1st	2nd	1st	2nd	1st	2nd
15,000	1,500	1,500	1,500	1,500	1,500	1,500
20,000	2,000	2,000	2,000	2,000	2,000	2,000
25,000	2,500	2,500	2,500	2,500	2,500	2,500
30,000	3,000	3,000	3,000	3,000	3,000	3,000
35,000	3,500	3,500	3,500	3,500	3,500	3,500
40,000	4,000	4,000	4,000	4,000	4,000	4,000
45,000	4,500	4,500	4,500	4,500	4,500	4,500
50,000	5,000	5,000	5,000	5,000	5,000	5,000

Annex B Examples of Women Taking Loans from P2K Income-Generating Program in East Java

Name	Village	Amount (Rp)	Activity	Benefits
Ibu Kus (Head of PKK/P2K)	Rejosari	50,000	rabbit raising	Purchased 20 rabbits @ Rp. 500; spent several thousand more on cages and medicine to protect against skin disease; her children provided grass daily; got immunization from government paravet in nearby town; within 5 months had 120 rabbits and sold 100 large ones @ Rp. 1,000.
Ibu Sryant	Sumboroto	10,000	shop owner	Increased her stock so that daily sales increased from Rp. 1,000 to Rp. 1,500 each day; wanted second loan of Rp. 30,000 to add fruit to her stock.
Ibu Kaniem	Sumboroto	10,000	palm sugar processing/ selling	Previously had to deal with *ijon* (broker) who provided capital and bought blocks of processed sugar @ Rp. 250/Kg.; with loan there was no need to deal with *ijon* and she can now sell sugar @ Rp. 500/hg. in market.
Ibu Suhinah	Sumboroto	20,000	palm sugar processing/ selling	After taking loan, no longer works through *ijon* and has increased production by an additional 40%.
Ibu Yatini	Sumboroto	25,000	chicken raising	Bought 50 chickens @ Rp. 500; none vaccinated and all died; repaid loan from husband's income.
Ibu Misiah	Sumboroto	15,000	dress	Bought 16 pieces of material to make children's cloths, ¼ meter in size, for total of Rp. 8,125; other supplies (thread, buttons, etc.) cost Rp. 4,875; made 13 children's garmets which sold @ Rp. 1,500 at the end of 5-month period.
Ibu Jumiati	Sumboroto	15,000	bamboo mat maker	Was able to purchase twice as much raw material; thus she had to make one trip to market each week rather than two as before; already working at optimal level, so that she has been unable to increase her production.
Ibu Kati	Sidomulyo	20,000	tempe production	Used to produce only palm sugar; continues that and has begun to produce tempe (fermented soybean) when she got loan; she processes 10 kg. of soy (@ Rp. 400/kg.) at a time—this produces 110 packets of tempe which she sells at Rp. 50; she does this 3 times a week; she recently took a 2nd loan for

				Rp. 25,000 and increased tempe production by 40%; she will use profits to educate her two children (pay for clothes and books).
Ibu Tamu	Nglaran	15,000	coconut oil production	She purchases coconuts at @ Rp. 80; needs 5 coconuts to product 1 liter of coconut oil which she sells for Rp. 500; in addition, she sells byproducts for another Rp. 300; loan has enabled her to double production and income has increased from Rp. 1,000-1,500/market day to Rp. 2,000/2,500/market day.
Ibu Parti	Nglaran	10,000	bamboo mat maker	She used Rp. 8,000 to purchase a goat for raising and Rp. 2,000 to purchase more hat-making material, so that she has to go to the market less frequently; no increase in production since working at optimal level; she sells 10 hats every week (2 markets), but could sell up to 50 more if production could be increased.

BIBLIOGRAPHY

Biro Pusat Statistik. *Statistical Profile of Children and Mothers in Indonesia* (Jakarta, 1982).

Kern, A. *A Project Proposal for a Village-Based Income Generating Scheme.* Jakarta: USAID, 1982.

Malone, P. *A Preliminary Study in Three Countries — Indonesia Report.* Washington, D.C.: Federation of Organizations for Professional Women/International Center for Research on Women, 1978.

Sajogyo, P., *The Role of Women in Different Perspectives.* Bogor: FAO/SIDA Project on Rural Household Economies and the Role of Women, 1980.

Sullivan, J. and Wilson, S. *The 1980 Baseline Round of the East Java Population Survey: A Final Report.* Chapel Hill: Poplab, 1982.

UNDP. Rural Women's Participation in Development. *Evaluation Study* No.3 (June 1980): pp. 121-67

USAID/Jakarta. *Background Information for USAID/Indonesia: Health Sector CDSS* Jakarta, 1983)

USAID/Jakarta. *Background Information for USAID/Indonesia: Indonesia Nutrition Strategy.* Jakarta, 1983.

USAID/Jakarta. *Indonesia Family Planning Program. Orientation Booklet* Jakarta, 1982.

USAID/Jakarta. *Village Family Planning/Mother-Child Welfare Project Paper. Jakarta, 1979.*

USAID/Washington. *Selected Statistical Data by Sex — Asia: Indonesia.* Washington: Office of Development Information and Utilization, n.d.

CHAPTER SIX

Tanzania:
The Arusha Planning and Village
Development Project

Prepared by Liz Wiley

CONTENTS

I. Country and Project Background

    A. Tanzania
    B. The APVDP Project

II. Context for Women

    A. National Policy & Programs
    B. Village Women
        1. Women and Village Government
        2. The Economic Role of Women

III. Project Description

    A. Project Objectives and Components
    B. Women in the ADVDP Project

TABLES

In early 1981, the Arusha Planning and Village Development Program, with the cooperation of USAID, carried out a short investigation to determine how rural women were being involved in the project. The project had been implemented in 1979, and while no special efforts had been undertaken to include women as project participants and beneficiaries, it was expected that the project would reach, involve, and benefit rural women in equal measure to rural men. Three project districts were examined, and it was anticipated that the findings would either confirm earlier expectations of women's full involvement in the project or would serve as a basis for reorienting project activities.

I. COUNTRY AND PROJECT BACKGROUND

A. Tanzania

Tanzania became an independent republic in 1961. Julius K. Nyerere, President since independence, heads the socialist Chama Cha Mapinduzi Party in the one-party state. The island of Zanzibar, close to the coast of Tanzania, has been formally federated with Tanzania since 1977 and provides the Vice President of the country. Historically, Tanzania was an important crossroads, a meeting place for different tribes and cultures, and later, explorers, traders, missionaries and colonizers. Today, this diversity finds some unity in the official Kiswahili language and emerging nationalism and 'Swahili culture.'

The country embraces 364,000 square miles of the east African coast. It is a country of diverse geography and includes within its boundaries the majestic Mount Kilimanjaro, immense grasslands sustaining the world's largest game population, waterless plains alongside well-watered highlands, and lake and sea coasts of immense beauty and varying fertility. Despite this variety, Tanzania is without significant mineral deposits and its economy depends almost entirely upon agriculture. The majority of Tanzania's 18 million inhabitants are peasants, subsisting on their small-holdings and livestock, many only tenuously involved in the money economy.

In late 1979, USAID/Tanzania described the country as "an economy in distress." It was among the 25 poorest countries in the world with a per capita GNP of $230 and one of the highest population growth rates in the world (3.3 percent). It was decreasingly able to feed itself, and did not have the surplus of export crops required to obtain essential foreign exchange. The country had entered a downward spiral of economic decline with immense international debt, critical shortages of commodities, rapid deterioration of stock, emergence of unofficial markets, poor management and rampant inflation. A variety of external and internal factors were considered to be responsible for this situation. There was the financial burden of the recent Ugandan War in which Tanzanian forces invaded Uganda to depose Idi Amin. World prices for coffee and other Tanzanian export crops had declined as petroleum prices increased. Mismanagement of scarce resources and agricultural production, pricing policies, and severe droughts were also blamed.

Tanzania holds considerable agricultural potential. The land to population ratio in most parts of the country is favorable. The diversity of agro-ecological zones allows for varied production, and there is considerable room for improved farm technology, management of crop production, and value-added processing of crops.

In the political sphere, Tanzania is known in the world community for its leadership in the quest for African independence, support of liberation movements, and for its own brand of agro-based socialism. The basic tenets of Tanzanian national socialism were articulatd in the Arusha Declaration of 1967 which called for the elimination of privilege and exploitation, and improvement in the quality of life for the peasant population. The most dramatic step to accomplish these goals was villagization (Ujamaa Vijijini), the grouping of scattered populations into cooperatively based villages. By world and African standards, the efforts of Tanzania towards egalitarianism have been regarded as successful. Income and asset distribution (most importantly, land) are comparatively even. Access to services, particularly health and education, is outstanding. Through a massive adult literacy campaign, eighty percent of the population has become literate since Independence.

B. The APVDP Project

The government has consistently moved toward decentralized government structures to provide a mechanism for decisions made at the central level to be carried out in villages, and to allow the Party to consolidate power. As one government official put it, "The Party is the bird that sings our song".

A 1972 decision to decentralize administration and create a Regional Integrated Development Programme (RIDEP) led the Tanzanian government to seek funds to initiate RIDEPs in all twenty regions. Ten have been implemented and are supported by donors which include the World Bank, and the British, Dutch, Swedish, German and U.S. governments.

RIDEPs have two aims:

i) to guide the regional governments in preparing a comprehensive and integrated development plan; and

ii) to provide the regional governments with capital funds to initiate developments in priority areas according to the development plan.

The Arusha Planning and Village Development Project (APVDP) is a USAID funded RIDEP. The twenty-one million dollar project began in late 1979 and will be completed in mid-1983.

There are six districts in Arusha Region: three are agriculturally-based (Hanang, Mbulu and Arumeru), and three are livestock-based (the Masai Districts—Monduli, Kiteto and Ngorongoro). The Arusha Region plays an important economic role in the country. It provides 80 percent of the wheat grown in the country and the bulk of seed-bean and coffee production which are the primary foreign exchange earners. In addition, Arusha town is one of four major industrial centers in the country. Table 1 provides a statistical profile of the Arusha Region.

II. CONTEXT FOR WOMEN

A. National Policy and Programs

When Tanzania became independent, it inherited a mixture of tribal customs and feudal-like hierarchies among most of the tribal groups which placed men in a significantly more advantageous position than women. Eighty years of colonialism had exacerbated traditional inequalities.[1] With independence and the emerging socialism of the 1960s, the issue of human equality became a major government concern, though it tended to focus on the questions of equality among socio-economic classes rather than between the sexes.

Women's rights have been discussed explicitly by President Nyerere:

> It is impossible to deny that women did, and still do more than their fair share of the work in the field and in the homes. This is certainly inconsistent with our socialist conception of the equality of all human beings and the right of all to live in . . . security and freedom . . If we want our country to make full and quick progress now, it is essential that our women live in terms of full equality with their fellow citizens who are men.[2]

National policy assumes that women's needs will be met through general programs and policies affecting all citizens. Women's development receives special attention in their traditional roles as bearers and caretakers of children. Villagization was heralded as helping women "by reducing the distance to water points and offering better childcare and educational facilities".

Official recognition of the low status of women in the country has been scant, but progress has been made when the issue of inequality has come to public attention. Employed women have achieved equal pay, benefits, and generous maternity leave. The Law of Marriage Act in 1971 ensured the equality of women in marriage and specified the right of wives to keep their union monogamous. It also established a minimum age for marriage and made some provision for inheritance by widows.

Primary schooling has long been compulsory for girls and boys, and women have been particularly encouraged to participate in adult literacy classes. Programs for establishing boarding facilities for girls at secondary and university level have been underway for some years. Girls now comprise 48 percent of primary school students, 30 percent of secondary school entrants, and 15 percent of university students.

Both Party and government have women's programs. The Party is explicitly concerned with politicizing rural women through the Umoja wa Wanawake Tanzania (UWT). Women are encouraged to establish a village UWT group and urged to understand Party principles and "speak Kiswahili" as evidence of their nationalism. Unlike other branches of the Party, the UWT is ill-supported financially. Its staff in each of Arusha Region's six districts includes one elected chairman and a government-paid and appointed officer of the Department of Community Development who is trained in domestic sciences.

In practice, the title UWT is applied loosely to any women's group in the village. Despite its political origins, the main task of the UWT organization is the promotion of women's income-generating and training projects. The latter are almost always associated with sewing or other domestic science-related areas. A village UWT without any income-generating project underway is considered deficient.

UWTs are well supported by village women. They appear to meet a need not only for participation in income-generating projects but for some form of solidarity among village women. However, they do not last very long. Of twelve projects started in ten Arusha villages, only three were active in 1979, and two of these were "failing." The reasons for these failures, were identified as problems with leadership, planning, and financial management. Most Councillors and local political leaders contend that women need their help to manage projects. One official told a group of women, "At home we (men) are the leaders and now, even in development, we will lead you and guide you".

UWT's do not engage in projects involving self-help or non-profit efforts or activities. Requests for the participation of women in such projects bypasses the UWT and are transmitted to individual women directly through the village council and Balozi (cell leaders). None of the UWTs examined in ten Arusha villages have ever initiated a self-help project and Village Chairmen could recall no instances when the UWT had presented the Council with any resolution.

The government sponsors women's programs through the Women's Division of the Department of Community Development. Over 70 economic projects for women were begun in the Arusha Region's 500 villages under the auspices of the government. Most are group farms or village shops. Very few of the projects are currently working well or are making a profit. The Department of Community Development staff provides limited assistance. It has 100 staff for the Region with a population of a half million. In 1981-1982, the government women's program in Arusha included:

1. conducting research into family life;

2. holding workshops for district Home Economics staff, Mother and Child Health Care leaders, etc.;

3. conducting training courses for village women in childcare, nutrition, health and sanitation, home management, sewing;

4. providing advice on Day Care Centers;

5. improving existing women's projects, and helping women start more economic (income-producing) projects.

The Arusha Region Development Council (RDC) made it qute clear in May 1981 that its long-term strategies should not include any reference to the problems of women in the region. On both district and village levels, the APVDP has found officials reluctant to promote women's projects beyond childcare or domestic-related activities.

B. Village Women

Data was gathered from a sample of women in ten diverse villages within the APVDP project area to determine the nature and extent of their activities and responsibilities. Three villages were located in remote highlands (Madunga ward) where a homogenous and distinct tribal group reside (Wairaq). The life style and agriculture practiced in this area has changed little in the last hundred years. Three other villages were located in mosquito-ridden floodplains (Magugu ward). Their population comprise a multitude of ethnic groups and a variety of agricultural practices. The remaining four villages were located in the grain bowl of the region (Gallapo ward) where the land is fertile and maize and bean production are extremely high.

There were many similarities among the three sites. However, the distinctions between them are illustrative of the range of differences in the role and status of women more broadly within the region, and within Tanzania as a whole.

1. Women and Village Government

The situation in the early 1970s was described as follows:

Social differentiation also existed between the women and the men. The men were represented on every institution of the village government, but the women did not have any representatives. Most of the decisions were taken by the men and explained to the women, and the women accepted them. It ws easy to see from the remarks of the men in meetings that they looked down on the women.

According to traditions which seemed to date from the colonial period, women were not allowed to speak in formal public gatherings. If they wanted to speak they had first to inform a man who would then address the meeting on their behalf.[3]

In 1980, the situation in the three APVDP Project districts in Arusha Region was described as follows:

. . . .In the project Districts, about *half* of the survey meetings were attended by anywhere from one to five women. However, with few exceptions, they played a very backstage role in the meetings, participating very little, if at all, in the discussion and answering of questions. The apparent regionwide lack of participation and poor representation by women in the survey is probably best explained by the fact that women have traditionally been excluded from formal leadership roles. That this tradition is still strong and prevalent, and changing only slowly, is obvious.[4]

Women do participate to some degree in the village governing system. There are two main levels of village government. The first is the monthly meeting of the Village Council attended by only those 25 villagers who have been elected Councillors. This is followed each month by a Village Assembly attended by all adults in the village. Table 2 provides a summary of data collected on a sample of Village Assembly meetings.

In Magugu and Gallapo, a system of fines provides an incentive for participation in village meetings. Usually a chicken comprises the fine, but in richer villages even a goat may be demanded. If a villager does not have these items, the house is visited and an article such as a chair or cooking pot taken and returned only when the individual has reformed by attending one or more meetings. In some villages, the fine system operates sporadically. One Village Chairman said, "When we call the people to the meeting, the women make sure they come so they won't be fined. But the men go to beer, so they forget about the fine".

In Magugu area, women's attendance at Village meetings appears to be high. The area secretary was emphatic that it is not fines that induce women to attend. "Women here are interested in developing themselves." One or two are known as talkers, but the majority of women keep quiet in the meetings. One Chairman said, "If a woman really wants something discussed, she will usually ask her brother or husband to say it".

Village officials gave the following reasons why women rarely attend meetings:

- women are still shy to attend public meetings;

- women are too busy at home to come;

- it is not the woman's job to roam and survey the village and attend things like meetings; it is her job to watch the house;

- women can't speak Kiswahili;

- women are uneducated;

- women don't understand the discussions;

- it's difficult for a woman to get a pass from the house to come; only one person from a household need come, so it is always the man;

- women don't need to come because we ask the men to tell them what we have discussed;

- women are not used to sitting together with men;

- there are still some men here who don't like to see women in meetings.

Women speak of preoccupations with childcare, housework, or work in the fields. Many women said that men preferred that they did not involve themselves in village affairs. In the Gallapo area a local UWT chairwoman was late to a meeting because "her husband wouldn't let her come until she had finished cooking his meal." Even the Village chairman was unable to persuade the husband to release her for the important meeting.

There are no rules or guidelines governing the election of women councillors. Village officials stressed that no pressure is put on the community to appoint women, or upon women themselves to stand for election. Women candidates are chosen for their willingness to speak out in public and their strong personalities. Many are reappointed. Most women councillors interviewed had at least two or three years of primary schooling. Only one had reached standard Seven. The ability to speak Kiswahili was noted as a factor in their appointment both by chairmen and women councillors themselves. Wealth did not seem important. However, half of the women councillors interviewed were either single or divorced.

In the Council meetings, women councillors did not express themselves as freely or frequently as male councillors. In contrast, all women in UWT meetings talked freely and debates became quite heated. Women councillors used their experience of council meetings to maintain order in UWT meetings.

Many women said representation and participation were "not important," that it did not change their circumstances in the village. Other comments on their status in the village:

"Now we are sitting in meetings, but my husband can still beat me if I complain. We are still dependent on men."

"Women are still the same because the money belongs to the husband still."

"A man can still refuse you anything because he owns all the things."

"Our main problem here is that the men are drinking our money and we have no way to get more."

"Things are better when we are working together as women. The men can't take the income from our field."

'In my opinion it would be better if the Council gave every woman one acre for herself."

"We are not equal with men. He can refuse anything, even to buy food for the children."

"Nothing has changed for us women. I was born from my father and now my husband is looking after me."

While being interviewed village officials complained:

"Water is a big problem for women. We can sit here all day waiting for food because there is no woman at home. Always they are going far to fetch water. . . . It is not the custom of our men to allow women a pass to leave the house. If they roam freely in the village, they will become bad women and forget their duties."

2. The Economic Role of Women in the Project Area

a. Agricultural Crops and Livestock

Women in Tanzania provide, on average, 60 percent of all required farm labor. In the project area, the overall input was judged to be higher than 60 percent. Table 3 shows which tasks household members undertake in cultivating the major crops. Table 4 differentiates household and farm maintenance tasks for Madunga Ward.

Perhaps the most labor-intensive activity is hoeing which is traditionally done by mixed working parties. The wife of the host brews beer, but no other payment is given the participants. A large number of respondents emphasized that harvesting, a task done elsewhere by both men and women, is usually done by women alone. No information was collected by the study to determine the hours spent on the storing and checking of crops and the processing of grain, but such tasks are routinely performed by women in all three areas.

In principle, national or regional control exists for what and where crops may be produced. However, farmers suggest what they will plant, and these suggestions are returned to the village as production guidelines. The role of the Village Council is important. In the high-production Gallapo area, the chairman stated:

> "It is the Village Council which decides when people shall start planting. We talk to the Bwana Shamba (agricultural extension officer) and make a decision. Then we call a meeting and tell the people. If a woman finds her husband not working properly, she can report him to the Village Council and he can be punished . . the men can report the women, too, but we only have trouble with the men forgetting to plough because of beer . . . We also set targets of what we shall produce each year and what each household must grow; usually, it is the same as last year. But we do not punish people for not growing what we say."

The Village Council also excercises control over the marketing of crops where it acts as a buying agent for the National Milling Corporation (NMC). Farmers make independent decisions about what to sell, and at what price, only when they sell in the unofficial market.

In all ten villages, both men and women indicated that the decisions about what to plant, when to weed, what inputs to use and who will provide the labor are made together by both male and female members of the household. Many added, "that man's say is final." No female respondent indicated that she was without influence in farm decision-making. In practice, if not by design, women tend to take a decision-making role by virtue of the fact that they so often do the work.

Farmers make the following decisions: when to plough; how many acres to plough; what to plant; spacing of seeds; when to weed and how often; whether to use manure and/or fertilizer; whether to use insecticides or herbicides; when to seek advice from the Bwana Shamba; when to harvest; when to sell; what price to sell for; and, in relation to all of the above, decisions as to who will provide the labor.

Interviews with female heads-of-households and other members of the community revealed that although a female head may do all the labor on her farm and has the final say on whether she plants in a given year, she seeks advice from male family members and neighbors. These men may purchase seed or insecticides for the woman, help her organize a hoeing work party (Madunga) or hire an ox-plough or tractor (Magugu, Gallapo). Women in households where husbands or fathers are temporarily absent will wait until their return at the ploughing season before hoeing or hiring a tractor. In other instances, they write to the husband asking him what he wants them to do that year. Women in all three areas emphasized that they can be chastised if the man, on his return, finds their work unsatisfactory. The Bwana

Shama in one area said that although there are a number of women farmers in the area responsible for their own farms, he never receives visits or requests from individual women.

In all three areas, many of villagers own livestock, and in Madunga Ward in particular, livestock rather than agriculture is often the primary source of income. While the labor involved in livestock-raising is less intensive, it does involve steady attention throughout the year. The division of labor between men and women in Madunga Ward for cattle keeping tasks is indicated in Table 5. A similar division of labor exists in Gallapo Ward, with the exception that women do little herding and do not collect fodder for the calves. Women do sometimes take the cattle to water, a time-consuming task in the Gallapo area. They frequently put the beasts in the kraal at night and milking is usually their responsibility.

Women and men agree that livestock is the business of men, and men make any decisions that are required regarding where cattle should be grazed, when cattle should be dipped, the purchase and sale of beasts, innoculation, husbanding, etc. Women carry out many of the routine tasks including milking, caring for calves, and kraaling. If they want to alter any of these practices, they first consult their husbands. No woman acquires or sells a beast without consulting the male head of the family. Both men and women interviewed laughed at the concept of women owning livestock. Men said, "If women owned cattle there would be corruption." Asked to explain, one man said, "If women owned cattle they could sell them without asking us. We would no longer be rulers of our women. They would be free to roam anywhere."

Women do not normally inherit livestock. If a husband dies, leaving a herd, this will almost always be taken over by an uncle or other male relative and only returned to the woman's male children when they are of age. Women do inherit or, in rare cases, purchase small stock, but decision-making concerning these animals rests with male members of the household or extended family.

Women said that they have more control over sheep and goats than over cattle. They may "even suggest to their husbands when to sell or slaughter a goat." Some men interviewed said that they have little interest in goats and sheep, that they are for the women. Nonetheless, men usually own the animals and the income derived from them.

Income generated from the sale of crops and livestock belongs to the men. Fathers and husbands provide for their wives and children. Very often, as soon as sales have been made and money secured, the husband will give the wife a portion to spend at once on household needs. He will often bring the wife a new *kanga* (cloth) for herself. Sometimes, the husband and wife will jointly decide how much money is required to maintain the household (new pots, clothes for children, etc.). The remaining funds are taken by the husband for his own use and the household's use over the coming year. These funds are used for purchasing seeds, hiring a tractor, and for men's traveling, beer drinking, etc. In the less traditional areas, some wives said that a husband gives his wife all money for safe-keeping. As he needs it, he asks her to give it to him.

Farms now "belong to the household" in Tanzania. However, plots are registered under the man's name and, in the event of a conflict, belong to him. Traditional inheritance in which land is passed from father to son is still the accepted pattern in modern villages. Some rural women do own land in their own right, but they generally have inherited it under special circumstances.

Village chairmen conceded the right of women to apply for land ownership, but noted that such applications would be unfavorably viewed if women had access to a household *shamba*. Their reasoning was that as long as land is short, villages can't affort two members of a household owning plots. However, councillors agreed that men do apply for and receive extensions or additional plots, in some instances involving quite large areas of land. No woman had applied for a plot in her own right.

The family home also belongs to the man. In the event of divorce, the women may be sent home to her father or elsewhere. In practice, widows usually keep the house after a husband's death, but a husband's family may take over the house. The Marriage Act of 1971 confirmed the right of women to retain all goods acquired by them personally since marriage, but fixed property was not covered in the Act.

Assets purchased as a result of both man's and woman's labor are viewed as the property of the man. In the ten villages studied, no oxploughs, tractors or carts are owned by women.

b. Income Generating Activities

Women in all three areas are involved in petty production which earns them independent income. The most wide-spread production is beer-making, from which a woman may earn 100/= a time (At official exchange rates 100/= is $11; at unofficial rates 100/= is worth only 2 or 3 dollars.) Few women brew more than three times a year. Pressures exist to prevent any one woman from taking over the market.

Women also derive income from handicraft production. Women in two areas produce mats and baskets for sale. In one area, it is estimated that 500 women produce mats or baskets for eight months a year. The average income for this activity is about 120/= per month.

In-kind exchange replaces cash; i.e., a basket exchanges for the amount of millet or maize it takes to fill the basket. Marketing is local, although in the case of mats, middlemen are emerging.

Some women earn an income from producing cloth items such as Muslim hats, embroidered tablecloths, etc. Others sell milk and ghee or produce and sell vegetables in the market. Bananas are a source of substantial income, sometimes up to 500/= per month. A range of other minor productive activities include cake-making and selling, cloth-selling, and collecting and selling bundles of firewood.

Although some women may earn up to 2,500/= a year, in these activities, the value is often in kind. If cash is received, it goes automatically toward the maintenance of the household. Several women expressed reluctance to earn too much money. "Then my husband will not give me any money at all. He will say I am now earning money and will keep all his money for beer."

Pressure to produce may be exerted by male members of the household, but the final decision rests with the women as to how much they produce and when. Women sell their own products, but do not have complete control over how their earnings are spent.

Women interviewed by the study in the ten villages added the following tasks which they considered to be time-consuming: child-watching, calf and pig caring, visits to maize mill, visits to clinic with sick children.

III. PROJECT DESCRIPTION

A. Project Objectives and Components

The goal of the APVDP was to improve the productivity, incomes and well-being of rural people of Arusha by strengthening the capability of the regions, districts and villages to plan, implement and evaluate development activities. A technical assistance team of nine permanent staff and 30 temporary and/or consultant staff spearheaded the program in the three agricultural Districts of the Region. Over 80 village-level projects were begun. Half were income-producing and the rest related to land use planning, improvement in extension delivery, or water development. APVDP staff and resources were integrated into the decision-making structure and processes of the Arusha Regional Development Directorate, with four main objectives:

1) to strengthen the planning, implementation and evaluation capabilities at the regional, district and village levels;

2) to improve agricultural production (crops, livestock and natural resources);

3) to identify and promote other economic activities (primarily rural industries); and

4) to improve the social and economic infrastructure directly related to productive activities (primarily water and road systems).

These objectives gave rise to four major project components which are described as follows:

1. Planning Activity

A major task of the project was to assist the Arusha Region government in preparation of an Integrated Rural Development Plan. This activity provided the focus of planning assistance at all levels of the region's administration. As of September, 1982, the following steps had been taken:

- A comparative analysis of RIDEPs was done and study tours to four regions were made to draw lessons from these experiences.

- The region specified village self-reliance, improved equity, economic growth, regional integration, and protection of natural resources as goals for resource decision-making.

- Two hundred forty-five distinct agro-ecological zones were then organized into planning units by district officials.

- An analysis of population growth and movement was made to determine the land pressures and other implications for the future.

- Village profiles for one hundred fifty-one villages were done to determine current economic activity and infrastructure.

- Sector-specific studies were undertaken for livestock, agriculture, rural industries, forestry, fisheries, beekeeping, mining, health, water, and transportation, and a set of background papers was prepared that analyzed problems that affected all sectors.

- regional and district planning committees were formed as working

Regional and district planning committees were formed as working groups to prepare the Regional Plan. The districts prepared Strategy and Priority Papers which identified key development issues and proposed solutions to those problems. The region prepared a similar paper, taking a more macroperspective.

- The conclusions of the District Strategies and Priorities Papers and the findings of the Regional Papers were synthesized into a document, entitled *Arusha Region: Decisions for the Future*, which has provided the basis for policy decision-making for the next twenty year plan period (1981-2001).

2. Productive Sector Development

The APVDP Project Paper identified the development and introduction of appropriate technologies for crop and livestock production to be undertaken by the project. The actual activities included:

- Sector assessments of agriculture, livestock, forestry, beekeeping and fisheries; planning and implementing a program to tackle the serious soil erosion problem; introduction of barley as a new crop;

- Training programs for local level livestock and agricultural extension staff and in soil conservation problems and methods;

- Provision of equipment and supplies;

- Provision of technical inputs for the development of local irrigation systems;

- Establishment of forestry and fruit tree nurseries and four village storage facilities (godowns); and

- Development of a Pilot Agricultural Extension Project (PAEP) to re-establish Farmer Contact Groups, improve extension management through seminars, field days and workshops with Agricultural Extension Staff and farmers, and development of comparable programs for livestock owners.

3. Small Industry Development

The identification and promotion of economic activities other than livestock and agriculture was a key project activity. In financial terms, it was budgeted at 7 percent of total project costs. The APVDP role was intended to be primarily supportive of existing initiatives and to facilitate linkages between villages and sources of funding and expertise. The APVDP was successful in developing and implementing technologies without establishing an Appropriate Technology Centre because there was an appropriate facility in Arusha. The APVDP played an important role in helping the region identify and promote economic activities at the village level. The mid-term evaluation of the APVDP concluded that more progress was made in this area than originally envisaged and strongly endorsed the consolidation of this initiative. The activities undertaken included:

- Establishing an Agricultural Implements Production Facility which produced a modified ox-drawn plough and steel parts required for the production of ox-carts;

- Establishment of ox-cart assembly and maintenance facilities in Hanang, Arumeru and Mbulu Districts;

- Establishment of brick and tile-making facilities in Arumeru, Hanang and Mbulu Districts;

- Technical assistance for the construction and development of a ceramic kiln to help with the local manufacture of ceramic tableware;

- Design and approval for a soap production industry;

- Pre-feasibility study for lime pozzalana cement production;

- Provision of grain grinding mills to 13 villages with an additional eight in the pipe-line;

- Other industries approved and/or initiated include woodcutting, beekeeping, woodworking, mat marketing and baking.

Research and development efforts undertaken in response to village requests included an improved irrigation pump, oil presses and expellers, and ox-drawn equipment in plows, weeders, etc. Other support activities included: financial arrangements with the Tanzanian Rural Development Bank and the National Bank of Commerce for funding commodity imports and development of an experimental loan program; village training in accounting and management; and establishment of a Regional Small Industries Coordinating Committee to coordinate efforts of government, parastatal and private institutions in developing small industries.

In developing these activities, the Rural Industries Specialist of the APVDP worked closely with both the Department of Ujamaa and Cooperatives, and the Small Industries Development Organization.

Actual project ideas arose from the village level through consultation initiated by Rural Development Specialists in conjunction with the sector specialist. It is this consultation that gave the rural industries program a strong emphasis for developing activities which support agricultural development. Under the APVDP, the three project Districts instituted revolving loans to village councils or village co-operative groups. This system guaranteed villages the opportunity to take out a consecutive loan of the same value once an initial loan was repaid. The mechanism encouraged the credit worthiness of villages.

4. Roads and Water Development

The intended outputs of the roads' component included: the rehabilitation of 276 miles of secondary roads; provision of resources to construct up to 200 miles of lower standard feeder roads, to connect project villages to the district road network; provision of equipment, selected operating costs and on-the-job training of district roads staff.

In addition, the project was mandated to improve the capability of the regional government to construct and improve roads. The mid-term project evaluation noted that roads had not been rehabilitated at the rate expected, nor was much accomplished in improving institutional capabilities.

Under the APVDP, shallow wells, boreholes, and spring catchments were to be developed in 52 villages. The criterion for selecting villages was the constraint on village production activities due to lack of water. Three water development crews were to be financed to carry out the construction work required, and vehicles and training were provided. A limited amount of low-cost, hand-dug irrigation development was also to be undertaken by the project. The mid-term evaluation of the project noted that progress was made in all areas, although not as anticipated in the original project design.

Women in the APVDP Project

The investigation initiated in 1981 to determine how rural women were involved in the project revealed that most APVDP initiatives took the form of village projects. They were processed through the Village Council which approved the project before its submission to district level APVDP. An APVDP staff member [Rural Development Specialist (RDS)] reviewed the project in conjunction with the appropriate sector officials. Each Village Council usually had at least one female member. These women members attended Council meetings where village projects were discussed, but the RDS who had attended all these meetings did not recall any instance when women had offered comments on a proposed project.

The RDS reported that women outside the Village Council were involved in planning the Gallapo Water Project. This project was designed to provide 8 villages in the area with shallow wells or other water facilities. Four representatives of each village were invited to attend the planning meetings and it was specified that at least one of these participants should be a woman. At the first meeting, five of the required women attended. At the second meeting, two appeared. In subsequent meetings, only one woman continued to attend. At one point in the proceedings, the RDS was tempted to refuse to continue the water planning meetings until all eight women were present. Pressure to mobilize the project quickly made this difficult and the project continued without the input of village women.

Village projects didn't always originate with the Village Council. Subsidiary village groups or co-operatives presented requests for assistance from APVDP, although the request ultimately had to be channeled through the Village Council. Woodworking, woodcutting and other small groups were formed, but none of these groups had female members.

Planning of village development at the district, division and ward level in support of village activities was carried out by the RDS in close consultation with District Sector heads and their staff, and Party officials. These posts usually were not filled by women. Only in one area was there a female Party officer and a female Community Development Officer. The RDS had worked with both of these women. The RDS had not made an effort to ascertain if there were any women's groups operating in the four pilot wards or how the APVDP might help them develop their productive capability. The government staff in the district which worked most closely with APVDP had not suggested that this area receive attention. Village chairmen had not brought projects to the attention of the RDS or government staff directly involved and concerned with groups of women in the village. Village women themselves had not made requests or suggestions to their Village Councils for assistance.

Village women were only vaguely aware of the purpose of the APVDP, and unaware that it could be tapped to their own advantage. Few women interviewed were even aware of APVDP projects (with the exception of one maize mill).

In all village projects which require labor, both men and women were called to participate, and in the Magugu Ward villages, women have generally contributed the greater share of self-help labor. However, where most APVDP projects have been initiated, Village Councillors reported they found it difficult to involve women. Women did provide labor for the construction of the Madunga Kati maize mill building and the establishment of experimental barley plots in all three villages of the ward. In the former project, a small group of women, called together by the woman village councillor, assisted in carrying water for brick-making, made the walls, and helped with the floor. In the barley project, women contributed labor for digging plots and planting, although not in numbers equal to men.

No women were involved in the implementation of the Gallapo Water Project. In Majengo village, women complained that the sites of two well constructions were inconvenient. When they were asked why they hadn't informed the drilling crew or Council, they claimed they either didn't know they were being dug, or that the Council hadn't listened to them.

TABLES
Table 1   Summary Statistical Profile on Arusha Region

Location:	North-central Tanzania, bordering Kenya on the Northeast
Size:	82,423.5 sq. km.
Climate:	Mild, average temperature 22°C. Considerable variation in rainfall between the mountains and the lowlands ranging from 500-1000 mm/year.
Natural Resources:	National forest 2,345.0 sq. km. (3% of the total land area). Game parks 10,460.0 sq. km. (8% of total land area) (wildlife population 1,870,000). Lakes & dams 3,571.0 sq. km. (4% of total land area). Grazing land 71,041.9 sq. km. (86% of total land area).
Population:	928,475—92% located in rural areas, annual growth rate—3%
Administrative Structure:	A regional government overseeing 1 Town Council, 6 Districts, 26 Divisions, 133 Wards, 463 Villages.
Physical Infrastructure:	Roads—2,525 kms. of which 962 kms. are murran/gravel, and 1,250 kms. are earth. Water systems—almost 48% of the population is provided with safe water.
Quality-of-Life Indicators:	Health—life expectancy 51 years. Infant mortality rate 130 death/1000 births. Percentage of population visiting health facility annually—3.8%. Education—adult literacy rate—37%. Percentage of school-age children enrolled in primary school—91%. Economic—gross regional product/capita T. sh. 1.650. Food production in Kcal/capita/day-3.818.

Source: Arusha Region Today: 1981, by RDD's Office, Arusha, Tanzania.

Table 2 Number of Women on Village Council and Sample Attendance at Village Assemblies

Village	No. Women Councillors	% of Village Assembly are Women
Gallapo Ward		
Gallapo	3	50
Qash	2	30
Gedamar	0	25
Halla	3	25
Ayamango	2	30
Tsamasi	0	20
Orng'adida	2	30
Majengo	2	45
Madunga Ward		
Utwari	1	20
Madunga Kati	1	20
Qameyu	2	20
Magugu Ward		
Magugu	4	55
Gichameda	3	55
Mapea	5	50
Matufa	4	ND
Masware	0	ND
Sarame	2	ND
Mawemairo	1	ND
Overall Average	2	34

Table 3 Gender Division of Labor for Cultivation of Major Crops by Geographic Area

Task	Major Crops				
	Madunga Area			Gallapo Area	Magugu Area
	Maize	Pyrethrum	Potatoes/Onions	Maize	Maize and Rice
Buy Select Seeds	Men	Men	Men/Women	—	—
Clear Land	Men	Men	Men	—	—
Plough	—	—	—	Men	Men/Women
Hoe	Men/Women	Men/Women	Men/Women	—	—
Plant/ Transplant	Women	Women	Men/Women	Women	Women
Thin/Weed	Men/Women	Women	Men/Women	Women	Women
Manure	Women/Girls	Women	Women	—	—
Scare Birds	Women/ Children	—	—	Children	Men/Women/ Children
Apply Insecticide	—	—	—	Women	Women
Harvest	Men/Women/ Children	Women/Girls	Women/Men	Women/Men	Women

Table 3   (Continued) Gender Division of Labor for Cultivation of Major Crops by Geographic Area

Task	Major Crops				
	Madunga Area			Gallapo Area	Magugu Area
	Maize	*Pyrethrum*	*Potatoes/Onions*	*Maize*	*Maize and Rice*
Carry Home	Women	Women/Girls	Women	Women	Women
Dry	Women	Women	Women	Women	Women
Thresh	Women/Men	—	—	Women/Men	Women/Men
Bag/ Transport	Women/Men	Women	Women/Men	Women/Men	Women/Men
Sell	Men	Men	Men	Men	Men

Table 4   House and Farm Maintenance: Madunga Ward

Women	*Hours per day*
Cleaning out dung from house every morning	½
Cooking food three times a day	2
Collecting fodder for calves	1
Watching over children	continuous
Collecting firewood	1
Cutting firewood	¼
Milking cows	½
Visiting sick relatives/friends	2 (not daily)
Cleaning house and surrounding	Continuous
Collecting water	1 (but often children)
Collecting wild vegetables, berries	2 (not daily)
Going to maize mill	2 (2 x per week)
Going to clinic	2 (1-2 x per month)
Farming	4
Washing clothes	½
Making baskets, mats	1
Fixing walls or grass roof of house	1 (not daily)
Shopping	1 (1 per week)
Processing grains	1
Checking stored foods	Not daily
Herding	2 (not daily)

Men	*Hours per day*
Farming	2
Building houses/fixing house etc.	1
Building kraals	(not daily)
Herding	3
Shopping	1
Meetings	4 (not daily)
Safaris	(not daily)
"Roaming and surveying the village (and beer drinking) for news"	3
Looking for food when shortages	(not daily)
Taking sick people to hospital	1 day

Table 5   Cattle-Keeping Tasks

Task	Performed by
Buying Beasts	Men
First herding (morning) (2-3 hours)	Boys (small)
Afternoon herding and taking animals to water (4-5 hours)	Men (sometimes Women & children help)
Milking (1 hour)	Women/Men
Supervising calves getting milk (½ hour)	Women
Kraaling in house (½ hour)	Women
Clearing house of manure (morning ½ hour)	Women
Drying	Women
Taking manure to shamba (¾ hour)	Women
Watching over calves in day	Women
Dipping	Men
Veterinary care	Men
Selection for sale	Men
Sale	Men
Husbandry (supervising, mating, calving, dehorning, etc.)	Men
Collecting fodder for calves (1 hour)	Women

NOTES

[1] See J. Koopman Henn's study *Women in the Rural Economy: Past, Present and Future* (University of Dar es Salaam: Institute of Development Studies, 1981) for an excellent analysis of this historical process.

[2] See President Nyerere. *Socialism and Rural Development*, (Dar Es Salaam: Tanzania, 1967).

[3] Micheala von Freyholt. *Ujama Villages in Tanzania: Analysis of a Social Experiment* (Heinemann, 1979) p. 145.

[4] David Peterson and Thad Peterson. *The Village Profile Excercise: Background Information.* (APUDP: Arusha, 1980). p. 127.

CHAPTER SEVEN

KENYA: EGERTON COLLEGE

Prepared by Mary B. Anderson

CONTENTS

I. Introduction

II. Country Background/Importance of Agriculture

III. Role of Women in Agriculture in Kenya

IV. Project Description/Background
   A. Government of Kenya
   B. Agricultural Systems Support Project
   C. Egerton College
   D. Needs for "Agriculture Manpower and Training"
   E. Proposed AID Project

V. Current Project Description

VI. Conclusion
   TABLES
   APPENDIXES

I. INTRODUCTION

"Information is power!" declared Dr. Maria Mullei, an Agriculture Projects Officer for USAID in Nairobi. "You must think in terms of how to get information and to transmit it," she admonished her friend. And, later, to another, she said, "It is very difficult to get Kenyan women to think this way. But it is a new time. We must recognize the importance of information and technology if we are to get ahead and if we are to play our part in helping Kenya get ahead."

In Kenya, information and technical know-how do exist and are constantly expanding. The educated, urban population and large farm owners and managers know how to get and use these resources. A basic development issue is how to broaden the dissemination of information and technology to others in the society on whom development also depends—particularly to smallholders in rural areas.

II. COUNTRY BACKGROUND

In 1976, agriculture employed approximately 85 percent of Kenya's labor force and contributed 29 percent to GDP while the services sector contributed 28 percent; government, 18 percent; manufacturing and mining, 15 percent; and construction and utilities, 10 percent. Agricultural products constituted 69 percent of total exports in 1976 and 86 percent in the first half of 1977. Of this, coffee accounted for 61 percent and tea, 19 percent.

Kenya's population was 14 million, of whom 87 percent lived in rural areas. Annual population growth was estimated at about 3.5 percent. This high rate of growth was forcing pressures on the land. Rural-urban migration was high and increasing, causing an annual urban growth rate of 7.1 percent. Most migrants to urban centers were male, under 30, and more than half were single. The migrants, as a group, had higher than average educational attainments for their age groups. For many of the young, wage employment was necessary as they owned no cultivable land; for others, their land holdings were insufficient to support their families and they, too, sought wage employment to make up for the failure of the land to support them. As a result of this migration by young, single males and some married men to cities for wages, rural areas have become populated predominantly by females, the very old and young, and people with lower than average schooling.

Also in response to land pressures, many families were moving to lower quality land areas for which they held no title or traditional rights of use. Thus, the number of people attempting to farm medium or low potential land areas was increasing.

Only 57 percent of rural household income was derived from farming, while 43 percent was earned from regular or casual labor or came from transfers, usually from relatives in urban areas. This fact is partially explained by the small size of typical farm holdings. While there were 3,264 large farms of 8 hectares or more in Kenya, there were 1.5 million small farms. With an average of seven persons per household, the smallholder group included almost 11 million people, or about 80 percent of the total population. Total acreage under smallholder agriculture was estimated at 3.5 million hectares, so that the average holding was 2.3 hectares, of which about 1.2 to 1.5 hectares were actually under cultivation. Thirty-two percent of these holdings were less than one hectare; almost 60 percent were less than two hectares; and about 75 percent less than three hectares (see Tables 1 and 2).

The trend, however, has been for the overall smallholder share of agricultural production to increase, going from 20 percent in 1960 to 51 percent in 1976 (see Tables 3 and 4). A major factor explaining the increase is smallholder expansion of acreage devoted to certain crops (see Table 5). But, while small farmers produced 57 percent of the value of coffee marketed in 1975-76, at the same time, they held 80 percent of the land under coffee cultivation. Smallholder productivity lags behind that of large farmers.

III. THE ROLE OF WOMEN IN AGRICULTURE IN KENYA

The primary contribution of women to the economy of Kenya comes through their work as smallholding farmers and as managers of their households. Approximately 88 percent of Kenyan women live in rural areas and 85-90 percent of them work on a family holding as compared to 55-60 percent of men in rural areas. Both traditionally and currently, women have responsibility for producing staple and supplementary food crops, performing all tasks except initial land clearance in cultivating, harvesting and preserving these crops.

Food crops that are grown both for family consumption and for sale, such as maize and beans, are also principally women's responsibilities. In other cash crop cultivation, women are often active though not usually primarily responsible. In cotton production, women do most of the weeding and work on the harvest. In coffee and tea, they, along with men, pick, sort and transport the harvest to processing factories. Some studies show that women in East Africa spend about one-third of their working time in actual field work and that women's work accounts for about 60 to 75 percent of all farm labor.

In household management, women perform all the functions including food processing and preparation, cooking, housecleaning, child-care, as well as collection of fuel, water, and, sometimes, feed for domestic or penned animals. These activities account, on average, for two-thirds of women's work time, the majority of this often in collection of fuel and water. In most parts of Kenya, women build and maintain the traditional houses of pole construction with mud and thatch.

Children are important contributors to the support of small farms, both in providing labor for crops and animal care and in household tasks. Older children also care for younger ones, and their roles increase in importance as adult members of the household migrate to cities for wages.

In the past, programs that were directed to increasing farm productivity and income have often increased the work burden of rural women. This occurs most often when a household adopts labor-intensive cash crops such as coffee, sugar cane, or pyrethrum, or when it adds livestock such as poultry, pigs, or dairy cattle. Also, male migration for wage income has increased women's farming responsibilities, as has the schooling of children which both diverts children's labor from the farm and necessitates school fee payment, usually from the earnings of women.

Women are active in small scale trade of food commodities and other household products. Studies by the Ministry of Transport and Communications showed that over 90 percent of sellers in area markets are women. Frequently, however, they are excluded from access to more formal and larger scale marketing channels.

Women also work in non-farm labor, but usually in the poorer paying informal sector. A survey in 1969 showed that women constituted less than 20 percent of the adult labor force in non-agricultural employment. Fewer than 5 percent of women from smallholdings are employed off-farm, as compared with 21 percent for men.

While this description of rural women's work is accurate in general, there is a great deal of variation among women and in the gender division of tasks, particularly between districts and ecological zones. Task division depends on family structure, traditional tribal customs, the degree of involvement in pastoralism vs. agriculture, and whether the family lives in traditional areas or has migrated.

An increasing number of women in Kenya are now heads of households. Estimates range from 19 percent to 40 percent for rural women, though official estimates are lower. Even among households headed by women, one finds variation. Some women are effective heads because their husbands have migrated to urban areas for wage income. Others are widowed, divorced, abandoned, or never married but with children. The age of children, especially sons, also affects the roles women play both in jobs performed and decision-making. Women whose husbands work in cities can sometimes be found hiring labor to do some of the farm work, or purchasing fuel and water with money sent by their husbands. Others receive virtually no remittances and have responsibilities and resources equivalent to widows or divorced women.

Age and stage in the life cycle also affect women's productive roles and status. Traditionally, while land was not privately owned, the rights of usage were established by land clearance done by men. Women, after marriage, were given access to plots for food crop production by their husbands or, if unmarried, by their fathers. With land reform in recent years in Kenya, title for land is being registered in individual names and this ownership is almost always granted to male family members. Sometimes, however, mature widows may be in a position to gain title to land. These women may also be owners and managers of other resources, such as herds or farm equipment, usually managed by men. Younger widows, on the other hand, may not have sufficient status and may be forced to rely on male family members for management of, and decisions about, major productive resources.

The importance of the differences which arise from variations in family status is indicated by a study of nutritional status of children. This study found that children of female-headed households fall into the two extremes with regard to nutrition. Those with absent but earning fathers who send monies home are found in the groups of greatest advantage nutritionally, while those without fathers are found at highest risk.

There are other differences among households headed by women. The average male head of household is 47 years old, and 27 percent of male heads of households have had more than a Standard 4 education. Of married female heads of households, the average age is 37, and 23 percent have had Standard 4 education or beyond. For unmarried females who head households, the average age is 55 and only 2 percent have had more than four years of schooling. A study in 1974-75 showed the mean annual income of male-headed households to be 19 percent greater than that for female-headed households. Table 6 shows the variations in the numbers of female-headed households by province. Tables 7, 8 and 9 show the percentage distribution of different labor by women and men depending on the type of household.

Another major source of differences among men's and women's roles in agriculture is that of ethnic background. Among the Kikuyu, women and girls traditionally do horticultural work, though men and women sometimes do the same work such as ground breaking, planting an already cleared field, and/or the first weeding of a crop. Kipsigis men work with women in the second weeding of millet fields and, with children, harvest the crop. While the Luo have a clear division of labor between men and women on millet in the pre-harvest activities, men and women harvest together.

There is extensive evidence that the roles of men and women in agriculture are in flux in Kenya. In particular, on the caring for and grazing of cattle on smallholdings, gender divisions have been blurred. Where no man is present in the family, women do all tasks, including those traditionally assigned to men. Household tasks, however, have not been adopted equally by men and women. Women and children have traditionally been, and continue to be, solely responsible for fetching firewood and water, and women continue to do food preparation, child care, and housekeeping.

Table 10 provides a breakdown by gender of educational attainment for three different age groups. The gap between male and female attendance at school has widened steadily since the colonial period, even as overall access to education has improved.

IV. PROJECT DESCRIPTION/BACKGROUND

A. Government of Kenya

The GOK has recognized the increasing importance of small-holdings in agricultural production and the increasing problems small-holders face as they move to marginal lands and/or experience increasing population pressures on their traditional lands. It has, therefore, emphasized services to this group and to pastoralists in its Third and Fourth Five Year Plans (1974-1978 and 1979-1983). Moreover, it has acknowledged that the institutional mechanisms needed to satisfy smallholder needs are simply not the same as those which have been developed to support the large farm sector. Two areas of critical need have been identified. First, systems of outreach and extension should be redesigned and/or improved to reach smallholders. Second, the information and technologies provided should be made relevant to smallholder conditions. An important avenue for serving the small-holder population is through the agricultural extension service.

B. Agricultural Systems Support Project

The Agricultural Systems Support Project (ASSP) was undertaken by USAID and GOK in 1978 to address the needs for increasing the trained personnel in agriculture, and for directing their training toward serving the needs of smallholders. The following two statements from the Project Paper illustrate the thrust of the project.

> The Agricultural extension service is a mechanism for delivery of technology and other information to the farmer. As such, it should respond through its structure and approach to the particular production objectives and client groups it is intended to reach. No single, ideal type of extension service system should be expected to perform equally well in reaching the diverse client groups or in meeting such diverse objectives as production for domestic food, for exports, or for industrial raw materials.

Increasing the pool of trained agricultural manpower and redirecting such training towards the needs of smallholders and the operation of smallholder-oriented extension and research systems will make a significant direct contribution towards addressing extension service problems of management/administration, staff numbers, pre-service training and technical support.

The ASSP was designed to address three principal constraints encountered by Kenya's agricultural programs and emphasized by the GOK:

1. insufficient numbers of trained personnel;

2. inadequate access by smallholders to agricultural credit insititutions, services and infrastructure; and

3. insufficient research focused on or adaptable to the needs of smallholders.

The six year commitment from 1978 to 1984 involved a total AID obligation of $49,800,000. Of this $26,200,000 was in the form of a grant and $23,600,000 was a loan. ASSP was multi-faceted and directed toward support of five interrelated systems, including:

1. training of agricultural personnel

2. credit

3. cooperatives

4. range research

5. storage of crops

Each component of the Project contained elements of research, training and extension.

C. Egerton College

One project component of ASSP was a major expansion of the facilities and teaching staff of Kenya's main training center for agricultural extension workers, Egerton College. Total costs of this component were $45,682,000. The GOK contributed $11,379,000 and AID contributed $34,303,000, of which $10,745,000 was a grant and $23,558,000 a loan (see Table 16). The Egerton College expansion was, therefore, a major part of the total ASSP accounting for just under one half of the grant funds and all of the loan funds.

Egerton College was founded in 1939 in the highly fertile Rift Valley of Kenya to train European farmers and their sons and daughters. In

1952 it was raised to the status of an agricultural college, and in 1955 it became a three-year, diploma-granting college. With Kenya's independence in 1963, the College became a centrally important training institution for Kenya's agriculturalists and for its agricultural extension service.

In Kenya's system of agricultural training, Egerton College occupies the middle ground. The Faculty of Agriculture at the University of Nairobi awards the BSc and MSc degrees. Three Agricultural Institutes, with two year courses, give certificates to their graduates. Students at Egerton College are required to have O-level and A-level passes at secondary school. As pressures on the spaces at the University of Nairobi have increased, more and more students entering Egerton are at the high A-level.

Enrollment at Egerton was 200 in 1964 and had grown to 686 by the beginning of the Project. The faculty numbered 42 senior and 32 junior staff. There were 431 support staff on the College payroll. Facilities included 14 teaching buildings; a dining hall; 3 administrative and support buildings; 6 dormitories; 344 staff houses for senior, junior, and support staff; a library; a 400 hectare teaching farm; a 1,100 hectare commercial/training farm.

The education that students gain at Egerton is geared to employment within the agricultural extension service of the Ministry of Agriculture. Eighty-two percent of Egerton graduates are initially employed by the Ministry of Agriculture and 14 percent are employed by the Ministry of Education as secondary school teachers. Those who enter the MOA do so as Technical Officers (TOs) assigned to the middle ranks of the extension service, as staff of the Research Division, or as teachers in the three Agricultural Institutes. Table 11 shows the division of these graduates in MOA assignments.

Technical Officers do some direct farmer-contact extension work. They also advise and supervise field extension agents who have direct contact with farmers, Technical Assistants trained at the certificate-granting Institutes, and Junior Agriculture Assistants who are younger employees of MOA without formal training. TOs also organize village-level training activities, teach special courses at Farmer Training Centers (FTCs), conduct in-service training for Technical Assistants and Junior Assistants, and take part in district and division level planning activities. Egerton graduates estimate that they spend two-thirds of their work time on administrative, supervisory or planning activities and one-third on direct farmer contact activities.

While the MOA hires 82 percent of the graduates each year, it employs only 49 percent of the total pool of Egerton graduates. Many former students go on to employment in the private sector or other parts of government. There is a delay in students' acceptance of other employment, however. Students at Egerton are "sponsored" by some government agency, private concern, or foreign donor. They then are "bonded" to that sponsor (or some designated agency in the case of foreign donor sponsorship) for a given period of time, usually three years.

At the start of the project, there were nine areas in which the diploma was offered by Egerton College. These have now been expanded to 16 courses discussed below. The nine which formed the core when the project began included:

1. Diploma in General Agriculture, providing general knowledge in many areas of agriculture and basic training in agricultural sciences with field experience in crop production from vegetables to cash crops.

2. Diploma in Agriculture and Home Economics, including basic agriculture, family life education and child development, food and nutrition, clothing and textiles, home management and economics, and home economics extension education.

3. Diploma in Animal Husbandry, teaching,the basic sciences, agricultural zoology, botany, and chemistry, and focusing on both large and small stock.

4. Diploma in Horticulture focused on the basic sciences, general agriculture and principles of crop production.

5. Diploma in Dairy Technology, emphasizing the production, treatment and collection of milk and management of dairy industries.

6. Diploma in Agriculture and Farm Management, providing applied training in agriculture, animal husbandry, farm machinery and economics.

7. Diploma in Agriculture Education, to strengthen the teaching of agriculture in the secondary schools.

8. Diploma in Agricultural Engineering, emphasizing workshop practice, farm machinery, soil and water conservation, structures, crop husbandry and economic management.

9. Diploma in Range Management, including grazing land management, inventory techniques, ranging schemes, wild life management and basic agricultural subjects.

In 1976, Egerton College, with FAO, undertook a major review of its teaching and curriculum in order to assess and increase its appropriateness to rural families and smallholders. Thus, each department at the College reviewed its approach and continues to do so to ensure that in both content and attitudes its teaching is geared toward the needs of the rural poor.

D. Needs for "Agriculture Manpower Training" in Kenya

A Study requested by the MOA in the late 1970s "to project the estimated supply and demand at all levels of trained manpower in agriculture" found that consistent shortfalls could be expected. Table 12 gives the figures for expected shortfalls of degree, diploma and certificate level graduates of Kenya's agricultural training centers. Table 13, compiled by USAID, shows the projections for demand from the agricultural sector for Egerton graduates, the diploma holders.

E. Proposed AID Project with Egerton College

Given the role of Egerton graduates in agricultural extension and the projected shortfalls of diploma recipients, AID agreed to support a major expansion of the College to raise the student capacity to 1,632 (with about 516 graduates per year). AID's inputs were to be in construction and in technical assistance.

Construction was to be funded with a loan over a three year period and to include new buildings, renovations and infrastructure. A careful feasibility study funded jointly by AID and GOK was conducted to assess the plant and equipment requirements to accommodate an increase in students. Current facilities were surveyed and alternative building/renovation options considered. It was determined that new construction should add to about twenty College buildings and build 513 new staff houses to replace a number of existent sub-standard houses. Many existing buildings would also have renovations in their plumbing, electrical and fire protection systems, and some remodeling for altered use. Infrastructure included additions to the water and waste water treatment systems, expansion of the electrical system, telephone installation and a minor realignment of one campus service road (see Appendix A).

Technical assistance support was to be through grant funding and included the provision of U.S. teaching staff and participant training (see Appendix B). Teaching staff was to increase from 42 to 76 overall. An assessment of needs within each diploma stream was made prior to the determination of staff needs.

During staff development, it was anticipated that a large number of U.S. personnel would be required in the College to: 1) teach in the courses when Kenya staff were away for training; 2) provide in-service training for staff in residence; 3) review and modify curriculum as appropriate; and 4) provide any other assistance necessary to help organize and smooth the growth. Eighty-six person years of U.S. technical assistance were budgeted to fill 28 teaching positions. In addition, 43 of Egerton's Kenyan teaching staff were to receive training in the U.S. for Ph.D., MSc., and BSc. degrees. The total training was projected at 139 person years (see Appendix C).

AID also financed five person years for a procurement/administrative officer to aid the expansion and provide support for the other U.S. staff. Tables 14 and 15 show the projected growth in student numbers by diploma specialty and the staffing growth over the years of the Project.

For its part, the GOK agreed: 1) to hire the additional Kenyan teaching and support staff required by the expansion; 2) to fund the incremental operating expenses incurred through the expansion; 3) to provide houses for U.S. teaching staff; 4) to finance architectural and engineering design fees and part of the construction; and 5) to purchase the furnishings required by the expansion. Table 16 shows the financial commitments of AID and GOK to the Egerton College Project Component.

Within the overall expansion plans, Egerton College's administration planned to increase the percentage of women students to 30 percent. This entailed expansion of dormitory and other facilities, and these were included in the AID support. This goal was seen as important for its own sake. Though taboos that limit the access of male extension workers to female farmers were important in the past and remain so in some provinces, they are reported to be of somewhat less significance in recent years.

V. CURRENT PROJECT DESCRIPTION

With only eight months remaining in the Project, much of the planned expansion of Egerton College has been accomplished. A new Administration building and a new library define the central campus area. A new and copious student dining hall is located beyond several blocks of new dormitories for men. Nearby, two older buildings have been renovated for women students. Many other buildings, both new and renovated, house the now 16 diploma-granting departments, training 1,442 students.

The increase from nine areas of concentration to sixteen reflects an increasing emphasis on specialized training. One previous course,

Agricultural Engineering, was sub-divided into two: Soil and Water Engineering; and Farm Power and Machinery. Animal Health, focusing on disease and disease control, was separated from Animal Husbandry. Ranch Management and Wildlife Management are now distinct courses, formerly included in Range Management. Additions to the College's offerings include Forestry, Food Science and Technology and Agriculture and Food Marketing.

The current principal of Egerton College, who assumed this post in 1980, emphasizes the continuing importance of keeping the curriculum focused, even as it becomes more specialized, on the needs and conditions of Kenya's small farmers. Citing the strengths and underlying good sense of many past agricultural traditions arrived at through direct experience and trial and error over centuries, he seeks to incorporate knowledge of these practices into the courses taught at Egerton. He sees this aspect as adding an important dimension to the otherwise technically modern and scientifically-based orientation of the courses. He believes that the education at Egerton Colege will improve, as the teachers are aware of and knowledgeable about traditions and include this knowledge in their curricula, even as they teach in the sophisticated laboratories and classrooms of the College.

Some courses can be seen to achieve a balance between traditional and modern methods. The working room in the Home Economics Department includes traditional charcoal cookers, simple electric stoves, and more complicated and modern electric and gas stoves. Students rotate in their use of the varieties of equipment during their course. The clothes washing, sewing, cleaning, and other equipment similarly ranges from traditional methods to modern machines. In many instances, equipment is made from local supplies. As part of the expansion, the Home Economics Department requested that two model homes be built for instruction purposes—one traditional and one modern. The modern one was constructed as a part of the project; the traditional house has not yet been built, though the College principal indicates that he plans to have it built in the traditional manner by College personnel.

Other departments reflect a far greater emphasis on modern techniques. The slaughterhouse is a completely modern facility and there is no training in traditional or ceremonial slaughter techniques. The dairy, while modest, is well equipped and run with high standards for sanitation, relying on electrical sterilization equipment. Laboratories are modern and well equipped, but the research is often focused on simple techniques related to small farmers' needs.

Planned faculty training has occurred almost entirely on schedule and expansion has surpassed original goals. The total faculty now is

150, sixty-one of whom have received advanced training in the United States (52 the MSc., and 9 the Ph.D.). In addition, Egerton is directly recruiting faculty to continue to meet the needs of the expanded curriculum. Of the current faculty, 12 are women. Though concentrated in the Home Economics Department, women now teach other subjects as well, including one in soil science, one in education, one in animal sciences, one in biology, one in chemistry, one in range management and one in wildlife management. There is also one woman who is a technician in the dairy technology course.

Women faculty at Egerton represent a broader spectrum of involvements than did the women among the U.S. technical assistance staff. Of the 31 U.S. faculty and advisors who were involved in the Project, seven were women; three of these were in the Home Economics Department and two in the Education Department.

The Home Economics Department has suffered particular misfortune in the training of its staff. Four members of the Department were scheduled to receive training in the U.S., three for the MSc degree and one for the Ph.D. Only one of these is currently teaching at Egerton. Two transferred to other parts of Kenya or overseas as a result of their husbands' transfers. The other died just before completing her Ph.D. course in the U.S. The Department is currently hiring directly in Kenya to fill these positions.

Of the 1,442 students enrolled in 1983 at Egerton College, 1,176 are men and 266 or 18 percent are women. The percentage of women admitted rose from 17 percent in the classes admitted in 1981 and 1982 to 22 percent in the class admitted in 1983 (see Tables 17 and 18).

Recruitment to Egerton occurs through listings in the Ministry of Education's Career Book, government in-service and newspaper announcements. Information about Egerton College is not a problem. For the class entering in 1983 in which 506 were admitted, 15,000 applications were received! A number of these came from GOK Ministries and Departments as nominations for in-service training. For example, the Forestry Department nominated 83 candidates to Egerton's entering class, of whom 10 were accepted. Nominations from the MOA and Ministry of Livestock were in the hundreds.

Egerton's acceptance is based on completion of secondary school with certain levels of competence overall and in biology, physics, chemistry and general science, mathematics and English and/or Kiswahili. Classes at the College are taught in English; the MOA extension service is conducted in Kiswahili. Candidates are rated by a composite of scores and listed by districts from which they come.

The acceptance procedure is based on a quota system by country districts with a strong effort to assure representation from the least progressive districts that had previously been left behind in development efforts. Table 19 shows a summary of the applications and admissions by gender of the candidates whose applications had been received by May, 1983 or a total of 2,325 out of the 15,000.

Students who are admitted to Egerton College seldom drop out. Only one or two students leave each year. Women who become pregnant are asked to take a year's leave of absence from the College, though they are automatically readmitted in the following year. This occurs also at about the rate of two per year. Virtually all of the women who take leave do return and complete their courses.

Placement of Egerton graduates is easy as they are both highly regarded and needed by Ministries and other sponsoring agencies. The bonding system described above also ensures post-graduate employment for students. In Kenya, men and women of equal employment rank receive equal pay in all aspects of government service.

VI. CONCLUSION

Planners for social and economic development in Kenya are sensitive to the methods by which information reaches various client groups and the probable differences in impacts from different methods and with different groups. One study shows that, while increases in educational status through schooling result in increases in rural household income overall, the same educational advantages, within a certain range, result in lower agricultural productivity. Schooling often prompts the recipient to seek off-farm employment as the more probable source of increased income. Another study, (Staudt, 1976) however, provides evidence that access to government agricultural services, including the information passed through direct agent contact, has a positive impact on agricultural productivity, primarily through increases in number and variety of crops and through increased adoption of cash crops. The same study indicates that, in general, more successful farmers are more apt to be visited by an agricultural extension agent than less successful ones, but that farms managed by a male, or jointly managed by husband and wife, are more often visited than female-managed farms. Less successful farms that are male or jointly managed are visited more often that more successful female-managed farms.

Egerton College enjoys a unique and important position in directing the thrust and determining the content of agricultural extension. It provides one of the principal sources of information and technology transfer to smallholders. Thus, the faculty at Egerton approach their jobs knowing that what they teach and how they teach it will have a direct and indirect effect on agricultural productivity among smallholders in Kenya.

TABLES

Table 1 Number of Holdings by Size and Percentage of Total 1965 and 1975

Size of Holdings (hectares)	Number of Holdings		Percent Share	
	1965	1975	1965	1975
8- 49	565	810	20.0	24.8
50-999	1,752	2,011	62.2	61.6
1000-over	503	443	17.8	13.6
	2,820	3,264	100.0	100.0

Source: Economic Memorandum, March, 1977, Tables 7.4 and 7.2. This data refers to ownership of holdings, not operational units.

Table 2 Small Farms: Percent Share of Total Holdings by Size 1975

Size of Holdings (hectares)	Percent Share 1975
0.0-0.5	13.9
0.6-0.9	17.9
1.0-1.9	27.0
2.0-2.9	15.1
3.0-3.9	8.9
4.0-4.9	7.2
5.0-7.9	6.5
8.0-over	2.5
	100.0

Source: Economic Memorandum, Table 7.5. In March, 1977.

Table 3 Value of Gross Marketed Production for Large and Small Farms, Selected Years (KSh million)

Year	Large Farms	Small Farms	Percent Share of Small Farms
1960	37.7	9.5	20.1
1965	33.3	23.8	41.7
1970	41.2	44.2	51.7
1976	124.5	127.8	50.7

Source: Economic Survey, various years.

Table 4 Share of Marketed Production for Large and Small Farmers, Selected Crops and Years

	Coffee		Tea		Pyrethrum		Maize	
Year	Large	Small	Large	Small	Large	Small	Large	Small
1960	80	20	99	1	79	21	57	43
1967	40	60	88	12	14	86	68	32
1971	53	47	79	21	55	45	54	46
1975-76	53	47	69	31	—	—	35	65

Source: Statistical Abstract, Nairobi, Kenya 1968; *Economic Survey* Nairobi, Kenya, various years.

Table 5   Acreage Allocated to Selected Crops by Large and Small Farmers, 1970 and 1974-75, '000 Hectares

	Coffee		Tea		Pyrethrum		Hybrid Maize	
Year	Large	Small	Large	Small	Large	Small	Large	Small
1970	29.7	62.5	23.8	19.6	3.3	13.5	59.3	155.8
1974-75	28.0	113.3	25.6	65.6	4.1	27.1	67.8	759.0

Source: Economic Survey, 1973; Statistical Abstract, 1976; Integrated Rural Survey Basic Report, 1977.

Table 6   Sex Ratios and Percentage of Female-Headed Smallholder Households by Province, 1974-75

Province	Sex Ratio	Women-Headed HH as % of all HH	Total # (000)	Percent of All Women-Headed HH
Central	101	23	73.8	22
Coast	86	27	18.9	6
Eastern	92	23	81.2	24
Nyanza	96	25	96.6	28
Rift	100	22	19.8	6
Western	98	19	48.4	14
Kenya	97	24	340.7	100

Source: Republic of Kenya, IRS 1974-1975: 23, 33, 52.

Table 7   Percentage Distribution of Regular Labor on Maize Among Households with Women and Men by Household Type

	Labor Inputs[1]				
	W or W+C	W+M or W+M+C	M or M+C	TOTAL %	No.
Planting					
(Household Types[2])					
Married Men	25	74	1	100	(1573)
Married Women	51	49	—	100	(59)
Unmarried Women	43	56	1	100	(130)
Total %	27	72	1	100	(1762)
Weedings					
Married Men	25	74	1	100	(1570)
Married Women	46	51	3	100	(59)
Unmarried Women	41	56	3	100	(130)
Total %	27	72	2	100	(1762)
Harvesting					
Married Men	27	72	1	100	(1578)
Married Women	50	48	2	100	(60)
Unmarried Women	44	55	1	100	(130)
Total %	29	70	1	100	(1768)

Table 7 (Continued) Percent Distribution of the Regular Labor on Maize Among Households with Women and Men by Household Type

	Labor Inputs [1]				
	W or *W + C*	*W + M or* *W + M + C*	*M or* *M + C*	*TOTAL* %	*No.*

1. Labor inputs are classified as women or women and children, women and men or women, men and children, men or men and children. Inputs of children in this survey were low, so results reveal more about adult workers.
2. Household types reflect household heads. Married-men households incude those with men present. Women-headed households include married women with absent husbands or unmarried women, usually widows.
Source: Carolyn Barnes, "Differentiation by Sex among Smallscale Farming Households in Kenya," p. 43. Nairobi, Kenya, USAID, n.d.

Table 8 Percentage Distribution of Regular Labor on Pyrethrum, Coffee, Tea and Cotton Among Households with Women and Men by Household Type

	W or *W + C*	*W + M or* *W + M + C*	*M or* *M + C*	*TOTAL* %	*No.*
Weeding					
Married Men	19	74	7	100	(664)
Married Women	58	32	10	100	(19)
Unmarried Women	26	66	8	100	(61)
Total %	21	72	7	100	(744)
Harvesting					
Married Men	19	77	4	100	(648)
Married Women	55	59	6	100	(18)
Unmarried Women	25	70	5	100	(61)
Total %	20	75	5	100	(727)

Source: Carolyn Barnes, "Differentiation by Sex among Smallscale Farming Households in Kenya," p. 44. Nairobi, Kenya, USAID, n.d.

Table 9 Percentage Distribution of Labor: Grazing Livestock and Fetching Wood Among Households with Women and Men by Household Type

	W or *W + C*	*W + M or* *W + M + C*	*M or* *M + C*	*TOTAL* %	*No.*
Grazing Cattle					
Married Men	26	27	47	100	(758)
Married Women	43	7	50	100	(30)
Unmarried Women	37	19	44	100	(62)
Total %	28	25	47	100	(850)
Fetching Wood					
Married Men	97	2	1	100	(159)
Married Women	97	3	—	100	(59)
Unmarried Women	97	3	—	100	(134)
Total %	97	2	1	100	(1784)

Source: Carolyn Barnes, "Differentiation by Sex among Smallscale Farming Households in Kenya," p. 45. Nairobi, Kenya, USAID, n.d.

Table 10   Educational Attainment in Three Age Groups (1977)

Schooling	Percentage 20-24 Years F	M	Percentage 35-39 Years F	M	Percentage 60-64 Years F	M
None	40	16	77	40	96	83
1-2 Years (Primary)	2	3	3	3	1	4
3-8 Years (Primary)	42	51	18	46	2	11
1-4 Years (Secondary)	14	28	1	9	—	1
5+ Years (Secondary)	1	1	—	1	—	1

Source: Unpublished data from the 1977 National Demographic Survey, Kenya.

Table 11   Egerton College: Placement of 1975 Class: MOA Sponsored Graduates

	Research Division	AHITA/ Bukura Institutes	Extension [1] Vet	LMD	An. Prod.	Other	Subtotal	Total
Agricultural Education		2				3	3	5
Agriculture (General)	10	1				17	17	28
Animal Science	7		20	5	6		31	38
Range Management	4	2			3	19	22	28
Home Economics						13	13	13
Farm Management	5					26	26	31
Horticulture	5					9	9	14
Agricultural Engineering						26	26	26
Dairy Technology			3				3	3
TOTALS	31	5	23	8	6	113	150	186
Percent	16.6%	2.7%	12.3%	4.3%	3.2%	60.8%	0.7%	

MOA/Total Egerton Graduates: 82%

1. LMD: Livestock Marketing Division
   An. Prod.: Animal Production
   Other: Includes Training and Extension Division, Food Crops Division, Land & Farm Management Division, Range Management Division, Industrial Crops Division, Horiculture Division. Graduates are mainly posted as Division Agricultural Officers and District Level Staff (TO).
   NB: The 1975 Class graduated in March 1978. (Class intake was in 1975.)

Table 12   Shortfalls in Training Output (Cumulative from 1977)

| | 1983 | | | 1988 | | |
	BSc	Dipl	Cert	BSc	Dipl	Cert
Low Effective Demand						
Output Required	1,136	1,782	6,390	2,350	3,876	14,052
Output at Current Rate	900	1,500	2,250	1,650	2,750	4,150
Shortfall	236	282	4,140	700	1,126	9,902
High Effective Demand						
Output Required	1,361	2,100	7,641	2,899	4,468	16,830
Output at Current Rate	900	1,500	2,250	1,650	2,750	4,150
Shortfall	461	600	5,391	1,249	1,718	12,680

Source: ATAC. Tables 11 and 13, pp. 43 and 45.

Table 13   Demand for Diploma Holders By Selected Area of Specialty. Agricultural Sector Request and Projected Graduates[1]

Areas of Specialty	Additional Request 1977-1988	Egerton Graduates 1977-1988	Excess (Shortfall)
Crop and Livestock Production[2]	940	691	(249)
Education[3]	185	468	283
Farm Management	983	348	(635)
Agricultural Engineering[4]	81	365	284
Animal Husbandry	732	437	(295)
Veterinary Medicine (Animal Health)	222	60	(162)

1. Unadjusted staff requests from ATAC Survey Data. See ATAC Report, Section II-D, for further comments. Does not include management/administrative specialties.
2. General Agriculture, Horticulture, Range Management.
3. Agricultural Education and Home Economics. NB: Survey data *does not* include Ministry of Education requirements and these are expected to be massive as agricultural education in secondary schools is to be greatly expanded assuming this recommendation of the National Commission on Education Objectives and Policies is implemented.
4. Additional requests considered to be unrealistically low. Other GOK estimates and extreme difficulties faced by employers seeking Egerton graduates suggest that demand is underestimated by a factor of ten.

Source: USAID/Kenya.

Table 14   Egerton College Projected Enrollment and Graduation (Month and Year)

Diploma Stream	CURRENT Enroll.	CURRENT Grad.	9/1981 Enroll.	7/1982 Grad.	9/1982 Enroll.	7/1983 Grad.	9/1983 Enroll.	7/1984 Grad.	9/1984 Enroll.	7/1985 Grad.	9/1985 Enroll.	7/1986 Grad.
Agriculture	72	28	76	22	88	22	96	30	96	30	96	30
Agricultural Education	90	40	90	28	90	28	110	29	130	28	150	48
Agricultural Engineering	80	25	102	26	123	26	192	46	240	46	288	91
Animal Husbandry	130	40	136	42	143	42	164	47	178	47	192	61
Animal Health	—	—	16	—	32	—	64	15	80	15	96	30
Dairy Technology	31	7	40	8	50	8	72	19	84	19	96	30
Food Technology	—	—	24	5	40	5	72	19	84	19	96	30
Farm Management	106	31	110	32	115	32	130	38	140	38	150	48
Home Economics	49	13	55	16	62	16	78	22	87	22	96	30
Horticulture	55	14	77	16	100	16	142	39	161	39	180	57
Range Management	81	8	86	25	91	25	128	31	160	31	192	61
Total	695	227	812	220	934	220	1,248	334	1,440	334	1,632	516

Table 15 Projected Staffing of Egerton College

	Current	9-79	9-80	9-81	9-82	9-83	9-84	Total New Hires/ Temporary Staff
1. LECTURES								
Lecturers in Residence[1]	42	32	29	33	46	61	76	
Lecturers in Training	—	22	37	40	27	13	—	139 PY
U.S. Teaching Staff	—	16	22	22	18	8	—	86 PY
Total Lecturers in Residence[2]	42	48	51	55	64	69	76	
Total Lecturers on Permanent Staff	42	54	66	73	73	74	76	
New Lecturers Hired	—	12	12	7	—	1	1	33
2. DEMONSTRATORS								
In Residence	19	25	28	37	45	55	57	
New Demonstrators Hired	—	6	3	9	8	10	2	38
3. ADMINISTRATIVE STAFF								
Senior Staff	11	12	13	15	17	17	19	8
Junior Staff[3]	98	108	110	130	150	160	177	79
4. PLANT STAFF[4]	335	350	380	450	475	500	524	189

1. Kenyan permanent staff.
2. Kenyan permanent staff plus U.S. Teaching staff.
3. Includes technicians, laboratory assistants, nurses, secretaries, typists, messengers.
4. Includes cooks, drivers, foremen, laborers, sweepers, security.

Table 16 Egerton College Project Component Financing

Financing ($'000')		AID	GOK	TOTAL
Grant:	Technical Assistance/			
	Implementation	$ 8,366	$ 5,864	$14,230
	Staff Training	2,379	43	2,422
	Subtotal	10,745	5,907	16,652
Loan:	Construction/Equipment	23,558	5,472	29,030
TOTAL		$34,303	$11,379	$45,682

Table 17 Women as a Percentage of Egerton College Students

CLASS of 1975	CLASS of 1976	CLASS of 1977	PROJECTED of 1983
13.7%	15.1%	20.3%	30%

Table 18 Student Numbers by Courses and Countries of Origin as of 14 September 1983

COURSE	KENYA								OTHER COUNTRIES								G. TOTAL	
	1981		1982		1983		TOTAL		1981		1982		1983		TOTAL			
	M	F	M	F	M	F	M	F	M	F	M	F	M	F	M	F	M	F
Agriculture	25	3	38	6	31	11	94	20	1	—	—	—	—	—	1	—	95	20
Agric. Education	28	12	34	14	39	5	101	31	—	—	—	—	—	—	—	—	101	31
Soil & Water Engineering	23	1	41	1	20	3	84	5	—	—	—	—	—	—	—	—	84	5
Farm Power & Machinery	23	1	31	—	31	—	85	1	—	—	1	—	—	—	1	—	86	1
Animal Husbandry	36	2	51	5	44	10	131	17	3	1	1	—	1	—	5	1	136	18
Animal Health	21	—	31	1	32	5	84	6	2	—	2	—	2	—	6	—	90	6
Farm Management	39	2	47	3	35	11	121	16	1	—	1	—	1	—	3	—	124	16
Horticulture	18	5	20	14	23	15	61	34	—	1	—	—	—	—	—	1	61	35
Dairy Technology	22	2	22	4	23	3	67	9	2	1	4	—	—	—	6	1	73	10
Food Science & Technology	14	4	14	2	8	6	36	12	—	—	2	—	—	—	2	—	38	12
Agriculture & Food Marketing	—	—	13	2	20	3	33	5	—	—	—	—	1	—	1	—	34	5
Agriculture & Home Economics	—	29	—	38	—	34	—	101	—	—	—	—	—	—	—	—	—	101
Wildlife & Management	16	2	10	1	7	1	33	4	—	—	—	—	—	—	—	—	33	4
Ranch Management	16	—	17	—	17	—	50	—	—	—	—	—	—	—	—	—	50	—
Range Management	34	—	40	—	41	—	115	—	—	—	1	—	1	—	2	—	117	—
Forestry	—	—	28	—	26	2	54	2	—	—	—	—	—	—	—	—	54	2
TOTAL	315	63	437	91	397	109	1149	263	9	3	12	—	6	—	27	3	1176	266
	378		528		506		1412		12		12		6		30		1442	
Women as % of Total	17%		17%		22%		19%		25%		—		—		12%		18%	

Information supplied directly by Egerton College Administration, October, 1983.

Table 19   Applications to Egerton Received by May 1983 by Field

	Applications			Accepted	
1. Agriculture	245 M	65 F		22 M	4 F
				9%	6%
			Total[1]	31	11
2. Education	74 M	41 F		18 M	5 F
				24%	12%
			Total	39	5
3. Agriculture and Food Marketing	90 M	25 F		22 M	3 F
				24%	12%
			Total	20	3
4. Home Economics	0 M	109 F		0 M	24 F
				—	22%
			Total		34
5. Animal Husbandry	110 M	30 F		37 M	9 F
				34%	30%
			Total	44	10
6. Animal Health	153 M	33 F		27 M	4 F
				18%	12%
			Total	32	5
7. Dairy Technology	47 M	9 F		17 M	1 F
				36%	11%
			Total	23	3
8. Food Science and Technology	260 M	95 F		8 M	2 F
				3%	2%
			Total	8	6
9. Farm Management	130 M	15 F		23 M	4 F
				18%	27%
			Total	35	11
10. Farm Power and Machinery	195 M	3 F		30 M	0 F
				15%	—
			Total	31	—
11. Forestry	82 M	10 F		—	—
			Total	26	2
12. Horticulture	63 M	33 F		15 M	7 F
				24%	21%
			Total	23	15
13. Soil and Water Engineering	137 M	12 F		25 M	1 F
				18%	8%
			Total	20	3
14. Range Management	89 M	6 F		30 M	0 F
				34%	—
			Total	41	—
15. Wildlife Management	29 M	3 F		8 M	1 F
				28%	33%
			Total	7	1
16. Ranch Management	no figures		no figures		
			Total	17	0

1. Total finally admitted in 1983 class.

APPENDIXES

Appendix A
Detailed Description of Capital Component
of Project Activity at Egerton College

Egerton College is situated approximately 10 miles west-south-west of Nakuru (headquarters for Rift Valley Province) on the foot hills of the Mau Escarpment, a fertile agricultural region of the Rift Valley. The altitude is approximately 7,400 feet above sea level. The College controls nearly 4,000 acres, most of which is agricultural land including Tatton and Ngong Ogeri Farms; the campus and residential areas occupying approximately 300 acres, containing approximately 4,700 people, including 686 students, teaching staff with families, administration staff and services staff with their families. Tatton Farm, approximately 1,000 acres, serves as the main teaching and experimental farm. Ngong Ogeri farm, approximately 2,700 acres, is run on commercial lines to generate income for the College and is used for the purpose of additional student demonstrations. The College has also leased 1,200 acres of land at Chemeron, Baringo District. This land is used for research and the training of students in Animal Production and Ranch Management.

Water supply for the campus is from bore holes located on grounds controlled by the College. Waste water treatment is by oxidization ponds or septic tanks depending upon the location of buildings. Electric power is supplied by the East African Power & Lighting Company and telephone service is maintained by Kenya Posts and Telecommunications.

Access to the campus is from the main (bitumen surfaced) Njoro-Narok road. This road also provides access to Tatton Farm. Various bitumen surfaced and gravel roads link the old campus (teaching and administration buildings) with Halls of Residences, Dining Hall, Tatton Farm and the Engineering Department.

To avoid wasteful use of good arable and pasture land for building development, which would at the same time provide an undesirable extension of the campus area, an increase in the density of the established campus area is proposed. The close relationship between residential halls, the teaching facilities, and farmland is maintained. The design of new facilities includes provision of adequate water supply, waste water treatment, electrical supply, telephone services and roads.

1. Renovations/improvements on existing facilities.
   A team of local consultants, engaged by the college, and Professor H. James Miller, of the University of Illinois, Urbana, undertook a detailed review of existing facilities. The majority of existing buildings are constructed of stone walls with pitched roofs of wood shingles, iron sheets, abestos sheets or roofing felt. The description of existing improvements/renovations is as follows:

   A. Animal Science Department (533 square meters, 1 building):
      The existing plumbing, gas supply, ventilation, fire fighting and electrical systems will be upgraded.

   B. Agriculture Engineering Department (1,000 square meters, 2 buildings):
      Relocate grain driers from the Processing room to Tatton Farm Barn and use the Processing room for other food processing, e.g., coffee and maize meal. The layout of the metal workshop will be modified to add more equipment. The woodwork workshop will be upgraded to woodwork machine shop. The farm machinery workshop will be converted to woodwork workshop. The electrical, fire fighting, and ventilation system will be upgraded.

The existing drawing room will be connected to the soil water conservation workshop/laboratory and renovated as water resources laboratory. The electrical, plumbing, fire fighting and ventilation systems will be upgraded. Ceiling will be repaired.

C. Crop Production Department (555 square meters, 1 bulding):
   The existing roof finish of the building will be repaired. Also, plumbing, fire fighting and electrical systems will be upgraded. The biology laboratory will be converted into two botany laboratories.

D. Biology Department (828 square meters, 1 building):
   The plumbing, electrical, gas, and ventilation systems will be upgraded. The biology laboratory will be converted into two botany laboratories.

E. Lecture Hall (538 square meters, 1 building):
   The plumbing, ventilation, and fire fighting systems will be upgraded. The existing roofing felt, including ceiling, will also be replaced.

F. Studies Department/General Classrooms (624 square meters, 1 building):
   The plumbing, ventilation, fire fighting, and electrical systems will be upgraded. Approximately 50 percent of the roof (wood-shingles), will be replaced.

G. Education Department and Extension Center for African Family Studies (440 square meters, 1 building):
   The plumbing, fire fighting, and electrical systems will be upgraded. Approximately 50 percent of existing roof (wood shingles) will be replaced.

H. Assembly Hall (1,286 square meters, 1 building):
   The plumbing, fire fighting, and electrical systems will be upgraded. The existing roofing felt will be replaced.

I. Economics and Range Departments (305 square meters, 1 building):
   The plumbing, electrical and fire fighting systems will be upgraded. The roofing (wood shingles) and ceiling will be replaced.

J. Administration Block (454 square meters, 1 building):
   The electrical, plumbing and fire fighting systems will be upgraded.

K. Transport Workshop (331 square meters, 1 building):
   The building will be remodelled to be used as Machine Workshop for the Agricultural Engineering Department.

L. Block "B" Dean's Office (340 square meters, 1 building):
   The building will be fully renovated (plumbing, fire fighting, electrical, roofing, ceiling).

M. Junior Common Room (502 square meters, 1 building):
   The roofing felt and ceiling will be replaced. The floor and walls will be repaired as necessary.

N. Students' Dining Hall and Kitchen (Kennedy Hall) (1,110 square meters):
   This building will be renovated and used as a students' common room.

O. Halls of Residences
   (i)   Men - One building 1,600 square meters, consisting of 55 rooms
   (ii) Women - One building 1,403 square meters, consisting of 52 rooms

(iii) Men - Three buildings 4,041 square meters, each building consisting of 64 rooms

(iv) One link block consisting of 16 rooms, 334 square meters

The plumbing, fire fighting and electrical systems will be upgraded. Existing roof (wood shingles) and ceiling will be replaced.

P. Staff Housing - Total area 19,032 square meters

(i)	Senior Staff	72	3-bedroom
		7	3-bedroom houses (under construction)
		4	Apartments
(ii)	Middle Staff	18	2-bedroom houses
(iii)	Junior Staff	44	2-bedroom houses
		28	2-bedroom houses without electricity
(iv)	Subordinate Staff	29	1-room temporary
		66	1-room temporary
		*71	1-room (thatch roof)
		5	1-room

*71 houses to be demolished as they are considered unhygenic.

Electricity will be provided for 28, 2-bedroom houses. All houses will be repaired as necessary.

Q. Tatton Farm: Demonstration Farm, 2, 415 square meters):
Will be remodelled as necessary

2. Existing facilities required no renovation

A. Chemistry Department (507 square meters, 1 building)

B. Home Economics Department (894 square meters, 1 building)

C. Food Science and Technology Department (1,227 square meters, 1 building)

D. Dairy Department (524 square meters, 1 building)

E. Medical Unit (553 square meters, 1 building, 20 bed capacity)

F. Library (620 square meters, 1 building)

Appendix B
Egerton College

U.S. Technical Assistance: Teaching Staff

Department Teaching Specialities:
1. Animal Science:	3 Technicians for	10 PY
2. Biology:	3 Technicians for	9 PY
3. Chemistry:	2 Technicians for	6 PY
4. Crops:	2 Technicians for	2 PY
5. Economics:	1 Technicians for	2 PY
6. Education:	3 Technicians for	10 PY
7. Home Economics:	2 Technicians for	4 PY
8. Range Management:	2 Technicians for	4 PY
9. Agricultural Engineering:	8 Technicians for	28 PY
10. Administrative/Procurement Officer:		5 PY

NB: Dairy Technology assistance being funded by DANIDA.

Appendix C
Egerton College

Participant Training

1. Animal Science:	6 Participants for **18** person years
2. Biology:	3 Participants for **15** person years
3. Chemistry:	4 Participants for **15** person years
4. Crops:	5 Participants for **15** person years
5. Economics	3 Participants for **6** person years
6. Education:	4 Participants for **12** person years
7. Home Economics:	4 Participants for **11** person years
8. Range Management:	2 Participants for **7** person years
9. Agricultural Engineering:	12 Participants for **48** person years
TOTAL:	43 Participants for **139** person years

SOURCES

1. American Technical Assistance Corporation. *Professional and Subprofessional Agricultural Manpower in Kenya,* March 1978.

2. Barnes, Carolyn. "Differentiation by Sex among Smallscale Farming Households in Kenya," forthcoming in Special Issue of *Rural Africans.*

3. Fleuret, Patrick and Greeley, Ned. "The Kenya Social and Institutional Profile," USAID/Kenya, Program Office, May 1982.

4. USAID/Kenya. Kenya Agricultural System Support Project Paper, Volumes 1 and 2.

5. Pala-Okeya, Dr. Achola. IDS, University of Nairobi, in private discussions regarding her research on Kenyan women's work.

6. Staudt, Kathleen Ann. "Agricultural Policy, Political Power, and Women Farmers in Western Kenya," PhD Thesis, 1976.

CHAPTER EIGHT

Dominican Republic: Program For Development of Micro-Enterprises

Prepared by Susan M. Sawyer and
Catherine Overholt

CONTENTS

I. **Country and Project Background**

A. Historical Background to Structural Unemployment
B. Unemployment and Underemployment Statistics
C. Projected Labor Demands for the Dominican Republic
D. Economic Activities within the Small Scale Enterprise (SSE) Sector

II. **Context for Women**

A. Gender Division of Labor
B. Family Structure

III. **Project Description**

A. Institution Background
B. Project Objectives
C. Project Identification
D. Components
E. Project Implementation
F. Progress at Midpoint Evaluation

Jeffrey Ashe, Senior Associate Director of ACCION International/AITEC, shut off the slide projector and turned to his desk. As a result of a query about women's involvement in the PISCES project, Jeff had been reviewing the pictorial history of the ACCION/AITEC assisted PISCES demonstration project in the Dominican Republic.

The slide series provided background information on the program and illustrated how successful the project had been at reaching entrepreneurs among poor urban dwellers. But Jeff wondered how well these slides represented the program participants. Only a few women borrowers were shown. The project statistics themselves did not reveal much more information about women's involvement since they had not been disaggregated by gender. However, Jeff thought much useful information regarding women's project involvement could be brought together and he began to systematically review project documents.

I. COUNTRY AND PROJECT BACKGROUND

A. Historical Background to Structural Unemployment

The social composition of most Latin American societies has been determined in part by four centuries of colonization by the Spanish, Portugese, English, French and Dutch. The strongest European influence in the Dominican Republic was that of Spain, which imposed Catholic tradition on more varied traditions. However, the influence of pre-Colombian and African civilizations as well as the experience of slavery resulted in a tremendous variation in the acceptance of European values.

The Spanish conquered the island toward the end of the Fifteenth Century and established a plantation economy based on sugar cane. In part because of the nature of the heavy labor requirements, African slave labor was imported. When the colonizers immigrated to richer lands, the sugar plantations lost their vitality, and systems of large cattle-raising farms which did not require slave labor and exploitation of precious woods were introduced. These were the dominant forms of agriculture in the Dominican Republic until the late 19th Century, and are in part responsible for the nation's present economic structure.

In the early 1800's the government abolished slavery and initiated agrarian reform with the objective of expanding agricultural production for internal consumption and export. The production for export included the development of coffee, cacao, and tobacco, as well as the continued production of sugar and beef cattle. These plantation export crops required large numbers of laborers on a seasonal basis at low cost. Although there were 12,000 ex-slaves living on the Spanish part of the island, 90 percent of them were employed as domestic servants. Consequently, the government required people who did not have a means of subsistence in urban and semi-urban areas to go to the interior to work the land. In addition, it promoted the immigration of North American Blacks. Between 1824 and 1828, approximately 13,000 North-American Black men were introduced into the Dominican economy as agricultural laborers.

During the latter part of the 19th and early part of the 20th centuries, the sugar industry began to employ imported Haitian labor at lower costs. By 1938, there were an estimated 20,000 Haitians working in the sugar cane fields. For that same year, other estimates indicated that 60,000 Haitians, including workers' families, were employed in agricultural work. Between 1967-70, the number of Haitian workers on Dominican sugar farms was estimated at 39,418, and three-fourths of them were permanent residents of the Dominican Republic.

Dominican agricultural workers have come to regard cane-cutting as an undesirable occupation—a conclusion based in part on the difficult conditions in which cane-cutters are forced to live during their seasonal work. Due to the profund prejudice which links cane-cutting to Haitians, the vast majority of poor Dominicans would rather do anything else than go to work in the cane fields. The industrial development in the Dominican Republic over the past 20-40 years has not been capable of absorbing this labor force and the D.R. has one of the highest rates of urban unemployment and underemployment in Latin America.

A dramatic effect of the displacement of Dominican agricultural workers by the migration of Haitian labor for seasonal agricultural tasks in the Dominican Republic is illustrated by the differences between urban and rural population growth rates. Between 1935 and 1950, the annual urban growth rate in the Dominican Republic was 4.3 percent. During the same years, the rate of rural population growth was 1.95 percent. Between 1960 and 1970, the urban growth rate in the Dominican Republic had risen to 6 percent, while rural growth rate dropped to 1.4 percent. During the decade of the seventies, the rural growth rate decreased to only 0.3 percent, while that of the urban areas was 1.8 percent.

B. Unemployment and Underemployment Statistics

During the period 1960-1970, men represented a total of 88.2 percent of the labor force and women only 12.2 percent. In these years, the female labor force in urban areas increased by 8.5 percent, while that of males increased by only 5.1 percent. About 35 percent of women in the active labor force of the Dominican Republic were classified under the category of "not well-defined occupations" in the

1970 Dominican Census. A 1974 Ministry of Public Health Survey illustrates the difficulty of translating work activities into occupations. Eight percent of the surveyed women indicated that they had "remunerated work of any type," and 2 percent stated that they were without jobs (see Table 1). However, when asked about their type of work, 16 percent of the women named an activity.

Official statistics from the 1970 census show a 22.7 percent urban unemployment figure for men and 26.2 percent unemployment for women. Tables 2-3 provide employment and unemployment profiles for the country. An ILO study of unemployment in Santo Domingo in February of 1973 emphasized the unequal distribution between men and women in the unemployment statistics. The incidence of unemployment among women was 30 percent, as opposed to 15 percent for men in that year. However, these labor force statistics typically underrate the proportion of women in the labor force.

The sub-employment rate for the Dominican Republic, defined as paid work for only part of each week, has been estimated to be close to 40 percent in the urban areas. A 66 percent subemployment is registered for those with no formal schooling.

C. Projected Labor Demands For The Dominican Republic

The most recent review of labor statistics for the Dominican Republic projects labor demands to the year 1990. The projections indicate that 916,000 jobs (or 60,000 jobs per year) will be needed by 1990 in order to keep the majority of the population actively participating in the economy.

> "If the Dominican economy performs as it did in the last two decades, it will not be possible to provide productive employment to more than a minor fraction of the new contingents which will be added every year to the labor force; consequently, the number of unemployed and underemployed people will continue to rise, arriving at more than a million, probably near to a million and a half (around 60 percent of the active population) in 1990. Applying the respective rates observed in recent years, that number of people will be distributed in 500 to 600 thousand 'open unemployed' and 750 to 900 thousand underemployed in 1990. It should be emphasized that this will take place in spite of the fact that in the period under study the growth rate of the active population will be in a process of descent, caused principally by the disminuition of fertility initiated twenty years ago."[1]

It is the structural nature of the unemployment produced by an earlier unequal development among the sectors of the economy which has now produced a need for innovative programs for generating employment and increased incomes among thousands of illiterate and semi-literate migrants to the cities. The sectors of the economy which have been most able to absorb great numbers of unemployed have been the informal and service sectors. The Program for the Development of Micro-enterprises aimed to strengthen the informal sector.

D. Economic Activities within the Small Scale Enterprise (SSE) Sector

The economic activities of the SSE or "informal sector" in Santo Domingo range from businesses which sell charcoal in their neighborhoods to coffee and food stands which sell to workers leaving for work at five in the morning, and to small beauty parlors or general stores in homes. Table 4 shows the involvement of men and women in informal sector activities.

In Santo Domingo, men run small grocery stores, butcher shops, or small stands where they sell ices or ice creams. Men are seldom found selling hot prepared food on the street corner or charcoal in the neighborhoods. Most men working the the informal sector in Santo Domingo, however, prefer to operate micro-businesses in a mobile fashion, using heavy cargo tricycles called "triciclos". At the lower levels of investment, it is generally possible to make more money per amount invested by operating one of these cargo tricycles than by having a stationary business. Aside from the greater flexibility in terms of markets offered by the tricycles, the vendor changes his products according to seasonal prices in the central market, the amount of working capital on hand, and his daily survey of the buyers' market.

Women in Santo Domingo do not operate cargo tricycles. One reason may be because of the weight of the tricycles with their load. Men who have done this work for years develop kidney problems after years of the heavy work involved. It is not known whether there are other strictly cultural obstacles to women entering this type of informal sector activity. The relationship of men and women to specific kinds of businesses changes, however, in different cities on the island, where there is often greater poverty and an even wider range of occupations.

II. CONTEXT FOR WOMEN

A. Gender Division of Labor

Industrial development in the Dominican Republic has been largely capital intensive, producing intense competition for jobs in the modern sector. Table 5 shows an employment profile for Santo

Domingo in 1974, and Table 6 shows a breakdown of the occupational categories which absorbed women in Santo Domingo in 1974. The service sector absorbed 61 percent of rural migrant women in that year. The use of a broad classification system for registering occupations tends to hide the true dimension of the gender division of labor in the Dominican Republic. At least one investigator who has studied the effect of these classifications suggests that many women classified as retail workers, office workers, as well as workers in the industrial and manufacturing sectors, are probably most often occupied in cleaning and other service work. Women workers themselves may exacerbate the confusion if it is more prestigious for a woman to say that she works in an office or in a factory than to say that she scrubs floors. Under the categories of machine operators and artisans, most women are seamstresses or dressmakers. Since 1969, most of those registered as machine operators are seamstresses working at low wages in the factories of the new Free Trade Zone in the Dominican Republic.

The general pressure on the existing jobs is increased by the rapid urbanization and monetization of the economy. These factors heighten the need for women to earn an income and contribute cash to the families' revenue stream. In addition, there are growing numbers of households in which women are the primary source of income. For the Central American and Caribbean countries, on average, 20 percent of households are women-headed. Among barrio women in Santo Domingo, 21 percent of households report that a woman is the household head; among women factory workers, 52 percent are heads of households.

For lower-income women in the Dominican Republic, a primary source of income is in the so-called informal sector activities. Many categories of women's work never appear in national income accounts, and these include both household services and informal sector activities.

B. Family Structure

Different kinds of conjugal unions exist in the D.R. as elsewhere, but "the economic position of both individuals exerts an important influence on the type and endurance of a conjugal union." The ideal of legal marriage and a male supported family is realized only among middle and upper class families. The patriarchal family ideal remains dominant for many reasons, including respectability, status, and economic stability. In the event that the wife must work to add to the family income, the husband must give the wife permission, especially for work outside the home. Many times, such permission is provided reluctantly, even if the women enjoy their work. For examle, in one study of women who worked outside the home, 45 percent of the women declared that their husbands disapproved. However, 30 percent of these women also said, "My husband does not like it, but we need the money."

When the man cannot provide the financial support necessary for family survival, new patterns of union for men and women occur. These may include regular living arrangements without the sanction of marriage, more casual but regular "visiting unions," or a pattern of successive male partners among some women. Several studies have documented that poor women in the Dominican Republic who have a pattern of consensual union change partners frequently and are far more likely to be the primary economic support of the family over a long period of time. For many low-income women who are entrepreneurs, their economic situation is such that they do not want to give up independence in economic decision making, so they faithfully carry out many household activities, such as cooking and laundering, which the man expects. A woman may wish to remain independent in order to maintain her own property, to be free to move to a different location to better her trade, or to decide on her own with whom she should leave her children if she has to go to a distant place to bring more income into her family.

One study concludes that the pattern of having successive husbands emerged as a very adaptive pattern for lower-class women in the Dominican Republic for exactly those reasons. Some women entrepreneurs live with women relatives, so as to have someone to care for their children when they need to travel for business reasons. One example of this pattern was a woman in her late thirties who had a tiny sewing business on the outskirts of Santo Domingo. However, during the spring, she traveled regularly to small towns in the interior to sell her clothes to the Haitians who came for the cane-cutting harvests. This woman's mother lived with her and stayed with the children whenever she travelled. The entrepreneur explained that a good part of her profit was derived from this secondary market, and it would soon allow her to expand into a second business.

III. PROJECT DESCRIPTION

A. Institutional Background to the Project

The initiative for the Micro-Enterprise Project of the Dominican Development Foundation evolved from the first phase of a larger Project called PISCES (The Program for Investment in the Small Capital Enterprise Sector). The Project was funded by the USAID Office of Urban Development. The main contractor for PISCES was an independent non-profit organization called ACCION International/ AITEC. Portions of the project were sub-contracted to two other non-profit organizations—The Development Group for Alternative Policies, and Partnership for Productivity.

Phase I of PISCES carried out research in 16 countries to identify the most adequate methodologies for assisting small scale economic activities of the urban poor. Under the requirements for Phase II of the PISCES Project, each of the three contracting organizations had to develop and evaluate two "demonstration projects" to show that such assistance could be effectively carried out through existing AID funding mechanisms. As the principal contractor, ACCION/AITEC intended to lead the way with a project that could be quickly grasped, implemented and proven effective. The demonstration projects were to be based on the research results of the first phase of the PISCES Project. These projects represented an institutional priority which gave assistance to the local implementing organization that funding would be forthcoming. Two other organizations which were interested in the design of the demonstration projects also helped to complete the funding.

The terms of the PISCES Project defined the maximum investment level of economic activities to be assisted, but did not specifically define which members of the small scale enterprise sector should be targeted or what form the assistance should take. The terms of the contract focused on developing mechanisms through which large numbers of SSE entrepreneurs could receive credit at low cost. It was left to the three contracted organizations for the PISCES Project to define the most appropriate target beneficiaries and the most appropriate methodology for assisting them.

Another set of constraints imposed on the design and implementation of the demonstration project related to the timing requirements for evaluation. Phase II of the PISCES Project required all the contracted organizations to have two projects implemented so that their impact could be evaluated. With a relatively short time to develop a project which would provide a convincing demonstration, ACCION had to find a target population which would lend itself to rapid project development with noticeable impact. A truly notable project would illustrate that ACCION's way of doing things provided a realistic response to the international debate regarding appropriate development strategies for the future.

The Program for Developent of Micro-Enterprise (PRODEME) was begun by the Dominican Development Foundation (DDF) in Santo Domingo in 1981, with a grant of US $500,000 Dollars from USAID/ Dominican Republic to generate income and employment among the poorest inhabitants in the urban centers of the Dominican Republic. The grant provided for technical assistance from ACCION International/AITEC to help design and provide assistance in the implementation of the program.

The Dominican Development Foundation is a non-profit institution which is financed by the private sector of the Dominican Republic. It had a long history of administering a broad credit program and implementing programs of economic and social development among the most marginal groups in the Dominican Republic. DDF's experience in dealing with credit and with international financing mechanisms were important aspects for the overall institutional setting of the project, and the institution came to be known among project participants as a very special kind of local bank. However, before this project, the DDF had only had experience with rural projects. Moving into urban areas was new for them.

B. Project Objectives

The objectives of PRODEME were:
1. to increase income among the poor;
2. to create new jobs;
3. to strengthen precarious jobs.

These objectives were a direct response to four major findings of a feasibility study carried out by the DDF with technical assistance from ACCION International/AITEC. The feasibility study, carried out by door-to-door surveys in 4 barrios of Santo Domingo and 6 secondary cities, revealed that micro-entrepreneurs in the Dominican Republic:

(a) did not have financing opportunities appropriate to their needs since traditional sources of financing directed their resources toward sectors of the national economy which offered more security and profit for their investments;

(b) have not received technical assistance from either the public or the private sector;

(c) were managed with an investment of less than $8,300 and employed six or less persons.

(d) had potential to improve the productivity of their businesses as well as generate new employment with a program of social promotion and technical assistance for business administration, management, and financing.

The PRODEME program was to direct credit and technical assistance to the smallest scale economic activities among the urban poor. The idea was to strengthen the economic viability of what people were already doing rather than teach new skills or create new activities for earning a living.

C. Project Identification

In Santo Domingo, 77 percent of the enterprises identified in the feasibility study qualified for the PRODEME Program, according to criteria established for the number of employees and level of total investment. Of the enterprises identified in the secondary cities, 87 percent also qualified. Fifty-six percent of these microenterprises were in commerce, 26 percent in services and 18 percent in manufacturing. A sample of 322 of the services and manufacturing businesses was selected and studied in depth. Commerce businesses were excluded because it was assumed that loans to commerces would not result in new jobs.

The in-depth study focused on the need for credit which would be met by the program. Three percent of the microenterprises in the in-depth study were owned by women, and the majority were seamstresses.

D. Components

The project had two major components: the Micro-Enterprise component and the Solidarity Group component. Each component was directed toward providing appropriate credit and technical assistance to small-scale enterprises, according to the size and characteristics of the businesses (see Table 7).

1. The Micro-Enterprise Component

This component provided management assistance and gave loans of between US$250 and US$3,500 to small production and service businesses such as tailors, shoemakers, mechanical repair shops, bakeries, etc. The objective was to increase the income to owners of these businesses and to create new jobs. To be accepted as a client for this part of the program, an entrepreneur had to:

a) be 18 years old or older;

b) be willing to receive management assistance;

c) have a minimum of one year's experience in the business;

d) have the potential of expanding the business and creating new jobs;

e) have a capital investment of less then US$8,300;

f) have six employees or less.

In addition to loans, assistance included formal courses in business management, and one-on-one management assistance. Program Coordinators assigned to individual businesses helped to determine the size of loans appropriate for the enterprises and delivered formal courses on management practices. Then, through a system of weekly visits to owners, they provided suggestions for improving the management of the enterprises and reviewed the owners' follow-up of the new skills learned. It was felt that the loans granted had a better chance of being used appropriately if owners received regular, individualized management assistance.

2. The Solidarity Group Component

The Solidarity Group Component was conceived as an appropriate way of delivering credit and management assistance to the hawkers, vendors and small cottage manufacturers from the low income neighborhoods. The Solidarity Group was intended as a mechanism to guarantee loans from the DDF. The contractual basis of the loan between the DDF and the Group made each member of the Solidarity Group responsible for the repayment of the loan to the DDF. Members were registered with the Foundation as contracting members for the total group loan. The size of each person's weekly quota was designated on the registration form. Requirements for entering the Program were:

a) be at least 16 years old;

b) have at least one year of experience in the business;

c) belong to a Solidarity Group officially recognized by the Dominican Development Foundation;

d) demonstrate solidarity with other members of the Group;

e) participate in a series of presentations on Basic Social Education.

The theory behind the use of this methodology was that "peer pressure" would be sufficiently strong to ensure prompt payback on the part of each member of the Group without having to rely on any material guarantees. By assigning to the clients themselves the major part of the responsibility for promotion, selection, group formation, and payback, this method was also expected to cut administrative costs significantly. In addition, the exchange of business information between members of the Groups was expected to strengthen the rudimentary business skills taught to group members and to lead to the formation of some kind of grassroots advocacy organization.

The Solidarity Group component was initially conceived as a mechanism to enable operators of cargo tricycles to purchase their own tricycle and break the cycle of paying one-fifth of their earnings in daily tricycle rental. The largest individual loan which was possible through the Solidarity Group mechanism was fixed at RD$300 (exchange rate for December, 1980, when first loans were made was 1:1). This amount covered the payment on a new tricycle and left RD$25 for "working capital." Weekly quotas were established according to the size of the loan and the amount of saving made possible through the loan. For operators of the cargo tricycles, the fixed daily repayment was established at RD$1.20, which represented a savings of at least RD$.30/day over the fee charged by the tricycle rental agencies. The loans were to be paid in fifty-two installments of RD$7.20 per week per person. Each member of the Solidarity Group was to repay, either on a daily or a weeky basis, to the Group president who then paid the total amount to the Foundation representative at the barrio-level meetings held each week.

Solidarity Groups also were formed by the market stall vendors and the "frituueras", and they had no obvious need for new capital equipment. Loans of RD$300 were permitted for straightforward working capital needs of these groups. For the Working Capital Loans, the weekly quotas were established according to the actual amounts borrowed and were worked out between each individual entrepreneur and the coordinator assigned to the Solidarity Group's neighborhood.

Working Capital Loans represented 17 percent of the total loan portfolio, and 75 percent of these loans went to women's Solidarity Groups. The average size of loans per group was RD$1,745 and the average size of loans per individual member was RD$282. All loans were to be paid within a year's time, at an annual rate of 24 percent interest. (The annual rate of inflation for 1980, 1981, and 1982 was 14.3%, 7.5%, and 8.3% respectively.)

Important personal characteristics of the working capital and *triciclero* Solidarity Groups are profiled in Table 8.

E. Project Implementation

1. The Solidarity Groups

The idea for this part of the PRODEME Program was that the essential principles would be simple and easy to grasp, and promotion of the Program would spread by word-of-mouth. If an individual wanted to enter, that individual could join together with 5 or 6 friends from similar businesses, and together they could contract for a loan from the DDF. It was assumed that individuals would not take the risk of signing for a collective loan unless they knew the other people and their businesses. It was also assumed that the person elected to be president of the group would take the responsibility for finding reliable ways to ensure 100 percent payback on the loans each week. The weekly neighborhood-level meetings with the coordinators were partly for the payment of the weekly loan quotas by Solidarity Group presidents. In this way, it became public knowledge when a payment was missed or incomplete and added to the peer pressure which was to be the principal guarantee for loan payback.

When problems of group disintegration and late payback occurred, another requirement was added. Prospective participants were required to participate in two short courses before being allowed to register as an officially recognized Solidarity Group. The two courses had been designed specifically to correct two misconceptions which it was felt had led to irresponsible Group formation. The courses were intended to clarify for new Solidarity Groups that they were taking on a serious responsibility when they applied for a loan. If the coordinator giving the courses felt that a new Group did not demonstrate real "solidarity," the group would not be alowed to register. This was the first official "filter." The second was the analysis of each Group's application for a loan by the DDF financial credit analyst. If the coordinator or the credit analyst decided that there were potential problems in the payback of the loan, the group would not be allowed to register. When a group was rejected, individuals of the group could not reform easily into new groups since they would have to be approved by the same coordinator and credit analyst.

On their own initiative, the first Solidarity Groups who entered the Program in Santo Domingo formed an Association. The Association helped to strengthen many aspects of the Program by serving as a means of communication for all groups and providing special services to its members.

2. Staffing and Delivery Systems

Two coordinators for the Solidarity Group component and two coordinators for the Micro-Enterprise component were trained by the local AITEC Director of Technical Assistance. The director had designed and carried out the feasibility study for PRODEME. The coordinators were young men who were university students in economics. One was doing his thesis on Micro-Enterprises.

The basic tasks of the Solidarity Group coordinators were:

a) to orient and train new groups;

b) to prepare credit proposals;

c) to collect weekly loan repayments;

d) to "troubleshoot" for groups having difficulty with their loan payments.

The basic tasks of the micro-enterprise coordinators included:

a) promoting the Program and recruiting new clients;

b) carrying out financial analysis on the viability of the business and assessment of willingness to accept management assistance;

c) assisting business owners in the preparation of credit proposals and planning of a rational strategy of investment for their businesses;

d) undertaking weekly supervisory visits to each business to provide new technical assistance where needed;

e) giving regular courses on business management to new clients;

f) collecting on loan repayments.

The loan proposals from the entrepreneurs from both components were submitted to the central Credit Department of the DDF for credit analysis and approval. The DDF formed a special loan committee to serve the Solidarity Groups and the Micro-Enterprises, and expedite the processing of these smaller loans. Similarly, the Program also established a new position of a program financial credit analyst in order to make the loan processing more agile.

The new PRODEME credit analyst was specifically trained to look for weaknesses in the economic activities served by the Program. Emphasis was put on making the reviews quickly, yet thoroughly, to defend each case before the loan committee. Loan proposals which were in doubt were rejected by the analyst before they even got to the loan committee. The financial credit analyst and the loan committee were all men.

The purpose of each component of the Program affected the degree of staff contact with clients and the pace of the delivery system. For the Solidarity Groups, the principal assistance was the credit itself and orientation to clients on how to handle a formal credit system. The assistance was expected to have a positive effect on the businesses by freeing the entrepreneurs from their former dependency on informal sources of credit and exorbitant interest rates. The costs of this assistance were kept low by raising the ratio of clients to coordinators.

The emphasis of the assistance to Micro-Enterprises was on teaching business owners to use rational business strategies and to work with them closely to overcome obstacles which inhibited new business growth. Growth was expected to lead to new employment possibilities within the SSE Sector.

Several changes were made in the staffing and delivery systems during the course of the Project. Because it was often difficult for the presidents of the Solidarity Groups to enforce regular repayment by all members, various procedures were invented along the way by those implementing the Program to ensure repayment. These procedures included:

a) elimination of some members and reformation of Groups;

b) collecting from individual members rather than from the group presidents;

c) re-possessing of vendor licences and/or tricycles from all members of groups who fell too far behind in their payments.

For the Solidarity Group component, a specific recommendation was made 8 months into the program to hire a woman as a coordinator. At that time, more than 80 male street-vendors had just formed their

Association of Tricicleros. Two small groups of women also were formed and had been admitted to the Program. With their entry, other women began to come to meetings and to inquire about the Program; they made up a tiny cluster of women in a huge garage filled with tricycles and their owners. These women stated:

> "We need someone here to talk with us . . . not just now . . . every week
> . . . There are things we cannot say to the men. We are not important . . .
> so they don't listen . . ."

A few months after the recommendation was made, a woman sociologist was hired as coordinator. However, she was not assigned to work in the neighborhood where these first groups of women had joined. She was assigned to a neighborhood where a woman political leader had earlier started a broad-based women's movement and several women's groups had been formed. Misinformation and political manipulation, as well as an apparent lack of attention to the women's real economic needs had led to many of these women becoming disillusioned and dropping out. Others had over-extended themselves on the credit and were unhappy with the lack of support. In spite of this difficult beginning, the interest of women entrepreneurs began to re-emerge with the entrance of a woman coordinator. That neighborhood eventually became the center for the biggest nucleus of women in the Program. By mid-1982, there was a movement on the part of many of these women to form their own Association.

When PRODEME became a separate division with the DDF, it expanded its staff to keep pace with Program growth and to organize its operation more efficiently. Separate departments were established for each component with procedures designed to match the special needs of each. The best coordinators were moved to supervisory positions in their respective departments. New coordinators were also hired in each department to keep up with expanding workloads. No new women were hired as new coordinators.

The principal contact which the clients had with program staff was through the coordinators assigned to their Groups. They met the financial credit analyst when he reviewed their loan proposal and sometimes saw the Solidarity Group Supervisor when he made occasional visits to observe neighborhood meetings. The program director and the technical advisor each spent about 40 percent of their worktime on the Solidarity Group Component. Some of that time was spent in supervision of office procedures rather than in direct contact with the Groups.

In the second year of the program, two men coordinators were hired—one of them to work in a secondary city as the program expanded into the interior of the country. There were no tricycles in that city and women who wanted to join the program at the Solidarity Group level seemed to outnumber the men.

3. Loan Disbursement

Decisions on how loans should be disbursed were made by the loan committee and the central credit department. A long-standing DDF method of disbursing loans to marginal clients was through a purchase order system. That system required the loan client to go to a store approved by the DDF and receive a quote on the cost of what he/she wanted to buy. The loan recipient received the merchandise directly and the merchant was paid in cash or by check by DDF. Under this system, money never passed through the hands of the loan client, and merchandise had to be bought in stores approved by the DDF. The credit department felt that this ensured that the money paid out in loans was actually going for business purposes. Loans for the purchase of a major piece of capital equipment used a similar method. The possibility of repossessing the equipment itself formed the guarantee for these kinds of loans.

When a purchase order was not possible, loans were disbursed to clients by checks from the DDF directly to the client. For example, working capital loans to food vendor Solidarity Groups were disbursed directly to individual members of the Groups.

The tricicleros, 83 percent of the program clients, received a combination of capital equipment loans and working capital loans. The capital equipment loans were disbursed through payments from the DDF directly to the tricycle manufacturers. Each triciclero received a check for RD$25 for his working capital loan.

Disbursement to clients receiving only working capital loans were made as follows:

1. disbursement of loans to food vendors was by a personal check from the DDF to the individual members of the group;

2. loan disbursement to seamstresses was entirely through the purchase order system at selected stores.

The types of micro-enterprises assisted included shoemakers, mechanical repair shops, tailors, dress-makers, a printing business and a ceramic-figure shop. All of the women clients but one were dressmakers. The average amount of capital invested in their businesses was close to RD$5,000 pesos, which was in the upper range of the overall investment in the microbusinesses. Loans to the seamstresses usually were disbursed through purchase orders. Sometimes the purchase orders were combined with a cash payment often related to the purchase of capital equipment. At other times, the purchase orders were combined with direct blanket payments to the company where the women would be buying their raw materials. This mechanism depended on the arrangements that the factory outlets would permit. If payment was made directly with a blanket check, the women could choose the amount and kind of merchandise needed at that moment. If the disbursement was only through a purchase order, the merchandise had to be specified in advance and did not permit any flexibility in production or pricing. Disbursement of loans to other types of micro-enterprises relied less heavily on the purchase order system.

For the Solidarity Group enterprises, business practices had to be highly flexible and responsive to daily and seasonal fluctuations in both buyers' and sellers' markets. The regular need for small amounts of working capital was related to that factor. Tricicleros in the program gained an edge on others in the sector because their mobility and daily savings combined to make it possible to make regular shifts in product lines in direct relation to market changes. Interviews with women program participants indicated that they also responded to the same kind of subtle changes in their markets. The most successful of these entrepreneurs were those who could keep enough capital on hand to respond to such changes. The most successful seamstresses, for example, seemed to have working capital to invest in other lines of business whenever there was a poor market for home-made clothing.

"I sell most of my clothes in December . . . a few in January, I guess . . . But most of my sales fall off after that, so I make my money on doing alterations and selling other items for the home when I can.

"I always start buying beauty products after Christmas, and towels and things like that for the home. Those are about the only things I can sell then. It's a low season until late July or August. People don't have enough to get by, really, so they only buy what's necessary. I keep sewing . . . you know, making things for myself and my family with old materials. But my earnings come from the other things, especially now that you have to buy where they have the purchase order. It's not the same . . .

"Well, I get along . . . in spite of the purchase order . . . but mainly because I always plan ahead for this low season . . . I have a lot of clothes already made and I take them to Barahona . . . A lot of Haitians go there for the cane-cutting season, and they like to take fancy Dominican things back with them when they return to Haiti . . . for gifts, and to feel important. The Haitians earn money when they come here, so they feel rich and want to buy things. They are good clients for me . . . Of course, I have to have the money to take the trip. So, I plan for it and save for it. That's how I manage to do fairly well in spite of the purchase order. Naturally, I could make a lot more money if I got the loan in cash.

"With the purchase order they won't let you buy where you know you can get your supplies at a lower price. And you have to buy everything at once. So, if sales aren't good you don't have anything left to try something else . . . It's their system that doesn't work."

"I've been in business for years and this is the first time I've had to worry constantly. It's because of the purchase order. It's making me lose business because I can't buy what I need to buy when I need it."

An analysis done by the program staff indicated that clients lost about 10 percent of the value of their loans through having to use the purchase order. That estimate was probably conservative since it did not emphasize all of the losses in business resulting from the lack of flexibility in making purchases.

F. Progress at Midpoint Evaluation

During the first seventeen months, AID funds were used for loans to assist 158 Solidarity Groups with close to 1000 members and 101 micro-enterprises that had 263 full-time equivalent employees (see Table 9). The characteristics of micro-enterprise owners of businesses most successful in terms of increased aggregate value are presented in Table 10. The net impact of the micro-enterprises component was RD$158,023 in new investment, RD$47,066 in increased sales, and 141 full-time equivalent jobs paying an average of RD$139 per month.

At the time of mid-point evaluation, 80 percent of the business owners in the micro-enterprise component were men and 89 percent of the employees of those enterprises component were also men (see Table 11). Sixty-two percent of the women employees earned less than the minimum wage compared to 51 percent of the men. Eighty-three percent of the solidarity groups were exclusively formed by men. Of the remaining 17 percent, about three fourths of the participants in the groups were women (see Table 11). Eighty-five percent of the solidarity groups had had one or more late payments. One hundred percent of the older groups have had late payments, compared to 80 percent of the newest ones. In a third of the triciclo groups, it had been necessary to either reposess a triciclo or remove a member. Despite policy changes, late payments continued to be a problem. In April, 1982, only 80 percent of payments were made on time, and the latest figure was 67 percent. Forty percent of the tricicleros and 13 percent of the working capital recipients had used up their working capital loans and returned to informal credit sources. Changes in daily income among Solidarity Group participants are presented in Table 12. Solidarity Group costs are presented in Table 13.

As Jeff finished reviewing the project documents, he reflected on the project's experience and began to formulate some conclusions about women's project involvement.

TABLES

Table 1   Previous Week Occupational Situation for Population Seven Years and Older by Sex: Dominican Republic, 1974.

	Dominican Republic	
Occupational Situation	*Male %*	*Female %*
Active Labor Force		
— Remunerated work of any type	57	8
— Without work (unemployed) and looking for first job	6	2
Household Chores	1	57
Non-Active Student	34	32
Retired, invalid, recluse, and profit income	2	1
	100	100

Source: Ugalde, Antonio—"Determinants of Female Participation in the Labor Force and Family Structure in the Dominican Republic," Published as 'La Mujer en la fuerza laboral en Santo Domingo; un estudio socio-demográfico. *Estudios Sociales*, Santo Domingo, vol. 17, no. 55 1984, pages 97.

Table 2   Unemployment Levels for the Economically Active Population From the Urban Area of the Country, by Sex and Age Group, According to the Population Census of 1970

	Men		Women	
Age Groups	*Unemployed*	*Rates*	*Unemployed*	*Rates*
TOTAL	75,264	22.7	40,047	26.2
10-14	5,029	34.8	3,289	31.9
15-19	12,281	34.7	7,590	30.7
20-24	11,993	23.8	7,190	26.3
25-29	9,146	20.7	4,723	23.0
30-34	7,248	17.6	3,628	21.9
35-39	6,476	17.2	3,243	21.4
40-44	6,248	19.9	2,505	21.8
45-49	3,945	17.8	1,861	22.6
50-54	4,085	22.2	1,784	28.3
55-59*	2,434	18.6	1,127	8.1
60-64	2,309	18.5	1,296	8.9
65-69	1,531	20.5	603	6.9
70-74	1,235	20.2	490	6.4
75 and older	1,304	19.0	718	6.9

*Due to the fact that the definitive data on the 1970 cencus of the economically active population was not broken down into groups for every five years beyond the age of 55, the values for those groups were obtained by applying the distribution observed in the sample of 20 percent of the population which was published earlier by the National Office of Statistics in the Dominican Republic.

Source: N. Ramírez, A Tatis and D. German: *Población y Mano de Obra en la República Dominicana*, Instituto de Estudios de Población y Desarrollo, January, 1983.

Table 3 Distribution of the Economically Active Population for the Next 10 Years by Occupation and Sex From the 1970 Census

Occupation Groups	Country Total			Urban Area			Rural Area		
	Total	Men	Women	Total	Men	Women	Total	Men	Women
TOTAL	1,211,704	899,656	315,048	472,450	321,445	151,005	739,254	575,211	164,043
Professionals, Technicians	34,060	17,927	16,133	27,813	14,435	13,387	6,247	3,492	2,755
Managers, Admin. and Directors	3,797	3,043	754	2,924	2,352	572	873	691	182
Office Employees and related	81,193	56,361	24,832	68,958	46,330	22,628	12,235	10,031	2,204
Salespersons and related	61,705	49,256	12,449	43,711	34,752	8,959	17,994	14,504	3,490
Agricultures, Cattle, Fishers, Hunters and related	551,617	458,638	92,979	47,325	40,060	7,265	504,292	418,578	85,714
Drivers and related	38,662	35,646	3,016	25,439	23,485	1,954	13,223	12,161	1,062
Artisans Shoes and Dress Makers	84,296	68,226	16,070	67,396	54,827	12,569	16,900	13,399	3,501
Other Artisans	51,717	46,368	5,349	16,928	14,556	2,372	34,789	31,812	2,977
Workers and Journalists, N.E.O.C.	66,825	39,251	27,574	57,783	33,591	24,192	9,042	5,660	3,382
Workers in Personal Services	63,171	23,664	39,507	48,199	17,198	31,001	14,972	6,466	8,506
Other Workers	174,661	98,276	76,385	65,974	39,859	26,115	108,687	58,417	50,270

Source: National Office of Statistics, Dominican Republic.

Table 4   A Typology of Informal Sector Activities in Santo Domingo

Activity	Gender	Level of Investment and Earnings
1. Retail of Charcoal; neighborhood markets; fixed location for storage; occasional delivery.	Female Dominated	Very Low to Low
2. Bottle & Cardboard Retail on foot.	Male Dominated	Very Low to Low
3. Bottle & Cardboard Retail on tricycle.	Male Dominated	Low, but profitable in quantity.
4. Coffee Stand; neighborhood route to work; semi-fixed location.	Female Dominated	Low, may expand to sale of food.
5. "Fritura"—Stands selling hot, prepared food; semi-fixed.	Female Dominated	Low, but slightly expandable.
6. Stand selling ices or fruit; semi-fixed.	Male Dominated	Low to medium.
7. "Tricicleros" selling fresh fruit, vegetables; non-fixed.	Male Dominated	Low to medium.
8. Street-corner stands selling chewing gum, candy, cigarettes; semi-fixed.	Female Dominated	Medium
9. "Ventorillo"—Street-side window selling candy, cigarettes; Fixed.	Female Dominated	Medium
10. "Fantasia"—Bigger, street-front store selling beauty items, toys, clothing, etc., fixed.	Female Dominated	Medium to High.
11. "Buhoneros"—Enclosed stands on side of street selling sundries, semi-processed foods, etc.	Mixed	Medium to High.
12. Neighborhood foodstands selling fruits, vegetables, chicken, etc.	Mixed	Medium to High.
13. Neighborhood Home Beauty Parlors, fixed location.	Female Dominated	Medium to High.
14. "Tricicleros" selling ice cream or packaged ices, non-fixed.	Male Dominated	High.
15. Neighborhood Butcher Shops, fixed.	Male Dominated	High
16. Neighborhood Seamstresses; fixed. (in home)	Female Dominated	High

Source: Susan M. Sawyer, Report prepared for ACCION, Santo Domingo, February-March, 1983 (unpublished).

Table 5   Female and Male Employment in Santo Domingo, 1974 [a]

Occupational Categories	Female	Male
Business and Professionals [b]	3%	6%
Health occupations	5	1
Teaching	11	2
Military	0	4
Managers and Administrators	3	4
Retail Operators	2	7
Sales Persons	4	6
Office Workers	16	19
Service Workers	42	10
Transportation	0	12
Construction	0	14
Machine Operators and Artisans	10	13
Industrial and Manufacturing Workers	4	3
	100%	100%

a) includes only persons who declared specific occupations (unspecified occupations are excluded)
b) does not include health professionals and teachers
Source: Ugalde, Antonio—"Determinants of Female Participation in the Labor Force and Family Structure in the Dominican Republic," published as "La Mujer en la fuerza laboral en Santo Domingo; un estudio socio-demográfico. *Estudios Sociales*, Santo Domingo, vol. 17, no. 55 1984, page 99.

Table 6   Female Occupational Categories by Selected Socio-Demographic Characteristics. Santo Domingo, 1974 (in percentages)

Occupational Categories	Household Position		Literacy		Marital Status		Social Class			Migration Status		
	Head	Spouse	Yes	No	S	M	Up	Mi	Lo	No	Rural	Urban
Business & Professional	4	4	3	0	2	5	16	3	2	5	3	5
Health Occupations	1	9	6	0	4	5	13	4	5	7	1	6
Teaching	13	8	15	0	12	11	11	21	4	18	6	11
Managers & Administrators	1	7	4	0	0	5	13	1	0	1	1	1
Retail Operators	3	5	3	5	1	4	0	3	2	0	1	1
Salespersons	6	5	5	0	3	6	0	7	2	4	8	2
Office Workers	8	21	21	7	16	16	47	22	8	28	3	29
Service Workers	42	24	28	72	50	33	0	27	61	28	61	35
Machine Operators and Artisans	20	10	11	16	10	10	0	10	11	4	12	3
Industrial & Manufacturing	3	8	4	0	1	6	0	3	6	3	3	5

Source: Ugalde, Antonio—"Determinants of Female Participation in the Labor Force and Family Structure in the Dominican Republic," published as "La Mujer en la fuerza laboral en Santo Domingo; un estudio socio-demográfico. *Estudios Sociales*, Santo Domingo, vol. 17, no. 55 1984, page 100.

Table 7   PRODEME Components

Solidarity Groups	*Microenterprise*
Promotion	
Word of mouth—informal conversation among friends, relatives and workmates;	Word of mouth—informal conversation between project participants and micro-business owners;
Meetings to explain program are set up and run by beneficiaries.	Response to announcements in newspapers.
Selection	
Consensual selection of group members who will share responsibility for loan payment.	Suitability of client is determined by the project staff through an economic analysis of the business;
	Loans are further guaranteed by property, inventory or co-signers.
Mechanism	
Clients form their own credit programs of from 5 to 8 business owners;	One-on-one assistance to individual clients
Group process is reinforced by regular meetings of the solidarity groups, in barrio-level meetings or through the Association.	
Assuring Loan Payback	
Group structure insures that those who do not repay will be pressured by other group members;	Coordinators are advised of late payments and visits are made to the business;
If this fails, program coordinators can, as a last resort, repossess property purchased through the loan.	If this is not sufficient, legal procedures are carried out.
Management assistance	
Exchange of ideas about improving business practices occurs informally through conversations with group members and more formally in meetings of the Association.	Program personnel teach clients how to improve their businesses in one-on-one sessions or in formal courses.
Beneficiary's role in the program	
Clients can assume increasingly important roles in meeting program goals: —membership —informing others about the program —taking an active role in the solidarity group —becoming a solidarity group president —participating more actively in the Association —assuming Association leadership.	Aside from the clients' activity in progam promotion and the courses, their role is limited.
Most appropriate client population	
Very smallest businesses.	Larger shops of 2 employees or more.
May be appropriate for larger businesses, but this needs to be explored.	Probably not suited for the smallest businesses as cost per beneficiary is higher and the supportive structure of the group is absent.

Source: Ashe, Jeffrey, *Assisting the Survival Economy: The Micro-enterprise and Solidarity Groups Projects of the Dominican Development Foundation* Vol 1 ACCION International/AITEC, Cambridge, MA.

Dominican Republic 239

Table 8   Comparison of Solidarity Groups

Tricicleros	*Working capital loan recipients*
Working as a vendor principally of fruits and vegetables or as a collector of botttles, cardboard or metal.	*Working as a sidewalk vendor, a market stall holder or a cottage artisan, most likely a seamstress.*
Male head of household (there are no female tricicleros): 88% are heads of households averaging 5 to 6 members.	*Female head of household:* are heads of households and 15% are wives; the rest are other adults living in the household; of the men loan recipients, 75% are heads of households; households average between 6 and 7 members.
Average age 30: virtually non are over 50;	*Average age 38:* three-quarters are between 21 and 50.
Poorly educated: average 4 years	*Poorly educated:* average 4 years.
Immigrant to Sto. Domingo: ony 4% were born in Sto. Domingo.	*Immigrant to Sto. Domingo:* only 5% were born in Sto. Domingo.
Long-term urban resident: average 9.6 years. Only 18% have been in Sto. Domingo 3 years or less.	*Long-term resident:* average 14 years. Only 2% have been in Sto. Domingo 3 years or less.
Lived in the barrio for several years: average 5.5 years.	*Lived in the barrio for several years:* average 6.5 years.
Works long hours and is experienced: work week averages 48 hours, 6 eight hour days. They have been tricicleros for an average of 5.3 years.	*Works long hours and is experienced:* Work week averages 47 hours over 6 days; worked at their current occupation for 8.7 years.
Percentage of Family Income Derived From Business: 87 percent of tricicleros; business is 75 to 100 percent of family income; for the remaining triciclero owners, their business was at least 25 percent of family income.	*Percentage of Family Income Derived From Business:* 42 percent of working capital recipients' business is 75 to 100 percent of family income; 25 percent of the recipients reported that their business was less than 25 percent family income.

Source: Ashe, Jeffrey, *Assisting the Survival Economy: The Micro-enterprise and Solidarity Groups Projects of the Dominican Development Foundation* Vol 1 ACCION International/AITEC, Cambridge, MA.

Table 9   Progress at Midpoint Evaluation

	MICROENTERPRISE			SOLIDARITY GROUP				
	# of loans	Total amount	Average amount	# of loans	# of Benefi- ciaries	Total amount	Average amount	Average per member
July-Dec. 81	49	$110,600	$2,257	64	418	$120,675	$2,010	$289
Jan.-June 82	14	32,962	2,354	40	236	67,881	1,697	288
July-Dec. 82	38	90,213	2,374	54	324	87,333	1,617	270
Total	101	233,775	2,314	158	978	275,909	1,745	282

All money is in RD$

Source: Ashe, Jeffrey, *Assisting the Survival Economy: The Micro-enterprise and Solidarity Groups Projects of the Dominican Development Foundation* Vol I ACCION International/AITEC, Cambridge, MA.

Table 10   Personal Characteristics Relating to Success of Micro-Enterprise

	Most Successful	Next two Categories	Unsuccessful
Age	33	39.5	41
Male	91%	68%	92%
Years of education	11	10	9.1
Years of experience	12	15.5	16
Business sole source of owner's income	89%	61%	75%
Years business has existed	4.5	7.9	6.6

Source: Ashe, Jeffrey, *Assisting the Survival Economy: The Micro-enterprise and Solidarity Groups Projects of the Dominican Development Foundation* Vol I ACCION International/AITEC, Cambridge, MA.

Table 11   Male and Female Participation in PRODEME During Different Phases

Phase	% Male	% Female
Planning Phase: Micro-enterprise owners chosen for in-depth study.	97	3
Implementation Phase: Mid-Point Evaluation (Sept. '82)		
—*Business Owners/Micro-enterprises with loans:*	80	20
—*Employees of those Enterprises:*	89	11
—*Solidarity Groups:**	83**	13***

*Recorded by Group, not by number of individuals.
**All-male groups of "Tricicleros."
***Estimate base on the following: 17% of Groups who received loans were Working Capital Groups; 75% of these were all-women's Groups; 4% were Mixed Groups.

Source: Ashe, Jeffrey, *Assisting the Survival Economy: The Micro-enterprise and Solidarity Groups Projects of the Dominican Development Foundation* Vol I ACCION International/AITEC, Cambridge, MA.

Table 12   Source of Family Income

Source of Income	Tricicleros	Working Capital
Spouse of owner	6%	46%
Another family member	13%	32%
Secondary employment of owner	2%	19%
Other source of family income (mainly renting rooms)	2%	17%

Source: Ashe, Jeffrey, *Assisting the Survival Economy: The Micro-enterprise and Solidarity Groups Projects of the Dominican Development Foundation* Vol I ACCION International/AITEC, Cambridge, MA.

Table 13   Percentage of Family Income Derived from Business

Percentage of Total Family Income	Tricicleros	Working Capital
75%-100%	87%	42%
50%-74%	9%	14%
25%-49%	4%	18%
0%-24%	0%	26%

Source: Ashe, Jeffrey, *Assisting the Survival Economy: The Micro-enterprise and Solidarity Groups Projects of the Dominican Development Foundation* Vol I ACCION International/AITEC, Cambridge, MA.

NOTES

1. Presidency of the Republic, Technical Secretariat, National Planning Office, *Bases para Formular una Política de Empleo para la República Dominicana*, PLANDES 19, Santo Domingo, 1974.

BIBLIOGRAPHY

La Condición de la Campesina Dominicana y su Participación en la Economía. Instituto Dominicano de Estudios Aplicados (Santo Domingo 1977-78).

Michel, Emilio Cordero. "Historia Social, Económica y Política Dominicana," Curso mimeografiado (Santo Domingo, 1970).

Hernández, Frank Marino. "La Inmigración Haitiana en la República Dominicana," *Eme-Eme, Estudios Dominicanos,* Vol. I, Numero 5, Marzo-Abril 1973.

Ramírez, E., Tatis, A. and German, D. *Población y Mano de Obra en la República Dominicana,* Instituto de Población y Desarrollo, (Santo Domingo, Enero 1983).

Newland, Kathleen. *Men, Women, and the Division of Labor,* Worldwatch Paper 37, May 1980.

Mota, Vivian M. *Burdened Women: Women's Work and Child Care in the Dominican Republic,* Overseas Education Fund, 1979.

Presidency of the Republic, Technical Secretariat, National Planning Office. *Bases para Formular una Política de Empleo para la República Dominicana*, PLANDES 19, (Santo Domingo, 1974).

Massiah, Joycelin. "Female-Headed Households and Employment in the Caribbean," *Women's Studies International,* No. 2, July 1982.

Brown, Susan E. "La Mujer Pobre en Santo Domingo," *Eme-Eme: Estudios Dominicanos,* Vol. I, No. 5, Marzo-Abril 1973.

Gross, Stephen. "Estudio de Factibilidad: Programa de Microempresas," Fundación Dominicana de Desarrollo, ACCION International/AITEC, 1980.

CHAPTER NINE

Peru: Banco Industrial del Peru Credit for the Development of Rural Enterprise

Prepared by Maria Eugenia Arias, a member of the Research Faculty of the Instituto Centroamericano de Administracion de Empresas (INCAE), under the supervision of Professor John Ickis of INCAE, Managua, Nicaragua

CONTENTS

I. Country, Project, and Women's Context

II. The Rural Enterprise Development Project
   A. Origin and Development of Phase I
   B. Phase II - Purposes
   C. BIP Organization and Staffing
   D. Integration of REF into BIP Operations
   E. Promotion and Outreach
   F. Loan Eligibility
   G. Collateral Requirements
   H. Terms
   I. Interest Rates
   J. Technical Assistance
   K. Loan Placements
   L. Repayments
   M. Economic Impact
   N. Borrower Experiences

ANNEXES

EXHIBITS

The Banco Industrial del Peru (BIP) was the country's only industrial development bank and its principal objective was to promote the industrial development of the country through the selective use of its financial resources. It provided the major single source of medium term credit to the small private industrial sector because commercial banks were prohibited from extending loans for greater than one year. The Government of Peru defined the rural sector to be an area in the most need of the Bank's resources.

The Bank had begun to shift away from large industrial clients to small scale enterprises in the early seventies. While small enterprise lending represented only 3.4 percent of total loans extended by the bank in 1974, by 1981, it had jumped to 50 percent. This dramatic increase in its lending programs to small enterprises was due partly to the Rural Enterprise Fund (REF) that officially started operations in November of 1975 after the signing of a loan agreement between the government of Peru (GOP) and the U.S. Agency for International Development (USAID). By 1982, over 6,000 loans were given to small entrepreneurs in the sierra and high jungle departments. Of the total number of loans, less than 25 percent had been given to women.

Humberto Osero, manager of the recently created Small Enterprise and Artisan Central Management Unit, had been asked by the U.S. Agency for International Development to review the results of the fund and analyze those results with respect to women. Humberto had asked José Quichero to consider why more women had not received loans and to make recommendations as to how the Bank could stimulate the demand for loans by women sub-borrowers. Jose was to present his report within a week, in time to review results prior to the visit from USAID Washington officials.

José Quichero, an agronomist in his early forties, had recently been promoted to head the branch division of the Banco Industrial del Peru. Prior to his transfer to the Bank's central headquarters in Lima, José had been the regional manager for the southern zone of the country. He was originally from Huaraz, had grown up on a farm and had been a dedicated "hacenadado," until the agrarian reform was implemented during Velasco Alvarado's military government. When he lost his land, José began working for the bank as a credit analyst in the Huaraz branch. He had spent the last 10 years with the Industrial Bank and was quite pleased both with his and the Bank's growth. The international funds that the bank had received, and channelled accordingly, had been one of the key reasons for the growth.

José had prepared information on the REF for AID officials before. They had visited him not only in Arequipa, but also in Puno, Huaraz, and Huancayo where he had been the Bank's administrator. The officials usually reviewed the files and interviewed a number of sub-borrowers. The REF had been a successful line; most of the results were well evaluated by the AID staff of consultants. The Bank expansion into distant communities (see Exhibit I) had profoundly affected the attitudes and actions of its credit officials.

José had not given thought to the number of loans from the REF directed to women. Frankly, he had never really wondered about the number of loans to women. Furthermore, the Bank reports for any credit line were not differentiated by gender. The people from USAID had never required the breakdown. As José Quichero left the office of Humberto Osero, he began to worry about the time it would take to gather the data that Humberto wanted. And how would he find it now, two years after the last project evaluation?

I. COUNTRY, PROJECT, AND WOMEN'S CONTEXT

Peru, the fourth largest country in Latin America, has a total area of 1,285,000 km², divided by the Andes mountains into three regions with extreme topographic and climatic contrasts. Along the 3,000 kms. of the Pacific coastline, there is a narrow strip of flat and dry land (the Costa), covering only 11 percent of the country's total area, but containing the major cities and nearly half of the total population. The Andean highlands (the sierra), above 2,000 meters, cover 26 percent of the country, are composed of steep mountain slopes and high valleys, and account for 44 percent of the country's population. East of the sierra are the vast tropical lowlands (the Selva), covering the remaining 63 percent of the country, but containing only 10 percent of the population. The rugged topography has limited trade and integration between the three regions. Modern economic activity has concentrated on the coast. The main coastal cities account for well over 80 percent of all industrial activity and commercial bank credit, the bulk of it concentrated in Lima.

Peru has its closest ties to the other Andean countries which stretch along the Andean chain from the southern tip of the continent to its northern extremes. These ties are not only geographical, but are also historical, cultural, linguistic, political and economic. All of these countries contain large Indian populations. The country was colonized by Spain in the sixteenth century and its fortunes were tied to those of the Spanish Empire until 1821. The Spaniards arrived and conquered the indigenous population, once a part of the Inca Empire.

Historians have referred to the Inca Empire as a form of agrarian socialism with vertically organized society that had a small ruling noble class and strong religious and military groups. The Incas had a high level of organization and relatively good communications. The population as a whole participated in working the land. Men, women, children, old and young, each had an essential role in agricultural production. Their official language was Quechua and, today, the Quechua and Aymara-speaking population comprise 30 percent of the total populalitical activity included men and women in more or less equal roles with men being the public representatives. There was a tradition of respect for the "yayas" or aged and an exchange of labor through the "minka" (a form of reciprocal labor obligations). These traditions have survived through Peruvian history. The small rural communities of the Andes have been little influenced by occidental patterns of living and are marginally involved in what their compatriots define as national life.

The Spaniards built their New World empire upon the already existing forms of organization. In Peru, the colonial administration was centered in the coastal city of Lima. The firmly religious "conquistadores" thought themselves superior to the local population and felt responsible for saving their souls. The church dedicated itself to convert them to Catholicism and teach them Spanish. The "varayoc," or religious hierarchy system, was introduced in the early 17th century, principally to reinforce the subordination of Indian populations to the elite of Spanish descent.

Ethnicity and language remain powerful determinants of social and economic position, power and wealth. As one Peruvian sociologist stated, "There is one axis which is decisive in distributing privilege, prestige, wealth and even chances of survival . . . that is the axis which locates on one side that which is European, white or groups assimilated by them, and on the other, that which is native Peruvian . . .". The ethnic composition of the population, according to primary school books, is 49 percent indigenous population, 37 percent mestizo and 14 percent white or other.

Peru's total population was estimated at 17.5 million in 1981. One quarter of the country's population lives in Lima which is 5 times larger than Arequipa, the second largest city in Peru. It concentrates resources even beyond what its size would indicate. For example, it is estimated that approximately two thirds of all medical specialists practice in Lima, and three quarters of all nurses are employed in the capital.

Approximately 35 percent of the total population lives in rural areas and of this group, almost 50 percent were female. The number of women is slightly higher in central sierra departments and much lower in the border provinces. The lower indices in sierra provinces could be explained by the migration of men to the coast and jungle areas, leaving women to head households. Women with better levels of education near the larger urban centers of the coast tend to go to these large cities in search of work.

The extremes of inequality in the distribution of wealth and social services in Peru were among the greatest to be found in Latin America. According to a World Bank study based on the 1972 census, the highest 20 percent of households held 61 percent of total income, while the lowest 40 percent of the households only 7 percent of the total income. Women in the poorer social groups frequently assume economic responsibilities and become the head of household. Some studies estimated that 60 percent of the total number of single heads of households were women. These women are unmarried, widowed, divorced or separated.

The economic crisis, which began around 1976 and continues to the present, has undone whatever redistribution of capital and income was achieved in the early 1970's. Poverty in Peru, while not exclusively limited to the rural area, can nevertheless be considered predominantly a rural phenomenon. Even urban poverty, fed by the high rate of migration from the countryside, has its roots in the lack of economic opportunities and harsh living conditions in the rural areas. Best estimates indicate that the national rate of unemployment remained constant at 7 percent for the last two years (11.2 percent for women and 5.4 percent for men). Underemployment was 51 percent in 1980; underemployment was almost twice as high among women. The 1972 census revealed a total of 800 thousand women among an economically active population of 3.4 million and of this number 204 thousand were women in the rural areas. Exhibits 1-3 classify the population by economic activity.

The agricultural sector has not kept pace with the rest of the economy. Fundamental problems in the rural area include the poor quality and scarcity of available land resources, low levels of technology, scarcity of physical infrastructure, difficult communications and lack of credit. As many as 21 percent of women in the sierra are farmers in their own right with husbands' income derived elsewhere, and higher concentrations of female headed households are located among the poorer strata of the peasantry. Women in near landless and smallholder households perform 35 percent and 27 percent respectively of agricultural field work in Cajamarca. Data also show that women are rarely accorded land or membership rights in agrarian reform or farm groups unless they are widows with no sons over the age of 18.

"Behind the facade of modern Peru, there exists a second nation of at least eight million sierra and urban slum inhabitants. Its inhabitants live in conditions of poverty more often seen in Africa and South Asia than in Latin America. These are not 'pockets of poverty,' they are vast regions where the majority of families exist on per capita income of less than $150 per year and entire cities in which more people live in slums than acceptable housing." (AID Project Papers, 1979).

Peru was under military rule from 1968 until a democratic government was elected in 1980. During this period, the government carried out one of the most massive agrarian reforms in Latin America. It also established a major educational reform to reorient the system toward the national majority and its needs. The adult rate of illiteracy, according to the 1972 census, was approximately 30 percent of the population over 14 years of age. For further data on education, refer to Exhibits 4-6. In practically every area of public life, the military government stressed participation, decentralization, balanced growth and economic justice. However, a combination of reduced production and lower international prices for Peru's traditional exports led to heavy commercial borrowing to cover balance of payments deficits and left the country unable to pay its large foreign debt. The military government initiated and implemented with relative success an economic recovery program which the new democratically elected government was committed to continue.

The new government was faced with a country in the midst of severe recession and an economic environment that was approaching crisis proportions. Indications of the seriousness of this situation included an annual inflation rate of over 10 percent, growing unemployment, dwindling international reserves, severely depressed fiscal revenues, and a negative growth rate projected by business sources at 8 percent. The government attempted to control inflation by reducing budget deficits, therefore restricting counterpart funding for development projects. Peru had been apparently successful in renegotiating its external debt with commercial creditors and was to renegotiate its debt to foreign governments in the near future through the Paris Club Mechanism. Nonetheless, credit had become limited at any interest rate for even the best business borrowers.

The situation of the agrarian sector, which was traditionally characterized by low income levels, high rates of underemployment, inability to absorb population increases and limited farm employment possibilities became worse. The rural population received incomes that were 40 percent of the average urban income. Access to education, health, and sanitary facilities by the rural population was either very limited or virtualy non-existent.

In 1979, the AID Mission developed a four year strategy to focus principally on the sierra poor, a secondary focus on the migrating poor, and a third focus on institutional innovation and reform. The strategy was to be refined through a sharper definition of poverty groups and called for an emphasis on priority programs for maximum impact on these groups. The target population was seen as Peru's sierra and high jungle inhabitants. AID's target group was disaggregated into 3 subgroups: 1) independent small farmers (minifundistas); 2) members of associative enterprises; 3) landless and near landless workers. The third group was to benefit through the expansion of employment opportunities.

The central long-term development problem in Peru was identified as the massive and persistent rural and urban poverty; therefore, areas of program emphasis were highlighted as: 1) improving farm productivity in the sierra, 2) creating off-farm employment in the sierra and to ameliorate the problems of landlessness, underemployment and income maldistribution, 3) exploiting the agricultural potential of the selva and 4) formulating new approaches to meet basic human needs through such activities as increasing the female high school enrollment in order to directly benefit women and influence indirectly the demand for family planning services.

The USAID/Peru Mission stated in its strategy paper its commitment to supporting projects which would have a strong positive impact on women. One mission official stated that "women should be an integral part of the project, not objects of special projects." The official went on to state that in the analysis of the role of women, "the biggest barrier facing campesino and poor urban women was the extreme poverty of these inhabitants of the marginal sector, not necessarily their status as women." The projects all had to have a section that told of the impact on women. This, "was not really taken very seriously . . . it's formally 2 or 3 paragraphs. When you're managing large financial projects, you're not able to handle little details . . . the health projects have the greatest impact on women." Another official revealed that he really had not read much on the status of women and that "maybe there is a wide array of projects that affect women in ways we don't even know."

During 1975-1981, the government of Peru took several measures that were to have a positive impact on the status of women. These included an article within the educational reform law that called for the revaluing of the role or status of women, the designation of 1975 as the Year of Peruvian Women, and the promulgation of a law requiring equal pay for equal work, regardless of sex.

Annexes I and II describe in more detail the gender roles in two rural areas in Peru believed to hold many similarities to much of the rural Andes.

II. THE RURAL ENTERPRISE DEVELOPMENT PROJECT

A. Origin and Development of Phase I

In 1970, Peru was hit by a devastating earthquake which affected most of the area of Huaraz. The Agency for International Development (AID) and the Government of Peru (GOP) created a fund to aid the private sector in this northern part of the country which had been severely affected. This fund was to be channelled through the commercial banks in the area. The Industrial Bank of Peru (BIP) had not been one of the entities channelling this newly created line. One of the bank officials commented that the bank began to worry about its lack of loans being placed in the area of Huaraz.

> "We asked our local manager what the reason for this was and he told us that commercial banks were giving easy loans with little requirements using ORDEZA funds (a government entity created by the GOP and responsible for earthquake reconstruction). We decided to knock on AID doors and get some of those funds. We did and when evaluation was carried out, we were told that we were the only institution that had met all the norms specified for giving those loans. It was then that we started discussing the possibility of a larger project and, somehow, Rural Enterprises was born".

The Rural Enterprises I loan was authorized in June, 1974 and in June, 1975, the conditions for disbursement were met. Originally, loan funds were allocated to two implementing agencies: ORDEZA ($4 million) and the Industrial Bank of Peru ($6 million). The ORDEZA portion of the loan was primarily an extension of the programs that had been developed as a result of the 1970 earthquake. The BIP portion was a pilot effort to develop a small rural enterprise credit line in four sierra departments.

ORDEZA apparently did not have the institutional capacity to fully utilize its portion of the loan and, during 1977, a loan amendment was signed with the GOP transferring an additional $2.4 million to the BIP. The amendment also expanded the geographical coverage to four additional sierra provinces.

The loan agreements established lending targets for BIP; the Bank met the targets in local currency terms, but the dramatic sol devaluation (more than 100 percent), which took place during the latter part of 1977 and 1978, caused it to start falling behind in dollar disbursement terms. AID requested and received approval for a one year extension of Phase I based on the sol devaluation. While this lengthened the total disbursement period needed for the loan, BIP was able to finance more enterprises that had been originally anticipated.

In summary, during this first phase of Rural Enterprises, the BIP implemented a pilot rural small enterprise lending program and promoted it so well that the resulting demand created for such credit was in excess of the government's current economic capability. USAID, through evaluation, had also found that the needs for such credit were large and yet the amount channeled toward rural areas and activities associated with rural enterprise development in Peru was severely limited. Estimates for demand in the sierra and high jungle were over 30 million dollars for the period 1979-1983. The first phase of the rural development fund had been a pioneering effort that would have to be discontinued without continued assistance. AID officials thought that this type of program should be continued, especially, in view of the gravity of sierra poverty and the particular attention given to employment and income generation activities. The positive results of Phase I, confirmed by the number of project audits, evaluations and other studies, prompted the design of Phase II of Rural Enterprises. The experience and information gathered by the BIP was not to be wasted and it would continue to be the executing agent.

B. Phase II

In May, 1979, a loan agreement was signed between the Government of Peru and the US Agency for International Development. The loan was destined to further expand the rural enterprise development fund created at the BIP in 1975. For purposes of this project, the rural sector was defined to include primary and secondary service centers whose economic roles and functions are closely and directly limited to agriculture and to the needs of the rural population. During this phase, AID was to commit 8 million dollars and the Government of Peru, 2.7 million. The project was designed to further expand and institutionalize the rural enterprise fund, the line of credit at the bank that promoted rural enterprise development. Credits were already being extended for the formation of new enterprises and for the expansion of existing ones in certain areas of the country. The new injection of funds would allow an expansion, both in terms of scope and geographical coverage. The REF was to continue providing credit access to enterprises that were not eligible for alternative financing on reasonable terms. In order to reach these rural clients and facilitate their access to medium and long term credit, the BIP would not only have to reduce high collateral requirements, but also simplify loan applications, reduce debt-equity ratios, provide loans for working capital requirements, and provide technical assistance.

BIP was to create new field offices to provide credit service and reach the population in all provinces in the project area. This expansion would require additional personnel, not only for promotional campaigns, but also to perform the increased administrative tasks this would require. The project had contemplated the expansion of the REF units and funds were allocated to the fund director for an adequate number of personnel and equipment. At the branch level, additional personnel would be assigned to both new and ongoing implementation areas to carry out promotion, administration of credit, and technical assistance.

At the end of the life of the project, it was expected that BIP would be servicing all the sierra and selva regions defined in the project. A total of 4,000 credits would be extended of which 1,600 were to be given to form new enterprises. The Bank would add 6 new offices to the already existing ones and add the technical and other personnel necessary to assure the successful implementation of the project. Through these credits to small rural enterprises, a total of 15,000 jobs were expected to be created with a maximum loan/employment generation ratio of $4,000 (1978 dollars). AID and the GOP also anticipated that the Fund would be fully institutionalized with the capacity to maintain its level of financing and that the Fund would continue to be an effective system to identify, promote and finance small enterprises.

C. BIP Organization and Staffing

A board of directors consisting of 10 representatives from the public sector named by the Minister of Economy and Finance controls the BIP. In 1983, BIP had approximately 1,400 employees of which almost 900 were at the central office in Lima and about 400 of the total number were women. In the branches, 98 out of a total of 500 people were women. None were in decision-making positions, although there were 3 women in the legal departments of 3 branches. One of the managers at the bank estimated that there were about 40 women in the approximately 240 professional and supervisory positions in Lima. He went on to say that the BIP employed a lot more women at higher levels than other banks and definitely had more professional women than any other bank. In 1983, some women did hold assistant manager and manager positions. One of the top women at the bank was head of the International Division and was the one in charge of relations with international donors such as AID and BID.

Until 1982, the bank had a general manager and all of the managers of divisions that existed at that time reported to him. Some of these were: the Finance Division, Small Enterprise and Artisan Division, the Credit Division, the Operations Division and the Administration Division. In 1982, five central management positions were created to which divisions reported. This change "was necessary; the general manager had to put his OK and review everything; he had many people reporting to him and sometimes things would take forever," commented the head of Economic Studies. Under the new structure (See Exhibit 7), the 5 general managers reported to the general manager and each had division managers reporting to them. At the province level, geographical zones were outlined and the regional managers' positions were created in 1982. Prior to the naming of regional managers, each of the branches had an administrator reporting directly to the manager of the branches divisions. A typical branch organization can be seen in Exhibit 8. "Everything has been divided because it has become specialized," commented a woman sub-manager in the Promotion Department. She added:

> "This was inevitable because we grew. For example, a Small Enterprise, Artisan and Administration Division was divided into the Small Enterprise and Artisan Division and the Operations and Central Administration Division in 1983."

D. Integration of REF into BIP Operations

The first phase of the REF program started slowly and, until 1977, the total number of loans and amount extended was very modest compared with budget allocations. Loan disbursements totalled only $66,200 in 1975 and $1,875,200 in 1976 before jumping to $3,166,600 in 1977 with the expansion of Phase I in August of that year. (See Exhibit 9 for exchange rates during project life). Slow implementation was mainly the result of a clash in lending between BIP's traditional lines of credit and the Rural Enterprise Fund. Branch administrators, credit officers, and other technical staff in the field had difficulty understanding the new lending concepts embodied by the fund. They reacted adversely toward the fund's vastly more flexible criteria with respect to credit and risk analysis, collateral and level of indebtedness. It was reported that, in some cases, branch level credit committees would meet an entire day to review loan applications and would adjourn without having approved one single loan, as traditional bank attitudes toward credit and legal matters proved insurmountable.

A former branch administrator explained the phenomena in the following way:

> "There was lots of resistance to the idea among various managers. The idea of authorizing credit bases on a report from the corner store in the village, that the man was honest, did not hit his wife, and there were people willing to confirm his good behavior, was shocking. Sometimes those were the only credit references we could obtain and the only criteria for approval. We had been used to asking for numerous personal and company documents proving the company status, credit references, and collateral. This new clientele demanded that we be more flexible with respect to requirements. We had to depend on informal references, simply accept that the artisan's license is being processed, and finance the total amount required by the project. This was a totally new thing and most of us were set in our ways and a bit scared."

During its first stage, the fund was managed as a section under the Studies and Development Division, a technical assistance and research section. It then became a unit of the Industrial Credit Division. The Bank and AID however began to take a more active role and pressured for closer administration of the fund. In order to provide this much needed impetus, REF coordinators were appointed at branch level. The REF coordinator had his own portfolio, own customers, and his own promotional activities. This caused problems for the organization as a whole. Humberto Osero, the central manager for the Small Enterprises and Artisan Division, remembered:

> "The REF became little special offices within the bank. My idea was that the fund should be integrated into the branches and these become offices for rural development credit extension. If you were going to have a whole different set of people handling the fund, when it was over you would have had to fire these people, and we would not gain much from that. They would not become part of the bank, but remain a separate entity. I, personally, had a big argument with the man who was for the idea of separating the fund. The man is no longer with the bank."

These problems were compounded by the different treatment and support received from the central office by branch officials. During the first phase of the program, REF coordinators were brought back to Lima for short seminars at the end of each month and received strong encouragement and operation support from the central office, whereas branch administrators and credit officers rarely had contact with Lima.

By late 1977, the REF was fully operational. The lending concepts for the REF were better understood at both central and branch levels. The credit experiences with individual borrowers was proving satisfactory, and the potential impact of the loan on the local economy began to be seen. The program was institutionalized in 1980 and the special REF coordinators disappeared at the branch level. The growing importance of the fund caused the bank to create a special unit for the fund. This unit, located in Lima, was staffed with professional banking specialists directly responsible to the financial manager. The REF portfolio was integrated within other BIP lending programs, while it kept its identity for accounting and reporting purposes. Since 1980, the REF fund was handled indiscriminately by credit officers. The loan approval process followed the same channels and was subject to the same approval level authority as other lines. (See Exhibit 10 for Branch approval levels).

E. Promotion and Outreach

The BIP was to publicize the REF programs through the design and development of pamphlets and brochures, and the use of mass media. In this process, the areas that were being opened for the first time were to receive the closest attention. With regard to these new areas, one of the branch promotion officers commented on the difficulties encountered:

> "Some areas that we opened up were located two or three hours distance on horseback after we had already traveled a couple of hours by car from our branch office. Due to the distances and the difficulty, we decided to take the applications and the forms for feasibility studies with us and proceed to bring them back already filled and signed."

The promotion of the bank and its REF fund was extensive: BIP officials from the branches, together with people from headquarters in Lima, traveled throughout the country advertising in any manner possible. The person who was in charge of promotion spoke of his experiences, such as one arriving in a community and using a megaphone to call the people to a meeting a central plaza. "It was like selling potatoes, screaming out from the pick-up that the bank was giving loans for those communities that had no radio station." Planning promotional campaigns was done at the central level in Lima and the process usually began with a meeting of the branch administrator and the credit analyst, along with the promotion or REF representative, in order to identify the zone's needs and decide how the campaign would be structured. After that meeting, a program of visits was outlined trying to cover as much territory as possible in a period of 8 to 10 days. In each of the districts, the bank officials tried to identify any existing associations, such as the mother's club, local artisans associations; if none existed, the priest, mayor or any government official were contacted to promote a meeting and gather the people from the community. At the meeting, the bank representatives would talk about the many services offered by the bank and specifically promote the use of REF resources.

The initial reluctance of bank officials towards the REF changed to enthusiasm for a program they strongly intended to pursue and extend to other areas of the country. At a local level, the REF took precedence over other lending programs in the sierra and was seen as the single most essential lending activity by branch staff. The Assistant to the General Manager at the bank stated, "most managers felt that REF helped to better its image and increase its scope of action due to the heavy promotional campaigns the fund had had . . . the REF was the credit line that opened the bank to areas it did not service previously".

F. Loan Eligibility

The eligible enterprises were cottage industry (including artisan), small-scale industry (manufacturing), services/commerce/tourism, and small-scale agribusiness. In addition, the enterprise could not be eligible for alternative financing on reasonable terms and had to be located within the project's defined geographical area (sierra and high jungle). Also, there had to be a maximum loan/employment generation ratio of $4,000 (1978 dollars).

Eligible uses would include construction, acquisition of capital goods, working capital requirements, and technical assistance. Sub-loans made exclusively for working capital purposes must show that the needs are for more than one year.

The maximum sub-loan size and maximum amount to be outstanding to any one sub-borrower would be $60,000 (1978 dollars). This would be established in soles and would be readjusted automatically based on the official exchange rate.

G. Collateral Requirements

In all cases, collateral was provided by the sub-borrowers. Loans for the purchase of machinery were always guaranteed by the machinery itself, occasionally aiding with existing machinery or other assets. For loans, outside the REF credit line, the bank would only lend 80 percent of needed amount and expect the client to put up 20 percent; collateral would be valued at 70 percent of its value.

Under the REF credit line, the collateral was valued at 100 percent of its value. The sub-borrower did not have to put up any amount at all.

The REF sub-borrowers offered 1) purchased machinery, 2) other existing machinery, 3) real estate owned by borrower or a third party as collaterals for their loans. From a sample surveyed, the following is the percentage distribution of type of collateral offered.

1 = 9%	1+2 =31%
2 = 14%	1+3 = 7%
3 = 6%	2+3 = 10%
	1+2+3 = 23%

Peruvian law requires that the husband countersign his wife's loan application form and grant approval prior to establishing any business venture. The law also requires the woman to have her husband's permission to work. Though not applied everyday, this is a right that can be enforced by the male.

H. Terms

The maximum term would be 10 years with a grace period not to exceed 2 years. No loans were to be made for a term of less than one year. The bank was to establish under these limitations, on a case by case basis, the actual term to be utilized for each project.

I. Interest Rates

Rates charged would approximate the rates established for development lines of credit in Peru and would be adjusted periodically by the Bank to maintain that approximation. Interest rates would be reduced to two differential rates for all eligible sub-borrowers under the REF. The extent to which rates were subsidized appears in Exhibit 11. These interest rates were to be increased fairly rapidly until positive rates were achieved. The Government of Peru was committed to achieving positive interest rates and had issued institutional guidelines in this regard. The project supported increased interest rates within the constraints of national economic policy. REF interest rates were substantially below Peru's inflation rate throughout the life of the program. They were negative in real terms by as much as 42 percent in 1979 and by as little as 12 percent in 1975.

J. Technical Assistance

All sub-borrowers received some kind of technical assistance. One analysis of 2490 clients showed that 64 percent had received assistance in filling out the application form, 21 percent had received assistance with feasibility studies, 22 percent had been given direct accounting assistance, 9 percent in marketing and 4 percent in product process. An evaulation of REF clients estimated that 75 percent of the total number of clients improved the quality of their accounting system. Courses in marketing, management and production were also being held in various provincial capitals for sub-borrowers. One of the instructors commented that there were few women at the courses, "at the most three or four, and usually relatives of the men present." Some women borrowers, when asked why they did not attend courses, commented that they had too much work at home and between that and taking care of the children, it was impossible for them to move.

K. Loan Placements

Rural Enterprises I made 3,249 loans as of January 1, 1979. Individual loans were generally under $5,000 with more than half of all loans made averaging less than $3,000. Approximately 80 percent of all loans were to small enterprises of which 58.7 percent were manufacturing enterprises, 26.5 percent artisan enterprises, 10.4 percent enterprise in the services sector, 1.2 percent in tourism, 1.3 percent in commerce, and the last 2 percent were to agriculture and fisheries. An illustrative list of the type of small scale enterprises that were financed in each sector is presented in Exhibit 12.

During 1980, the fund extended the greatest number of loans totalling 2,268. That year was characterized by a sharp increase in loans to the small enterprise and artisan sector. According to bank records, loans for this sector, which were 24.2 percent of the total number of loans extended in 1979, jumped to 40 percent in 1980. In 1981, the number of loans extended was down to 1,450 and, by 1982, the REF fund had decreased in importance and the bank extended less than 500 loans through the fund. The branches, however, were approving loans to small entrepreneurs utilizing funds from other international donors. The Interamerican Development Bank, the World Bank, and the Agency for International Development were channelling funds through the Industrial Bank for small entrepreneurs.

Exhibit 13 disaggregates the loans during the 1980-82 period by the gender of the recipients. Exhibit 14 reveals the gender distribution of 1982 loans by size of loan.

The loans approved and given by the Industrial Bank utilizing the Rural Enterprise Fund were well diversified geographically with none of the participating branches accounting for more than 16.5 percent of total lending. The bank had branches divided into five regions, the north, south, central, central sierra and jungle. According to an analysis of bank documents, approximately 46 percent of all REF loans were given to rural enterprises outside the provincial capitals.

The distribution of loans according to the sub-borrower's economic activity remained fairly consistent after 1978. The small industry sector had the largest share of loans in all branches. The artisan sector, which consisted of processing alpaca products into garments and tapestries, ceramics productions and other tourist items, received the second largest share of loans in the sierra departments of Cajamarca, Junin (Huancayo), and Cuzco. Women, commented a bank official in Huancayo, "usually are involved in artisan activities such as weaving, textiles, making sweaters, dressmaking; in general, activities that are appropriate for women". Another official that had administered the Huaraz branch stated that "I don't remember many women as sub-borrowers, but normally they were involved in the type of everyday activities of small communities . . . they were the ones with the bakery, or the small corner store and in the provincial capitals, they were basically into pharmacies, corner stores and selling of agricultural products". Sonia Bregon, recently promoted to head the Development Program Department, affirmed the "women are not usually involved in the industrial loans. Few women dedicate themselves to industry; they don't dare. They engage in home industries—sewing". Finally, Maria Tuesta, from the Promotion Department at the Bank, stated that "women in the sierra are more in the artisan activity. Apparently they dedicate themselves to their home, their land and this activity of weaving is secondary; they do it only when they finished working the land." Approximately 60 percent of loan funds were used to purchase fixed assets, usually equipment, whereas 40 percent were given for working capital to buy raw materials and supplies.

L. Repayments

The relatively low level of delinquencies was a major factor in the institutionalization of the program and its acceptance by bank management as a feasible and effective lending practice. Real delinquencies were estimated to be in the seven to eight percent range on the aggregate. The REF delinquencies were apparently at very acceptable levels and compared favorably with those of other BIP lending programs.

The supervision burden of monitoring REF loans had been much lower than expected. Bank officials assumed that, given the nature of small business, recovery of outstanding debt would lead to high supervisory costs. The average loan cost to the Bank to process and collect a loan was $49. This was $18.30 higher than loans to borrowers paying commercial rates of interest with normal loan guarantees. The officials believed, however, that the lower delinquency and default rates of REF loans should offset high administrative costs.

The general opinion of the branch administrators and other top level bank officials was that the delinquency rates for women was probably lower. In their experiences with REF loans, they usually remembered having better exeriences with the loans to women than to men. Some comments made by the men bank officials were: "women are very able and the ones in charge in this zone of Huancayo, they have a lot of drive and are very orderly . . . my experience has shown that they are more responsible." A Division Manager that had been a Branch Administrator for one of the larger branches told us that once he realized that women were willing to pay the debt before spending it on a "fiesta", he decided to set as a rule that women co-sign a loan with their husbands. He went on to state that "in my own very personal concept, when the woman discovers that she is a good entrepreneur, she catches on what the details of good administration are; the woman is definitely more careful. Of course, all this holds true until the woman falls in love . . . ".

The two women officers that were involved with REF at some point also agreed that women were probably more punctual. One stated that "women are more constant; they go into something with soul, heart and life . . . they maintain good records but they usually lack accounting knowledge even more so than men." The other seemed to think that both men and women from low income rural families were similiar in this regard. They agreed that women borrowers usually dedicated themselves to artisan activity to complement their farm work, and that they treated their relationship with the Bank with much care. They pointed out that it was the first time that most of the borrowers, women or men, had entered a bank and acquired a loan.

M. Economic Impact

A sample survey[1] of 85 entrepreneurs interviewed in four RDF branches indicated that, on average, between the time of the first RDF loan and the present:

- real sales increased overall by 160 percent of 28 percent per year;
- real gross income increased by $16,000;
- real net income grew by over 50 percent per year;
- real total assets increased by 260 percent, of 72 percent per year;
- real net worth almost quadrupled, representing a yearly increase of over 56 percent; and
- the debt to equity ratio fell from 2.39 to 0.49.

In addition, on average:

- paybacks period per loan was three and one half years in terms of economic value added;
- loan repayments represented 31 percent of total net income before interest costs at current prevailing interest rates; and
- present net return on sales was 29 percent for industrial, artisan, commercial, and agricultural firms, while service enterprises showed a healthy 43 percent return.

Extrapolations from these surveyed results indicate that total loan funds disbursed since the program's inception have helped to generate each year:

- $60 million in net profits and salaries to owners;
- $19 million in income to new employees; and
- $50 million in sales to Peruvian suppliers.

Each dollar of loan funds, thus, has contributed to about $3.00 in estimated new income.

Approximately $7,000 of loan funds helped generate one additional full-time job; thus, the entire program has helped to create about 6,150 jobs. On average, about $2,700 of loan funds helped sustain jobs existing at time of first loan disbursal or create new jobs. Thus, approximately 15,700 jobs have been sustained or created.

Exhibit 15 reveals the jobs produced by the loans to the surveyed borrowers, disaggregating the recipients by gender. Exhibit 18 analyzes the financial statements of selected rural enterprises. Exhibit 19 provides detailed data on the characteristics of these surveyed borrowers and their loan experiences.

N. Borrowers' Experiences

1. Mauro Meza

Mauro Meza, a sub-borrower from a small community outside Huancayo, commented on his experience in obtaining a loan for machinery. He had heard of the loan from the silversmiths' association in his community. Since he was single and did not possess a home or other assets, a loan with no collateral requirement was difficult to get. He went to the bank and, with the assistance of a friend, asked for his first loan. Mauro stated he encountered problems getting the loan, especially meeting the requirements for the artisan's license and the proforma statements for buying the machines. Mauro's parents served as his guarantors. With the loan, Mauro bought machinery and the bank payed the supplier directly. "Now," he states, "I owe only three payments and I am looking forward to buying more machinery."

The work at the Meza house was divided among the members of the family. These included Mauro, his mother and two brothers with their wives. The children were still little and did not participate. The women did the finer work in processing the silver, the "filigree" part, giving the earring, clip or spoon head its desired shape and elegance. The Mother, Doña Hortencia, went to the market on Sundays and together with her daughter-in-law, sold the finished product. Doña Hortencia was over 70 years old and still in charge of cleaning, cooking and doing work in the family plot. She does much less now, she comments; her sons and daughter-in-law helping about, she now enjoys taking care of her grandchildren. In a separate room, inside the small compound with dirt floors, admiring her plants, Hortencia spoke of her son Mauro and the fact that he was not married yet. She worried and made everyone laugh with her humorous comments. Doña Hortencia was a proud mother; she had been able to put her son through school and even though she had 4 years of grade school, Mauro had finished high school. Hortencia was pleased that her son was proving to be responsible and was paying the bank on time.

2. Isabel Santibañez de Larco

Isabel was a woman who not only payed punctually, but cancelled her loan before it was due. Isabel, while sitting at a fashion show at the Rotary Club, commented on her loan experience. She had heard from friends that the Industrial Bank was giving medium and long term loans and had gone to borrow money to buy four weaving machines. Isabel was in the textile business; she made sweaters and other goods of "tejido de punto". At first, she made the same sweaters everyone else did and was having problems selling them. She stated, "there was too much competition in sweaters made of dralon . . . my husband and I did a small market survey and found that the market was good for fine sweaters, with special designs from European magazines . . . exclusive things like what was being shown at the fashion show."

Her BIP loan was her first loan and her first experience with any bank. When telling of the process of getting the loan, Isabel commented on how long it took.

> "I had to open books, do the accounting, establishing a business formally, get a municipal license, the industrial register and so forth . . . it was easier for me to get the papers because of my friends and relatives in the various organisms. While there, I was able to see the kind of treatment others were getting . . . those poor Indian men and women who are so humble and never protest . . . you could tell that the tellers were exasperated by having to explain things so much . . ."

Isabel did so well that instead of paying her monthly amortization and interest amount for over a five year period, she was able to cancel her loan in a year and a half. She was proud of that and planned to work with short term credit from commercial banks, avoiding further long term obligations.

In mid-1983, Isabel had 6 employees, four women doing the weaving on the machines and two women doing the finishing touches. She did not employ family members and she closely supervised the production. "I know exactly what each machine should do," commented Isabel, "and therefore I can control well." The finished goods were sold in a small boutique that she now has in the center of Huancayo. In her spare time, Isabel enjoys her children and belongs to a masonic lodge. She has two full time maids that do the housework for her and take care of her children. Isabel was pleased with the business and appreciated the kindness and helpful assistance of the bank officials in Huancayo.

3. Rosa Peña De Guamani

Rosa owned a bakery and a small grocery store. She had taken out a loan to expand her bakery and to buy machinery. She learned about the REF program through the newspaper. Her business was in her name because she had not married her husband when the loan was processed. Rosa was the one who went to the bank and was impressed by the attentiveness of BIP officials. The process of getting the papers from government offices, agreed Rosa, was the one that took the longest.

A typical day for Rosa meant getting started before 6:00 am to supervise the early shift, then sending the girls off to school and serving breakfast to her husband. Her husband supervised the distribution of the bread and managed their second bakery in Tambo, a suburb of Huancayo. Rosa normally spent the day at the cash register, though her nieces sometimes took over in her absence. Her day usually ended around 10 or 11 pm. After all this, she was not ready for a course. "I do not think that after this I can attend a course. This week my husband is attending the quality control course."

4. Máxima Ramos

Maxima, a 27 year old woman had borrowed 300,000 soles at a 48.5 interest rate in 1980 for looms. She was selling her goods at the market and commented about her loan and her worries. "I live with my father who is 74 years old; I am the only daughter. My two brothers live on the coast. My father's house was offered as collateral for the loan. I not only weave, but also work the family plot. We have workers to help in the family plot and also to do the weaving. I cook for my father and the workers and do the cleaning for the house." Maxima had had few problems getting her loan, but when it was time for the disbursement, she had to go into the bank various times. They had told her that it would be ready on a Friday, but she arrived that day and it was not. Traveling between her community and the city was expensive and difficult for Maxima, and she complained of the expense and the wasted time.

5. Eliza Meza

Eliza was a 60 year old woman who had a third grade education. She was dedicated to weaving "tapices," famous for their design and quality in the San Pedro de Cajas community. Eliza learned about the loans through her "compadre" who was the bank administrator in Puno. She took the loan out in Puno, and later moved near Huancayo. Eliza, dressed in the traditional flowing ankle-length skirts that rested on top of several layers of embroidered felt underskirts, told how she had borrowed 350,000 soles in 1980 in order to buy material to weave tapices. She followed all the instructions given to take out the loan. She was told to bring a register for artisan activity which she did not have. The bank officials helped her fill out the application. She went to the government offices to obtain her artisan register and had to wait in lines and "listen to the nasty people" telling her over and over how she should fill out the forms and what she should do next. She even thought of paying a "paper processor" to do the forms for her, but that was definitely too expensive. She returned to the bank and brought a certificate that stated she was in the process of getting her permit.

Eliza had given her house as collateral. She dedicated herself to the weaving and also worked the family plot when there was rain. Eliza cooked, washed and did the cleaning around the house. The bank did not ask her husband to sign the loan because, at that moment, she was not married. She had lived with him for many years before marrying. The whole family helped her with the weaving and she went to the market on Sunday to sell her tapices. Eliza was selling her tapices well and wanted to borrow more money perhaps, to make lots of tapices and take them to Lima. However, she was concerned about the high interest rates and the rumor that when the loans were paid in full the bank would charge additional interest. If that were the case, she feared that when it came time to finish repaying her loan, she would not have the money to cover the additional interest charge.

JOSE QUICHERO AND THE REPORT

After reviewing the information regarding the REF credit line and looking at the records of sub-borrowers, José wondered how he would present the information. While Quichero was aware of the bank's and USAID's preoccupation with loans to small entrepreneurs, he did not know how they were dealing with the woman component and was wondering why the Washington officials were interested in reviewing this particular project in that light. Nonetheless, José felt it was important to distill from the information the extent to which women had benefitted from the REF program and how bank procedures affected the women entrepreneurs' participation. Furthermore, he believed that it was incumbent on him to make recommendations for any program changes that would increase women's participation in REF and, consequently, the program's effectiveness.

ANNEXES

Annex I
Description of Gender Roles in the Andes

The following exerpts from Susan C. Bourque's and Kay Barbara Warren's book *Women of the Andes: Patriarchy and Social Change In Two Peruvian Towns* (Ann Arbor: The University of Michigan Press, 1981) provide a partial view of gender roles in an agricultural community and in a small trading center.

Description of the Sites Studies (pp. 1-3).

"The fieldwork for this study was carried out in a rugged area of the Andes, relatively isolated from national society until the twentieth century. The towns of Mayobamba and Chiuchin, located in the districts of Checras and Santa Leonor, lie on the western slopes of the Andes in the hinterlands between the departments of Lima and Cerro de Pasco. The settlements are small. Chiuchin is a trade center, located at 2,400 meters, of about 250 residents; Mayobamba, located above Chiuchin at 3,400 meters, is an agricultural community of about 450 residents. A precipitous road, carved into the mountainsides along the river basin in the 1940s, connects Chicuchin to the coast. Local residents completed a twisting, vertical extension of the road between Chiuchin and Mayobamba in 1968. This is a bilingual, Quechua-Spanish region where, according to the 1972 census, 62 percent of the population was literate in Spanish. Neither community has electricity or sewage, and potable water, while available since the 1960s in public faucets, is rarely found in people's homes.

"Chiuchin's entrepreneurs own and operate general stores, supplying dry goods, beer, coca leaves, alcohol, tin goods, shoes, and necessities brought in by truck and bus from the coastal towns some six hours away. The most enterprising townspeople have also converted their second floor or spare rooms into boardinghouse hotels to accommodate the students from the neighboring peasant communities who study in Chiuchin, and the steady trickle of Peruvian tourists who come to use the hot spring baths located on the property of a *hacienda* (a large estate) that adjoins the town.

"Chiuchin is composed of people actively interested in pursuing the opportunities that the extension of coastal contact offers. Despite its small size, it has the air of an important trade center, an interesting place to be where there is much action, especially in contrast to the highland towns. After spending even a week in one of the surrounding agricultural communities, one experiences in Chiuchin a heightened sense of activity: so much is available, there are strangers present, and the bus and trucks arrive every day. The town conveys this sense of activity without the benefit of a paved street, electricity, running water, or central plumbing.

"Chiuchin is also the seat of several extensions of the central government's bureaucracy, despite the fact that it is not the district capital—that honor is reserved for one of the highland agricultural communities. The national police force (*guardia civil*) and the agricultural extension agent have their local headquarters in the town. The secondary school operates there as well. In short, it is a town with extensive ties to both coastal urban society and to the rural Andean agricultural communities which surround it.

"Mayobamba, in contrast, is a much more traditional agricultural community. Registered officially as an Indigenous Community (now termed a Campesino Community) on December 18, 1935, the total extension of the community is approximately 4,000 hectares which are located at altitudes ranging from 3,000 to 4,600 meters. About 1,000 hectares are under cultivation. The system of land tenure involves both communal and private holdings. All non-irrigated pasture land south and west of the town has been retained in communal ownership and the town cultivates 4 hectares of alfalfa for the community's dairy herd. Also, communal lands for dry farming potatoes, the staple crop, are made available to all *comuneros*, or officially inscribed heads of household. *Comuneros* are assigned two fields in each of eight annually rotated areas. The community as an entity plants two large, central fields of potatoes each year as well. Despite the continuing importance of communally controlled land, private property has increased in economic importance and virtually all irrigated, high quality land is now in private hands. Water flow to the irrigated fields, however, is regulated by the community.

"In Mayobamba, wealth is determined by the extent of irrigated land a family owns, which in turn determines the amount of cattle that can be raised. Both men and women inherit land, although there is a preference for males to inherit more extensive lots."

Economic Activity and Gender Roles in Mayobamba (pp. 118-120, 124, 125)

"Despite the broad overlap in the work that men and women undertake, there are culturally important differences in men's and women's patterns of economic participation. First, women believe that they are centrally involved in agriculture while men tend to see female involvements as peripheral. Second, men's labor is valued more highly than women's. Both sexes explain this difference in value largely as a result of men's ability to work with heavier tools and to engage in more strenuous labor. Third, women are effectively barred from such agricultural tasks as plowing by their lack of access to tools and draft animals. Fourth, there are some types of labor such as clearing the fields, irrigation, and fixing loads on burros that women traditionally do not do for social and cultural reasons. Fifth, in addition to their agricultural involvements, women work a double day in Mayobamba. They are responsible for child care, cooking, spinning, and care of the home. By any standards, these tasks are especially laborious in rural society. They contribute to longer work days for the women than for the men of all social classes.

"In Mayobamba, women recognize a sexual division of labor, marked by differences in strength and in the tools appropriate for each sex, but they indicate their own full range of involvement in agricultural tasks. One woman described women's work in the following words:

We cook, we wash, we go to the fields, collect wood, harvest beans and potatoes. Women earn less than men because the work is less. Men have shovels and picks. Women aren't going to use shovels because it can't be done. We don't have the strength; we would become ill with the exertion. We cultivate beans and corn with smaller tools, collecting the earth and turning it over. Men use the shovels and picks.

"Here is an account by another Mayobamba woman:

"Women don't participate in rotating and aerating the soil before planting [called the *chakmayo*]. That is men's work. The women don't go. They prepare lunch for the work crews and stay home to prepare the afternoon meal. There is no need for women to participate in the *chakmayo* because it is men's work. There's nothing a woman could do. Women don't use those tools; they're too heavy. But they say in other places that women do this. In Santa Cruz, located in the [neighboring] Leoncio Prado district, it is the custom that women work with shovels and picks. Perhaps this is because of necessity or perhaps because of custom. But here they don't. However, in the harvest, we do the same thing as men. Women also participate in the planting. The men just leave the rows, and the women plant. In the planting of corn, it's the same as potatoes; the women plant after the men have made the rows. The only work in which women don't participate is the *chakmayo* and that lasts about two days.

"Only in the harvest of the community fields for the town's treasury do men significantly outnumber women. In this case, officially recognized heads of households are required to harvest the community fields as a communal labor project. As men are designated as heads of household in disproportionate numbers, they are overrepresented in the one-day community harvest. Widows and older single mothers who officially head families also participate. These women are given precisely the same amount of work as men during the community harvest.

"In Mayobamba, the male-controlled, community government enhances the significance of men's contributions to work such as irrigation. The community government reaffirms that the crucial aspect of irrigation is the task of opening up the channels. A community official (*el juez de agua*) determines the order of rotation for heads of households (*comuneros*) to irrigate their fields. Access to water at the appropriate intervals is crucial for the successful production of cash crops and fodder, and can only be gained through the community.

"Women oversee the sorting and storage of the family's harvest, the selection of seed potatoes, and, finally, the consumption of the family's stores from one harvest to the next. This management function retains importance to the extent that the family is dependent on this production for consumption throughout the following year. However, as a family increases the cultivation of cash crops and gears consumption to commercial products, women tend to lose their control over the management of family resources. While it is true that many men give their wives money, an action consistent with a women's role as financial administrator of the household, both men and women report that men ultimately maintain decision-making power over the use of money."

Economic Activity and Gender Roles in Chiuchin (pp. 126-131)

"Businesses in Chiuchin cater to the agricultural communities, providing them with staples not produced in the region as well as with housewares, clothing, and liquor. With the exception of bread, which is baked in Chiuchin, all commodities are brought into the town from the coast by bus and trucks. Boardinghouses and small restaurants serve visitors from the high towns; students continuing their education in the regional school; teachers, policemen, and extension agents who are stationed in the region; as well as Peruvian tourists visiting the thermal baths.

"Most hotels and restaurants are incorporated into people's homes, although the growing tourist trade has sparked second-story additions built expressly to meet the growing demand for rooms. Agriculture and stock raising are clearly secondary activities in Chiuchin because landholdings of the high towns extend to just above the town, leaving very little land for non-commercial use. Most families own small plots of land below the town, which are used to grow corn, wheat, beans, and to pasture small numbers of dairy cattle, sheep, and horses. In some cases, Chiuchinistas rent land from the high towns or manage to retain *comunero* status in other communities so that they have rights to communal lands. Commerce, however, remains the principal economic activity of almost all inhabitants of Chiuchin.

"Relative to Mayobamba, Chiuchin offers an expanded set of occupations to women. Given the commercial nature of the town, women have established themselves as rooming house operators, shopkeepers, and restaurant owners and managers. These specialized commercial activities simply do not exist as options for either men or women in agricultural communities like Mayobamba. In Chiuchin, women work full time in the six major commercial enterprises in town. Each of these businesses operates a store, rents rooms, and, more often than not, serves meals. In the cases of the two enterprises with the highest capital investment, men established the businesses and have expanded them over the past ten years in response to the opportunities offered by tourism. In both cases, wives are thoroughly involved in all local aspects of the establishments. Men play a much larger role in the running of these stores and hotels than in the establishments where women are the proprietors.

"In four other major businesses, women are the sole proprietors who make all financial and management decisions, regardless of whether or not they are married. In three of these cases, women are directly assisted by adult kin, generally a mother or a brother and his spouse. In addition to women directly involved in major businesses, the entrepreneurial nature of the town has generated emprst began their businesses and that they are less likely to be deceived by coastal suppliers. Moreover, they feel that they are better prepared than their husbands and brothers to strike fair bargains in local trade situations. For example, here is a typical comment by a Chiuchin woman: 'My brother is impossible. It is a mistake to send him for purchases. He doesn't know how to bargain. He will pay any price the merchants ask. Even the taxi drivers [on Lima buying trips] take advantage of him. He's embarrassed to haggle over the costs.'

"In Chiuchin the patterns of economic involvement for women present a sharply contrasting picture. Rather than the *comunero*-centered family defining the economic unit, in Chiuchin the business delimits the household. Widows, single mothers, and married women (whose husbands work outside of the town) may set up economically independent units with the assistance of kinsmen and kinswomen who join the household. In maintaining a large labor pool, such households are able to diversify their businesses.

"Of course, diversification is also a response to the economically difficult circumstances in which undercapitalized enterprises are forced to operate. Businesses are vulnerable to strong local competition, to changeable markets in the agricultural towns, and to the vagaries of the national market where government policy fixes prices of commodities such as flour and gasoline. Unable to count on agriculture for subsistence, the businesses of Chiuchin tend to incorporate several income-generating activities.

"Women in Chiuchin (as in Mayobamba) are paid about two-thirds the typical male wage for day labor. The difference in wages is explained by men and women in terms of the different tasks that men and women perform. Men earn money by working in the fields or in construction, while women generally work washing sheets for hotels and cooking for restaurants.

"Both sexes run stores, wait on customers, engage in economic trans-actions, and purchase stock from wholesale merchants who visit the town. In local restaurants and rooming houses, however, women proprietors or the wives of couples who own businesses specialize in the supervision of cooking and domestic maintenance for guests. Men never work in restaurant kitchens as cooks or supervisors. In fact, wives of store owners have effectively blocked their husbands' desire for an expansion of the family businesses to incorporate a restaurant by simply refusing to organize or involve themselves in food preparation for customers. In addition to their commercial ventures, Chiuchin women accomplish the full spectrum of agricultural activities if men are unavailable. While men generally follow the sexual division of tasks common in agrarian communities, women will stand in for a missing man to accomplish tasks such as loading burros or opening irrigation channels, often with the assistance of their children or a paid laborer.

"Access to wages and education is not equivalent for men and women in Chiuchin. Moreover, in the context of regional economics, which depend on profitable contacts with the coast, men benefit from their monopoly of two critical tasks: wholesale purchasing and the transportation of goods from urban centers to Chiuchin. Regionally, men are the truck and bus drivers; locally, men have higher levels of experience with coastal society than women. Thus, despite the fact that women perceive themselves as more competent than their fathers, husbands, or brothers to bargain and assess local demands for coastal products, family businesses are often represented by men on the coast.

Annex 2 EXTRACT FROM "Estatus De La Mujer"—Problemas Poblacionales Peruanos

Violeta Sara-Lafosse, Translation-Beatriz Glover

Women of higher classes enjoy comfort, have access to services, and have economic resources. The majority, however do not go to the university nor do they exercise a career; consequently, their intellectual development and their interests are limited. Sexual segregation in this social strata is marked. Women's world is marked by fashion, a need to consume, entertainment and personal looks. In contrast, men's world involves politics, business, sexual adventures. Family life revolves around his economic interests and he decides what is important.

The situation of middle class women is more heterogeneous in comparison to upper class women. An important number of them have developed intellectual abilities through university education. However, marriage to men of patriarchal ideology often prevents them from cultivating a profession. Those that do pursue a career, generally daughters of working mothers, face disadvantages in finding employment and obtaining promotions due to the hostility towards women in decision-making positions.

Analysis of agriculture and livestock activities reveals that the work of campesina women is underestimated quantitatively as well as qualitatively. The concept of "housewife" corresponds to the urban occidental world. When a campesina defines herself as "housewife," it includes agricultural and livestock activities. Urban notions of rural work also is valued on the basis of physical strength required and men generally carry out heavy physical work.

Efforts to help the campesina are not oriented to improving her knowledge of agriculture and livestock technology, but to offer her training in handicrafts or lower tasks. One of the legal instruments that tends to exacerbate the situation of the campesina is the Law of Agrarian Reform which does not recognize women as beneficiaries of land and as members of cooperatives in their condition of land workers.

A great number of blue collar working women are concentrated in the garment industry (9% of the female PEA). However, there are a large number of women that do this job at home. They work 12 to 15 hours per day and do not have vacations or enjoy the benefits of social security. They use their own sewing machines, pay for electric energy, location, etc., but receive salaries for their work.

Retail commerce is another activity that absorbs an important number of women. This type of occupation is variable and includes selling from one room in the house, groceries in the neighborhood, market vendors, and ambulatory vendors.

Source: Problemas Poblacionales Peruanos, R. Guerra García et al, editors, Asociación Multidisciplinaria de Investigación y Docencia en Población, Lima, 1980.

EXHIBITS
Exhibit 1   Total Population and Economically Active Population by Gender and Location

	Total Population	Economically Active	%
Total	13,538,208	3,871,613	28.6%
Urban	8,058,495	2,388,827	29.7
Women	4,030,326	595,319	14.8
Men	4,028,169	1,793,508	44.6
Rural	5,479,713	1,482,786	27.1
Women	2,723,352	204,896	7.5
Men	2,765,361	1,277,840	46.5

Source: VI National Population Census, Peru.

Exhibit 2   Employed Female Population, Six Years and Older by Category of Economic Activity

Total		741,586	100%
Agriculture, Hunting, Forestry		147,942	19.95
Agricultural Products	146,138		
Other	1,804		
Fishing		437	0.06
Mining		1,349	0.18
Manufacturing		124,995	16.86
Spinning	27,697		
Stitching	11,165		
Clothes making	55,476		
Bakery	3,337		
Pharmaceuticals	1,759		
Others (89)	16,699		
Not specified	5,862		
Electricity, Gas Water		353	0.05
Construction		1,548	0.21
Trade, Restaurants, Hotels		122,533	16.52
Retailing	91,750		
Wholesaling	5,615		
Restaurants and Hotels	25,168		
Transport, Warehousing, Communications		6,543	0.88
Financial Services		7,699	1.04
Community, Social and Personal Services		290,259	39.14
Public Administration	11,382		
Public Instruction	66,054		
Medical Services	23,331		
Entertainment	18,561		
Laundries	11,422		
Domestic Service	146,649		
Hairdressing	5,871		
Other (24)	6,989		
Not Specified		37,928	5.11

Source: VI National Population and Housing Census, Peru.

Exhibit 3 Percentage of Employees 15 Years and Older by Gender, Category of Activity, and Salary Level (in soles, 1972)

	Total employed	Under 500	500-4,000	5,000 and over	Not specified
Agriculture					
Men	19,907	12.0	45.9	17.2	25.4
Women	2,032	20.8	39.5	12.4	27.3
Manufacturing					
Men	70,063	—	48.7	42.9	8.4
Women	17,433	—	44.3	24.0	11.7
Commerce					
Men	69,593	—	60.0	32.0	8.0
Women	28,116	—	76.2	13.7	10.1
Transport					
Men	38,439	—	59.6	33.7	6.7
Women	5,499	—	72.0	25.1	2.9
Finance					
Men	26,588	—	35.2	61.7	3.1
Women	7,341	—	56.3	40.2	3.5
Services					
Men	204,708	—	44.3	48.4	7.3
Women	125,353	—	68.9	24.8	6.3

Source: VI National Population Census, Peru.

Exhibit 4 Population Over 5 Years According to Level of Education

	Urban		Rural	
	Males	Females	Males	Females
Not in school	415,439	730,318	854,760	1,424,960
Preschool	212,682	218,505	147,750	118,686
Primary	1,674,558	1,640,528	1,116,084	641,833
Secondary	865,823	680,108	91,479	36,164
Teachers College	15,692	29,062	2,146	1,606
University	186,580	88,515	6,558	2,286
Superior	1,414	1,556	183	16
Not specified	42,691	35,835	12,940	10,437

Source: IV National Population Census, Peru.

Exhibit 5   Population 5-14 Years According to School Attendance and Location

	Attending				Not Attending			
	Urban		Rural		Urban		Rural	
	Male	Female	Male	Female	Male	Female	Male	Female
5	40,983	40,521	5,558	4,844	77,087	75,605	91,086	85,376
6	82,847	81,124	30,103	25,299	33,019	34,127	69,346	71,223
7	104,902	100,104	52,911	42,681	12,896	14,475	40,042	46,762
8	106,421	103,046	62,645	51,713	6,393	8,210	26,413	36,508
9	99,281	97,341	58,359	47,563	3,758	5,009	13,706	20,731
10-12	304,949	285,557	200,538	149,308	12,816	19,380	37,839	65,372
13-14	180,464	165,545	98,646	60,879	15,607	27,923	31,747	53,551

Source: VI National Population Census, Peru.

Exhibit 6   Illiterate Population

	Males	Females	Total
Over 5 years	1,356,683	2,229,710	3,586,393
5-14	730,614	785,485	1,516,099
15 and over	624,018	1,438,852	2,062,870
Not specified	2,051	5,373	7,242

Source: VI National Population Census, Peru.

Exhibit 7 Banco Industrial Del Peru Central Headquarters: Organization Chart

(1983)

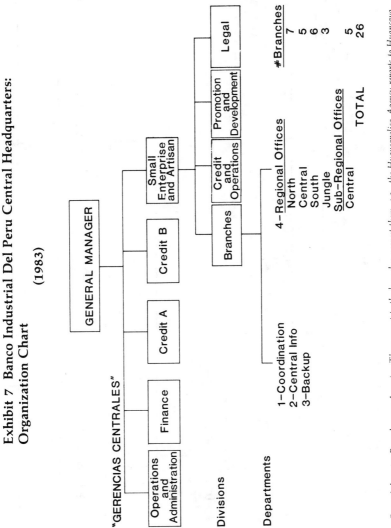

¹*Four of these 26 Branches are Agencies. These report to the branches nearest them, e.g., the Huancavelica Agency reports to Huancayo.*

Elaborated based on information from BIP records and conversations. Only overall data relevant to the case and not a complete organization chart is presented. The only "Gerencia Central" shown with its respective layers is small enterprise and artisan.

Exhibit 8 Banco Industrial Del Peru Typical Branch: Organization Chart

(1983)

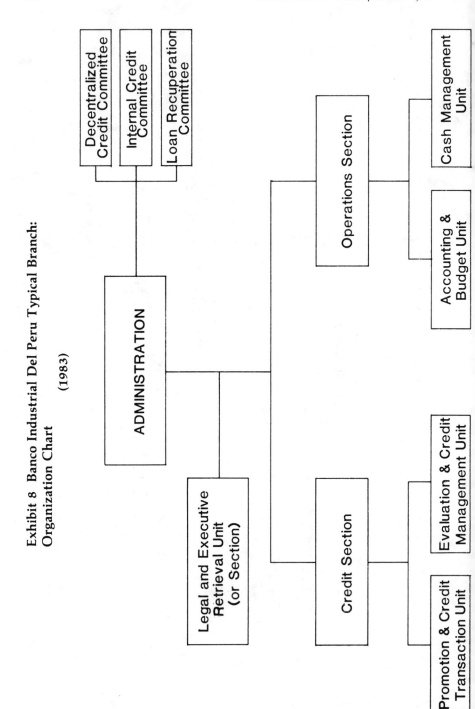

Exhibit 9   Peru: Exchange Rates, 1976-1983 (number of Soles to U.S. $1)

	Weighted Averages	End of Year
1976	57.43	69.37
1977	83.81	130.72
1978	156.34	196.68
1979	224.55	250.75
1980	289.20	342.73
1981	422.30	503.80
1982	697.50	989.67
1983	1,679.32	2,271.70

Source: BIP: Departamento de Estudios Economicos

Exhibit 10   FDR Branch Approval Levels (as of February 1982)

	Soles	Dollars ($1 = 548 Soles)
Credit Committee		
Arequipa, Huancayo, Piura and Trujillo	15,000,000	27,372
Callao, Cusco, Chiclayo, Chimbote Huanuco and Tarapoto	12,000,000	21,898
Cajamarca, Ica, Jaen, Pucallpa, Puno, San Ramon and Tacna	8,000,000	14,598
Ayacucho, Huaraz and Iquitos	5,000,000	9,124
Decentralized Committees		
Arequipa, Huancayo, Piura and Trujillo	20,000,000	36,496
Cusco, Huanuco, Chiclayo, Chimbote and Tarapoto	16,000,000	29,197
Cajamarca, Ica, Jaen, Pucallpa, Puno, San Ramon and Tacna	12,000,000	21,898
Ayacucho, Huaraz and Iquitos	8,000,000	14,598
Other		
The Administrator	10,000,000	18,248
The Credit Committee	80,000,000	145,985
The Regional Staff	150,000,000	273,723

Exhibit 11 Change in Main Interest Rates[1]

	1975	1976	1977	1978[4]	1979	1980	1981[3]	1982	1983
Artisan Sector	7.0	7.0	7.0	15.5[5]	18.5[8]	18.5	34.0	42.5[16]	48.5[16]
Small Loans	10[2]	10.0	18.5[6]	18.5[6]	21.5[9]	18.5[11]	40[14]	44.0[17]	50.0[17]
Large Loans	12[3]	12.0	12.0	22.5[7]	25.5[10]	25.0[12]	49.5[15]	54.0[18]	63.0[18]
Commercial Bank Lending Rates	12.0	17.5	19.5	29.5	34.5	34.5	49.5	54.0	63.0
Central Bank Rediscount Rate	9.5	12.5	14.5	28.5	31.5	33.5	44.5	54.0	63.0
Annual Inflation Rate	23.6	33.5	38.0	57.8	67.7	59.2	72.0	44.5	60.0
Interest Rate Differential (highest FDR rate minus inflation rate)	11.6	21.5	26.0	35.3	42.2	34.2	22.5	72.9	130.0

Source: BIP Records and IBRD, *Peru Staff Appraisal Report: Second Industrial Credit project,* February, 1981 Annex 4, T-24.

1. Interest rates include the FDR's 2% commission charge. Only nominal interest rates and commissions charged by commercial banks are included; the standard practice of discounting loans causes their affective interest rates to approximate the prevailing inflation rate.
2. Ten percent interest was charged on loans for purchase of fixed assets up to soles 2,000,000 in private industry, tourism, and fisheries; only 5.7% was charged for working capital loans to the same clients.
3. Twelve percent interest was charged for loans between 2 and 10 million soles made to associative enterprises for fixed assets' purchases. Only 7.7% interest was charged for working capital loans to the same clients.
4. FDR interest rates from August to November 1978, in November all FDR interest rates were increased by 3%.
5. Loans under S/.1,000,000.
6. Loans to industry and hotels under S/.10.000.000; loans this size to service enterprises had a 22.5% interest rate.
7. Loans over S/.10.000.000 to industry and hotels; 26.5% was charged to service enterprises.
8. Loans under 1 million soles to artisans.
9. Loans under 10 million soles to industry and hotels; service was charged 27% more interest.
10. Loans over 10 million soles to industry and hotels; service was charged 27% more interest.
11. All loans under 3 million soles.
12. All loans over 3 million soles.
13. Rates as of May 15, 1981.
14. Loans under 15 million soles to all types of small enterprises.
15. Loans over 15 million soles to all types of small enterprises.
16. Loans under 5 million soles.
17. Loans over 5 million soles.
18. Loans over 100 million soles to all types of small enterprises.

Exhibit 12 Types of Small Scale Enterprises Financed by Rural Enterprises I

Industry	*Artisan*	*Services/Tourism*
bakeries	weavings	auto repair shops
carpentry shops	stone carvings	farm machinery repair shops
shoe manufacture	leather	print shops
machine shops	rugs	hostels
roofing tile production	filigree	bicycle shops
tea processing	dolls	restaurants
furniture manufacture	carvings	plumbing shops
lime and plaster production		radio repair shops

Commerce	*Agriculture/Fisheries*
pharmacies	apiaries
grocery stores	cheese production
bottled gas	chicken production
agricultural supply	guinea pig production
hardware stores	trout production
	sausage production
	chocolate refining

Exhibit 13 BIP Rural Enterprise Fund Loans 1980-82

	1980	*1981*	*1982*
Number of Loans	3,256	1,006	436
Amount (Soles 000)	3,390,850	3,270,397	1,490,994
Portion to Women	13%	19%	11%
Portion to Men	87%	81%	89%
Average Loan Women	609,736	2,616,806	2,505,287
Average Loan Men	1,165,069	3,368,092	4,508,993

Exhibit 14 BIP Loans by Gender and Loan Size, 1982 Soles (000)

	Women			*Men*		
	# of Loans	*Amount*	*%*	*# of Loans*	*Amount*	*%*
Up to 1,800,000	28	13,068	10.0	117	117,572	90.0
1,800,000 to 5,407,020	33	99,339	17.2	127	477,111	82.8
5,407,020 to 8,651,092	2	11,861	7.3	22	149,745	92.7
Over 8,651,092	3	36,029	6.5	32	520,661	93.5

Exhibit 15   Jobs Sustained and Created Among Sampled Firms

	HUANCAYO			HUANUCO			CUSCO			CAJAMARCA			TOTAL No.			TOTAL %		
	M	F	T	M	F	T	M	F	T	M	F	T	M	F	T	M	F	T
Current Employment (in person years)																		
Owners	18	3	21	20	1	21	18	8	26	21	12	33	77	24	101	77%	23%	19%
Unpaid Family	19	16	35	12	5	17	12	12	24	6	4	10	49	37	86	57%	43%	16%
Salaried Employees	45.5	3	48.5	115	4	119	28	7	35	57	9	66	245.5	23	268.5	91%	9%	51%
Apprentices	14	0.25	14.25	4.75	0	4.75	3	0	3	0	0	0	21.75	0.25	22	99%	1%	4%
Daily Workers	5	0.08	5.08	6.25	0.5	6.75	6	0	6	13	2	15	30.25	2.58	32.83	92%	8%	6%
Seasonal Employees	4	0	4	4	6	10	0	0	0	0	3	3	8	9	17	47%	53%	4%
Total	105.5	22.33	127.83	162	16.5	178.5	67	27	94	97	30	127	431.5	95.83	527.33	81%	19%	100%
Jobs Created (in person years)																		
Enterprise																		
Owners	4	0	4	5	0	5	3	4	7	3	3	6	15	7	22	68%	32%	10%
Family Members	7.75	6	13.75	8	1	9	6	7	13	4	3	7	25.75	17	42.72	59%	40%	20%
Salaried Employees	22.5	1	23.5	59	3	62	14	3	17	33	2	35	128.5	9	137.5	93%	7%	65%
Apprentices	2.4	0	2.4	2.25	0	2.25	3	0	3	0	0	0	7.65	0	7.65	100%	0%	5%
Total	36.7	7	43.7	74.25	4	78.25	26	14	40	40	8	48	176.95	33	209.95	87%	13%	100%
Jobs created/Firm			2.08			3.73			2.0			2.09			2.47			
Loan (PV)/Number of Jobs Created			$8,395			$8,246			$3,518			$7,768			$6,981			
LT Liabilities, Capital/ Total No. of Jobs sustained and created			$5,732			$7,622			$4,339			$5,444			$5,784			
Average Net Worth per Enterprise			$29,230			$68,000			$27,361			$16,212			$35,201			
Fixed Assets/ Number of Jobs			$5,836			$4,319			$2,752			$8,042			$5,237			

Source: Development Alternatives Inc., *An Impact Evaluation of the Industrial Bank of Peru's Rural Development Fund* (a random sample of 85 FDR sub-borrowers interviewed during the first quarter of 1982). p. 62.

Exhibit 16   Analysis of Financial Statements of Selected Rural Enterprises

Table 1:   Income Statement Analysis (Averages for all enterprises visited during survey)

	Huanuco	Huancayo	Cuzco	Cajamarca	Average
Current Yearly Sales (US$), based on end-1981 monthly figures	$44,121	$25,050	$33,582	$31,667	$33,605
Ratio of Present Sales to Sales at Time of First FDR Loan (At Present Values)	1.73	2.51	2.71	3.44	2.60
Average Yearly Sales Increase Since FDR Loan (Present Values)	19.9%	32.0%	28.7%	32.3%	28.2%
Current Yearly Gross Income (US$)	$19,871	$11,751	$15,052	$16,989	$15,915
Ratio of Yearly Increase in Value Added To Loan Amount(s) (At Present Values)	(2.26)	.10	.89	.45	.29
Current Salaries Paid on Yearly Basis (US$)	$ 3,617	$ 3,261	$ 2,644	$ 2,850	$ 3,092
Average Yearly Increase in Net Income (Present Values)	121.4%	16.1%	18.6%	58.1%	53.5%
Present Net Return on Sales —Non-service Enterprises	22.5%	25.2%	34.5%	33.8%	29.0%
—Service Enterprises	65.5%	20.7%	37.2%	49.2%	43.2%
Ratio of Present Yearly FDR Loan Payments to Net Income Before Interest Payments	24.2%	45.0%	26.3%	28.5%	31.0%

Source: Development alternatives International, INC: *An Impact Evaluation of the Industrial Bank of Peru's Rural Development Fund* (A random sample of 85 for sub-borrowers were interviewed during the first quarter of 1982).

Table 2: FDR Enterprises Balance Sheet Analysis

	Huanuco	Huancayo	Cuzco	Cajamarca	Average
Ratio of Current Total Assets to Total Assets at Time of First FDR Loan (Present Values)	3.59	3.73	3.51	4.57	3.85
Average Yearly Increase in Total Assets (Present Values)	49.6%	89.0%	108.4%	42.5%	72.4%
Ratio of Current Working Capital to Inventory (Liquidity)	1.94	1.80	.96	1.24	1.26
Ratio of Current Net Worth to Net Worth at Time of First FDR Loan (Present Values)	3.89	3.56	3.74	4.24	3.86
Average Yearly Increase in Net Worth Since First FDR Loan (Present Values)	54.4%	65.5%	70.7%	35.4%	56.5%
Debt to Net Worth at Time of First FDR Loan (Including FDR Loan Amount)	3.32	2.23	1.94	2.08	2.39
Outstanding Debt to Net Worth Ratio (At Present)	.46	.25	.38	.89	.49

Source: Development alternatives INC: *An Impact Evaluation of the Industrial Bank of Peru's Rural Development Fund* (A random sample of 85 for sub-borrowers were interviewed during the first quarter of 1982).

NOTE

1. Development Alternatives Inc., *An Impact Evaluation of the Industrial Bank of Peru's Rural Development Fund* (A random sample of RDR sub-borrowers interviewed during the first quarter of 1982).

CHAPTER TEN

India: Gujarat Medium Irrigation Project

Prepared by Dr. C. Gopinath and Dr. A. H. Kalro of the Indian Institute of Management, Ahmedabad, India

CONTENTS

I. Introduction

II. Agriculture in India

III. Socio-Economic Status of Women

IV. The State of Gujarat

V. Gujarat Medium Irrigation Project (MIP)

VI. The Fatewadi Sub-Project

VII. Villages in the Project Command

VIII. Profile of Selected Villages

IX. Women's Activities in Selected Villages

I. INTRODUCTION

Ellen Treacy settled into a comfortable chair in her hotel room to look over the materials that had been left by her Indian colleagues. Her five member team, sponsored by the U.S. Agency for International Development (AID), had arrived earlier in the day in Ahmedabad to explore the possibility of collaborating with an Indian institution on a brief, intense investigation of a nearby irrigation system slated for rehabilitation.

The AID mission in India is committed to supporting the Government of India (GOI) in its expansion of small and medium scale irrigation projects. Since the investment levels are high, both the Indian government and the donors want to assure the highest possible returns from these projects. Yet, in many parts of the world, developers have made the same discovery; irrigation systems are not producing expected levels of benefits. Water does not actually reach all the farms on a reliable basis, and crop increases, while substantial, are often not as great as projected. Concern has also been expressed that unequal distribution of water may increase inequity in rural economic structures. Both the GOI and the donors agree that efficient design and management of irrigation projects depend on a greater understanding of the functioning of the total system—what happens to the water at the village and farm levels, as well as in the main canals. Hence, their interest in on-site investigations of a few functioning systems, to improve the rehabilitation of these older systems as well as the design of new ones.

Ellen's university had participated in a number of these collaborative investigations in the past 5 years. Typically, the teams included agronomists, economists, irrigation engineers and sociologists. Since both the Indian government the the AID mission were interested in how the design and operation of irrigation systems are related to women's roles, Ellen had been included in this team. She knew that her Indian colleagues had already done a substantial amount of research in the study area, the Fatewadi subproject of the Gujarat Medium Irrigation Project. She was interested to see what they had found, and what questions would emerge in tomorrow's joint discussions. As she looked over the material, she asked herself, "What do these data tell us? What else will we need to learn to improve the functioning of this irrigation system?"

II. AGRICULTURE IN INDIA

India is a vast country, with a population of over 700 million, which is growing 2.3 percent annually. It is also one of the world's poorest countries, with a per-capita GNP in 1975 of U.S. $150, and a conservatively estimated 300 million people living below the poverty line of US $70 per capita per year. Therefore, the government's development plans emphasize alleviating poverty and creating employment, especially in rural areas.

Agriculture dominates the Indian economy. It contributes about 45 percent of the GNP and engages about 70 percent of the labor force. The gross cropped area increased from about 132 million hectares in 1950-51 to about 163 million hectares in 1975-76. Approximately 75 percent of this area is planted in food grains. In 1975-76, there were 81.5 million farms, with an average size of approximately 2 hectares.

Fifty-five percent of the land holdings are 1 hectare or smaller, and 73 percent are 2 hectares or smaller. The average varies from 0.4 hectares for marginal holdings (below one hectare) to about 18 hectares for large holdings (above ten hectares).

Unfortunately, only 31 percent of the net sown area receives adequate rainfall, and only 17 percent has any form or irrigation, leaving more than half of the cultivated area dependent on the vagaries of the monsoon rains. The government has sought to increase food grain production by increasing the use of fertilizers and plant protection chemicals, and developing higher-yield varieties. The most important component of public investment for agricultural development, however, has been the expansion of public irrigation works, particularly canal irrigation. Private investment for groundwater irrigation has also been encouraged through subsidized institutional credit. Major investments in irrigation have been planned for the future as well.

Over the past two decades, India's irrigated area has more than doubled, from 22.6 million hectares in 1950-51 to 52.6 million hectares in 1979-80. About three-fifths of this area is surface-irrigated, and two-fifths groundwater-irrigated. Until 1964-65, the irrigated area increased at a rate of only about 2.1 percent per year. Since then, the rate of increase has about doubled, mainly through an accelerated program of groundwater development.

In most completed projects, however, actual crop production is significantly less than the potential created by the irrigation systems. Overall, the increase in food production over the past 20 years has barely kept pace with population growth. Increased attention is therefore being devoted to improving water use efficiency at the farm level. Attention is also being paid to improving planning and design criteria for irrigation works and to the management of water from the main system through to the fields. Actual water distribution losses have been much higher than the assumed figures, and water allocation and canal operation procedures have also not matched the exacting requirements of modern agriculture. Major programs are under way to modernize existing irrigation systems.

III. THE SOCIO-ECONOMIC STATUS OF INDIAN WOMEN

Indian society implicitly accepts a sharp distinction in the roles of men and women and their spheres of activity. Decision-making for the community and the exercise of political power are generally considered male prerogatives. Women are associated primarily with the home and their role in the outside world has not yet been accepted as desirable, although according to the 1971 census, the number of women in the paid labor force in India numbered 31 million. Of these, 81 percent were engaged in agriculture, and 89 percent of all female workers were illiterate.

In the rural areas, except perhaps in the large cultivation households, rural women shoulder a greater workload than men. In addition to sharing the field work as paid or unpaid family labour, they are responsible for child-rearing, domestic tasks such as fetching water and fuel, and caring for the family's health.

The early age of marriage, high rates of mortality and illiteracy, and low participation in the country's paid labor forces are indicative of women's lower status in society. During 1961-71, the mean age at marriage for females was 16.7 in the rural areas and 19.2 in the urban areas, versus 21.6 and 24.3 years for males. Female life expectancy was 45.6 years, versus 47.1 for males. In rural areas, the infant mortality rate for females was 148 per 1,000 live births, compared with 132 for males. In 1971, only 18.4 percent of women were literate, versus 39.5 percent of men, and the percentage of women in the total paid labor force dropped from 31.5 in 1961 to 17.3 in 1971. Exhibit 1 summarizes the male-female disparities in India and in Gujarat State with regard to a number of demographic characteristics.[1]

The gap between the position and roles accorded to Indian women by the constitution and the laws and those imposed by social traditions is wide. Religious traditions have a strong bearing on the role and status of women. Hindus are the predominant religious communities in India, while Christians, Sikhs, Buddhists and Jains are important minorities.

Among Hindus, women are viewed solely as mothers and wives, and these roles are idealized. Historically, movements within the Hindu fold such as Buddhism, Jainism, and Sikhism contributed to some improvement in the status of women, but these groups, too, continued to regard women primarily as mothers and wives and as inferior to men in society. Though the Koran regards Muslim men and women as equals, the various interpretations of Koranic injunctions over the centuries have accorded women an inferior position. Islam recognizes women's rights to inherit property, but in practice, these rights are not upheld. Though Christianity is less restrictive to women, Indian Christian women are still regarded as inferior to men in a number of respects. There is thus no radical difference in the position of women in India across diverse religious communities. Changes accompanying economic development are reflected in Indian women's lives in very complex ways.

IV. THE STATE OF GUJARAT

Gujarat State, in western India, covers an area of about 19.8 million hectares and has a population of 30.7 million (1977) that is increasing 2.6 percent per year, one of the highest rates in India. About a third of the population lives in towns and cities. About 40 percent of the rural population lives below the poverty line, with some sections of the state being much poorer than others.

The average farm size in Gujarat is 4.1 hectares, but varies considerably from district to district, from a minimum of 1.8 hectares to a maximum of 8.4 hectares. The distribution is determined largely by agro-climatic conditions. Approximately one-fourth of the land holdings belong to the marginal category (less than one hectare) and one-tenth to the large category (more than ten hectares). With strict enforcement of tenancy legislation, 97 percent of all holdings are fully owned. Land ceilings are applied according to soil type and are 10.9 hectares per family for irrigated lands and 8.1 to 21.9 hectares per family for unirrigated lands.

Agriculture contributes about 40 percent of the state's domestic product, employing about 65 percent of the labor force. The net cultivated area as a percentage of total reporting area has been as high as 50 percent. Cropping intensity, on the other hand, is one of the lowest in India, because of the low and uncertain rainfall. The state average is reported to be 108 percent. The main crops are irrigated paddy, wheat, millet, sorghum, maize, groundnuts, cotton and tobacco. There are three cropping seasons: Kharif (June-October); Rabi (November-February); and hot weather, (March-May). Most of the cropping is done during Kharif, the monsoon season. One-fifth of the area is cultivated with bi-seasonal or perennial crops.

Potential for further increase in agricultural production is limited by a number of factors, including climate, topography and soils, present land use, and supporting services. Further increases in production (and incomes) are primarily dependent on yield increases arising out of improved practices, expansion of irrigation, and shifts to higher-value crops.

Only one-sixth of cultivated land in Gujarat is irrigated. Groundwater resources have been developed to almost 70 percent of their potential, higher than in any other Indian state. There is an acute need, therefore, to expand and improve surface irrigation. Tapping available water resources for other uses is also of paramount importance in this drought-prone state. Provision of safe and potable drinking water is a serious problem in approximately one-third of the villages, where the groundwater is unreliable and often saline.

V. GUJARAT MEDIUM IRRIGATION PROJECT (MIP)

Because of direct impact of irrigation projects on increased agricultural production, as well as the considerable indirect economic and social benefits, the government of Gujarat is emphasizing the development of surface irrigation. Major effort will be devoted to medium scale projects, such as the Gujarat Medium Irrigation Project, which is being funded jointly by AID, ($30 million), the International Development Association ($85 million), and the Government of Gujarat ($100 million). AID funding began in 1978. The goals of the AID project, as stated in the project paper, are:

1) to increase the level and security of small-farmer income;
2) to expand rural employment opportunity; and
3) to increase the availability of food to the rural and urban poor.

To meet these goals, the three stakeholders will share the cost of constructing 13 new irrigation systems covering 88,000 hectares, and of modernizing or rehabilitating 20 existing systems, covering 61,000 hectares. The direct responsibility for planning, implementation, operations and maintenance rests with the irrigation wing of the Gujarat Government's Department of Public Works. Final approval of each subproject plan rests with the Government of India Central Water Commission. Each new system will generally consist of:

1) an earthfill storage dam with a gateway spillway;
2) a fully lined canal network which can deliver water through outlets serving eight-hectare blocks and
3) a drainage network connected to natural drains.

Modernization of existing systems involves

1) canal extension to outlets serving eight-hectare blocks;
2) lining of all the canal systems;
3) additional control structures to make possible better regulation of water delivery; and
4) local drainage works.

In addition to the construction, the International Development Association (IDA) is also financing development of a computerized approach to scheduling water distribution, so that limited water can be allocated more efficiently. It will also finance a reorganization of the extension service. Currently the extension agents are village-level workers (VLWs) from the Department of Community Development who have many duties other than agricultural. The reorganization will transfer these VLWs to the Department of Agriculture to "strengthen applied agricultural research, establish a better link between research and extension and increase staff mobility at all levels".[2]

VI. THE FATEWADI SUBPROJECT REHABILITATION

The Fatewadi irrigation project is located on the right bank of the Sabarmati River in Ahmedabad District. The area receives an average of 24 inches of rain per year. In addition to being low, this rainfall is highly uncertain and unevenly distributed. During heavy rains, the Sabarmati used to spill over its banks. There were a number of depressions in the area in which farmers stored water from the spills for use in irrigation, but because of insufficient run off, the earthen tanks were generally not filled. In 1950, a head regulator was built on the river, and the Nani Fatewadi canal was constructed to fill some of these tanks during the monsoon. The success of this project led to the construction of another regulator and the Moti Fatewadi canal, which was completed in 1967-68. Each year, when the monsoon receded, temporary embankments were built downstream of the regulators and approach channels to divert water to the Nani and Moti Fatewadi canals. To overcome the difficulties of building temporary embankments each year, the Wasna barrage was built in 1979, with a lined feeder canal to divert flows into the Nani and Moti Fatewadi canals, which are unlined.

The available water for the Fatewadi project comes from three sources:
1) the flows in the river Sabarmati, resulting from the available free catchment (about 4,584 km[2]);
2) treated sewage flows discharged into river Sabarmati by the Ahmedabad Municipal Corporation (0.40 mcum, average daily flow, 1980);
3) monsoon flows into the existing tanks from their respective catchments.

The project area has a large number of tanks. Most are used for irrigation, some are village tanks. The 181 tanks of the Fatewadi irrigation system have a storage capacity of 62.3 mcum. There are other tanks (both village and village-cum-irrigation) in the area, not connected to the Fatewadi canal network, but drawing limited supplies from their own free catchments.

The area has a number of open dug wells, which draw from groundwater supply. Unfortunately, a high proportion are saline, which limits their usefulness both for irrigation and drinking. The chief source of drinking water in the area are deep tube wells, constructed and managed independent of the Fatewadi project by either the village panachayats or other governmental agencies.

The project area soils are recent to sub-recent alluvials, having a medium to fine texture. They are very deep in the entire command area. In about 97 percent of the command, the land is almost level (0-1 percent) and gently sloping (1-3 percent) in the rest of the area. Details of the command area are provided in Exhibit 2.

Irrigation is currently practiced not only from the tanks, but also directly from the canals. In the head reaches of the canals, some lift irrigation is also practiced. In existing practice, most of the diverted river water is used for paddy cultivation during the monsoon season (Kharif). Depending on water availability and requirements, the tanks are filled once or twice. The irrigation tanks, which submerge private lands, are generally emptied by the end of October, and the moist tank beds are then used for cultivating wheat in the Rabi season. Any water left in the tanks at the end of Kharif is used to inundate the surrounding lands for Rabi cultivation. The only river flows diverted during Rabi are used to irrigate the land directly under the command of the canals. Since during this season there is no storage, the Rabi wheat area is restricted by the availability of water in the river.

The canal supplies are also used to fill village tanks connected to the Fatewadi system. Water from village tanks is chiefly used for washing vessels and clothes, for bathing and for animals, but in some cases provides limited irrigation. Water from these tanks is not used for drinking. Most of these village tanks have either dug wells or deep tube wells at their deeper end from which supplies are drawn for drinking water and other community uses during lean periods. The village tanks, in general, have inadequate provision of washing platforms, steps, drinking water troughs for animals and such other community facilities.

Water release for both the canals and tanks is scheduled by the Irrigation Department (ID) of the Government of Gujarat. The ID also regulates lift irrigation from the canals. At the beginning of the cropping season, (chiefly Kharif), the ID functionaries in consultation with the cultivators in the command area assess the extent of crops (chiefly paddy) to be planted. This information is compiled for different reaches of the irrigation system and is aggregated for the project as a whole. Employing a duty of 3 acres per cusec for the area under canals/tanks, 4 acres per cusec for the area under lift irrigation and an irrigation interval of 20 days, the ID assesses the crop water requirements and the demand. During the irrigation season, the flow computed from demand is compared with the available flows and if the supply is less than demand, the irrigation interval is proportionately adjusted and lengthened. Generally, village tanks are given priority over irrigation tanks in periods of shortage. Although the farmers are consulted in decisions related to scheduling, decisions in the system down to the irrigation outlets are made by the ID. Shortages of water, particularly for the tail enders, are often reported from the project area.

Conflicts in water use are largely resolved locally or through forums such as the Irrigation Advisory Committee comprising selected non officials (15) and officials (4), with the Executive Engineer of the project as the Secretary of the Committee. The Advisory Committee has no membership for women. In the lift-irrigated part of the command, about 10 Lift Irrigation Cooperative Societies are reportedly in operation. The use of water from the village tanks was primarily managed by the panchayats.

The Fatewadi project has a command area of 95,883 hectares, of which some 30,000 are targeted for irrigation. This target has never been met, because of erratic rainfall and high water loss in the canals. Exhibit 3 provides information on the actual area irrigated for selected years, during the pre and post modernization phases of the Fatewadi system.

An impact evaulation of the Fatewadi Project[5] done prior to the AID funded rehabilitation reported that because of the high ground water levels and salinity in the area, further cultivation of paddy would be very detrimental to the total ecosystem. Paddy has a low resistance to salinity and the study suggests that crops more resistant to salinity need to be introduced. Unfortunately, paddy now occupies a major portion of the area in Kharif and with increased water availability from the Fatewadi as a result of modernization, in the normal course of events, paddy is expected to increase. The study also notes that because growth in farm income and improvement in employment have been assumed to follow automatically on the development of irrigation, in the past little effort to integrate the various processes of water management was made. The result has been inadequate development of irrigation facilities at project level and poor water management at the farm level. Of the total water released from storage to the head reaches of the main canal, only one third meets the demand of crops. The rest is lost in conveyance and application.

To decrease canal water loss, the project will line the major canals and reduce the size of the turnout blocks from 40 to 8 ha. Some of the existing tanks will also be strengthened. The cost of improvements has been estimated at approximately Rs 180 million and benefit cost ratio 1.1 using a social discount of 12 percent. It is expected that after completion of the work, 26 percent of the command area will be irrigated for paddy cultivation in Kharif, and 9 percent for wheat in Rabi. This would extend the growing season for many farms by increasing the number of farms growing 2 crops a year. The cropping intensity during Kharif and Rabi would be 85 percent and 30 percent, respectively. Both the longer growing season and the increases in production from irrigated land would contribute to total increase in crop production.

The project paper also indicates a possible increase in the production of cash crops such as cotton, and notes that irrigated cotton production requires 140 person days per acre of labor, in contrast to 40 person days per acre for rainfed cotton. Two shifts are likely to occur with increased availability of irrigation water. One is a shift in the types and amounts of crops to make the best use of the new resource. The second is an increase in labor demands as double and triple cropping increases. Labor demand is likely to spread out across the year, both for agricultural labor and for crop processing and storage. How this will affect gender-segregated labor markets is not clear. Exhibit 4 provides the current pattern of rainfed and irrigated crops in the project area.

VILLAGES IN THE PROJECT COMMAND

There are more than one hundred villages in the project command. Although they vary in size, they share certain characteristics. Most have a primary school, and a health center, and a nearby secondary school, hospital and cooperative society. They are nuclear settlements, each containing a number of groups belonging to different castes and religions. The different castes and communities are, in general, integrated in their economic, social and ritual patterns by ties of mutual and reciprocal obligation. The villages are administered by statutory-elected Panchayats (village councils), with reserved seats for women and certain minorities. In the nine member panchayat committees, usually two seats are held by women. Women members invariably come from the older age groups and are uneducated. Though they attend panchayat meetings once a month and exercise voting rights, they are generally passive members of the panchayat and are not involved in decision-making on irrigation-related or other major issues affecting the village community. Their role is generally confined to organizing devotional and religious discourses and other activities for the community.

Each village comprises the following classes:[3]

1) Landowners (landlords), who are mainly prosperous farmers or money lenders and traders.

2) Peasants, the majority of whom hold tiny, uneconomic holdings.

3) Tenant farmers and sharecroppers.

4) Landless agricultural laborers, who sell their labor to the richer farmers.

5) Artisans and others rendering a variety of services.

The primary unit of the village social structure is either a large joint family or the elementary family maintaining close contact with allied families. The next unit is the caste. Different castes have well-defined positions and functions in village rituals and norms. In most villages, the caste system determines to a considerable extent the socio-religious, political and economic subsystems in the community. The caste of an individual generally dictates a distinctive way of life, norms and standards of behavior. The larger circle of neighbors mostly consists of caste fellows. Social distance is far wider than physical distance between the classes, but boundaries of kin and caste are transcended in types of interdependence entailed by economic relationships.

The social structure of the village is largely determined by kinship and caste. Common features of these communities are shared values, individual identity and recognition of unity, an economy built largely around agriculture, a love of land and ascription of great value to it, and a sharing of common community problems and influences. With development, the changing rural scene and changing attitudes have resulted in significant variations in social organization, particularly with reference to family, caste and village council, which are summarized in Exhibit 5.[4]

The age factor is also important. Young children do odd tasks, but no responsibility is thrust upon them. As they grow up, girls must accept an increasing share of the domestic tasks. "Grown-up" boys and girls are gradually entrusted with some responsibility. The main responsibility for all work rests with the young men and women. The middle-aged continue to do a part of the work, but their time is more occupied with planning, direction and supervision. Older persons continue to supervise and direct, but gradually retire and devote most of their time to grandchildren and community affairs.

Most of the work differentiation is based on sex. Exhibit 6 illustrates the traditional division of work between men and women. Ideally, woman's place is at the hearth. She cooks the meals, cleans the house, collects firewood, tends the cattle, bears and rears the children, and attends to the sick. She also participates in agricultural work, depending on her social position and the time she has available. During the illness or absence of his wife, a man may have to perform some of her domestic duties, but this is a compromise with necessity. In the poorer families, women, besides doing domestic work and assisting their husbands in agriculture and caste occupations, also work for wages. Divorced and widowed women often are the primary support of their families.

Women spend considerable time providing water for cooking, drinking, bathing and the washing of utensils and clothes. Water facilities in villages vary considerably. In most villages, there is no piped water supply to individual houses, and domestic needs are supplied from either a dug well or deep-tube wells. In some cases, the village well is used for drinking water only, with water for other domestic uses coming from village tanks. Separate tanks are sometimes constructed to provide water for animals. Water scarcity is not uncommon, particularly during the hot summer months. In such cases, the village council establishes some form of rationing. In many villages, the council has constructed a central piped water facility where women collect their domestic water requirements. These facilities are also used for washing utensils and clothes, and at times as a meeting place for women.

PROFILE OF THE SELECTED VILLAGES

Three villages, (Adroda, Sanathal and Khoda) within the Fatewadi Command and one village, (Telao) just outside the command were selected for primary level investigations. All four villages are small to medium sized with road and public transport (bus) serving them. Adroda and Khoda are located about 40 km from Ahmedabad city towards the lower half of the command area. Sanathal and Telao are in the upper reaches of the command, about 15-20 km from Ahmedabad.

Exhibit 7 shows the occupational patterns of households in the villages. There is no marked difference in the caste composition and economic and other characteristics of households across the villages. The Harijans (untouchables), the landless labor and the Bharwards (graziers) form the weakest segments of the village society and they provide the labour input to agriculture. Amongst the upper castes (Darbars), women do not participate in field work. The rich farmers form a small but powerful section of the village society. During critical periods of farm work, labour shortage is experienced in the villages, particularly by the larger farmers. On such occasions, labour (both men and women) is brought from outside the area on a contract basis.

Adroda has been served by the Fatewadi system since 1970-71, with the canals and canal-fed tanks providing the chief source of irrigation. Open wells provide drinking water supplies and limited irrigation in the village. Tube wells are noticeably absent in the village. *Khoda,* though within the command, has limited access to canal waters from the Fatewadi. The sources of irrigation in the village are a rainfed tank and open wells. A tube well provides drinking water to the village. *Sanathal* is served by flow and lift irrigation from the canals and tanks fed by canals. Open wells provide limited Rabi irrigation and drinking water. *Telao* is a comparatively dry village with limited irrigation supplies from a rainfed tank, a few open wells and a tube well. A second tube well provides drinking water to the village. Exhibit 8 shows the nature of access in the villages to tank, canal and groundwater sources. In the villages, during periods of water availability (monsoon and a few months thereafter) the village tanks provide the source of water for washing clothes and vessels, for bathing and for animals to drink. Water for cooking comes from open wells or tube wells. With village tanks getting depleted, particularly during lean summer months, there is heavy demand on groundwater for all the uses specified above. Field investigations reveal Adroda and Sanathal to be the better off in length of availability of water in village and irrigation tanks. Khoda, though falling within the overall command, has limited access to canals and draws part of its supplies from a rainfed tank. The length of availability of water from this tank was reported to be low compared to that from canal fed tanks.

Agriculture and dairying form the main economic activity in all the villages. Paddy and wheat comprise the principal Kharif and Rabi crops. Farming is largely traditional with draft animals and wooden (and some iron) plows. Tractors, chiefly owned by larger farmers, are appearing on the village scene, primarily for tillage and transport (both on and off the farm).

Along with agriculture, dairying forms an important subsidiary occupation of households in the villages. Data on cattle population are given in Exhibit 9. Dairying as an economic activity is a major feature in the rural areas of Gujarat State and is generally organized through milk cooperatives. The primary village societies are organized by the producers at the village level. Any family owning a milch animal, if it promises not to sell milk to any other buyer, can join the cooperative by purchasing a share for one household member. Each primary village society averages about 100-300 members. It is reported that even though women share a greater burden in dairying activity, most of the members are the household males. Twice a day, once in the morning and once in the evening, milk is taken to the cooperative office, generally by women, where the weight and fat content is measured and recorded. Payment on the basis of fat content is made in cash the next day. Milk is collected from the village primary societies either by the milk producers union or dairy which produces this milk. Transportation networks for collection of the milk are worked out by the milk producers union or the dairy as the case may be. Members of the primary village societies are provided free veterinary services and other inputs against cash payment. These inputs are provided by the village society itself. New cooperatives are organized by various agencies. Some training is provided to promising leaders to run the cooperatives. These persons are usually males. Women receive minimal or no training. The societies offer no services beyond these connected with animal care.

WOMEN'S ACTIVITIES IN SELECTED VILLAGES

In a typical day, woman in these villages undertake a number of activities that involve water. Since water facilities for domestic and other purposes vary, data on access to these facilities during two seasons (Kharif and summer) were gathered (Exhibit 10.) Though a quantitative assessment of the per-capita domestic water requirements in the villages was not possible, secondary data from similar environments are presented in Exhibit 11.

An examination of the economic activities and work patterns of women in the selected villages showed that they are typically involved in agriculture, domestic and community-related activities. Among their agricultural duties, transplanting (for paddy), weeding, harvesting and threshing are prominent. In Khoda, many women also work as paid laborers in cotton.

Because it was difficult to quantify women's involvement in various agricultural activities precisely, a semiquantitative approach using scaling techniques was employed. For the selected villages, women's labor on the principal crops, in two categories of farm size (large, medium and small), are shown in Exhibit 12.

Although not reflected in the field crop data, women in the households with cattle (cows and buffaloes) invest considerable time in caring for cattle and in dairy production. They wash and water them, tether them in shelters at day or night, collect dung to make into cakes for fuels, clean their stalls and milk them twice a day. In addition, women chop, collect and carry fodder for the animals. These activities, on an average, take 2-4 hours every day. The milk is taken to the village cooperatives, primarily by women, who are paid cash the next day. Daily earnings were reported by women to vary from Rs 5-10 per day. The income is generally retained by women and utilized by them for household expenses. A survey by the Department of Economics at Sardar Patel University, Gujarat found that milk constitutes about half the household income of families belonging to the milk cooperatives compared to one-fifth in case of families who were not members of such cooperatives. Unlike sporadic income from crops or wage labor, income from sale of milk or ghee made from milk by women is reliable and paid daily in cash. Women reported selling on an average two-thirds of the milk produced in the morning and one-third of that produced in the evening. The rest is used for the families own consumption. The poorer women sell a higher proportion of milk. One of the major constraints in the project area in promoting this activity further is the acute shortage of fodder in the lean summer months and shortage of irrigation water.

EXHIBITS

Exhibit 1   Male-Female Disparity in Regard to Selected Demographic Characteristics in India and Gujarat State

		Female per 1,000 Males	
		India 1971	Gujarat 1971
1	TOTAL POPULATION	930	934
	Rural	949	951
	Urban	858	893
2	EDUCATIONAL LEVEL		
	Illiterate	1,342	1,304
	Literate and Educated	474	580
	Middle	371	355
	Matriculation or Higher Secondary	277	359
3	MARITAL STATUS		
	Never Married	762	800
	Married	1,024	999
	Widowed	2,772	3,078
	Divorced or Separated	1,630	1,050
	Unspecified Status	328	748
4	WORKERS		
	Total	210	187
	Cultivators	135	141
	Agricultural Laborers	498	513
	Livestock, Forestry, Fishery, Hunting, Plantations and Orchards	232	73
	Mining and Quarrying	155	178
	Manufacturing, Processing, Servicing and Repairs		
	a) Household Industry	265	131
	b) Other	88	53
	Construction	101	157
	Trade & Commerce	59	37
	Transport, Storage & Communications	34	25
	Other Services	165	178
	Non-Workers	1,726	1,719
5	NON-WORKERS ACCORDING TO MAIN ACTIVITY		
	Full-Time Students	480	533
	Households	6,734	9,637
	Dependent and Infants	1,084	1,043
	Retired and Persons with Independent Means	356	551
	Beggars, Vagrants, etc.	587	234
	Inmates of Penal, Mental and Charitable Institutions	354	235

Exhibit 2   Details of Fatewadi Command Area

1) *Area Under Command*

	Hectare
Gross Command Area (GCA)	129,500
Cultivable Command Area (CCA)	95,883
Irrigable Command Area	29,792

2) *Water Table*

Water Table Below Ground Surface (meters)	*Percent of Area*
0-1.5	0.3
1.5-3.0	15.9
3.0-5.0	47.5
More than 5.0	36.3

3) *Land Irrigability Class*

Class	*Hectares*	*Percent*
1	475	1.6
2	10,819	36.3
3	14,961	50.2
4	2,189	7.4
5	101	0.3
Unsurveyed	1,247	4.2
Total	29,792	100.0

4) *Salinity Groups*

Salinity Class	*Pecent Area*
Free	24.9
Slight	27.1
Medium	34.1
Strong	13.6

Exhibit 3   Area Irrigated for Selected Years in Fatewadi Project (Area in Hectares)

Type of Irrigation	Season	Pre Modernization Period		Post Modernization Period	
		1973-74	*1977-78*	*1978-79*	*1982-83*
Lift Irrigation	Kharif	1,099	1,169	1,270	1,791
	Rabi	1,278	1,162	619	1,240
	Total	2,377	2,331	1,889	3,031
Canal Irrigation	Kharif	4,856	7,960	7,721	9,890
	Rabi	4,944	2,681	92	2,206
	Total	9,800	10,641	7,813	12,096
Tank Irrigation	Kharif	1,642	11,106	10,615	11,383
	Rabi	2,292	1,643	—	40
	Total	3,934	12,749	10,615	11,423
Lift/Canal/Tanks	Kharif	7,597	20,235	19,606	23,064
	Rabi	8,514	5,486	711	3,486
	Total	16,111	25,721	20,317	26,550

No irrigation is provided during the hot weather.

Exhibit 4   Existing Cropping Pattern in Command Area of Fatewadi Project

Season	Crop	Percentage Area		
		Rainfed	*Irrigated*	*Total*
Kharif	Jowar (millet)	18.9		18.9
	Bejra (sorgum)	4.7		4.7
	Oilseeds	0.6		0.6
	Paddy	1.3	18.2	19.5
	Pulses	1.9		1.9
	Grass — fodder	3.5		3.5
	Misc.	3.6	0.3	3.9
Rabi	Wheat	16.0	7.7	23.7
Bi-Seasonal	Cotton	28.9	0.4	29.3
	Tobacco	0.9	—	0.9
	Total	80.3	26.6	106.9

Exhibit 5   Changes in Social Organization in Indian Villages

I *FAMILY*

THEN	NOW
(1) Insistence on family solidarity and cohesion.	(1) Growth of individualism.
(2) Greater attachment to the soil and settlement.	(2) Migrations more frequent.
(3) Intra-family relations governed by regard for age and kinship status.	(3) Less regard for these traditional principles.

II *CASTE*

THEN	NOW
(1) Occupational specialization on the basis of caste	(1) Caste no longer the final and only determinant for occupation.
(2) Prohibition on inter-dining with some equal castes and all lower castes.	(2) Rules of inter-dining less rigid.
(3) Hierarchy and permanent distance between different castes.	(3) Mild protest against social hierarchy: some modification in actual practice.

III *VILLAGE COUNCIL*

THEN	NOW
(1) Constituted on hereditary principles.	(1) Also admits people with "achieved status."
(2) Little outside intervention.	(2) Considerable outside pressure.
(3) Decisions generally accepted.	(3) Defiance or avoidance possible.

Exhibit 6   Work Differentiation Based on Sex

Activity	Women's work	Men's work
1. Domestic work	Assisting husband in repairs to the house	Occasional repairs to the house
	Keeping house clean (sweeping, swabbing etc.)	Looking after bullocks
	Fetching water	
	Cooking and serving food to menfolk and children	
	Grinding grains	
	Milking cows/buffaloes and taking care of them	
	Washing clothes	
	Collecting fuel	
	Looking after children	
2. Agriculture	Helping in cutting shrubs and repairing field bunds	Cutting shrubs, and repairing field bunds
		Ploughing
	Helping in sowing	Sowing
	Weeding	Irrigation and weeding
	Transplanting	
	Harvesting and threshing	Harvesting and threshing
	Carrying crops home	Carrying crops home
		Buying imputs and marketing outputs
3. Village Administration	Passive role in village council	Active role in village council

Exhibit 7 Occupational Pattern of Households in Selected Villages of Fatewadi Command Area

Villages	Farmers			Landless Labourer	Cattle Rearing	Business	Skilled Labour	Others	Total
	Large	*Medium*	*Small*						
1. Adroda	10	41	40	86	60	6	10	4	257
2. Sanathal	10	243	68	265	15	15	7	20	643
3. Khoda	20	90	36	52	106	2	1	7	168
4. Telao	48	90	78	60	30	15	12	—	333

Exhibit 8   Access to Irrigation Sources in Selected Villages of Fatewadi Command Area

Sr. No.	Villages	Tank	Canal	Tube Well	Village Well	Irrigated Well
1	Adroda	2[a]	1	—	2	15
2	Sanathal	1	1	—	1	17
3	Khoda	1	—	1	[c]	26
4	Telao	2[b]	—	2[c]	1	8

[a] one of these tanks is a small one used for domestic water requirements.
[b] one of these tanks is used only for domestic requirements during monsoon months, as the tube well cannot meet all the requirements.
[c] one tube well is for domestic water requirements, and another for irrigation.

Exhibit 9   Cattle Population in Selected Villages of Fatewadi Command Area

Sr. No.	Villages	Total Cattle	Total No. of Households	No. of Families Owning Cattle	Average Heads of cattle per family
1.	Adroda	599	257	150	4
2.	Sanathal	1,405	643	225	6
3.	Khoda	631	168	150	4
4.	Telao	997	333	200	5

Exhibit 10 Access to Water for Domestic and Other Purposes in the Selected Villages of Fatewadi Command Area

Total number of respondents: 15
Figures in the table gives frequency

Items	Kharif					Summer				
	Tank	At Home at the Tap	At Home with water from Well/Tank	At the Well	At the Water Works	Tank	At Home at the Tap	At Home with water from Well/Tank	At the Well	At the Water Works
I. ADRODA VILLAGE										
1. Clothes	14	—	1	—	—	7	—	1	6	—
2. Vessels	12	—	3	sometimes	—	6	—	2	7	—
3. Animals	1	—	—	1	—	1	—	—	1	—
II. SANATHAL VILLAGE										
1. Clothes	11	4	—	—	—	4	11	—	—	—
2. Vessels	10	5	—	—	—	3	12	—	—	—
3. Animals	10	5	—	—	—	3	12	—	—	—
III. KHODA VILLAGE										
1. Clothes	10	5	—	—	—	—	9	—	—	6
2. Vessels	10	5	—	1	—	—	9	—	—	5
3. Animals	9	2	—	4	—	6	2	—	1	1
IV. TELAO VILLAGE										
1. Clothes	12	1	2	—	—	—	1	10	3	1
2. Vessels	12	1	2	—	—	—	1	10	2	2
3. Animals	2	—	—	—	2	1	—	1	1	1

Exhibit 11   Water Requirements per Capita per Day

Purpose	Consumption per head per day in liters	
A Humans		
Drinking	2.25	
Cooking	4.5	to 9
Washing Clothes	15	to 30
Water Closets	25	
Utensils and House Washing	15	to 25
Bathing	45	to 90
B Cattle	15	

Source: *A Text Book on Water Supply Engineering,* R.P. Singhal. Indian Institute of Management, Ahmedabad, India, p. 43.

Exhibit 12 An Assessment of Women's Involvement in Agricultural Work in Two Categories of Farm Sizes for Principal Crops in Selected Villages

Paddy: Large Farms*

Average** Days Required	Operations	Family Males				Family Females				Hired Males				Hired Females			
Villages:		A	S	K	T	A	S	K	T	A	S	K	T	A	S	K	T
13	1. Primary tillage	L	NA	H	H	—	NA	—	—	H	NA	—	—	—	NA	—	—
	2. Secondary tillage	L	H	H	H	—	—	—	L	H	—	—	—	—	—	—	M
2	3. Nursery work	—	H	L	L	—	—	—	—	L	L	L	L	M	M	M	M
15	4. Transplanting	L	H	H	H	—	—	—	—	M	L	—	—	M	M	—	—
2	5. Irrigation	L	H	L	H	—	—	—	—	H	L	L	—	—	—	—	—
6	6. Weeding/Interculture	—	—	L	L	—	—	—	L	M	L	L	M	M	M	M	M
12	7. Harvesting	—	—	L	L	—	—	—	L	M	M	L	L	M	M	M	M
4	8. Threshing	—	L	L	L	—	—	—	—	M	M	M	M	M	M	—	—
2	9. Marketing	H	H	H	H	—	—	—	—	—	—	—	—	—	—	—	—
Total 56																	

Paddy: Medium Small Farms*

Average** Days Required	Operations	Family Males				Family Females				Hired Males				Hired Females			
Villages:		A	S	K	T	A	S	K	T	A	S	K	T	A	S	K	T
13	1. Primary tillage	H	H	M	H	—	—	—	—	L	—	L	—	—	—	—	—
	2. Secondary tillage	M	H	M	M	—	—	—	M	M	—	L	—	—	—	—	—
2	3. Nursery work	M	H	M	M	—	—	—	M	M	L	L	L	M	M	M	M
15	4. Transplanting	L	L	L	L	—	—	—	L	L	L	—	—	M	M	M	M
2	5. Irrigation	H	H	H	H	—	—	—	—	—	—	—	—	—	—	—	—
6	6. Weeding/Interculture	L	L	H	H	—	—	—	—	M	L	—	M	M	H	M	M
12	7. Harvesting	L	—	L	—	—	—	—	L	L	M	M	L	M	M	—	M
4	8. Threshing	L	—	M	L	—	—	—	L	L	—	M	M	M	M	—	—
2	9. Marketing	H	H	M	L	—	—	—	L	—	—	—	L	—	—	—	L
Total 56																	

Exhibit 12 (Continued)

Wheat: Large Farms*

4	1. Primary tillage	L	H	NA	NA	—	—	—	—	NA	NA	—	—	—	—	NA	NA
	2. Secondary tillage	L	H	M	H	—	L	—	—	L	L	—	—	—	—	—	—
6	3. Sowing	L	H	M	H	—	—	—	—	—	L	—	—	—	—	—	—
3	4. Fertilizer appl.	L	—	H	H	—	—	—	—	—	—	—	—	—	—	—	—
2	5. Irrigation appl.	L	H	L	NA	—	—	—	—	M	NA	—	—	—	M	—	NA
	6. Weeding/Interculture	—	NA	NA	—	—	NA	L	L	NA	—	—	NA	NA	M	M	—
10	7. Harvesting	—	L	L	M	—	L	L	L	L	—	—	L	M	M	M	—
8	8. Threshing	M	L	L	M	—	M	M	L	M	M	—	M	M	—	—	—
1	9. Marketing	H	H	H	H	—	—	—	—	—	—	—	—	—	—	—	—
Total 34																	

Wheat: Small Farms*

Villages:	A	S	A	S	A	S	A	S
4 1. Primary tillage	L	NA	—	NA	H	NA	—	NA
2. Secondary tillage	L	H	—	—	H	L	—	L
6 3. Sowing	M	H	—	—	M	L	—	L
3 4. Fertilizer appl.	L	H	—	—	H	L	—	L
2 5. Irrigation appl.	M	NA	—	NA	M	NA	—	NA
6. Weeding/Interculture	—	—	—	—	—	L	M	L
10 7. Harvesting	—	H	—	—	M	L	M	L
8 8. Threshing	H	H	—	—	M	L	M	L
1 9. Marketing	H	—	—	—	—	—	—	—
Total 34								

Exhibit 12 (Continued)

Cotton: Large Farms*

	Villages:	K	T	K	T	K	T	K	T
4	1. Tillage	—	H	—	—	H	—	—	—
2	2. Sowing	M	H	—	—	M	—	—	—
12	3. Interculture	L	H	—	M	M	—	M	—
10	4. Harvesting pod	—	M	—	NA	L	—	H	—
7	5. Separating cotton from pod	—	NA	—	—	L	NA	H	NA
2	6. Marketing	H	H	—	—	—	—	—	—
Total 37									

Symbols:

Involvement

L — Low involvement
M — Medium involvement
H — High involvement

0 — 40% of workers
40 — 70% of workers
70 — 100% of workers

Villages

A — Adroda
S — Sanathal
K — Khoda
T — Telao

*Large farmer is specified as one having a holding size of 10 acres (4.05 ha) or more. Medium and small as less than 10.

**Figures are for raising a unit acre of the crop (.405 ha.).

NOTES

1. Committee on Status of Women in India. *Towards Equality: Report of the Committee on Status of Women in India,* (New Delhi: Dept. of Social Welfare, Government of India), 1974.
2. Water Management Synthesis Project, *Irrigation Projects Document Review: The Indian Subcontinent,* (Logan, Utah: Utah State University, 1981).
3. A.R. Desai, "Rural Sociology," *Popular Prakashan,* Bombay, India.
4. S.C. Dube, *Indian Village,* Allied Publishers Private Ltd., Bombay.
5. An Impact Evaluation of Fatewadi Medium Irrigation Project within the Perspective of Modernization, CEPT Study Cell, Centre for Environmental Planning and Technology, Navrangpura, Ahmedabad, 1981.

CHAPTER ELEVEN

Kenya: Kitui District Arid and Semi-Arid Lands Project

Prepared by Mary B. Anderson

CONTENTS

I. Country Background

II. Kitui District Background

III. Women, Families and Work in Kitui

IV. Project Background and Description
   A. Government of Kenya
   B. The AID ASAL Development Project
   C. Status of Project

TABLES

REFERENCES

Only a two hour drive takes us from Nairobi to Kitui. In Nairobi, water pure enough to drink and plentiful enough to water gardens and wash cars flows from the faucets. In Kitui water can scarcely be found. The night before going, I ask an agricultural officer who is familiar with the area if there is any drip irrigation in Kitui. "Irrigation!" he rejoins, "In Kitui, we are only trying to locate enough water for basic human consumption."

I. COUNTRY BACKGROUND.

About eighty-two percent of Kenya's total land area is classified as arid or semi-arid. These lands support about 50 percent of Kenya's livestock and about 18 percent of the country's population (2.6 million people). The people are heterogeneous, including twelve major ethnic/tribal groupings, and live as nomads, semi-sedentary pastoralists,

pastoralists engaged in farming, or cultivators and ranchers.

Drought is common in the arid and semi-arid lands (ASALs). Regional drought, lasting one or two seasons, affects maize growers every three or four years, growers of special drought resistant maize every eight years, and growers of millet (which is also more drought resistant than maize) every five years. The impact of droughts and the extent of evaporation of low rainfall is greatly affected by the herding and agricultural practices of the residents of the areas.

Recent large migration into some ASAL areas is the result of several factors. First, pressures on high quality and traditional farm land are increasing due to population growth (estimated at 3.5 percent or more per year). Thus, many people are seeking new areas to settle and to raise their families. Second, there is migration among the semi-arid and arid zones as populations exceed the carrying capacity of the land and people try to spread out to survive. Third, resettlement and irrigation schemes have been established in some ASALs by the government.

ASAL immigrants have often used technologies and approaches not ecologically suited to their new areas which cause additional damage to and deterioration of the land. Some traditional adaptation techniques, such as moving herds and shifting cultivation areas, become more difficult with increasing population. Kenya's land reform, through which land is being transferred to individual title holders, undermines traditional migratory patterns. Land reform is also altering traditional social insurance systems which had supported survival. For example, nomads often held communal rights to the critical limited resources of salt licks, watering places, and grazing lands. Agriculturalists shared drinking water sites, participated in cooperative work practices, and had taboos surrounding irrigation waters. They hedged against drought by mixed reliance on crops and cattle. Individual land ownership, and the disruptions introduced by the influx of new dwellers, undermine these traditional systems and introduce new uncertainties.

Land deterioration further diminishes the quantity and quality of food produced. Many families in the ASALs now seek off-farm employment in order to overcome perennial food shortages. It is not atypical for 70 percent of all male and female adults to engage in off-farm income producing activities at some time during the year. These activities include collecting and selling firewood and thatching grass, and making and selling charcoal. Other male adults are employed full-time in off-farm occupations, and two thirds of these are outside their district, leaving their families behind.

Excluding remittances, 58 percent of household income is in-kind and 42 percent is cash from such activities. Families spend about 50 percent of total income for food.

II. THE KITUI DISTRICT BACKGROUND

One major arid and semi arid area in the Eastern Province is Kitui. The total land area of Kitui District is 3,109,000 hectares of which approximately 61 percent is classified as low potential. Estimates show that 180,000 hectares or 5.7 percent of the entire area is under crops. The Kamba, a Bantu-speaking group, are the majority. They combine agricultural production with livestock for their livelihoods.

In the Central Division of Kitui where the population density is highest, about one-half of the farms are smaller than two hectares with one-fourth between two and six hectares and one-fourth larger than six hectares. It is estimated that there are 50,000 small farms in the district. Average farm size is actually larger in the poorer ecological zones of the district, and in most areas agricultural production has been limited in the past by the shortage of labor rather than land. However, population growth and immigration, as well as the GOK policy of registering land to individual owners, have resulted in some land pressures in recent years.

Traditionally, as sons came of age in Kitui, they left their father's household and land and established their own families on unoccupied lands. The youngest son remained to inherit his father's land. As land became scarcer it was still possible to acquire a plot by asking a nominal "owner" for rights to settle and cultivate. Usually this was granted with payment of a goat. Once rights were established through settlement and cultivation, eviction was not possible. Land that had once been cleared and cultivated could be claimed by the descendants of the original clearer. Though land was thus claimed for cultivation, livestock was free to graze on other people's land and water rights were shared, not owned.

Though the purpose of the GOK land reform policy is to prevent the loss of time spent in quarrels over land rights, to discourage land fragmentation, and to encourage long-term capital investments, in Kitui this effort has altered some basic survival methods. Grazing has been curtailed and access to watering points for both household and animal consumption cut off. The legal assignment of land has also introduced the concept and reality of landlessness in Kitui District for the first time.

As might be expected given its harsh conditions, Kitui lags behind other areas of Kenya in certain development indicators. As Table 1 shows, only eight other districts in Kenya suffer from as high or higher child mortality. The incidence of malaria is higher than for most other areas and, while female literacy in Kitui falls in the middle range for all districts, it lags significantly behind Central, Nyanza, Western and much of the Rift Valley Provinces. Kitui also has one of the lowest rates of high potential agricultural land per capita in all of Kenya.

Table 2 shows enrollment rates in secondary schools in Kitui at only 7 percent. This again ranks in the middle range for Kenya's districts but behind the provincial averages for all but the North Eastern Province.

The range of crops that can be grown in Kitui is limited by climatic conditions. Only those that require little rainfall or that are drought resistant are suitable. Principle food crops are maize, cowpeas, pigeon peas, millet, sorghum, beans, green grams, cassava, and sweet potatoes. Bananas, guavas, mangoes, onions, tomatoes and cabbages are grown on a small scale. In some instances, each of these crops may be raised for sale.

Cash crops are cotton, sunflower, castor, sisal, and to a lesser extent, tobacco, cashew nuts and coffee. Cotton and sunflower are grown all over the district in small plots of .4 hectares each. There are no sisal plantations in Kitui but sisal plants are used to mark the boundaries between fields under cultivation with other crops and are harvested for use and cash. Tables 3 and 4 show the Kitui District Five Year Plan projections for these crops, and Table 5 shows the same for livestock. While crops are seen to increase by from 2 percent to 11 percent, the entire increase is projected through increases in hectarage under production. Land reclamation is a central part of the District's Five Year Development Plan.

III. WOMEN, FAMILIES AND WORK IN KITUI DISTRICT

In Kitui District, as in all parts of Kenya, the family is the central social unit. Marriage is traditionally, therefore, extremely important. Polygamy was common among the Kamba, but it is now gradually diminishing.

A woman's family pays bridewealth to a prospective husband and, upon marriage, a woman leaves her father's home and joins her husband's extended family. Before she bears her first child, a bride is expected to serve as an apprentice to her mother-in-law. Only after she has a child does she receive a piece of land from her husband to cultivate for herself. In Kamba culture, a marriage without children is incomplete. If a woman dies soon after marriage without having borne a child, the bridewealth is usually returned to her father.

Children are highly valued. The belief is that God determines how many children a woman should have. Average households in Kitui include 6 to 8 people, and 20 percent of the population is below five years of age. Boys are valued over girls and are, therefore, more often educated by their families than their sisters. Boys stay within their fathers' households to protect and support their parents as they grow old. Women, of course, move away and join another family. Only occasionally does a widowed or divorced woman move back into her parents' household.

Table 6 shows the population in Kitui District for 1978 and 1979. While the growth rate in the district is estimated at 3.2 percent, below the national average of 3.5 percent, the demographic patterns result in 30 percent more adult women in the area than adult men. Fifty-nine percent of the small farms in Kitui are operated solely by women.

Traditionally, men and women in Kitui divided their agricultural work. Men were responsible for clearing fields and plowing as well as applying fertilizers when they were used. Men also cared for cattle and small livestock such as sheep and goats. Men traditionally raised bees but with the introduction of new bee hive techniques, women have also begun to keep bees.

Women's responsibilities included selecting seeds, planting, hoeing and weeding, harvesting and treating and storing food crops. They also maintained the households with sole responsibility for food preparation and processing, fetching water and firewood, caring for children, grinding grain, and making beer, honey, pots and baskets. Women also milked cattle. In the drde. Table 7 shows the percentage of female headed households in Eastern Province where Kitui is located. Eastern Province accounts for almost one-fourth of all the female-headed households in Kenya. Many observers feel that these official figures greatly understate the numbers of female headed rural households. Some estimates go as high as 45 percent. Women are now seen performing all of the jobs named above, including those formerly designated as male. They do so either alone or alongside men.

There is no diminution of their household tasks, however, so with their combined agricultural and household production women work 15 hours per day on average. As water has become scarcer, women have had to walk farther to find it. Frequently they travel as far as 6 kilometers, a trip averaging five hours. In drought periods, they go as far as 15 kilometers. Sometimes women use donkeys to carry their water jugs. Even where water catchments have been constructed so that distances to water are reduced, women find that time spent in collection has not been correspondingly reduced. This is because they often must wait in line for their turn. Problems of water collection are clearly worse in dry seasons and droughts, causing women to spend even more time in walking to water points and in waiting for water levels to rise enough after each dip that they can gather more. The help of young girls is frequently required for women to complete all aspects of their work.

Work on most crops is now either done solely by women or shared by men and women. Cotton, which is thought of in Kitui as a "men's crop" is, one observes, actually cultivated by women. During the growing season, women spend an average of 17 hours each week in weeding alone. During this season, they also spend one hour/ each day guarding their fields against incursions by monkeys. Care of animals and poultry involve women throughout the year for an average of eight hours each week and marketing, in which about one-half of Kitui women are engaged, takes five hours each week.

As has been mentioned, activities in Kitui District follow a distinct seasonal pattern with cropping and cultivating assuming major importance during the rains, and water collection requiring much time in the dry seasons. Cattle care is consistent year-round except as finding water and forage becomes more time-consuming. Most construction work is done in dry seasons. When a surveyor in Kitui District asked women what they would like to do if they had more time to take care of their homes, farms and children, one woman answered:

> "I would terrace my farm and introduce crop rotation, which my husband has been insisting on for a long time. I would also wash my clothes and the children's more often than I do these days."

Others said:

> "I would plant vegetables and plant green grams for sale. I would spend more time with my children and wash them more systematically than I nowadays do."

> "I would be harvesting my green grams and peas in time before they split and scatter all over the garden. I would wash my children's clothes more often."

A significant portion of residents in Kitui District belong to organized self-help groups, called mwethya, which undertake local development activities. The groups construct schools, nurseries, dams, water catchments, and cattle dips and do most of the land terracing. Members contribute labor, cash and materials. Over 2000 such groups are registered in Kitui and 80 percent of the members are women. Mwethya groups usually form around a specific project and, if they qualify for registration by membership and probability of project success criteria, they are eligible for technical advice and support from government agencies. In addition to construction, these groups get together to grow tomatoes, cabbages, and other vegetables as cash crops; to raise bees, goats or poultry; to start small enterprises such as bakeries or shops; and to do handicrafts. It was on these groups that the GOK relied to provide the labor contribution to the ASAL pilot project in Kitui District.

IV. PROJECT BACKGROUND AND DESCRIPTION

In 1979 AID agreed to fund an ASAL Project in the Kitui District of Eastern Province costing a total of $17,991,000 of which AID was to contribute $12,346,000 and the GOK, $5,645,000 (See Table 8).

A. The Government of Kenya

In its 1979-1983 Five Year Development Plan, the Government of Kenya stressed as its main theme the alleviation of poverty and the provision of basic human needs to all Kenyans. The focus was on rural development and the agricultural sector. Among seven major programs in agriculture was the development of arid and semi-arid lands. The other six included: 1) increasing the intensity of land use and development; 2) development of appropriate technology; 3) development of smallholder agriculture; 4) alleviation of poverty; 5) improvement of market incentives for agriculture; and 6) increasing access to and employment on the land.

The emphasis on ASALs in the Fourth Five Year Plan grew out of a policy paper prepared by an interministerial Task Force in 1978-79 entitled "Arid and Semi-Arid Land Develoment in Kenya: The Framework for Implementation, Program Planning, and Evaluation."

This paper identified four objectives of the Kenyan government's program for ASALs.

1. Development of human resources because the people of the ASALs are among the most disadvantaged of Kenya;

2. exploitation of the ASAL productive potential based on the knowledge that similiar areas in other countries, such as the Middle East, North America, and Australia, do in fact realize far greater output than is realized in Kenya;

3. conservation of the land; and

4. integration with the national economy, partly to redress past imbalances in development investments.

Through a series of seminars and consultations, the GOK sought broad international donor support for its ASAL efforts. The complexities and interrelationships of geographical and conservation programs with physcial and social infrastructure meant that all major Ministries of Kenya were included in the planning and programming for ASALs.

International donors agreed to support different parts of the program. The EEC financed an integrated development project in Machakos District. The IBRD planned a ten-component project in Barengo District. The UK took on activities in Isiolo/Meru/Embu Districts, and the Norwegians funded assistance in Marsabit and Turkana Districts.

B. The AID ASAL Development Project

As early as 1974, the GOK asked AID to finance a comprehensive study of resources, problems and potential investment opportunities in parts of the Eastern and Rift Valley Provinces. In 1977-78, this survey was carried out by a team of eight Kenyans and eight Americans and produced a ten volume "Pre-Investment Inventory" of the marginal and semi-arid lands in these areas. AID was, therefore, prepared and willing to take on a major role in the ASAL program of the Fourth Five Year Plan.

AID was particularly concerned with two things. First, because of the potentially high risks associated with large projects in unstable and deteriorating land areas, AID emphasized the importance of careful research and data base collection. Second, AID agreed to fund certain pilot scale projects where information seemed sufficient and the projects' success was not dependent on any highly complex set of other related interventions. Subsequent to successful involvement in these two activities, AID was prepared to support larger, action-oriented investments under other AID agreements.

The ASAL AID Project had three distinct components.

1. Planning. AID was to assist in ASAL planning by placing one technical assistant in the Ministry of Economic Planning, one in the Ministry of Agriculture and one in Kitui District. The project provided 12 years of planning assistance, 12 months of consultancies and nine years of participant degree training to increase the Kenyan capacity for ASAL planning.

2. Data Collection and Analysis. This component included: a.) pre-investment inventories of resources; b.) mapping aids such as aerial photography and remote sensing imagery; and c.) feasibility and project design studies. For the pre-investment resource inventories, 17 person years of technical assistance were to be supplied, including two soil scientists, one soil and water engineer, a forester and a range ecologist. The mapping activities would involve one technical advisor and, while all ASAL areas were to be included, Kitui District was specifically designated for ortho-photo maps of a pilot area, landsat imagery and interpretation over a two year period for the entire district, and black and white and multi-spectral photos for the district.

3. Soil and Water Conservation. This component was focused on testing various soil and water conservation techniques in a pilot area in parts of two divisions in Kitui District. Activities in afforestation and in supplying free implements for agriculture were included. Twenty-five years of technical assistance were planned, including advisers in land use planning, soil and water engineering, soil science, forrage crops, agronomy, farm equipment and agricultural economics.

A pilot area of 333,000 hectares was designated, in Kitui, comprising 11 percent of the total district, with a population of 173,000 or 37 percent of the District. USAID assistance included:

1. major soil and water conservation measures;
2. development of the infrastructure;
3. development of non-agricultural economic activities;
4. mapping;
5. improvement of district level planning capability; and
6. feasibility studies for small irrigation schemes, afforestation, food production and rural roads construction.

Much of the thrust of the actual project work in Kitui was focused on involving local people. The government of Kenya's contribution to the project was to equal 31 percent of which 75 percent was to be in the form of field labor in the soil conservation component. Imputed costs of labor were used to estimate the contribution through self-help voluntary groups. The GOK labor commitment arrived at in this way represented 2,500,000 person days or almost 3 percent of the labor force in the pilot area. (This calculation was done in a project evaluation by Richard M. Hook, "Consultancy Report to USAID/Kenya on Review of the Arid and Semi Arid Lands Development Project" April 6, 1983, p. 20.) Actual construction of dams, ditches, water catchments, terraces, etc.—all essential to supplying and retaining water—was to be done by local groups. No provision for wages was possible in the project so people were to be encouraged to volunteer. To elicit a sufficient number of volunteers and to use this project process for the broader dissemination of new agricultural and animal technologies, project planners devised a system for providing equipment and implements to groups of volunteers. This equipment could be used both for project-related work and for the groups' own activities. The system of distribution of the implements allowed for comparative testing of their effectiveness under different soil conditions and this, in turn, allowed for refinements in their design during the project.

Population density in the pilot area was 52/sq. km. compared with 13 for the district as a whole. The pilot area contained more medium-potential and semi-arid land, as compared to arid land, than the district as a whole.

Demonstration plots were planned on 350 acres belonging to the Better Living Institute, a training center in Kitui which also serves as a Farmers Training Center under the Ministry of Agriculture. The land in these plots was of medium potential and, therefore, better quality than most of the surrounding area.

Training was also important in the pilot program. Three month training courses in land use planning and soil and water conservation were planned for 55 people at the Better Living Institute. Trainees would become soil-conservation technicians in parts of the pilot area. An additional 67 years of participant training in planning, data collection and soil conservation were designated for staff from the Survey of Kenya, the Ministry of Water Development and the Ministry of Transport and Communications.

C. Status of the Project

Delays in funding and staffing meant that the USAID Project in Kitui did not begin until 1982. During this time, the GOK suffered a deterioration of its budgetary resource base as the coffee and tea boom of the 1970's ended and petroleum prices rose. Nonetheless, the government retained a very high commitment to its ASAL program and projected an expansion of it in other Districts. While a number of the projects are preceeding well, problems of coordination have emerged as a result of the necessity for involving all Ministries.

Table 10 shows a summary of the status of the donor-sponsored ASAL Projects that were in place when AID undertook the Kitui project. The Table shows a higher level of technical assistance in the USAID project than in any of the others. A consultant who evaluated the Kitui project noted that this high cost and the relative emphasis AID placed on research and data collection created a disjunction between community expectations and actual project accomplishments.

As of March 1983, a number of targets set for 1982 had not been met (See Table 11). One explanation for this lag is found in a severe budget curtailment of project activity by the GOK. Whereas the targeted activities were based on a budget of KSh 395,000, the actual budget approval was only KSh 95,000. This forced even greater reliance on the labor of volunteer Mwethya groups.

The Kitui project has not achieved its projected targets to date. At least some part of this failure can be attributed to start-up delays, project design emphasis on research, and shortages of funds. Project redesign and rescheduling address these problems. However, another factor affecting outcomes is the availability of labor, particularly volunteer labor, as it is matched with project labor requirements both overall and seasonally. Project redesign might be improved if greater care were taken to assess these patterns of local labor availability as plans were made for future project activities, technical assistance, and community involvement.

TABLES

Table 1   Child Mortality Rates by District and Relted Variables

District/Province	Child Mortality	Percent Malaria Cases	Percent Female Adults Literate	Per Capita High Potential Agr. Land
NAIROBI	93	—	67.84	—
CENTRAL				
Kiambu	70	4.53	46.50	0.289
Muranga	68	11.29	38.41	0.289
Nyeri	49	1.35	46.59	0.329
Kirinyaga	82	14.35	44.99	0.336
Nyandarua	64	1.74	39.42	1.136
NYANZA				
Kisumu	199	34.71	31.88	0.451
Siaya	211	32.62	24.12	0.451
South Nyanza	216	31.56	25.35	0.692
Kisii	101	20.91	36.50	0.253
WESTERN				
Kayamega	143	31.03	33.22	0.315
Bungoma	140	30.38	37.16	0.502
Busia	198	27.60	22.45	0.547
COAST				
Mombasa	120	18.29	43.96	—
Kilifi	212	26.09	8.65	0.241
Kwale	190	23.79	9.84	0.437
Lamu	200	17.55	3.23	0.165
Tana River	181	28.22	7.90	0.790
Taita-Taveta	116	23.93	21.42	0.284
RIFT VALLEY				
Laikipia	77	5.97	32.40	0.966
Narok	95	13.71	8.33	4.398
Kajiado	75	18.70	18.46	0.148
Turkana	133	13.84	2.09	0.084
Samburu	77	14.08	4.91	1.820
Nakuru	97	9.16	37.47	0.557
Baringo	171	16.25	19.33	0.814
Kericho	91	14.92	27.69	0.600
Uasin Gishu	92	19.81	34.06	1.087
Nandi	110	13.84	27.01	0.782
Trans-Nzoia	114	17.50	29.53	0.802
Elgeyo Marakwet	127	13.23	23.69	0.699
West Pokot	188	23.63	6.35	0.649
EASTERN				
Meru	75	15.71	26.84	0.290
Isiolo	127	27.00	5.86	0.000
Kitui	148	24.98	18.57	0.144
Machakos	98	19.63	36.14	0.122
Marsabit	130	18.76	2.08	0.042
NORTHEASTERN				
Garissa	131	23.21	2.83	0.000
Wajir	129	16.42	1.72	0.000
Mandera	146	19.82	1.23	0.000

Table 2   Secondary School Enrollment Ratios Age Group 13-16: 1974, 1977

	1974	*1977*
Coast	9%	9%
Taita/Taveta	10%	12%
Kiliffi	3%	3%
Tana River	5%	3%
Lamu	3%	4%
Kwale	3%	4%
Mombasa	22%	23%
Central	14%	23%
Nyandarua	7%	16%
Nyeri	16%	27%
Kirinyaga	13%	27%
Murang'a	13%	22%
Kimbu	16%	23%
Eastern	8%	12%
Machakos	12%	17%
Kitui	5%	7%
Embu	7%	9%
Marsabit		2%
Isiolo	3%	2%
Nairobi	25%	41%
Rift Valley	5%	8%
Nakuru	12%	18%
Kericho	3%	6%
Nandi	3%	7%
Laikipia	11%	13%
Kajiado	4%	5%
Narok	3%	4%
Baringo	3%	7%
Elgeyo-Marakwet	4%	5%
Uasin Gishu	7%	12%
Turkana	3%	1%
Samburu	2%	2%
Trans Nzoia	8%	14%
West Pokot	2%	3%
Nyanza	6%	9%
Kisumu	5%	7%
Kisii	7%	14%
South Nyanza	5%	7%
Siaya	6%	6%
Western	7%	15%
Busia	7%	11%
Bungoma	4%	15%
Kakamega	8%	15%
North Eastern	1%	1%
Garissa	1%	1%
Wajir	1%	1%
Mandera	3%	4%
Kenya	8%	13%

Source: CBS data files

Table 3 Projected Hectarage and Production Food Crops for Period 1979/83 Kitui District

	Growth Rate	Units	1979	1980	1981	1982	1983
GREEN GRAMS	2%	Ha.	6,500	6,630	6,763	6,898	7,036
		Ton	2,250	2,295	2,341	2,388	2,436
NJAHI	3%	Ha.	325	335	345	355	366
		Ton	3,590	101	104	107	110
PIGEON PEAS	3%	Ha.	10,500	10,815	11,139	11,473	11,817
		Ton	6,300	6,489	6,684	6,885	7,092
CASSAVA	3%	Ha.	1,100	1,133	1,167	1,202	1,238
		Ton	7,700	7,931	8,169	8,414	8,666
MILLET	4%	Ha.	17,000	17,680	18,387	19,122	19,696
		Ton	76,550	79,612	82,796	86,107	89,551
SORGHUM	4%	Ha.	17,000	18,387	19,122	19,887	20,683
		Ton	765,500	796,120	827,965	861,084	695,527
SWEET POTATOES	3%	Ha.	380	391	403	415	427
		Ton	760	783	806	830	855
COWPEAS		Ha.	13,000	13,390	13,792	14,206	14,632
		Ton	4,450	4,584	4,722	4,864	5,011
KATUMANI MAIZE	3%	Ha.	15,500	1,596	16,444	16,937	17,445
		Ton	31,000	31,930	32,888	33,875	34,891
BEANS	4%	Ha.	6,000	6,240	6,490	6,750	7,020
		Ton	3,600	3,744	3,894	4,050	4,212

Table 4 Projected Hectarage and Production of Cash Crops for Period 1979/83 Kitui District

	Growth Rate	Units	1979	1980	1981	1982	1983
TOBACCO	7.9%	Ha.	550	593	640	691	746
		Ton	89	96	104	112	121
SUNFLOWER	4%	Ha.	5,000	5,200	5,408	5,624	5,849
		Ton	750	780	811	843	877
COTTON	11%	Ha.	7,000	7,770	8,625	9,574	10,627
		Ton	1,400	1,554	1,725	1,915	2,126
SISAL	2%	Ha.	45,000	45,900	46,818	47,754	48,709
		Ton	200,000	200,400	208,080	212,242	2,164,487
CASTOR	4%	Ha.	6,500	6,760	7,030	7,311	7,603
		Ton	600	624	650	676	703
COFFEE		Ha.	30	30	30	30	30
		Ton	3	3	3	3	3
CASHEW NUT		Ha.	100	200	400	500	800
		Ton	3	4	4	4	6

Table 5   Projected Livestock Population For Plan Period 1979/83 — Kitui District

	1977	1978	1979	1980	1981	1982	1983
CATTLE (Beef)	213,300	218,325	223,783	329,378	235,113	240,991	247,016
Dairy	150	300	300	330	386	438	497
GOATS	312,204	321,570	331,217	341,154	351,389	361,289	372,289
SHEEP	81,603	84,050	86,572	89,169	91,844	94,599	97,437
POULTRY (LAYERS)							
(i) Grade	48,003	15,000	15,000	52,500	90,000	127,500	165,000
(ii) Local Birds	68,817	76,463	380,000	380,000	830,000	980,000	1,130,000
KENYA TOP BEE HIVES (Improved Hives)	53	360	360	2,235	4,110	5,985	7,880

ed Population Kitui District 1978

	Total	Male	Male Children	Male Adults	Female	Female Children	Female Adults	Area KM 2	Density Per KM 2
	140,934	66,481	35,969	30,512	74,512	34,781	39,672	2,640	53
on	45,437	21,161	10,648	24,276	24,376	10,265	14,011	5,736	7
vision	70,789	33,062	17,018	16,044	37,725	16,245	21,480	7,148	10
Mw... vision	101,881	48,112	27,292	20,720	53,769	26,649	27,120	2,231	45
Kyuso Division	69,083	32,086	17,342	14,744	36,997	17,115	19,882	7,031	10
Sub-totals	428,008	200,849	108,207	92,643	227,159	105,026	122,132		
Kitui Town	6,100								
Totals	434,108	200,849	108,207	92,643	227,159	105,026	122,132		

Table 6 (cont.) Projected Population Kitui District 1979

	Total	Male	Male Children	Male Adults	Female	Female Children	Female Adults	Area KM 2	Density Per KM 2
Central Division	145,408	68,591	37,111	31,480	76,817	35,885	40,932	26,400	55
Eastern Division	46,880	21,833	10,847	10,986	25,047	10,591	14,456	5,736	9
Southern Division	73,036	34,113	17,559	16,554	38,923	16,671	22,162	7,148	11
Northern Division	105,116	49,640	28,262	21,378	55,476	27,495	27,981	2,231	48
Far North Division	71,278	33,105	17,893	15,212	38,173	17,659	20,514	7,032	10
Sub/total	441,718	207,282	111,672	95,610	234,436	108,391	126,045		
Kitui Town	6,100								
Totals	447,818	207,282	111,672	95,610	234,436	108,391	126,045	18,787	

Table 7 Sex Ratios and Percentage of Female-Headed Smallholder Households by Province, 1974/5

Province	Women-headed HH as % of all HH	Total # (000)	% of all Women headed HH
Central	23	73.8	22
Coast	27	18.9	6
Eastern	23	81.2	24
Nyanza	25	96.6	28
Rift	22	19.8	6
Western	19	48.4	14
Kenya	24	340.7	100

Source: Republic of Kenya, IRS 1974/5:23, 33, 52.

Table 8 Project Agreement (000's of $)

	AID	GOK	Total	
Planning	2,010	390	2,400	13%
Data Collection	3,880	1,175	5,055	28%
Soil Conservation	6,456	4,080	10,536	59%
Total	12,346	5,645	17,991	100%

Table 9 Percentages of Land by Classifications for Kitui District and Pilot Area

	Pilot Area	Kitui District
Medium Potential Land	12%	3%
Semi-Arid Land	45%	5%
Arid Land	42%	92%

Table 10 Status of Donor Sponsored ASAL Projects, 1983

	Started	Donor	1982/83 GOK Budget-Kb	% of Request Budgeted	Est. Ta a % of GOK Budget
Machakos	1978	EEC	3,258,000	95	20
Embu-Meru Is	1979	Brit	328,500	43	40
Barino	1980	IBRD	647,000	44	45
Kitui	1982	USAID	286,000	39	400
Turkana	1980	NORAD	306,000	na	na
W. Pokot	1981	DUTCH	na		
Elg. Mar.	1981	DUTCH	na		
Ndeiya/Karai	1978	DUTCH	very small		

Source: Richard M. Hook, "Consultancy Report to USAID/Kenya on Review of the Arid and SemiArid Lands Development Project," Nairobi, Kenya, USAID unpublished report.

Table 11   Kitui Project Targets, 1982 and March 1983 Achievements

Activity	Original to end of 1982	March 1983 Estimated Position
No. of farms to be terraced	2,080	over 2,000[1]
Meters of cut-off drains	156,000	over 40,000 est.[2]
Gully Control Areas	9.0[3]	(See Note 3)
Rehab. Overgrazed Land	640 ha.	over 300 ha.
Fenced eroded areas	6.5 km2	over 3 sites
Rock Catchment/Sub Surface dams	8	3 sites in progress
Rehab. of small dams	4	2 in progress
Nurseries establ./improved	4	2 in progress
Bulking fodder crops	4.5 ha.	over 5 ha.
Demonstration Plots	--	200

Source: Richard M. Hook, "Consultancy Report to USAID/Kenya on Review of the Arid and SemiArid Lands Development Project."

Notes: 1. Both estimates refer to partial rather than complete terracing of farms. Estimates to date of terraces constructed total about 125,000 meters.

2. In future reporting, the team will shift from meters dug to areas protected.

3. Now included in "Fenced eroded areas."

SOURCES

1. AID/Arid and Semi Arid Lands Project Paper, June 1979.
2. AID/ASAL Preliminary Social Soundness Analysis, n.d.
3. Richard M. Hook, "Consultancy Report to USAID/Kenya on Review of the Arid and SemiArid Lands Development Project." April 6, 1983.
4. "Arid and Semi Arid Lands Development in Kenya," Government Printer, 1979.